Environmental Law in Hong Kong

Environmental Law in Hong Kong

Third Edition

Anton Cooray

This book was originally published as a monograph in the International Encyclopaedia of Laws/Environmental Law

Founding Editor: Roger Blanpain
General Editor: Frank Hendrickx
Volume Editor: Kurt Deketelaere

Wolters Kluwer

Published by:
Kluwer Law International B.V.
PO Box 316
2400 AH Alphen aan den Rijn
The Netherlands
E-mail: international-sales@wolterskluwer.com
Website: lrus.wolterskluwer.com

Sold and distributed by:
Wolters Kluwer Legal & Regulatory U.S.
7201 McKinney Circle
Frederick, MD 21704
United States of America
E-mail: customer.service@wolterskluwer.com

ISBN 978-94-035-3682-8

e-Book: ISBN 978-94-035-3683-5
web-PDF: ISBN 978-94-035-3684-2

The Author

Professor Anton Cooray, LLB, PhD (London), PhD (Sri Lanka), Professor of Law at City, University of London, and Senior Associate Research Fellow of the Institute of Advanced Legal Studies, University of London, was formerly Professor of Law at City University of Hong Kong, where he was Head of the Department of Law and Associate Dean of Law.

Professor Cooray specializes in public law and planning law. He was a member of Hong Kong Town Planning Board from 1996 to 2004 and Chairman of Town Planning Appeal Board and Deputy Chairman of Town Planning Appeal Board panel (2004–2012). He is the author of *Halsbury's Laws of Hong Kong* titles on *Town Planning* (6th reissue 2018), *The Environment* (5th reissue, 2020), *Constitutional Law* (5th reissue, 2019) and *Constitutional Law in Hong Kong* (3rd ed., 2019: Kluwer International). He is the editor of the *Journal of International and Comparative Law* (Sweet and Maxwell).

The Author

Table of Contents

Table of Contents

List of Abbreviations

EIA	Environmental Impact Assessment
EPD	Environmental Protection Department
EU	European Union
NIA	Noise Impact Assessment
NSR	Noise Sensitive Receiver
SSSI	Site of Special Scientific Interest

General Introduction

§1. Geography and Population

I. Geography

1. Hong Kong is located to the south-east of the Mainland of China, adjoining the Province of Guangdong, and lies between latitudes 22° 37' and 22° 9' N and longitudes 113° 52' and 114° 30' E. Hong Kong covers Hong Kong Island, Lantau Island, the Kowloon Peninsula and the New Territories, including 262 outlying islands. Hong Kong has a land area of 1,104 km^2.[1] Between Hong Kong Island and the Kowloon Peninsula lies Victoria Harbour, one of the world's most renowned deepwater harbours. Hong Kong's climate is subtropical, with temperatures dropping below 10° Celsius in winter and exceeding 31° Celsius in summer. It is warm, sunny and dry in autumn, cool and dry in winter, and hot, humid and rainy from spring to summer.

II. Population

2. Hong Kong is one of the most densely populated countries. Its population was approximately 7.37 million in 2016. People of Chinese descent comprise the vast majority of the population, with foreign nationals comprising 8%.[2] The New Territories has the largest share of the population, with its share increasing from 50% in 2001 to 52.3% in 2016. The share of the population on Hong Kong Island decreased from 20% in 2001 to 17.6% in 2016. During the same period, the share for Kowloon remained at around 30%. Population density, as measured by the number of persons per square kilometre of land area, increased from 6,237 in 2001 to 6,777 in 2016 for the territory as a whole. The most densely populated district was Kwun Tong District, with a density of 55,530 persons per square kilometre in 2016. The population densities in districts in the New Territories were generally lower than those in districts on Hong Kong Island and in Kowloon. In 2016, 45.6% of the

1. The information contained in this paragraph and the following paragraphs on Hong Kong population was taken from the website of the Hong Kong Census and Statistics Department, the bi-census of 2016 http://www.bycensus2016.gov.hk/en/bc-mt.html. The Hong Kong Government's website is a rich source of updated information and also contains the Hong Kong Yearbook.
2. *See* http://www.gov.hk/en/about/abouthk/facts.htm.

population was in public housing (29.2% in rental housing and 16.4% in subsidized home ownership scheme) while 53% of the population was in private housing sector.[3]

Hong Kong has enjoyed an impressively low rate of unemployment. From January 2012 to January 2014, it ranged from 3.2% to 3.5%, and in 2016 it came down again to 3.2%. The labour force increased from 2.8 million in 1991 and 3.724 million in 2011 to 3.91 in 2016.[4]

3. Census and Statistics Ordinance (Cap 316) makes provision for the taking of a census of population and the collection, compilation and publication of statistical information concerning Hong Kong. A population census is generally taken every ten years and the last exercise was carried out in 2011. A bi-census is taken in between two census, and the last bi-census was conducted in 2016.

§2. Legal and Political Structure

4. Hong Kong is a Special Administrative Region of the People's Republic of China. Since the hand over by the British of its sovereignty to the People's Republic of China, Hong Kong is governed by the Hong Kong Basic Law, operating within the unique 'One Country, Two Systems' concept, which guarantees that the Chinese socialist system and policies will not extend to Hong Kong. The system of government that the Basic Law has introduced is virtually a continuation of the previous system of colonial government, subject to a number of technical and substantive modifications.

5. The Basic Law vests legislative power in the Legislative Council, executive power in the executive branch of the government headed by the Chief Executive, and judicial power in the courts. The Legislative Council is an elected body returning thirty-five members through geographical constituencies and thirty-five members through functional constituencies. The Chief Executive, the Head of Hong Kong Government, is selected by the people of Hong Kong and appointed by the Government of the People's Republic of China. The Basic Law provides for the appointment of a broadly representative election committee to select the Chief Executive. The most recent election of a Chief Executive through the election committee was held in March 2017, and the newly elected Chief Executive assumed office on 1 July 2017. The intention of the Basic Law is for Hong Kong to gradually move to a system where the Legislative Council and the Chief Executive are directly elected, on a one-man-one-vote basis. Judicial appointments are through a system of appointment, with safeguards to secure independence of the judiciary.

6. Hong Kong has an Executive-led system of government, where the Executive initiates financial and other public policies for debate and approval by the Legislative Council and is responsible for their implementation. The executive branch of

3. *See* https://www.gov.hk/en/about/abouthk/factsheets/docs/employment.pdf.
4. *See* https://www.censtatd.gov.hk/hkstat/sub/so30.jsp.

the government consists of the Chief Executive, the Head of Hong Kong Government; the Executive Council, appointed by the Chief Executive to advise him; and the Public Service, headed by three secretaries, namely the Chief Secretary, Financial Secretary and the Secretary for Justice.

7. In this constitutional arrangement, the Legislative Council is in many ways subordinate to the Chief Executive. Article 74 imposes a significant limitation on the power of the Legislative Council to initiate legislation:

> Members of the Legislative Council of the Hong Kong Special Administrative Region may introduce bills in accordance with the provisions of [the Basic Law] and legal procedures. Bills which do not relate to public expenditure or political structure or the operation of the government may be introduced individually or jointly by members of the Council. The written consent of the Chief Executive shall be required before bills relating to government policies are introduced.

A Bill passed by the Legislative Council becomes law when it is assented to by the Chief Executive. An Ordinance takes legal effect from the appointed date, that is, the date on which the Chief Executive directs the Ordinance to come into effect. Thus, an ordinance which is not promulgated, or brought into effect, by the Chief Executive will remain in the statute book, but will have no legal effect. A legislative measure that falls outside the restrictions in Article 74 may be proposed by a private member and passed by the Legislative Council, but it cannot become law until it is assented to and promulgated by the Chief Executive.[5]

The Chief Executive must report any law that has been enacted by the Legislative Council to the Chinese Central Government for record. The reporting of a statute duly enacted in Hong Kong for record does not affect the entry into force of such law. If in the view of the Central Government the law does not fall within the legislative competence of the Legislative Council, it may return it in which case it stands invalidated. Such invalidation does not have retrospective effect unless otherwise provided for in Hong Kong law.[6]

8. The Legislative Council has no power to remove the Chief Executive. It may persuade the Chinese Government to remove him by impeaching him as provided by Article 73(9) of the Basic Law:

---

5. *Leung Kwok Heung and Another v Chief Executive of the HKSAR* [2006] HKEC 239 concerned the Interception of Communications Ordinance (Cap 532), which was introduced as a private member's bill and passed by the Legislative Council, over the opposition of the administration, and assented to by the Governor just three days before the British colonial rule came to an end on 1 July 1997. Realizing that the Bill could not be implemented without the support of the government, the Legislative Council specifically provided in the Bill that it would become operative on a day to be appointed by the Governor (after 1 July 1997 the Chief Executive). Until 2005 when the judicial review application was made, the Chief Executive had not promulgated the bill. The Court of First Instance refused to issue a declaration that the Chief Executive had failed in his duty to promulgate the Ordinance or to issue an order in the nature of mandamus directing the Chief Executive to bring the Ordinance into effect. Affirmed by the Court of Appeal: [2006] HKEC 239.
6. Basic Law, Art. 17.

> If a motion initiated jointly by one-fourth of all the members of the Legislative Council charges the Chief Executive with serious breach of law or dereliction of duty and if he or she refuses to resign, the Council may, after passing a motion for investigation, give a mandate to the Chief Justice of the Court of Final Appeal to form and chair an independent investigation committee. The committee shall be responsible for carrying out the investigation and reporting its findings to the Council. If the committee considers the evidence sufficient to substantiate such charges, the Council may pass a motion of impeachment by a two-thirds majority of all its members and report it to the Central People's Government for decision.

In January 2013, an unsuccessful attempt was made to impeach the Chief Executive.[7]

9. Hong Kong's constitutional system, therefore, relies for its successful operation on close cooperation between the legislative and executive branches of the government. The Government of the Hong Kong Special Administrative Region must abide by the law and be accountable to the Legislative Council of the Region: it must implement laws passed by the Legislative Council and in force; it must present regular policy addresses to the Legislative Council; it must answer questions raised by members of the Legislative Council; and it must obtain approval from the Legislative Council for taxation and public expenditure.

10. The judicial branch exists and operates independently of the other two branches of government. Courts have unlimited constitutional jurisdiction in the sense that they can question the constitutionality of legislation, in addition to their extensive powers to review legality of administrative action. As in other common law jurisdictions, the existence of special tribunals is a special feature of the system of dispute settlement in Hong Kong. Being an international centre for commercial dispute resolution, Hong Kong has embraced alternative dispute resolution and the judiciary has taken a special interest in encouraging amicable dispute resolution as an alternative to litigation. The judiciary is also committed to aggressive modernization of litigation processes in order to make courts more accessible.[8]

I. The Relationship Between the Chinese Central Authorities and Hong Kong

11. Hong Kong is an inalienable part of China, but has been authorized to exercise 'a high degree of autonomy'. Hong Kong is one of the two Special Administrative Regions of China, the other being Macau, both created in pursuance of Article 31 of the Chinese Constitution. The Basic Law is unique because it was

7. *See* https://asiancorrespondent.com/2013/01/hk-lawmakers-try-to-impeach-beijing-backed-leader/.
8. *See* http://mediation.judiciary.hk/en/index.html.

enacted as a national law of China but for the purpose of giving effect to an international treaty between Britain and China, the outgoing and incoming sovereigns.[9] The Basic Law sets out how relations between China and Hong Kong are to be conducted.

12. The power to amend the Basic Law remains with the National People's Congress of China. However, before exercising the power of amendment, the National People's Congress is required to consult the Committee for the Basic Law, which is an advisory body consisting of Mainland and Hong Kong representatives.[10] There have been so far no amendment of the Basic Law. The ultimate power of interpreting the Basic Law rests with the Standing Committee of the National People's Congress.[11] There have so far been five interpretations of the Basic Law. In adjudicating cases, the courts of Hong Kong must follow any interpretation pronounced by the Standing Committee.[12]

13. Hong Kong was a British Crown Colony until the resumption of sovereignty over it was resumed by the People's Republic of China in 1997. Hong Kong is an integral part of China and is not a sovereign independent state. It is an autonomous region within the People's Republic of China, officially known as Hong Kong Special Administrative Region. Hong Kong's interests are represented in international relations by the sovereign state, the People's Republic of China. There is a basic division of powers and functions between the Chinese central authorities and the Hong Kong Special Administrative Region. For instance, foreign affairs and defence are matters for the Central Government. However, a fair proportion of activities of that description may be carried out by the Hong Kong Government, upon authorization.[13] Recognizing Hong Kong's special historical development, socio-economic, cultural, legal and political system, China has granted a high degree of autonomy to Hong Kong.[14] This essentially means that in domestic matters Hong Kong government has freedom to make policies and implement them without any approval being necessary from the People's Republic of China. The Basic Law expressly provides that Chinese national laws, except those which are specified in the Basic Law, have no application in Hong Kong. National laws of China do not apply in Hong Kong, except those relating to 'defence and foreign affairs as well as other matters outside the limits of autonomy of the Region as specified by [the Basic Law]', through their incorporation in Annex III of the Basic Law.[15] The Basic Law

9. Namely, 'The Joint Declaration of the Government of the United Kingdom of Great Britain and Northern Ireland and the Government of the People's Republic of China on the Question of Hong Kong', signed on 19 December 1984.
10. Basic Law, Art. 159.
11. Basic Law, Art. 158.
12. *See*, for instance, *Chief Executive of HKSAR v President of the Legislative Council* [2017] 1 HKLRD 460 (CA). On 16 January 2017, the Court of Appeal refused leave to appeal to the Court of Final Appeal: *Chief Executive of HKSAR v President of the Legislative Council* [2017] HKEC 53.
13. Basic Law, Arts 13 and 14.
14. Basic Law, Art. 12.
15. Basic Law, Art. 18.

provides that there shall be no interference in Hong Kong's affairs by any department of the Central Government or any local or municipal authority in the rest of China.[16]

II. Hong Kong's System of Government: The Executive Branch

14. Hong Kong has been given a high degree of autonomy and enjoys executive, legislative, and independent judicial power, including that of final adjudication, in accordance with the Basic Law. As provided by Article 62 of the Basic Law, the Hong Kong Government formulates and implements policies; conducts administrative affairs; conducts external affairs as authorized by the Central People's Government under the Basic Law; draws up and introduces budgets and final accounts; drafts and introduces bills, motions and subordinate legislation; designates officials to sit in on the meetings of the Legislative Council and to speak on behalf of the government.

15. The executive branch of the government is headed by the Chief Executive, appointed for a term of five years by the Chinese Central Government, after having been selected or elected through consultations held locally.[17] The main powers and functions of the Chief Executive include: determining government policies; approving the introduction of motions regarding revenues or expenditure to the Legislative Council; signing bills passed and budgets approved by the Legislative Council; and making judicial and public appointments.[18] There is an Executive Council to assist the Chief Executive in policymaking, but the Chief Executive is not bound to accept its advice.[19] The Chief Executive is required to consult the Executive Council before making important policy decisions, introducing bills to the Legislative Council, making subordinate legislation, or dissolving the Legislative Council, except for the appointment, removal and disciplining of officials and the adoption of measures in emergencies.[20] Currently, the Executive Council consists of sixteen official members (Chief Secretary, Secretary for Administration, Secretary for Justice and thirteen Secretaries, who head bureaus) and fifteen non-official members.[21]

The Chief Executive is assisted by three secretaries: Chief Secretary for the Administration, Financial Secretary and Secretary for Justice. The Secretary for Justice oversees the Public Service Commission, the Department of Justice, Independent Commission against Corruption, Office of Ombudsman and Audit Commission. The Chief Secretary for the Administration oversees nine bureaus dealing with civil service, education, home affairs, security, constitutional and mainland affairs, environment, transport and housing, labour and welfare, and food and health. There are four bureaus under the supervision of the Financial Secretary: Development, Commerce and Economic Development, Financial Services and

16. Basic Law, Art. 22.
17. Basic Law, Arts 43, 45, 46.
18. Basic Law, Art. 48.
19. Basic Law, Arts 54, 55, 56.
20. Basic Law, Art. 56.
21. *See* http://www.ceo.gov.hk/exco/eng/.

Treasury, Innovation and Technology. Each bureau is headed by a Secretary (such as Secretary for Education) and has under it several government departments and other administrative units such as agencies (for instance, Working Family and Student Financial Assistance Agency), commissions (for instance, the University Grants Commission) and authorities (for instance, Communications Authority). The Chief Secretary for the Administration oversees the Policy Project Coordination Office, Administration Wing and the Efficiency Unit. The Financial Secretary oversees the Hong Kong Monetary Authority and Economic Analysis and Business Facilitation Unit. The Central Policy Unit and the Belt and Road Office are directly under the Chief Executive. Currently, there are thirteen bureaux, of which the ones directly relevant to environmental protection being Environment Bureau, Development Bureau, Transport and Housing Bureau and Food and Health Bureau. Environment Bureau has the smallest number of divisions. It only has one department under it, namely the Environmental Protection Department. Development Bureau and Financial Services and Economic Development Bureau have the highest number of subdivisions. Each Bureau has ten departments or other units under it.[22]

16. Prior to 2002, the heads of bureaux were civil servants and they operated under the leadership of the relevant Secretary. In 2002 a system of accountability was introduced and bureaux heads were no longer to be civil servants but political appointees appointed by and answerable to the Chief Secretary for the Administration, retitled secretaries (such as Secretary for the Environment). In 2008, bureaux were assigned a deputy secretary and an assistant secretary who were likewise politically answerable. Secretaries, deputy secretaries and assistant secretaries could be drawn from the civil service and outside.[23] With the introduction of the political appointments system for the principal officials in 2008, the Civil Service Bureau adopted a Civil Service Code which civil servants are expected to uphold. It sets out the framework within which civil servants are expected to work with politically appointed officials.[24]

III. Hong Kong's System of Government: The Legislative Branch

17. Hong Kong's legislature, the Legislative Council, is elected for a term of four years.[25] The Legislative Council has the power to pass legislation, approve taxation and public expenditure, debate government policies and matters of public interest and scrutinize government.[26] The power of the Legislative Council to initiate and pass legislation operates in the following way. Any Legislative Council member may propose any bill. A bill introduced by a member is known as a Member's Bill. Where a bill is sponsored by the government, it is called a Government bill. Any member of the Legislative Council may introduce a bill so long as it does

22. *See* https://www.gov.hk/en/about/govdirectory/govchart/index.htm.
23. *See* 'Consultation Document on Further Development of the Political Appointment System' of 2006 *http://www.info.gov.hk/archive/consult/2006/pa_consultation_e.pdf.*
24. *See* Civil Service Code of 2009 at http://www.csb.gov.hk/english/admin/conduct/1751.html.
25. Basic Law, Art. 69.
26. Basic Law, Art. 73.

not relate to public expenditure or political structure or the operation of the government. A bill relating to government policies may be introduced in the Legislative Council only with the written consent of the Chief Executive.[27] The primacy of the Legislative Council in its relationship with the government is clearly set out in Article 64 of the Basic Law, which provides as follows:

> The Government of the Hong Kong Special Administrative Region must abide by the law and be accountable to the Legislative Council of the Region: it shall implement laws passed by the Council and already in force; it shall present regular policy addresses to the Council; it shall answer questions raised by members of the Council; and it shall obtain approval from the Council for taxation and public expenditure.

A member's bill may deal with any matter that is not excluded by Article 74. For instance a member may introduce a bill which deals not with a matter of general public interest, but a private matter such as the incorporation of a religious or educational institution. Such a bill is known as a private bill.

A bill passed by the Legislative Council will become law when it is assented to and promulgated by the Chief Executive (Article 76 of the Basic Law).

18. Legislative power is entrusted to the Legislative Council which is wholly elected, although not all members are elected by universal franchise on a one-man-one-vote system. Thirty-five of its seventy members are elected from geographical constituencies on the basis of universal franchise, while the other thirty-five members are elected from functional constituencies.[28]

19. Decisions in the Legislative Council are generally taken by a majority vote. Bills sponsored by the government may be passed with a simple majority of those present and voting. However, the passage of motions, bills or amendments to government bills introduced by individual members of the Legislative Council requires a simple majority vote of each of the two groups of members present: (1) members returned by functional constituencies and (2) members returned by geographical constituencies through direct elections.[29]

20. A bill passed by the Legislative Council of the Hong Kong Special Administrative Region may take effect only after it is signed and promulgated by the Chief Executive. If the Chief Executive considers that a bill passed by the Legislative Council is not compatible with the overall interests of the Region, he or she [the first woman Chief Executive was elected in March 2017 and is scheduled to assume office on 1 July 2017] may return it to the Legislative Council within three months for reconsideration. If the Legislative Council passes the original bill again by not less than two-thirds of all the members, the Chief Executive must sign and promulgate it within one month. If he does not do so, and if consensus still cannot be

27. Basic Law, Art. 74.
28. *See* Annex II of the Basic Law, as amended in 2010.
29. *See* Annex II of the Basic Law, 'II. Procedure for voting on bills and motions in the Legislative Council'.

reached after consultations, the Chief Executive may dissolve the Legislative Council.[30] To counter balance his power of veto, Basic Law provides that if the Legislative Council formed after such dissolution passes the same bill with a two-thirds majority, the Chief Executive must sign and promulgate the law. Otherwise, he must resign.[31] Similar provision has been made in relation to the refusal of the Legislative Council to pass the budget presented and any legislation proposed by the government.[32]

IV. Hong Kong's System of Government: The Judicial Branch

21. Judicial power is exercised by the courts of Hong Kong, which are to be established by ordinary legislation.[33] Article 83 of the Basic Law provides that the structure, powers and functions of the courts of Hong Kong at all levels shall be prescribed by law. The Basic Law sets out the courts system as consisting of the Court of Final Appeal, the High Court (Court of Appeal and the Court of First Instance together), District Courts, Magistrate's Courts and other special courts.[34] Article 81 further provides that 'the judicial system previously practised in Hong Kong shall be maintained except for those changes consequent upon the establishment of the Court of Final Appeal of the Hong Kong Special Administrative Region'. The Court of Final Appeal has replaced the Privy Council as Hong Kong's highest court of law. Article 82 of the Basic Law provides that the power of final adjudication of the Hong Kong Special Administrative Region shall be vested in the Court of Final Appeal of the Region, which may as required invite judges from other common law jurisdictions to sit on the Court of Final Appeal. Such overseas judges are referred to as overseas non-permanent judges.[35] The establishment of the system of courts in Hong under the Hong Kong Basic Law may be briefly explained as follows: The intention of the Basic Law is to continue the system of courts, and their jurisdictional remits, as prevailing at the time the Basic Law came into effect; the only significant change was to set up a new Court of Final Appeal to take over from the Judicial Committee of the Privy Council which was the highest judicial tribunal in Hong Kong under British colonial administration. The Basic Law therefore makes

30. Basic Law, Arts 49, 50.
31. Basic Law, Art. 52(2).
32. Basic Law, Art. 52(3).
33. Basic Law, Art. 80.
34. Basic Law, Art. 81. Special courts in Hong Kong include the Juvenile Court established by the Juvenile Offenders Ordinance (Cap 226) which exercises the powers of a magistrate in proceedings under this ordinance, Lands Tribunal established under the Lands Tribunal Ordinance (Cap 17), Labour Tribunal established under the Labour Ordinance (Cap 25) which has exclusive jurisdiction in relation to matters such as claims in relation to a breach of term relating to minimum wage, Small Claims Tribunal established under the Small Claims Ordinance (Cap 338) and Obscene Articles Tribunal established under the Control of Obscene and Indecent Articles (Cap 390) which can exercise the powers of a magistrate in dealing with matters within its jurisdiction.
35. *See* http://www.hkcfa.hk/en/about/overview/index.html.

special reference to the Court of Final Appeal. It also makes provision for the jurisdictional limitations on Hong Kong courts, in the form of the final authority of constitutional interpretation vested in the Standing Committee of the National People's Congress of the People's Republic of China.

22. Article 158 of the Basic Law provides that the Standing Committee of the National People's Congress of China has the power to interpret any provision of the Basic Law. It goes on to provide that the Standing Committee authorizes the courts of Hong Kong to interpret, on their own, provisions of the Basic Law which are within the limits of the autonomy of Hong Kong. Article 158 provides that Hong Kong courts may interpret provisions of the Basic Law concerning affairs which are the responsibility of the Central People's Government or concerning the relationship between the Central Authorities and the Region. However, if such a question of interpretation of such reserved powers comes before the court and the determination of that question is necessary for the case to be finally disposed of, the court must refer the question to the Standing Committee for its binding interpretation.[36] The relevant provision, Article 158 clarifies the effect of an interpretation: 'When the Standing Committee makes an interpretation of the provisions concerned, the courts of the Region, in applying those provisions, shall follow the interpretation of the Standing Committee. However, judgments previously rendered shall not be affected.'

23. Articles 88, 89 and 90, which are discussed in this and the following three paragraphs, are pivotal to the guarantee of judicial independence. Article 89 provides that judges of Hong Kong courts shall be appointed by the Chief Executive on the recommendation of an independent commission composed of local judges, persons from the legal profession and eminent persons from other sectors.[37] Article 90 of the Basic Law provides that judges and other members of the judiciary of the Hong Kong Special Administrative Region shall be chosen on the basis of their judicial and professional qualities and may be recruited from other common law jurisdictions. This follows the guarantee Article 81 holds out: 'The judicial system previously practised in Hong Kong shall be maintained except for those changes consequent upon the establishment of the Court of Final Appeal of the Hong Kong Special Administrative Region' and the direction in Article 84 that the courts of the Hong Kong Special Administrative Region shall adjudicate cases in accordance with the laws applicable in the Region and may refer to precedents of other common law jurisdictions.

24. The Basic Law provides for the independence of the judiciary. Article 85 of the Basic Law provides that the courts of the Hong Kong Special Administrative Region shall exercise judicial power independently free from any interference and that members of the judiciary shall be immune from legal action in the performance

36. *See* Part VIII of the Basic Law 'Interpretation and Amendment of the Basic Law'.
37. *See* Judicial Officers Recommendation Ordinance (Cap 92).

of their judicial functions.[38] Article 88 provides that judges of the courts of the Hong Kong Special Administrative Region shall be appointed by the Chief Executive on the recommendation of an independent commission composed of local judges, persons from the legal profession and eminent persons from other sectors.

25. Article 89 provides that a judge of a court of the Hong Kong Special Administrative Region may only be removed for inability to discharge his or her duties, or for misbehaviour, by the Chief Executive on the recommendation of a tribunal appointed by the Chief Justice of the Court of Final Appeal and consisting of not fewer than three local judges. It also provides that the Chief Justice of the Court of Final Appeal of the Hong Kong Special Administrative Region may be investigated only for inability to discharge his or her duties, or for misbehaviour, by a tribunal appointed by the Chief Executive and consisting of not fewer than five local judges and may be removed by the Chief Executive on the recommendation of the tribunal and in accordance with the procedures prescribed in the Basic Law.

26. Article 90 provides that in the case of the appointment or removal of judges of the Court of Final Appeal and the Chief Judge of the High Court of the Hong Kong Special Administrative Region, the Chief Executive shall, in addition to following the procedures prescribed in Articles 88 and 89 of the Basic Law, obtain the endorsement of the Legislative Council and report such appointment or removal to the Standing Committee of the National People's Congress for the record.

§3. Sources of Law

27. Article 18 of the Basic Law provides that the laws in force in the Hong Kong Special Administrative Region shall be the Basic Law, the laws previously in force in Hong Kong as provided for in Article 8 of the Basic Law, and laws enacted by Hong Kong's legislature. Article 8 describes what is meant by laws previously in force in Hong Kong as 'the common law, rules of equity, ordinances, subordinate legislation and customary law … except for any that contravene [the Basic Law]'. Article 160 of the Basic Law provides as follows: 'Upon establishment of the Hong Kong Special Administrative Region, the laws previously in force in Hong Kong shall be adopted as laws of the Region, except for those which the Standing Committee of the National People's Congress declares to be in contravention of [the Basic Law]. If any laws are later discovered to be in contravention of [the Basic

38. *See Ma Kwai Chun v Leong Siu Chung* [2001–2003] HKCLRT 286 (CA), and *Tam Mei Kam v HSBC International Trustee Ltd* [2014] HKEC 1189 (CA), where Chu JA observed at [5] as follows: 'The common law principle of judicial immunity is both ancient and well settled. That a judge is absolutely immuned from personal civil liability for any judicial act done in his capacity as a judge, irrespective of whether he acted under gross error or negligence, or was actuated by envy, hatred and malice and all uncharitableness is well recognized by the law: *See Sirros v Moore & Others* at pp 132D & 140A and *Ma Kwai Chun v Leong Siu Chung* [2001-2013] HKCLRT 286, [9].'

Law], they shall be amended or cease to have force in accordance with the procedure as prescribed by [the Basic Law].' The Standing Committee declared that certain pre-existing statutes contravene the Basic Law.[39] An example of a pre-existing legislation so ruled out is the Application of English Law Ordinance (Cap 88). Similarly, the Standing Committee of the National People's Congress declared sections 2(3), 3 and 4 of the Bill of Rights Ordinance to contravene the Basic Law and those sections were expunged from the Ordinance. The hierarchy of law in Hong Kong, as in other common law jurisdictions, would be the Basic Law, primary legislation, subsidiary legislation, common law and equity, and custom. International law, which exercises an ever-compelling influence on domestic legal systems, has no direct binding force of law in Hong Kong. A principle of international law will gain binding effect in Hong Kong only if it is incorporated into the domestic law. Several international treaties and conventions, some of environmental concern, have been expressly adopted or given expression in local law.

28. As we have already seen, legislative power is vested in the legislature and laws made by the Legislative Council, which are known as Ordinances, are the primary sources of law, so long as they are consistent with the Basic Law. Hong Kong courts may enquire into the constitutionality of legislation and any law that contravenes the Basic Law may be declared invalid. Article 17 if the Basic Law requires all legislation to be reported to the Central Chinese Government for the record. The Standing Committee of the National People's Congress of the People's Republic of China may invalidate any such law that is not 'in conformity with the provisions of [the Basic Law] regarding affairs within the responsibility of the Central Authorities or regarding the relationship between the Central Authorities and the Region'. As in other common law jurisdictions, administrative agencies may be given power to make subsidiary legislation, a power which must be granted by 'parent legislation'. Environmental statutes, for instance, grant power to the Chief Executive to make regulations, which are subsidiary legislation. To be valid, subsidiary legislation must be consistent with the parent legislation and any other primary legislation in force, and must also be consistent with the Basic Law. It means that a subsidiary legislation which is consistent with the parent statute may become ineffectual because the parent statute itself is unconstitutional.

29. Common law and equity rank below legislation as a source of law. Common law in one sense refers to judge-made law. When used in conjunction with equity, common law refers to the body of jurisprudence that was developed in common law courts in England, while equity refers to the jurisprudence that was developed in courts of equity in England. After the amalgamation of courts of common law and equity, courts of law came to be courts of common law and equity administering the two systems of law according to their own peculiar characteristics.

39. *See* Decision of the Standing Committee of the National People's Congress on Treatment of the Laws Previously in Force in Hong Kong in Accordance with Art. 160 of the Basic Law of the Hong Kong Special Administrative Region of the People's Republic of China (Adopted at the Twenty-Fourth Session of the Standing Committee of the Eighth National People's Congress on 23 February 1997). This appears as Instrument sixteen appended to the Basic Law of Hong Kong. It is also published as A 206 in 'Hong Kong E-Legislation'. https://www.elegislation.gov.hk/.

30. Equity which was developed as a gloss on common law, and administered by equity courts to ensure justice and fairness, came in later years to be dependent on, and rather strictly regulated by, judicial precedent just as the common law is. While there is some overlap between common law and equity, these two branches of law continue to retain their inherent characteristics. In relation to environmental law, common law plays a more important part. For instance, criminal law provides an important enforcement mechanism to environmental regulation. Equity plays a minor role, for instance, by making its equitable remedies such as injunctions a useful devise to ensure compliance with environmental regulation.

31. Local custom as a source of law is rather unimportant in Hong Kong. Chinese customary laws play a limited role in relation to family matters as well as religious matters such as administration of Buddhist temples. Chinese customary laws may not have a part to play in environmental regulation at all.

32. In the area of environmental law, the primary source of law is legislation, the principal statutes being Air Pollution Control Ordinance, Water Pollution Control Ordinance, Noise Control Ordinance, Waste Disposal Ordinance and Environmental Impact Assessment (EIA) Ordinance. Primary legislation is supported by a network of regulations, notices, technical memoranda and codes of practice. The origins of the environmental regulation may be traced to common law regulation of relations between neighbours, especially in relation to nuisance. Common law remedies continue to provide some control over environmentally harmful acts. Hong Kong statutes rely on remedies in the nature of civil enforcement action, such as injunctions, as well as on criminal law for enforcement. The relevance of common law is illustrated in the substantive parts of this work.

33. Common law is primarily concerned with disputes between individuals. In the area of tort law common law intervened to protect property rights against unlawful intrusions. The principal areas where tort law played an important incidental part in protecting the environment are negligence, nuisance and the rule in *Rylands v Fletcher*.[40] Where a person caused harm to the property of the claimant, such as by letting water from his land flood the claimant's, there lay either a claim in negligence, nuisance, or for strict liability under the rule in *Rylands v Fletcher*, depending on the nature of the intrusion and the surrounding circumstances. The common law remedies exist for the protection of private rights, and protection of the environment can be described as an incidental benefit to the public.[41] Apart from the fact that no action in tort lay except at the suit of a claimant whose personal rights are affected, common law was also deficient in relation to remedies that were available. The onset of environmental legislation addressed both these deficiencies in common law: first, it set up a comprehensive environmental regulatory machinery to

---

40. [1868] UKHL 1.
41. A common law remedy, such as for nuisance, could coexist with the possible preventive, enforcement or remedial action taken under environmental legislation. In *Chan Ying Wah v Bachy Soletanche Group Ltd* [2005] 2 HKLRD 176, a claim in negligence, nuisance and under the rule in *Rylands v Fletcher* succeeded in relation to an escape of water which damaged a neighbour's crops, in a water pollution control area.

take preventive, enforcement and remedial action; and, second, it provided a diversity of appropriate monitoring and supervisory mechanisms supported by the use of modern technological advances and effective remedies to prevent and remedy environmental harm.

34. As Lord Goff of Chieveley succinctly stated in the celebrated case of *Cambridge Water Co Ltd v Eastern Counties Leather plc*:

> The protection and preservation of the environment is now perceived as being of crucial importance to the future of mankind; and public bodies, both national and international, are taking significant steps towards the establishment of legislation which will promote the protection of the environment, and make the polluter pay for damage to the environment for which he is responsible – as can be seen from the WHO, EEC and national regulations to which I have previously referred. But it does not follow from these developments that a common law principle, such as the rule in Rylands v Fletcher, should be developed or rendered more strict to provide for liability in respect of such pollution. On the contrary, given that so much well-informed and carefully structured legislation is now being put in place for this purpose, there is less need for the courts to develop a common law principle to achieve the same end, and indeed it may well be undesirable that they should do so.[42]

35. Lord Goff concluded:

> I incline to the opinion that, as a general rule, it is more appropriate for strict liability in respect of operations of high risk to be imposed by Parliament, than by the courts. If such liability is imposed by statute, the relevant activities can be identified, and those concerned can know where they stand. Furthermore, statute can where appropriate lay down precise criteria establishing the incidence and scope of such liability.[43]

36. Legislative regulation in the area of environmental protection, as in other regulatory areas, is more efficient than common law which is developed by judges through cases which come up before them for resolution.

37. The first advantage of legislation is that it can set up a comprehensive legislative regulatory framework, setting out environmental standards,[44] prohibiting

42. [1994] 2 AC 264 at 305 (HL).
43. *Ibid. See* Anton Cooray, '*Environmental Torts*', in Kemal Bokhary (ed.), *Tort Law and Practice in Hong Kong* (Sweet & Maxwell, Hong Kong, 2014).
44. For instance, Part II of the Water Pollution Control Ordinance, Cap 358, enables the Chief Executive to declare any part of Hong Kong a water control zone (s. 4) and requires the Secretary to establish for each such water control zone a water quality objective, meaning 'the quality which, in the opinion of the Secretary, should be achieved and maintained in order to promote the conservation and best use of those waters in the public interest'(s. 5). Once a water quality objectives has been established, it is the duty of the Authority to achieve the such water quality objective as soon as reasonably practicable and thereafter maintain the quality so achieved (s. 6).

certain acts (such as polluting the environment),[45] requiring a person convicted of a pollution offence to take remedial action where environmental harm has been done (such as under the Water Pollution Control Ordinance, Cap 358),[46] carrying out such remedial work by the Authority if such person fails to comply with such requirement,[47] regulating certain potentially harmful activities through licensing,[48] mandating certain action (such as carry out an environmental impact assessment for any proposed designated project,[49] obtaining and complying with an environmental licence), setting up agencies to ensure environmental friendliness of developmental activities (such as by overseeing EIAs), ensuring that regulated activities conform to the relevant standards and requirements (such as by requiring regular reporting by operators and through site inspections), and taking enforcement action (such as requiring operators to comply with licence conditions or prosecuting offenders).

38. An important feature of environmental legislation is the use of criminal sanctions as a deterrent. The five main environmental statutes (Air Pollution Control Ordinance, Water Pollution Control Ordinance, Noise Control Ordinance, Waste Disposal Ordinance and Environmental Impact Assessment Ordinance) create several types of offences: they include substantive environmental offences such as emitting smoke, discharging effluents or making noise in contravention of statutory prohibitions or restrictions; offences of failure to comply with statutory notices which require compliance with environmental regulations. Where an environmental statute requires a licence or permit for the carrying out of certain activities, such as discharging matter into Hong Kong waters, offences are created to serve two purposes: (a) to ensure due compliance with the conditions of the licence or permit and (b) to ensure that the licence or permit is not obtained by withholding material information or by providing materially incorrect information. It is common for environmental statutes to create offences in relation to the enforcement powers of the

45. For instance, Part III of the Water Pollution Control Ordinance (Cap 358) prohibits the discharge of any waste or polluting matter into the waters of Hong Kong and internal waters (s. 8) and the discharge of any prohibited matter into communal waters and communal drains (s. 9).
46. Where any person has been convicted of an offence of prohibited discharge under section 8 (such as discharging any waste or polluting matter into the waters of Hong Kong in a water control zone, or discharging any poisonous or noxious matter into the waters of Hong Kong) or section 9 (such as discharging any matter into a communal sewer or communal drain in a water control zone, other than discharging domestic sewage into permitted communal sewers and communal drains), the Authority may, if he is of the opinion that: (a) any part of the waters of Hong Kong suffered continuing damage as a direct result of the commission of the offence; and (b) it is reasonably practicable to restore or partially restore that part to the condition it was in before the commission of the offence, by notice in writing require the person so convicted to carry out such work as is specified in the notice to effect such restoration or partial restoration. Such restoration work must be carried out as directed by the Authority in the manner specified and before the date specified in such notice (s. 13).
47. Section 13(3) of the Water Pollution Control Ordinance (Cap 358) provides that (as seen in footnote 64) where the person on whom a notice requiring restoration of waters has failed to comply with the notice to carry out such restoration work or any part of restoration, the Authority may carry out such restoration work and recover the cost of doing so.
48. Licensing is a common regulatory mechanism in environmental regulation.
49. Under the Environmental Impact Assessment Ordinance, Cap 499.

Authority and of authorized officers: (a) offences of failure to cooperate with authorized officers as required by law and (b) offences of unauthorized disclosure of information that an authorized officer has acquired in the course of carrying out his duties.

39. Courts have recognized that, because of the vital importance of protecting the environment by punishing acts detrimental to the environment, the legislature is justified in imposing strict or absolute liability for environmental offences. The discussion of offences under the various environmental statutes will provide illustrations of such offences of strict and absolute liability. We may now briefly consider the difference between strict liability offences and absolute liability offences.[50] Strict liability refers to a situation where the prosecution needs to establish only *actus reus* (that is the commission of the prohibited act or failure to act) but the defendant may set up a common law or statutory defence. Absolute liability refers to situations where the statutory formulation of the offence leaves no room for the defendant to plead a statutory defence or a common law defence. In *Kulemesin v HKSAR*,[51] Ribeiro PJ reformulated the approach that he had proposed in *Hin Lin Yee v HKSAR*,[52] in identifying the different alternative interpretations that are possible of statutory offences that exclude or do not refer to *mens rea*:

(a) The presumption of *mens rea* has not been displaced by the statute presumption. (the prosecution must prove both *mens rea* and *actus reus*).
(b) The prosecution must prove only that the defendant is responsible for the prohibited act or failure to act. However, if there is evidence capable of raising a reasonable doubt that the defendant may have acted or omitted to act in the honest and reasonable belief that the circumstances of his conduct were such that, if true, liability would not attach, he must be acquitted unless the prosecution proves beyond reasonable doubt the absence of such exculpatory belief or that there were no reasonable grounds for such belief.
(c) The presumption of *mens rea* has been displaced so that the prosecution need not prove *mens rea* but the accused has a good defence if he can prove on the balance of probabilities that he acted or omitted to act in the honest and reasonable belief that the circumstances of his conduct were such that, if true, he would not be guilty of the offence.
(d) The presumption has been displaced and the accused is confined to relying on the statutory defences expressly provided for, the existence of such defences being inconsistent with the second and third alternatives mentioned above; and
(e) The presumption is displaced and the offence is one of absolute liability so that the prosecution succeeds if the prohibited act or omission is proved against the accused, regardless of his state of mind regarding the relevant elements of the offence in question.

---

50. See Anton Cooray 'Environmental Offences' Chapter 40 in *Archbold Hong Kong 2021* (Sweet & Maxwell, Hong Kong, 2021).
51. (2013) 16 HKCFAR 195 (CFA), [83].
52. (2010) 13 HKCFAR 142 (CFA), [96].

40. As a general rule of common law, the prosecution must prove that the prohibited conduct is attributable to the defendant who acted with a guilty mind. This is commonly referred to as coincidence of *actus reus* and *mens rea*. The need to prove the mental element of an offence may be relaxed by legislation. Sometimes an environmental statute expressly provides that no mental element has to be established. For instance, section 10 of the Water Pollution Control Ordinance provides that where 'it is alleged that the defendant caused matter to enter the waters of Hong Kong or inland waters or a communal sewer or communal drain or caused matter to be deposited as provided in s. 2(3) it shall not be necessary for the prosecution to prove that the acts or omissions in question were accompanied by any intention, knowledge or negligence on the part of the defendant as to any element of the offence'. However, liability is not absolute because the defendant may plead any of the defences set out in section 12, as appropriate, such as that the discharge or deposit was made in an emergency in order to avoid danger to life or property and as soon as was reasonably practicable he informed the Authority thereof in writing, or that he acted under instructions given to him by his employer and he exercised the care and took the steps that the court, having regard to his position as an employee, considers reasonable in the circumstances to avoid the occurrence of the prohibited discharge or deposit. There, the liability is strict and not absolute.

41. Sometimes, statutory offences do not explicitly refer to any mental element as part of the definition of the offence. It is then the role of judges to decide as a matter of statutory interpretation whether *mens rea* is or is not an element of the offence. The starting point is the presumption that *mens rea* is an essential element of any common law or statutory offence. The presumption may be displaced only when it is clearly or by necessary implication the intention of the legislature to do so. In what circumstance may the legislature be justified in displacing the presumption of *mens rea*, which conflicts with the presumption of innocence? The presumption may be displaced where the relevant statute is concerned with an issue of social concern. As the Privy Council emphatically stated in the case of *Gammon (Hong Kong) Ltd v Attorney General*, even where a statute is concerned with such an issue, the presumption of *mens rea* stands unless it can also be shown that the creation of strict liability or absolute liability will effectively promote the object of the statute by encouraging greater vigilance to prevent the commission of the prohibited act.[53] This decision of the Privy Council has been followed in relation to environmental offences for the following reasons:

53. *Gammon (Hong Kong) Ltd v Attorney General* [1984] 2 All ER 503 (PC),508. *See also Hin Lin Yee v HKSAR* (2010) 13 HKCFAR 142 (CFA), where the Court of Final Appeal endorsed the view taken in *Gammon* case that absolute liability only arises where such conclusion compelling and that regulatory nature of such offence was insufficient for imposition of absolute liability; it must serve some useful purpose which cannot be sufficiently met by making the offence subject to common law defence of honest and reasonable belief.

(1) environmental offences are regulatory offences and not truly criminal in character;
(2) they are concerned with issues of social concern; and
(3) imposition of strict liability promotes the objective of the statute by encouraging greater vigilance to prevent activities which are detrimental to the environment.

We may take an example from a case that clearly illustrates the difference between a strict liability offence and an absolute liability offence. *HKSAR v Paul Y-ITC Construction Ltd*[54] concerned a prosecution for contravention of section 6 of the Noise Control Ordinance (Cap 400) which created the offence of causing mechanical equipment to be used for construction work without a permit. Section 6 did not use any qualifying words such as 'knowingly' in creating the offence, unlike section 4 of the Ordinance which made it an offence to 'knowingly permit' any annoying noise to emanate from domestic premises. Section 6(1)(a) provided as follows: '[A]ny person who … causes … to be used any powered mechanical equipment … in respect of which a construction noise permit is not in force … commits an offence.' The Court of Appeal held that as long as the *actus reus* is established, namely the use of powered mechanical equipment without a construction noise permit, no *mens rea* needed to be proved. Section 6(1)(a) clearly indicated that no mental element such as intention, knowledge or negligence needed to be proved. The section was held to create a strict liability offence in the sense that the prosecution was not required to prove any form of *mens rea* as an element of the offence. However, the liability created by the section was not absolute because the defendant could rely on any statutory defence[55] provided by section 33 of the Noise Control Ordinance, such as that the prohibited act was done 'in pursuance of the purpose of the prevention of injury to any person or the saving of the life of any person' or any common law defence such as that he believed for good and sufficient reason, though erroneously, that the provisions of the Ordinance had been complied with.[56] In *R v Leung Kam-Hung*[57] the charge against the accused persons related to importing

54. [1998] 2 HKLRD 35 (CA).
55. Examples of cases of strict liability where a statutory defence was available are *R v Fanta Construction Co Ltd* [1996] HKLY 450 (CA)—unauthorized dumping at sea; *HKSAR v Sims Trading Co Ltd* [2002] HKLRD (Yrbk) 437)—prohibited discharges into communal sewers and communal drains under the Water Pollution Control Ordinance (Cap 358).
56. In *HKSAR v Paul Y-ITC Construction Ltd* [1998] 2 HKLRD 35 (CA), the Court of Appeal referred, obiter, to the possibility of pleading the common law defence of reasonable but mistaken belief to strict liability for carrying out noisy construction work without a construction noise permit. *Sunley Engineering and Construction Co Ltd* [2001] 2 HKC 318, [2001] HKLRD (Yrbk) 322 is a case where the defendant company, which was charged with contravention of a condition of its licence to discharge water from its construction site, had failed to prove that it had a reasonable, if mistaken, belief that the proper preventative steps had been taken to comply with the conditions of the licence.
57. [1986] HKDCLR 39.

ivory tusks and crocodile leather into Hong Kong, in breach of section 4(1) of the (repealed) Animals and Plants (Protection of Endangered Species) Ordinance (Cap 187), which provided as follows: 'Subject to s. 18, no person shall, except under and in accordance with a licence issued under s. 7(1), on his own behalf or on behalf of any person, import any scheduled species.' There was no reference in section 4(1) to any requisite mental element. There were also no defences that a defendant could plead. The District Judge held that this created an absolute offence and observed that the only way the provisions of the Ordinance can be effected is by imposing absolute liability on those concerned with the importation into Hong Kong of specified goods without a licence.

42. It is a matter of statutory interpretation whether a person charged with the commission of a strict liability offence is entitled to rely on any common law defence in addition to the relevant statutory defences. In *HKSAR v China State Construction Engineering (Hong Kong) Ltd*[58] the relevant provision was section 5 of the Air Pollution Control (Construction Dust) Regulation (Cap 311R) which provided as follows: 'The contractor responsible for a construction site where a regulatory work is being carried out shall ensure that the work is carried out in accordance with the Schedule.' Section 7 of the Regulations makes it a defence for the defendant to prove that his failure to comply with the statutory requirements was due to circumstances such as inclement weather and that he exercised due diligence to prevent the commission of the offence.[59] The magistrate had doubted whether the common law defence of 'honest but mistaken belief' was available to the defendant in addition to the statutory defence and found that, even if the common law defence was available, the defendant had failed to bring himself within its protection. While deciding that the magistrate had committed no error of law or fact, the Court of First Instance did not express any opinion regarding whether the statutory defence operated to the exclusion of the common law defence of honest but mistaken belief.[60]

The legal principles which apply in determining whether a statutory provision creates an offence of strict liability or absolute liability, which is not subject to any

58. [2005] HKEC 381.

59. *See also* s. 16A(3) of the Waste Disposal Ordinance which provides that a person charged with an offence of unlawful depositing of waste has a defence if he proves that he took all reasonable precautions and exercised all due diligence to avoid the commission of the offence.

60. *See also HKSAR v Kwan On Construction Co Ltd* [2009] HKEC 926 and *HKSAR v Kwan On Construction Co Ltd* [2009] HKEC 926 where the defendant failed to establish the defence of due diligence (both prosecutions under the Air Pollution Control Ordinance) and *HKSAR v Kwan On Construction Co Ltd* [2009] HKEC 978 (prosecution under the Water Pollution Control Ordinance). *See also HKSAR v Dragages Hong Kong Ltd* [2015] 2 HKLRD 1165 where the common law defence was not applicable in the absence of evidence that the defendant had good and sufficient reasons to believe that it had complied with the Ordinance and the conditions of the construction noise permit.

statutory or common law defence,[61] have been set out in the decisions of the Court of Final Appeal in *Hin Lin Yee v HKSAR*[62] and *Kulemesin v HKSAR*.[63]

Where a person is acting or has acted in breach of an environmental statute, there are various measures that the Authority may take to prevent the commission of the breach or to remedy the effects of the breach. They include supervision by the Environmental Department followed by advice, warnings, and, orders to take remedial measures or desist from taking measures that may cause contribute to environmental harm. Prosecution for the commission of a criminal offence is only one of the measures that may be taken. It is instructive here to refer to the non-statutory Prosecution Policy of the Environmental Protection Department, which is modelled on the prosecution policy of the Department of Justice of the Hong Kong Government. The policy is not to institute criminal proceedings in respect of every breach of environmental law. To determine whether criminal proceedings are appropriate, the department reviews the available evidence and all other factors, including those favourable to the offender. The department will institute criminal proceedings only when it is in the public interest to do so. In assessing public interest, the relevant considerations include the seriousness of the breach, the consequences of the breach, the attitude of the suspect such as remorsefulness, how the decision to prosecute affect other people, how serious a view is the court likely to take of the offence as regards sentencing in the event the offence is proved, the availability of a civil remedy and the likely effect a prosecution will have on others (paragraphs 5 and 7). The Policy recognizes the importance of the separation of the prosecutor and the investigation team in the Environmental Protection Department in order to ensure that the prosecutor acts independently of the investigators (paragraph 4.1). The Policy states that the power to prosecute for environmental pollution offences has been delegated by the Secretary for Justice to officers of the Environmental Protection Department (paragraph 2.2).

The existence of a comprehensive environmental regulatory system is in place is a relevant consideration in determining whether an activity which complies with

---

61. For instance, the offence of permitting the use of a motor vehicle on a road without third party insurance, where the honest and genuine belief that the vehicle is insured was not a defence as in *HKSAR v Wai Lung Shing* [2005] 4 HKLRD J3. In *HKSAR v Shun Tak Properties Ltd* [2009] 3 HKLRD 299, the Court of Appeal considered the nature of the offence created by s. 4(e) of the Factories and Industrial Undertakings (Suspended Working Platforms) Regulation (Cap 59, Sub Leg AC), which provided that 'the owner of a suspended working platform shall ensure that it is not used for carrying persons unless it is properly maintained'. This provision for held to have created an absolute liability for two reasons: (i) Neither the Factories and Industrial Undertakings Ordinance (Cap 59) nor the Regulation, refer to any requisite mental element such as 'knowingly' or 'without lawful excuse'. The offences are not subject to any statutory defence, and it was not possible to assume that the common law defence of honest and reasonable mistaken belief; (ii) policy considerations made it necessary to treat offences involving public safety under the Ordinance and the Regulation as one of absolute liability. This promoted the objects of the statute by encouraging greater diligence to prevent the commission of the prohibited act. And otherwise, the intention of the Legislature to ensure public safety could easily be defeated by entrusting the duty to maintain to an independent contractor, and the contractor was not liable because he was not an 'owner' within the Regulation. Absolute liability is generally viewed with disfavour: *So Wai Lun v HKSAR* [2006] 3 HKLRD 394 (CFA).
62. (2010) 13 HKCFAR 142 (CFA).
63. (2013) 16 HKCFAR 195 (CFA).

such system may nevertheless amount to a breach of common law standards that are applicable to negligence, nuisance and even *Rylands v Fletcher*.[64]

43. The second advantage of legislation is that environmental legislation commonly provides for regulatory bodies who are responsible for setting standards, monitoring compliance and taking enforcement action including instituting civil or criminal litigation. In contrast, enforcement of compliance with common law has to be through private litigation which is prohibitively expensive. An individual who is aggrieved by a breach of environmental legislation may indirectly enforce environmental standards by making a complaint to the regulatory body which may take enforcement action. Once a valid complaint is made, costs of investigation and enforcement, including litigation, will be by the publicly funded regulatory agencies. Unlike in some other jurisdictions, there is no statutory provision in Hong Kong enabling private individuals to have direct access to courts for the purpose of enforcing environmental legislation.[65]

44. The third advantage of legislation is that environmental legislation promotes unification of law. There is a great amount of international agreements and conventions on environmental protection, and when domestic legislation is passed, there is an inevitable tendency to make it compatible with the universal practice. Sometimes domestic legislation is passed to give direct effect to international conventions. Even where a particular international convention or practice is not incorporated in the domestic law, domestic courts may have legitimate recourse to international material in interpreting domestic legislation.

45. The fourth advantage is that environmental legislation, however comprehensive, does not exclude the possibility of private citizen's access to courts of law. *Lloyds Bank plc v Guardian Assurance plc* provides a good example where it was

64. In *Barr v Biffa Waste Services Ltd* [2011] 4 All ER 1065 (QBD), at [3], Coulson J referred to the dilemma courts face in such situations: 'It is therefore right to note at the outset that this dispute involves a clash between two potentially irreconcilable principles. On the one hand, the claimants contend that they have inalienable common law rights in nuisance which have not been affected, let alone excluded, by the relevant environmental and landfill legislation and the detailed terms of Biffa's permit; on the other hand, Biffa submit that it would be unfair and unrealistic if the cascade of legislation and the terms of their permit were ignored, so that they could comply with all their numerous obligations and the detailed provisions of their permit, and still find themselves liable to the claimants in nuisance, as if the legislation and the permit did not exist.'

65. *See* Anton Cooray, 'Environmental Litigation in Hong Kong: The Role of the Judiciary and Statutory Tribunals' in John Hatchard & Amanda Perry-Kessaris (eds), *Law and Development: Facing Complexity in the 21st Century* (Cavendish Publishing, London, UK, 2003), 226–245. In the United Kingdom the Environmental Protection Act 1990 provides that a private citizen may move the Magistrate's Court for the abatement of a statutory nuisance (s. 82) in addition to the regulatory action that a local authority may take by way of issuing an abatement notice. In the USA, there is so much scope for private initiation of environmental regulation that we refer to 'environmental citizenship'. *See* JG Miller, 'The Standing of Citizens to Enforce against Violations of Environmental Statute in the United States' (2000) 12:3. J. of Env. L. 370–384. *See also* Professor Andrew Dobson, *Environmental citizenship and pro-environmental behaviour. Rapid research and evidence review* (November 2010: Sustainable Development Research Network). *See* below, '*V. Towards Environmental Citizenship?*' Paras [56]–[59].

argued on appeal that the lower court should not have exercised its discretion in favour of granting an injunction because the matter was controlled under the Control of Pollution Act 1974, and that it was, at the least, an undesirable duplication for the court to intervene to exercise its discretionary powers. Sir John Arnold P observed as follows:

> There is, in my judgment, nothing to be derived from the language of the Act or from any principle of jurisprudence, known to me at least, to justify the conclusion either that there would be some impropriety in the court exercising a jurisdiction to restrain a nuisance merely because a statutory power is given to a local authority to proceed by notice to control a similar nuisance, or from granting, if it thought proper so to do, larger relief than that prescribed by an existing or threatened notice.[66]

§4. Land Tenure in Hong Kong

46. A striking feature of Hong Kong's landholding system is that the government is the sole ground landlord.[67] The land and natural resources within Hong Kong are state property, meaning property of the People's Republic of China. However, it is the Hong Kong Government that is responsible for the management, use and development of land in Hong Kong. The Hong Kong government has the authority to lease land for use or development. The revenue derived from any such land grants is at the exclusive disposal of the Hong Kong Government.[68]

47. As a result of being the ground landlord, the government of Hong Kong is in a position to decide for what purposes any leased land may be used. Unlike in a freehold land system, a leaseholder has no right to unrestricted use of his land.[69] Even if a leaseholder (colloquially, but inaccurately, referred to as landowner)

66. (1986) 35 Build LR 38, 41 (CA).
67. *See* Anton Cooray, 'Government as Ground Landlord and Land Use Regulator: The Hong Kong Experience' in Kotaka and Callies (eds), *Taking Land: Compulsory Purchase and Regulation in Asian Pacific Countries* (University of Hawaii Press, USA, 2002), pp. 96-142.
68. Article 7 of the Basic Law.
69. Decisions taken by the Director of lands relating to grant, refusal to grant, renewal, and modification of land leases are not amenable to judicial review, unless there is a dominant public law element involved. *See Chau Tam Yuet Ching v Director of Lands* [2013] 3 HKLRD 169 (CA), where it was held that decisions to grant, modify or terminate a Government lease; to grant or modify or terminate a short-term waiver; or to grant and to cancel (for a breach of the terms of the licence) a licence for the occupation of unleased land were not reviewable. They were 'commercial decisions' which were guided by the interest of the government as landowner or landlord and governed by the private law of contract or land law as in the case of a lease or short-term waiver. The mere existence of some public interest considerations in the decision-making process did not per se render it amenable to public law remedies. As Lam JA explained: 'The mere presence of some public element in the Government's decisions is not sufficient to transform such decisions into public law decisions. After all, the Government administers land in Hong Kong, whether qua landowner or landlord or covenantee, for the benefit of the general public and it is difficult to imagine a case where a public official can make such decision without affecting the public interest either directly or indirectly.' The Court of Appeal referred to and followed the following previous decisions on this point: *Hang Wah*

secures planning permission for a development, he will not be able to implement it unless the lease conditions permit such development in its proposed density and manner. Where an existing lease does not permit the proposed development, the leaseholder has to apply for a lease modification which is granted at the discretion of the government; if a modification is granted, the government may impose a premium for the additional property development right.[70]

48. Similarly, the government is able to specify any environmental protection measures in relation to the use of a land by way of lease conditions. It is a standard practice for environmental type lease conditions to be imposed whenever a lease is granted or modified to enable a major development such as a housing scheme or commercial development.

49. Secan Ltd v Attorney-General[71] provides a good illustration. The lease, which in this case was an exchange of land agreement, relating to a proposed residential development contained the following condition:

> (12)(a) The Grantee shall within six months from the date of this Agreement submit to the Director for his approval proposals to mitigate any environmental problems as identified and notified to the Grantee within two months from the date of this Agreement by the Director of Environmental Protection, which may directly affect the lot or neighbouring lots or premises and shall implement such ameliorative measures as deemed necessary by the Director of Environmental Protection.

In pursuance of this, the developer agreed to erect a noise barrier along the road which fronted the residential building, but subsequently decided not to build it. When the government informed the developer that no occupation permit would be issued unless a noise barrier is erected as agreed, the developer unsuccessfully applied for judicial review contending that the noise barrier requirement was not binding on him.

A somewhat common environmental type lease restriction is the 'offensive trade clause'. In *Uni-Creation Investments Ltd v Secretary for Justice* [2017] 2 HKLRD 139, the Court of First Instance concluded that whether the construction of a columbarium could be regarded as falling fowl of the lease restriction prohibiting 'any noisy, noisome or offensive trade or business' in question depended on factors such

---

Chong Investment Co Ltd v Attorney-General [1981] HKLR 336 (PC), *Canadian Overseas Development Co Ltd v Attorney-General* [1991] 1 HKC 288 (CA), *Polorace Investments Ltd v Director of Lands* [1997] 1 HKC 373 (CA), *Rank Profit Industries Ltd v Director of Lands* [2009] 1 HKLRD 177 (CA), *Rank Profit Industries Ltd v Director of Lands* [2009] HKEC 1021, CFA, *and Anderson Asphalt Ltd v Secretary for Justice* [2009] 3 HKLRD 215.

70. In *Shun Shing Hing Investment Co Ltd v Attorney-General* [1983] HKLR 432, at 434, Hunter J said: 'A peculiar, if not unique, feature of life in Hong Kong is that the Government is the sole ground landlord. It is the provider of land and can combine the functions of landlord and planning authority. Thus, Hong Kong Government can do what many planning officers in the UK would give their eye-teeth to be able to do. They can charge developers a premium for the benefit of the permission they are giving them.'

71. [1995] 2 HKLR 523; [1995] 2 HKC 629.

as: (a) the nature of the business; (b) the locality of the business; (c) the nature of its operation; and (d) its effect on the neighbourhood.

Litton V-P explained at p 529: 'What we are concerned with here is, in effect, a commercial agreement: one which is intended to give the Government a very large measure of control over the development of this very large site on Ap Lei Chau. In construing the agreement, a court should not be too astute or subtle in finding defects and must give effect to what the parties by their agreement have clearly intended.'

50. The leasehold system in Hong Kong enables the government to decide for what purposes government land may be leased, such as for residential, commercial, and, educational or other community purposes. The inherent disadvantage of lease control as a method of land-use regulation is that leases are site specific. Although the government might have a land development policy for a particular area, grant of leases is not the ideal way of implementing such policy unless all the leases for that area are granted or modified all at the same time. Moreover, government policies may change over time. It is in this context that land-use planning regime becomes helpful. In Hong Kong, town planning and land lease systems operate rather disjunctively, in the sense that where planning legislation requires planning permission for a proposed development, the planning authorities are free to reject the application notwithstanding that the proposed development is permitted by the land lease. Conversely, the Town Planning Board may grant permission for a development which is not permitted by the applicable government lease, and it is then the responsibility of the landowner (leaseholder) to obtain a lease modification in order to implement the grant of planning permission. It has been asserted more than once that while the land leases serve the interests of the government as if it were a private landlord, planning permission system operates maintaining the correct balance between the leaseholder's private interests and the public interest.[72]

51. Hong Kong land-use regulation is a rather simple system. Development plans made by the Town Planning Board permit certain developments in designated zones as of right, for instance, a house in a residential zone, or a shop in a commercial zone. Any other type of development may be undertaken only if the proposed development is listed as a development which may be undertaken with planning permission.[73] An application for such development may be made to the Town Planning Board which may approve the application with or without planning conditions or refuse to approve it. A development which is permitted by the development plan or by a grant of planning permission may be implemented provided that it complies with other regulatory regimes such as lease control, building control and fire safety control.

---

72. *See United Bright Ltd v Secretary for Justice* [2015] 2 HKLRD 633 (CA), and cases referred to therein.

73. Because of this rather inflexible nature of a development plan, meaning that no planning permission may be granted for a type of development which is not listed in the plan as a development that may be permitted by the Town Planning Board, there have been many attempts to challenge the legality of a plan by way of judicial review. For a successful challenge, *see Hysan Development Co Ltd v Town Planning Board* [2014] HKEC 1869 (CA).

52. In considering applications for planning permission, the Town Planning Board must take all relevant planning considerations into account, and environmental considerations constitute such a material consideration.[74] Town Planning Board Guidelines specifically require a planning application to provide information on its environmental impacts and measures that are proposed to prevent or minimize such environmental impacts.[75] Where the Town Planning Board is not satisfied that any possible adverse impacts can satisfactorily be mitigated, planning permission would be refused.[76] In case of major land-use developments, the Town Planning Board requires a formal EIA conducted under the Environmental Impact Assessment Ordinance.

53. In granting planning permission, the Town Planning Board may impose planning conditions, including conditions for environmental protection which have to be met to the satisfaction of the Director of Environmental Protection or the Town Planning Board. In order to assist the Town Planning Board in its deliberations on environmental issues, the Director of Environmental Protection serves as one of its members. It is the practice of the Town Planning Board to receive comments from relevant government agencies, including the Environmental Protection Department, when it considers planning applications. Input from the Environmental Protection Department plays an important part in the proceedings of the Town Planning Board when it considers planning policies.

§5. Environmental Regulation

54. Hong Kong does not have an integrated environmental system, governed by a single environmental statute. Its environmental regulatory system developed piecemeal and is presently dependent on four principal environmental statutes and a number of supplementary statutes. Air Pollution Control Ordinance, Water Pollution Control Ordinance, Noise Control Ordinance and Waste Disposal Ordinance deal with distinct types of environmental pollution. The Environmental Impact Assessment Ordinance provides for a formal assessment of environmental impacts

---

74. The Town Planning Ordinance, unlike the Town and Country Planning Act 1990 of England and Wales, does not expressly require the Town Planning Board to take 'any other material considerations' (i.e., material considerations other than the relevant plan) into account. However, as a matter of administrative law principles the Town Planning Board, and indeed the Town Planning Appeal Board, must take all relevant considerations into account in arriving at its decisions. In this way, the idea and content of 'any other material considerations' in English planning law has found its way into Hong Kong planning law *See Halsbury's Laws of Hong Kong*, authored by Professor Anton Cooray (6th reissue, 2018) [385.270] 'Material Considerations' 368–382, at 369.

75. *See*, for instance, Town Planning Board Guidelines for Application for Development within Green Belt Zone under s. 16 of the Town Planning Ordinance, TPB PG-No. 10, para. 2 'Main Planning Criteria': '1. The proposed development should not be susceptible to adverse environmental effects from pollution sources nearby such as traffic noise, unless adequate mitigating measures are provided, and it should not itself be the source of pollution.'

76. As Professor Anton Cooray wrote in the Town Planning Appeal Board Decision in *Larkincil International Ltd v Town Planning Board* (2009) Appeal No. 2 of 2008: 'It is only where such impacts are unavoidable or uncontrollable that rejection of planning permission is justified.'

generated by major land-use developments. It is worth noting here that private property rights protected under the Basic Law need to be balanced with the need to protect public interest. Many planning regulations such as limitation on building rights on land are imposed in order to protect significant public interests such as prevent overcrowding or environmental pollution. Common law recognizes the validity of justifiable limitations on private property rights, and the Court of Final Appeal has recently clarified that such limitations would be justified only if they satisfy the proportionality test.[77]

I. Setting Up Environmental Standards

55. Hong Kong environmental statutes adopt several strategies for environmental regulation. The first strategy is to set out environmental standards that must be observed. For instance, the Air Pollution Control Ordinance provides for the adoption of Air Quality Objectives that must be met. The second strategy is to adopt a permit or licence system to ensure that certain activities cannot be undertaken without obtaining a permit or a licence, which ensures that the environmental authorities have an opportunity to assesses whether a proposed relevant activity is likely to be carried out in an environment-friendly manner and also to set out any conditions that the operators have to comply with. The threat of cancellation is an effective deterrent against breach of licences or permits. Environmental statutes also provide that breach of a licence or permit is a criminal offence for which deterrent punishments are prescribed. The third strategy is to make certain acts or omissions criminal offences, such as the discharge of prohibited matter into the waters of Hong Kong. The fourth strategy is to order the cessation of certain activities which are harmful to the environment and in case of non-compliance to authorize the environmental authority to take remedial measures. The fifth strategy is to warn an offender of an environmental wrong by issuing an abatement notice, the failure to comply with which is a punishable offence.

II. Absence of a Specialized Environmental Litigation System

56. An important feature of Hong Kong's environmental governance is the absence of a specialized environmental litigation system.[78] Hong Kong does not have a dedicated environmental court and all criminal cases relating to the environment are litigated in ordinary criminal courts. There is an administrative appeal system, as under the Town Planning Ordinance, under the following environmental legislation: Noise Control Ordinance, Water Pollution Control Ordinance, Air Pollution Control Ordinance, Waste Disposal Ordinance and the Environmental Impact

77. *See Hysan Development Co Ltd v Town Planning Board* [2016] HKEC 2081, CFA.

78. Anton Cooray, 'Environmental Litigation in Hong Kong: The Role of the Judiciary and Statutory Tribunals' in John Hatchard & Amanda Perry-Kessaris (eds), *Law and Development: Facing Complexity in the 21st Century* (Cavendish, London, UK, 2003), 226–245.

Assessment Ordinance. These Appeal Boards hear appeals against regulatory decisions such as to refuse a licence or impose conditions on a licence. There is no appeal to a court of law against a decision made by an Appeal Board.

57. Judicial review provides an avenue for a person aggrieved by a decision of an Appeal Board to question the legality of the appeal process or the decision, but not the merits of such Appeal Board decision. A recent example is *Serge Berthier v Noise Control Appeal Board*[79] where the applicant challenged the rejection of his appeal against a noise abatement notice. The court rejected the challenge based on the legality of the Appeal Board's decision and observed in relation to the applicant's attempt to introduce a new challenge to the noise abatement notice:

> Judicial review is not an appeal and the function of the Court is not to rehear the case on its merits. It is not for this Court in a supervisory role to consider an issue (in particular a fact sensitive one) that was never raised and argued before the Appeal Board. Not only is that this could not be relied on by the Applicant to show that the Appeal Board was wrong (in the public law sense) in coming to the decision as this had not been argued before it, this would also effectively allow an applicant to mount a second or alternative appeal under the pretence of judicial review. This should not be permitted unless there are good reasons to do so.[80]

Commenting on the proper role of the courts in general, the Court observed:

> This Court in judicial review is not concerned with the merits of the findings, in particular factual ones, of the Appeal Board. It would only interfere in those findings and the decision if they contain errors of law, are unreasonable or irrational in the public law sense, or are a result of procedural errors or unfairness.[81]

III. Limited Judicial Control of the Environmental Regulatory System

58. This hesitance on the part of the courts to second-guess the decision of an Appeal Board reflects the general judicial reluctance to transgress the area of government policymaking. *Clean Air Foundation Ltd & Another v Government of HKSAR*[82] illustrates this judicial attitude. There the applicants, in effect, invited the judiciary to declare that the government had failed in its legislative and constitutional duty to take effective measures to control air pollution. The applicants asserted that Government had a constitutional obligation to guarantee the right to life of all residents, which included the duty to provide the best possible health care, and that in failing to take more stringent steps to combat air pollution Government

79. [2011] HKEC 1432.
80. *Ibid.*, [104].
81. *Ibid.*, [97].
82. [2007] HKEC 1356.

had failed in that duty. It had failed, so it was asserted, because it had not ensured that there is adequate legislation in place and/or has not pursued effective policies. This failure, it was argued, constituted a breach of the Basic Law, the Bill of Rights and various international covenants which have been extended to Hong Kong.[83]

The Court of Appeal agreeing with the Court of First Instance decided that the judicial review application was directed at merits of government policy. Hartman J said that a government policy may be questioned in a court of law only on grounds of legality and that a policy does not become unlawful because it is 'unwise, short-sighted or retrogressive'. He rightly observed: 'It has long been accepted that policy is a matter for policy-makers and that to interfere with the lawful discretion given to policy-makers would amount to an abuse of the supervisory jurisdiction vested in the courts.'[84] Hartman J concluded that the judicial review application was 'fundamentally misconceived. While it purports to seek the determination of issues of law, on an objective assessment it is clear that it seeks in fact to review the merits of policy in an area in which Government must make difficult decisions in respect of competing social and economic priorities and, in law, is permitted a wide discretion to do so. While issues of importance to the community may have been raised, it is not for this court to determine those issues. They are issues for the political process'.[85]

83. *Ibid.*, [4] and [5].

84. *Ibid.*, para. [32]. In *Ng Ngau Chai v The Town Planning Board* [2007] HKEC 1207, [28], Reyes J said that he fully sympathized with the applicant's concerns about the deteriorating quality of the environment around his neighbourhood, by observed that 'the Court can only apply law. The Judiciary cannot manage the environment. That is the role of the Executive. … the Court cannot proceed with a judicial review in the absence of information pinpointing an administrative decision … and setting out the precise basis on which that decision is challenged'. *See*, generally on judicial deference to the legislature and the executive, Anton Cooray, 'Entering the political thicket: The role of the judiciary as an arbiter in relation to the making and interpretation of public policy' in Shimon Shetreet (ed), *Judicial Independence: The Rule of Law and World Peace* (Martinus Nijhoff: 2014) 200-216.

85. *Ibid.*, [43]. As Zervos J rightly explained in the case of *Reid, Peter Anthony v Environmental Bureau* [2017] HKEC 1304, [11]: 'As is well recognised, judicial review is the means by which the Court of First Instance exercises its general supervisory jurisdiction over inferior courts, tribunals and other bodies performing public functions. In general terms, the nature and scope of the judicial review jurisdiction is largely defined by the relief that a court may grant. The court on review is required to check the exercise of the public function that either has no lawful basis or has a lawful basis but has been exercised unfairly or unreasonably. It will not review the merits of a decision or attempt itself to perform the task that has been entrusted to the public authority by law.' The Court of Final Appeal has on more than one occasion emphasized the need to recognize the demarcation between the province of the judiciary and of the other two branches of government. For instance, in *Fok Chun Wa v Hospital Authority* (2012) 15 HKCFAR 409 the Court of Final Appeal observed that that the role of the judiciary was to apply the law, and matters of state or community policies were predominantly those for the executive or legislature. It would not usually be in the province of the courts to adjudicate on the merits or demerits of government socio-economic policies. In delivering the decision of the court, Ma CJ made it clear that courts would not hesitate to intervene in matters of government policy where such intervention is warranted. Ma CJ said at [66] that 'it would not usually be within the province of the courts to adjudicate on the merits or demerits of government socio-economic policies. That said, where appropriate … the court will intervene, this being a part of its responsibility to ensure that any measure or policy is lawful and constitutional. This has been the consistent position of the courts'. The circumstances where courts may or may not look into the legality of government policy are set out in [75]. Such intervention is justified where a policy choice

IV. Hong Kong Ombudsman

59. Hong Kong Ombudsman is a non-judicial institution which has been given the power to investigate into complaints of maladministration in the government and to propose recommendations for improvement. The Ombudsman has the power to find maladministration on the part of a government agency, but it has no power to order any remedy, such as payment of compensation, although it may recommend the making of an ex gratia payment. The Ombudsman has investigated into complaints against government agencies for environmental pollution activities. For instance, in Case No. 2291 of 2000, the Ombudsman enquired into a complaint that the Environmental Protection Department had failed to take action to prevent pollution caused by an illegal septic tank. In Case No. 3081 of 1998, the Ombudsman enquired into a complaint that the Environmental Protection Department failed to take enforcement action against the Housing Department under the Noise Control Ordinance. Both complaints were unsuccessful. The Ombudsman may also conduct direct investigations into acts of maladministration, but may more importantly conduct general enquiries. For instance, in January 2011, newspapers reported that the Ombudsman has enquired from the administration why Hong Kong's air quality objectives have not been updated for many years.[86] Later in the year, the Ombudsman recommended that air quality objective are outdated and that action must be taken to update them.[87] In 2015, the Ombudsman carried out a direct investigation into the implementation of the new emission control measures the government had introduced in 2014 to address the worsening roadside air pollution. The Ombudsman identified eight inadequacies in the implementation measures effected by the Environmental Protection Department and the Transport Department.[88]

V. Towards Environmental Citizenship?

60. Recourse to the judicial process is open to citizens only where a decision is taken by the administration which directly affects them, for instance, where a criminal prosecution is instituted for an environmental wrong, or a decision is taken affecting a person directly such as when a licence application is rejected.[89]

---

made by the government is 'manifestly beyond the spectrum of reasonableness' [76]. Even where the government may be said to be under a positive constitutional obligation to enact legislation, the decision as to how to comply with such obligation is necessarily a matter for the government, subject to the supervision of the courts to assess the practical efficacy of the measures adopted. Whether it had provided practical and effective protection would depend on the facts of any given case: *ZN v Secretary for Justice* (2020) 23 HKCFAR 15.

86. *See* http://www.independent.co.uk/travel/news-and-advice/ombudsman-probes-outdated-hong-kong-air-pollution-rules-2179232.html.

87. *See* http://www.foe.org.hk/e/content/cont_page.asp?cat_id=470&content_id=751#.WeouILpFyUk.

88. *See* summary of the investigation report: http://ofomb.ombudsman.hk/abc/files/Annex_1_E-28_1_2016.pdf.

89. Anton Cooray, 'Environmental Litigation in Hong Kong: The Role of the Judiciary and Statutory Tribunals' in John Hatchard & Amanda Perry-Kessaris (eds), *Law and Development: Facing Complexity in the 21st Century* 226–245 (Cavendish, London, UK, 2003).

61. Recent litigation, such as those in relation to air pollution, indicate that a member of the public may have sufficient standing to bring litigation questioning the legality of administrative action such as issuing an environmental permit. *Clean Air Foundation Ltd & Another v Government of HKSAR*,[90] which we have seen immediately above, is a case where the court held that an interested citizen might have sufficient interest to bring a judicial review application. There, the first applicant was a limited liability company, its principal aim being the protection of the 'environmental rights' of Hong Kong people. The second applicant was an environmental advocate, who had established the Clean Air Foundation in order to galvanize support of Hong Kong residents in actively promoting the improvement of Hong Kong's air quality. Hartman J agreed that the judicial review application was not an abuse of judicial process because it was at least prima facie arguable that the constitutional right to life might apply in the circumstances advocated by the applicants; that is, by imposing some sort of duty on the government to combat air pollution.[91] Hartman J, however, refused leave to proceed with the application because the court considered that the application was misconceived: it was aimed at challenging merits of government policy, which is not within the province of courts.

The Clean Air Foundation litigation shows how litigation may be used as a public forum to raise issues of public concern and interest. The judicial review application was directed at highlighting the failure of the government to exercise effective control over air pollution and one of the concerns raised was that the air quality objectives were out-of-date. We shall see in the chapter dealing with air pollution control that the Ordinance was amended in 2013 to provide for periodic review of air quality objectives and that a new set of objectives was adopted in January 2014. Thus, although the applicants were unsuccessful in their judicial review application, they were able to influence the government to improve its policy in relation to maintaining high standards of air quality.

62. A recent development of importance to public interest litigation is the willingness of Hong Kong courts to make protective cost orders, at the commencement of the proceedings or at any time during the proceedings, whereby an applicant litigating to save a public interest is protected from adverse costs orders in the event of failure of litigation, following upon what are known as the Corner House principles. For the latest articulation of the relevant principles, *see Designing Hong Kong Ltd v Town Planning Board* [2017] 2 HKLRD 60 (CA), affirmed by the Court of Final Appeal.[92] 'Corner House Guidelines' which are especially relevant to environmental litigation were set out in *R (Corner House Research) v Secretary of State for Trade and Industry* [2005] 1 WLR 2600 (CA). The court, obviously, has a discretion at the conclusion of the proceedings not to make an order for costs on the 'costs follow the event' principle on similar grounds. For instance, in *Lai Pun Sung v the Director of Agriculture, Fisheries and Conservation* [2009] HKEC 1425, which will be discussed under country parks in Chapter 7, the Court of First Instance decided not to order the unsuccessful applicant to pay the costs of the

90. [2007] HKEC 1356.
91. *Ibid.*, [17].
92. (2018) 21 HKCFAR 237.

respondent for the reason that that the unsuccessful applicant had no personal interest in the outcome of the litigation and that the case afforded an opportunity to the court to clarify an important point of law. Lam J said that the litigation has resulted in a clarification of the law that 'a country park can be re-designated, the map can be amended or replaced, but there has to be a good purpose': In other words, the discretion to amend an approved plan is not absolute.[93] In determining whether a case before the court can be said to be in the public interest, the court takes into account issues raised and decided in the proceedings, not the wider problems which a litigant hopes to resolve incidentally with the commencement of proceedings. In *Chu Hoi Dick & Another v Secretary for Home Affairs* Lam J formulated the three criteria that guide the court: (a) a litigant properly brought proceedings to seek guidance from the court on a point of general public importance so that the litigation is for the benefit of the community as a whole to warrant the costs of the litigation be borne by the public purse as costs incidental to good public administration; (b) the judicial decision has contributed to the proper understanding of the law in question; and (c) that the litigant has no private gain in the outcome.[94]

63. After some initial hesitation to recognize that a public-spirited citizen may seek judicial assistance where a public authority has failed to exercise its power to ensure environmental protection, courts of Hong Kong have been willing to encourage such public participation in environmental regulation and enforcement. Recall that in *Clean Air Foundation* case Hartman J accepted that there was at least a prima facie arguable case that there was 'some sort of duty on the Government to combat air pollution'. The application for leave to proceed with the judicial review application was unsuccessful because the purpose of the application was to question the merits of government policy. However, if a judicial review application seeks to question the failure of a public servant to take enforcement action, it is arguable that such an application will be better received by courts, although the courts are likely to defer to administrative discretion because the decision to take enforcement action is closely linked to policy considerations.

64. Lau Oi Kiu v Man Chan Shing[95] clearly illustrates that where an environmental agency fails to bring enforcement action, that itself does not enable a private individual to found a private claim. There, the defendant had dumped waste on the plaintiff's land. The plaintiff brought a private action on the basis of trespass, nuisance and breach of statutory duty and succeeded on the first two grounds. The Court did not uphold the plaintiff assertion she was entitled to bring a private suit for breach of statutory duty against the Environmental Protection Department for its failure to bring criminal prosecution against the defendant for breach of section 16A of the Waste Disposal Ordinance, which prohibits dumping of waste in any place

93. *Lai Pun Sung v the Director of Agriculture, Fisheries and Conservation* [2009] HKEC 1425, [18]. Two previous decisions that considered the relevant principles in making a cost order are *Chu Hoi Dick v Secretary for Home Affairs* [2007] HKEC 1640 and *Chan Noi Heung v Chief Executive in Council* [2009] 3 HKLRD 362 (CA). For Ma CJ's formulation of the principles *see Chan Noi Heung* case, [12].

94. *Chu Hoi Dick & Another v Secretary for Home Affairs* [2007] HKEC 1640, [29], Lam J.

95. [2015] HKEC 563.

without lawful authority or excuse or without the permission of the owner or occupier of the place. It was held that where a statute has been enacted for the public benefit and not to a limited class of the public to which the plaintiff belongs, a private action for breach of statutory duty is not available.

The Court cited with approval what Lord Browne-Wilkinson said in *X (Minors) v Bedfordshire CC*: 'The basic proposition is that in the ordinary case a breach of statutory duty does not, by itself, give rise to any private law cause of action. However a private law cause of action will arise if it can be shown, as a matter of construction of the statute, that the statutory duty was imposed for the protection of a limited class of the public and that Parliament intended to confer on members of that class a private right of action for breach of the duty. There is no general rule by reference to which it can be decided whether a statute does create such a right of action but there are a number of indicators. If the statute provides no other remedy for its breach and the Parliamentary intention to protect a limited class is shown, that indicates that there may be a private right of action since otherwise there is no method of securing the protection the statute was intended to confer. If the statute does provide some other means of enforcing the duty that will normally indicate that the statutory right was intended to be enforceable by those means and not by private right of action … However, the mere existence of some other statutory remedy is not necessarily decisive. It is still possible to show that on the true construction of the statute the protected class was intended by the Parliament to have a private remedy.'[96] In *Kwok Cheuk Kin v Director of Food and environmental Hygiene*,[97] the Court of Appeal agreed with the High Court that a public officer's refusal to take enforcement action under environmental protection legislation is amenable to judicial review. A Rural Committee had allowed residents of the area to use a piece of land, neighbouring a residential area, for the purpose of holding funeral services, on the payment of a fee. A resident of the area drew the attention of the Director of Environmental Protection to this activity which he considered to be unlawful in the absence of a licence permitting the Rural Committee to conduct this business, as required by regulation 4 of the Funeral Parlours Regulation.[98] When the Director decided not to take any action the complainant applied for judicial review of the refusal. Upon the grant of his application by the High Court, the Director appealed to the Court of Appeal arguing that the activity concerned did not come within the meaning of funeral parlour in the Funeral Parlours Regulation. The Regulation provides that a funeral parlour is 'any premises or place set apart or habitually used for reception, storage or treatment of human remains'.[99] Giving these words a liberal interpretation, the Court of Appeal held that the activity in question was within the meaning of a funeral parlour and the provision of service without a valid licence was a punishable offence. The Court of Appeal held that the Director was under duty to take enforcement action against the unlicensed funeral parlour, as requested by the applicant.

96. *X (Minors) v Bedfordshire County Council* [1995] 2 AC 633 at 731D-732B.
97. [2016] HKEC 613 (CA).
98. Funeral Parlours Regulation, Subsidiary Legislation AD passed under the Public Health and Municipal Services Ordinance (Cap 132).
99. Public Health and Municipal Services Ordinance (Cap 132), s. 2 (interpretation section).

§6. INSTITUTIONAL STRUCTURE

65. The following authorities or agencies play an important role in environmental regulation: (1) the Chief Executive of the Hong Kong Special Administrative Region; (2) The Secretary for the Environment; (3) the Director of Environmental Protection; (4) the Advisory Committee on the Environment; (5) the Environmental Appeal Board.

I. The Chief Executive of the Hong Kong Special Administrative Region

66. The Chief Executive is the Head of the Hong Kong Special Administrative Region, who takes the place occupied by the Governor of Hong Kong under the British colonial administration. The Chief Executive plays a part in the environmental regulatory regime in several ways: The Chief Executive (1) performs a legislative function by making regulations to supplement provisions in the primary legislation; (2) exercises power of appointing members of the Appeal Board and authorized officers; (3) exercises power under most of the environmental statutes by determining date on which the Ordinance or certain provision of an ordinance come into effect, or appoint day for regulatory provisions of the Ordinance such as a day for the determination of what discharges into the waters of Hong Kong are to be regarded as existing discharges; (4) exercises advisory powers, such as when giving such directions as he thinks fit, either generally or in any particular case, with respect to the exercise or performance by the Secretary or the Authority of any powers, functions or duties under the Water Pollution Control Ordinance (section 3); (5) may act as an approving authority such as when the Authority decides to make certain variations of a licence issued under the Water Pollution Control Ordinance (section 24); (6) may act as a reviewing authority, for instance, under the Water Pollution Control Ordinance which provides that a decision of the Appeal Board may be referred to him for review.[100]

II. The Chief Secretary for the Administration

67. The Chief Secretary, the Financial Secretary and the Secretary for Justice are the highest ranking members of the executive branch immediately below the Chief Executive. The Chief Secretary for the Administration is also the head of the public administration. He does not play a significant part in the administration of the environmental regulatory system. His only important function is in relation to breaches of environmental statutes attributable to government officers. As we will see, public officers are exempt from criminal liability for breaches of an environmental statute, but if environmental damage has been caused by such breach, remedial action has to be taken. It is the duty of the Chief Secretary for the Administration to order the taking of such remedial action. There are two secondary functions that he performs:

100. The current Chief Executive of Hong Kong, who assumed office on 1 July 2017, Carrie Lam, is the first woman to lead the Hong Kong government.

(1) to determine any question regarding who are members of the Advisory Council on the Environment; (2) to determine which government department is responsible for a breach of an environmental statute.

III. Secretary for the Environment

68. The Secretary for the Environment exercises: (1) legislative functions when he makes regulations, for instance, under the Noise Control Ordinance, or exercises limited powers of amending legislation such as in relation to intruder alarms under the Noise Control Ordinance; (2) powers of a quasi-legislative nature when he establishes air quality objectives or water quality objectives or when he prepares Codes of Conduct under Waste Disposal Ordinance; (3) powers of an administrative nature when he determines the dates for the purposes of a statute, for instance, when he exercises the power to amend relevant dates specified in the Schedules of the Waste Disposal Ordinance; (4) advisory powers, for instance, when he gives directions to the Authority how he should exercise his powers in a particular way in relation to achievement or maintenance of air quality objectives; (5) supervisory powers, such as when he removes an exemption that the Authority has given under the Air Pollution Control Ordinance.

IV. The Director of Environmental Protection

69. As we have already seen, the central environmental agency is the environment bureau, headed by the Secretary for the Environment, which is the agency charged with the responsibility of making and implementing environmental policy. The Environmental Protection Department, the only division operating under the bureau, is the administrative body which is responsible for assisting the Secretary for the Environment in his policymaking function. The Department plays a central role in implementing the government's environmental policy. Its Director exercises most of the regulatory functions, assisted by the Advisory Committee on the Environment. The Director is the Authority for the principal environmental statutes. The following are illustrative of his many powers: (1) it is the Director who has been given the legislative power of preparing a waste disposal plan, and to issue Codes of Practice and guidance under the Waste Disposal Ordinance; (2) under the same Ordinance he has administrative power to amend relevant dates in the Schedule to the Ordinance; (3) acting under the direction of the Secretary for the Environment, the Director has the duty to achieve and maintain air quality and water quality objectives; (4) he exercises enforcement powers including the serving of abatement notices and granting of licences; (5) prosecutions are authorized by him.

V. The Environmental Protection Department

70. The Environmental Protection Department was established in 1986 to coordinate and carry out pollution prevention and control activities. Between 1986 and

March 2005, it was mainly engaged in enforcing environmental laws and implementing environmental policies as determined by the relevant policy bureaux. To enable the Environmental Protection Department to play a more efficient role and concentrate on the environmental protection work, the Environment Branch of the then Environment, Transport and Works Bureau, which was responsible for environmental policymaking, merged with the Environmental Protection Department in April 2005.

This development has placed the Environmental Protection Department in the position of both determining and implementing environmental policies. Subsequent to the reorganization of government bureaux in July 2007, a new Environment Bureau was formed to oversee the formulation and implementation of policies such as those on environmental protection, conservation, energy and sustainable development.

The Environmental Protection Department is responsible for developing policies covering environmental protection, nature conservation; enforcing environmental legislation; monitoring environmental quality; providing collection, transfer, treatment and disposal facilities for many types of waste; advising on the environmental implications of town planning and new policies; handling pollution complaints and incidents; and raising awareness and support in the community for environmental initiatives.

VI. The Advisory Council on the Environment

71. The Advisory Council on the Environment's members (currently numbering twenty-one) and its Chairman are appointed by the Chief Executive. They are all prominent figures from the community and comprise members of the Legislative Council and the Urban Council, academics, businessmen, professionals and representatives of the major green groups, and trade and industry associations. The Secretary for Planning, Environment and Lands, the Director of Environmental Protection, the Director of Planning, the Director of Agriculture and Fisheries and the Director of Health attend Council meetings.

The Advisory Council on the Environment, formerly known as the Environmental Pollution Advisory Committee, is government's principal advisory body on matters relating to pollution control and sustainability of the environment. It is consulted on a wide range of issues relating to new legislative proposals and the implementation of existing pollution control and conservation measures. Major policy initiatives are also referred to it for advice before they are adopted by the government.

VII. Appeal Board

72. There is an Appeal Board under each of the environmental statutes. This is an independent body, which does not have any public officers as its members. An Appeal Board is constituted under each environmental statute, and the membership of one Environmental Appeal Board does not prevent cross-membership of other environmental appeal boards. Cross-membership may in fact be beneficial. Each environmental statute provides for the composition of the Appeal Board and its powers, which are not dissimilar to the provisions in other environmental statutes. Each statute specifies the decisions against which an appeal lies to the Appeal Board and provides for the procedure for appeal hearing and determination. Appeal Board's decision is final except under the Water Pollution Control Ordinance where its decision may be reviewed by the Chief Executive.

Chapter 1. Air Pollution Control Ordinance

§1. INTRODUCTION

73. Being a small state with a high concentration of population, street-level air pollution has been a serious challenge. Situated adjacent the Pearl River Delta, a region of high industrial activity in Mainland China, Hong Kong also has to struggle with poor regional air quality – especially smog. Diesel vehicles are the main source of street-level pollution. Smog is caused by a combination of pollutants from motor vehicles, industry and power plants both in Hong Kong and in the Pearl River Delta region. Because of these air pollution problems, Hong Kong has yet to fully achieve its air quality objectives. As we shall see later, the Air Pollution Control Ordinance was amended in 2013 to mandate periodical review of Hong Kong air quality objectives, and the prevailing air quality objectives were updated in January 2014. Hong Kong's failure to achieve the pre-2014 air quality objective standards, which came under public scrutiny as a result of *Chu Yee Wah* case[101] in 2011, is a reflection of how serious a challenge air pollution control is.[102]

In order to understand measures that the Hong Kong government has taken to alleviate the problem of air pollution, it is useful to see what the Environmental Protection Department says about the problem and its response. What follows is based on information found on the website of the department of environmental protection.[103] The main strategies that the Hong Kong government has adopted to control street-level air pollution and smog include: implementing a wide range of measures to control emissions from motor vehicles, power plants, and industrial and commercial processes locally; and working with Guangdong Provincial Authorities to implement a joint plan to tackle the regional smog problem.

I. Reducing Emissions from Vehicles

74. Over the years, roadside levels of respirable suspended particulates and nitrogen dioxide have far exceeded the indicative air quality objectives. Motor vehicles, especially diesel vehicles, are the main sources of these pollutants. To overcome this problem, the government has implemented a series of measures, such as an incentive programme to phase out pre-Euro IV diesel commercial vehicles, modification of LPG taxis and light buses, the adoption of tighter fuel and vehicle emission standards, an incentive programme to retrofit old diesel vehicles with particulate reduction devices, providing grants to help vehicle owners to replace their old vehicles with ones which comply with the prevailing emission standard for

101. *Chu Yee Wah v Director of Environmental Protection* [2011] 5 HKLRD 469; [2011] HKEC 1275 (CA).
102. Generally, *see A Concise Guide to the Air Pollution Control Ordinance* (2020: The Environmental Protection Department). https://www.epd.gov.hk/epd/english/environmentinhk/air/guide_ref/guide_apco.html.
103. *See* http://www.epd.gov.hk/epd/english/environmentinhk/air/air_maincontent.html.

newly registered vehicles, stepping up the control on smoky vehicles, and a reduction of the first registration tax for environment-friendly vehicles.

75. The Environmental Protection Department has introduced several additional measures to reduce vehicle emissions. It has commenced a trial of retrofitting Euro II and III franchised buses with selective catalytic reduction devices, which, together with the diesel particulate filters installed in these buses, could upgrade their emission performance to the level of Euro IV or V buses. Subject to satisfactory trial results, the government will fund the full cost of retrofitting Euro II and III franchised buses with Selective Catalytic Reduction devices. It has set up a HKD 300 million Pilot Green Transport Fund to support the testing of green and innovative transport technologies for the public transport sector and goods vehicles. The government is currently consulting stakeholders on proposals, including the use of roadside remote sensing equipment and chassis dynamometer testing, to strengthen the control of emission from petrol and Liquefied Petroleum Gas (LPG).

II. Reducing Emissions from Industrial Sources and Power Plants

76. The Air Pollution Control Ordinance and its subsidiary regulations provide for the control of emissions from power plants, industrial and commercial sources, construction activities, open burning, asbestos, petrol filling stations and dry-cleaning machines. A regulation passed in 1990 limiting the sulphur content of industrial fuel has reduced sulphur dioxide pollution to very low levels. The regulation was amended in 2008 to mandate the use of ultra-low sulphur diesel (with sulphur content not more than 0.005% by weight) in industrial and commercial processes.

77. Power generation is the main source of air pollutant emission in Hong Kong. To reduce emissions from power generators, installation of new coal-fired power plants was banned in 1997 to encourage the use of natural gas for electricity generation. Since 2005, stringent emission caps are imposed on power plants. The two local power companies' rate of return is linked to their compliance with the emission caps requirements. In 2008, the Environmental Protection Department, through a Technical Memorandum, prescribed stringent emission caps for 2010 and beyond. In 2010, the First Technical Memorandum was reviewed, tightening the emission caps for the power sector from 2015 onwards. Compliance with these standards will require the power sector to maximize the use of existing gas-fired generation units and prioritize coal-fired generation units retrofitted with emission abatement facilities. As a result of the stringent control measures implemented over the past years, emissions from power plants have been substantially reduced even though demand for power has increased.[104]

---

104. Generally, *see* 'Air Pollution Control Strategies' (Environmental Protection Department). www.epd.gov.hk/epd/english/environmentinhk/air/prob_solutions/strategies_apc.html.

III. Tackling Regional Air Pollution

78. Vehicles, industry and power plants in Hong Kong and the Pearl River Delta region all contribute to regional air pollution. The Hong Kong and Guangdong governments are working on a joint plan in the short term to reduce the total amount of emissions and stop air quality from further deteriorating and in the long term to achieve good air quality for the whole region. These joint efforts have seen improvement of air quality through the retrofitting of power plants with flue gas desulphurization devices, the phasing out of highly polluting industrial plants in the region, and the introduction of cleaner motor vehicle fuels and motor vehicles.

§2. Legislative Framework

79. The Air Pollution Control Ordinance (Cap 311) is the principal statute relevant to air pollution control. Other relevant Ordinances that are examined here are: Road Traffic Ordinance (Cap 374), Ozone Layer Protection Ordinance (Cap 403) and Shipping and Port Control Ordinance (Cap 313). Regulations made under these ordinances as well as the Factories and Industrial Undertakings Ordinance (Cap 59 sub leg AD) are also relevant and examined here.

80. The Air Pollution Control Ordinance adopts the following strategies to tackle problems of air pollution:

(1) *Establishing and maintaining air quality objectives*: Air quality objectives set out the quality of air that the government seeks to achieve. The first set of quality objectives were set out in a Technical Memorandum which was gazetted in June 2004. The Air Pollution Control Ordinance was amended in 2013 to take away the setting of air quality objectives from Technical Memorandum. They are since then prescribed in Schedule 5 of the Air Pollution Control Ordinance. The legislative amendment also introduced a mechanism to review prevailing air quality objectives every five years. A new set of air quality objectives was gazetted in January 2014 and published as Schedule 5 of the Ordinance.[105]
(2) *Licensing specified processes*: The air quality objectives must be taken into account when issuing and reviewing licences to conduct specified processes (namely, major stationary air polluters such as power plants, incinerators and concrete batching plants).
(3) *Regulating activities other than specified processes*: The Ordinance makes provision directed at specific activities, which do not pose as high a pollution risk as specified processes. Regulations made under the Ordinance seek to control emission of dust, grit and smoke from furnaces, ovens or industrial

105. *See* http://www.epd.gov.hk/epd/english/environmentinhk/air/air_quality_objectives/air_quality_objectives.html. As will be observed elsewhere the results of the second review are expected to be incorporated in Schedule 5 and the bill for the amendment of Schedule 5 was presented to the Legislative Council on 24 March 2021. *See* below para. 129.

plants; Air Pollution Control (Fuel Restriction) Regulations are aimed at reducing the sulphur content in fuels used in commercial and industrial processes; Air Pollution (Smoke) Regulations are intended to control the emission of dark smoke from chimneys, furnaces, engines, ovens or industrial plants; Air Pollution Control (Construction Dust) Regulation aims to control the generation of dust from construction sites and Air Pollution Control (Open Burning) Regulation prohibits open burning in construction sites.

(4) *Vehicle emission control*: Air Pollution Control Ordinance makes provision for the regulation of emissions from motor vehicles and these provisions are supplemented by Road Traffic Ordinance (Cap 374).

(5) *Asbestos control*: Air Pollution Control Ordinance makes special provisions for the control of harmful effects of asbestos, including provisions that prohibit importation or sale of harmful asbestos, and makes provision in relation to activities involving harmful asbestos. A major aspect of asbestos control is clearing premises of harmful asbestos. Of equal importance are the provisions which aim at protecting workers from exposure to harmful asbestos.

(6) *Air pollution abatement notices*: Air pollutants, emanating from places other than places licensed for a specified process or places which are regulated by licensing under the Public Health and Municipal Services Ordinance (Cap 132), which threaten the maintaining of air quality objectives are controlled through air pollution abatement notices. Failure to comply with an air pollution abatement notice is a punishable offence.

81. Just as other environmental statutes, the Air Pollution Control Ordinance relies on criminal offences and an enforcement regime to ensure the effective implementation of the various regulatory methods (such as licensing and serving of abatement notices) and provides for public access to information as well for the protection of sensitive information that may have been gathered by public officers.

82. There are several statutes which provide supplementary provision for the control of air pollution. They include the Shipping and Port Control Ordinance (Cap 313), Merchant Shipping (Local Vessels) Ordinance (Cap 548) and Merchant Shipping (Prevention of Air Pollution) Ordinance (Cap 413), all of which relate to marine air pollution. The Ozone Layer Protection Ordinance (Cap 403) has been enacted for the purpose of protecting the ozone layer.

§3. Air Pollution Control Ordinance

83. The Ordinance is designed to make provision for abating, prohibiting and controlling pollution of the atmosphere and for connected matters.[106] The regulation of air pollution commences with the setting of air quality objectives for Hong Kong with mechanisms to achieve and maintain desirable air quality standards. An important mechanism for enforcement is air pollution abatement notice. Certain large scale activities which are highly likely to contribute to air pollution have been

106. Cap 311, Long Title.

identified as 'specified processes' and are regulated through a system of licensing. The Ordinance provides special control regimes in relation to asbestos works, construction work and motor vehicle emissions. The Ordinance provides for the creation of criminal offences for the purpose of enforcement and provides for an Appeal Board which hears appeals against appealable decisions. The provisions of the Air Pollution Control Ordinance are supplemented by regulations. Further details are provided by Technical Memoranda and Codes of Practice.

I. Regulations

84. The Secretary has the power to make regulations for the purposes of the Air Pollution Control Ordinance and regulations may be made for a number of purposes prescribed in the Ordinance such as for: (a) the designation of noxious or offensive emissions; (b) the abatement, prohibition and control of the emission into the atmosphere of air pollutants; (c) methods to be used for the measurement of the composition, concentration, quantity, quality or density of any air pollutant emitted from any polluting process or passing through any chimney and for the better carrying out generally of the provisions and purposes of the Ordinance.[107] Regulations made under the Ordinance are subject to control of the Legislative Council as provided by Part V of the Interpretation and General Clauses Ordinance (Cap 1).

II. Technical Memoranda

85. Technical Memoranda set standards to be followed in the control of air pollution. Section 9 of the Ordinance enables the Secretary for the Environment to issue Technical Memoranda setting out principles, procedures, guidelines, standards and limits for:

– the prediction, measurement, assessment or determination of air pollution caused, or contributed to, by the operation of a polluting process;
– the issue of pollution abatement notices; and
– the determination of whether or not an air pollution abatement notice is being complied with.

Where the Secretary for the Environment decides to issue a Technical Memorandum, he must make available a copy of it for inspection by the public free of charge at such offices of the government as he directs during business hours. He must publish it in the Gazette and lay it on the table of the Legislative Council and a Technical Memorandum becomes effective on expiry of twenty-eight days of laying it before the Legislative Council, providing that the Legislative Council has not disapproved or amended it. The Legislative Council may within such period of twenty-eight days, pass a resolution amending the Technical Memorandum in any manner

107. *Ibid.*, s. 43(1).

consistent with the power to make a Technical Memorandum. Such an amended Technical Memorandum comes into effect when the resolution is published in the Gazette.[108]

86. Nine Technical Memoranda have been issued. They include the Technical Memorandum for Issuing Air Pollution Abatement Notices to Control Air Pollution from Stationary Polluting Processes and the first Technical Memorandum for Allocation of Emission Allowances in Respect of Specified Licences (2008) followed by seven technical memoranda updating it.[109]

III. Codes of Practice

87. For the purpose of encouraging reduction and the better control of air pollution, the Secretary may, after consultation with the Advisory Council on the Environment, issue general advice in the form of Codes of Practice directed at persons operating or maintaining a chimney, relevant plant, machinery or equipment; conducting a specified process; operating, maintaining, repairing, modifying or adapting a motor vehicle; engaging in any asbestos-related activities; engaging in any other polluting process, as to any matter concerning:

- the construction, operation and maintenance of a chimney, relevant plant, machinery, equipment or containment;
- the conduct of a process or activity or the carrying out of any work;
- the storage, transportation, distribution, handling or use of materials;
- the preparation of asbestos investigation reports, asbestos management plans and asbestos abatement plans; and
- the maintenance and manner of using motor vehicles.[110]

88. Failure on the part of any person to observe the provisions of any such Code or to accept any such advice shall not of itself render that person liable to criminal proceedings of any kind, but any such failure may, in any proceedings whether civil or criminal and including proceedings for an offence under the Ordinance, be relied upon by any party to the proceedings as tending to establish or to negative any liability which is in question in those proceedings.[111]

89. Several Codes of Practice have been issued and they all relate to asbestos control: Code of Practice on Asbestos Control – Preparation of Asbestos Investigation Report, Asbestos Management Plan and Asbestos Abatement Plan; Code of Practice on Asbestos Control – Safe Handling of Low Risk Asbestos Containing Material; Asbestos Work Using Full Containment or Mini Containment Method; and Asbestos Work Using Glove Bag Method.

---

108. *Ibid.*, ss 37A, 37B, and 37C.
109. *See* https://www.epd.gov.hk/epd/english/envir_standards/statutory/esg_stat.html.
110. *Ibid.*, s. 37(1).
111. *Ibid.*, s. 37(2).

IV. Practice Notes

90. The Environmental Protection Department has issued several Practice Notes for Professional Persons. These non-statutory practice notes include: Practice Note on Control of Air Pollution in Vehicle Tunnels; Control of Air Pollution in Car Parks PN 2/96; and Handling of Asbestos Containing Materials in Buildings PN 2/978.

§4. The Application of the Air Pollution Control Ordinance

I. The Impact of the Ordinance on the Government

91. The Air Pollution Control Ordinance binds the government, subject to the following qualifications:

- The Ordinance grants immunity to public officers in respect of administrative functions they perform.
- No liability rests on the government or any public officer by reason of the fact that any licence to carry out a specified process is granted renewed, varied, transferred or cancelled or that any exemption from the need for a licence is granted, continued or cancelled under the Ordinance.
- A public officer is not personally liable for any act or omission done in the honest belief that it was required or authorized in the exercise of any function, duty or power under the Air Pollution Control Ordinance.
- Such protection of public officers does not affect in any way the liability of the government in tort for that act or omission.[112]
- The provisions relating to failure to comply with abatement notices, failure to use best practicable means for preventing the emission of noxious or offensive emissions from any premises used for a specified process, and for preventing the discharge, whether directly or indirectly, of such emissions into the atmosphere, and, where an emission takes place, for rendering any such emissions harmless and inoffensive and use of premises for any specified process without a licence do not impose criminal liability on the government or any person who causes or permits to be emitted any air pollutant or conducts any specified process which he is required to emit or conduct in the course of carrying out his duties in the service of the government.[113]
- This does not mean that the government can freely carry out such polluting activities. The Ordinance provides that if it appears to the Authority, namely the Director of Environmental Protection, that there is a contravention of these statutory provisions by any person in the course of carrying out his duties in the service of the government, the Authority must report the matter to the Chief Secretary for Administration, where the contravention has not been forthwith terminated to his

112. *Ibid.*, s. 42.
113. *Ibid.*, s. 44(2).

satisfaction. The Chief Secretary for Administration must enquire into the circumstances, and if the contravention is continuing or likely to recur, ensure that the best practicable steps are taken to terminate the contravention or avoid the recurrence.[114]

- Where the government is responsible for the conduct of a specified process, a notice or application under the Ordinance concerning the emission of an air pollutant from such process may be given or made by any public officer on behalf of the government.[115]
- Any notice the Authority wishes to serve concerning an air pollutant or the conduct of a specified process which has to be given to the government may be served on the principal officer of the government department which appears to the Authority to be responsible for the emission or conduct. In the event of any question arising as to which Department is responsible, such notice must be given to such public officer as the Chief Secretary determines.[116]
- The government is exempt from paying any fee or charge under the Ordinance.[117]

II. Key Personnel

92. The Chief Executive of Hong Kong SAR, The Chief Secretary for Administration, The Secretary in charge of the subject of environment, and the Authority for the purpose of the Ordinance, namely the Director of Environmental Protection, have certain powers and functions under the Ordinance. In addition, there is an Environmental Appeal Board which exercises important adjudicatory functions under the Ordinance.

A. *The Chief Executive of Hong Kong SAR*

93. The Chief Executive has three main powers or functions: First, the Chief Executive in Council may declare any part of Hong Kong to be an air control zone for the purposes of the Ordinance.[118] Second, the Chief Executive makes appointments to the Appeal Board Panel. Third, the Chief Executive may give advice or directions to the Authority, where the Authority is required to consult the Chief Executive, such as when cancelling or varying a licence relating to a specified process.[119]

114. *Ibid.*, s. 44(4).
115. *Ibid.*, s. 44(5).
116. *Ibid.*, s. 44(6).
117. *Ibid.*, s. 44(7).
118. *Ibid.*, s. 6.
119. *Ibid.*, s. 22.

B. The Chief Secretary for Administration

94. The Chief Secretary for Administration has one important function, namely to investigate any contravention of sections 10, 12 and 13 of the Air Pollution Control Ordinance by a public officer in order to direct remedial action, in view of the exemption of public officers from criminal liability.[120]

95. The Chief Secretary's intervention is set in motion in the following manner. If it appears to the Authority that any emission of an air pollutant or conduct of a specified process is being, or has been, emitted or conducted in contravention of section 10 (the emission of air pollutants from a polluting process which is causing or contributing to air pollution which exists or which is imminent); section 12 (failure to use the best practicable means for preventing the emission of noxious or offensive emissions from such premises, and for preventing the discharge, whether directly or indirectly, of such emissions into the atmosphere, and for rendering such emissions where discharged harmless and inoffensive); or section 13 (using any premises, or permitting any premises to be used, for the conduct of a specified process without a licence to use the premises for the conduct of a specified process), by any person in the course of carrying out his duties in the service of the Crown, the Authority must, if the contravention is not forthwith terminated to his satisfaction, report the matter to the Chief Secretary for Administration.[121] On receipt of such a report, the Chief Secretary for Administration must enquire into the circumstances and, if his enquiry shows that a contravention of sections 10, 12 or 13 is continuing or likely to recur, he shall ensure that the best practicable steps are taken to terminate the contravention or avoid the recurrence.[122] The Chief Secretary for Administration may also determine any question as to the membership of the Advisory Council on the Environment.[123]

C. The Secretary in Charge of the Subject of Environment

96. Schedule 5 of the Ordinance prescribes the air quality objectives for an air control zone.[124] The Secretary must from time to time review the air quality objectives for an air control zone to ensure that they are the objectives that should be achieved and maintained in order to: (a) promote the conservation of air in the zone in the public interest; and (b) promote the best use of air in the zone in the public interest.[125] He may give directions to the Authority whose duty it is to implement air quality objectives. The Authority must comply with any such directions.[126]

120. *Ibid.*, s. 44(4).
121. *Ibid.*, s. 44(3).
122. *Ibid.*, s. 44(4).
123. *Ibid.*, s. 45.
124. As provided in s. 7A(1) of the Ordinance. *See* http://www.epd.gov.hk/epd/english/environmentinhk/air/air_quality_objectives/air_quality_objectives.html.
125. *Ibid.*, s. 7(A). *See* http://www.epd.gov.hk/epd/english/environmentinhk/air/air_quality_objectives/aqoreview2016.html. *See also* paras 102 and 103 below.
126. *Ibid.*, s. 8(3) and (4).

97. The Secretary also performs the following functions: (1) he makes regulations, and issues Technical Memoranda and Codes of Practice, which are all useful means of implementing the legislation; (2) he may direct that an application for renewal or transfer of a licence must be publicly notified enabling the public to object to such application; (3) he may specify particulars and information regarding the existing use of any premises for a specified process that must be submitted to the Authority, who may exempt such premises from the requirement of a licence; (4) the Secretary has the power to remove an exemption that has been so granted by the Authority; and (5) he may grant an application for the withholding of private information from public disclosure.

D. *The Authority*

98. The Chief Executive may appoint a public officer to be the air pollution control authority[127] and has designated the Director of Environmental Protection to be the Authority, whose aim must be to achieve the relevant air quality objectives and to maintain such quality.[128]

99. The Authority has extensive enforcement powers, including the power to issue air pollution abatement notices, powers in relation to licensing, imposition of conditions on exempted premises, regulatory powers over asbestos-containing materials and vehicle smoke emissions. Prosecutions for offences against the Air Pollution Control Ordinance are brought in the name of the Authority, without prejudice to the general power of the Secretary of Justice in relation to prosecutions.[129]

E. *Appeal Board*

100. The Chief Executive must appoint a panel of persons who are not public officers and who in his opinion are suitable for appointment as members of an Appeal Board and as Chairman of Appeal Boards a person who is not a public officer and is qualified in law, that is, a person qualified for appointment as a District Judge.[130]

101. The Appeal Board has extensive powers of admitting evidence, including evidence inadmissible in a court of law.[131] On appeal, the Appeal Board may confirm, reverse or vary the decision, requirement or specification appealed from.[132] It

127. *Ibid.*, s. 4(1).
128. *Ibid.*, s. 8(2).
129. *Ibid.*, s. 47.
130. *Ibid.*, s. 32.
131. *Ibid.*, s. 33(5).
132. *Ibid.*, s. 33(2).

may refer any contempt of the Appeal Board, such as when a witness fails to appear when summoned, to the Court of First Instance for investigation and punishment.[133]

§5. Establishing and Maintaining Air Quality Objectives

102. The overall policy objective for air quality management in Hong Kong is to achieve as soon as reasonably practicable and to maintain thereafter an acceptable level of air quality to safeguard the health and well-being of the community and to promote the conservation and best use of air in the public interest. It is for this purpose that air quality objectives for seven widespread air pollutants were established in 1987, based on international standards of air quality management. These air quality objectives apply to the whole of Hong Kong. The Ordinance provides for the taking of preventive and enforcement measures to control excessive emissions.[134]

103. The Air Pollution Control Ordinance provided in section 7, which was repealed by Ordinance No. 12 of 2013, that air quality objectives mean the quality which, in the opinion of the Secretary, should be achieved and maintained in order to promote the conservation and best use of air in the public interest.[135] In place of the repealed section 7, a new section, section 7A, was inserted and came into effect on 1 January 2014. It provides that Schedule 5 of the Ordinance prescribes the air quality objectives for an air control zone or a part of an air control zone. Schedule 5 prescribes air quality objectives which are applicable in every air control zone by reference to maximum concentration of air pollutants such as sulphur dioxide, fine suspended articles, respirable suspended particulates, nitrogen dioxide, ozone, carbon monoxide and lead. Section 7A also provides that the Secretary may from time to time review the air quality objectives for an air control zone to ensure that they are the objectives that should be achieved and maintained in order to: (a) promote the conservation of air in the zone in the public interest; and (b) promote the best use of air in the zone in the public interest. A review must be carried out at least once in every review period, meaning the first five years beginning on 1 January 2014 and each successive five-year period. As soon as reasonably practicable after a review is carried out, the Secretary must submit to the Advisory Council on the environment a report of the review.[136]

133. *Ibid.*, s. 38(9).
134. Environmental Protection Department 'AFI and air monitoring background information', *see* generally, http://www.epd.gov.hk/epd/english/environmentinhk/air/air_quality_objectives/air_quality_objectives.html.
135. Air Pollution Control Ordinance, s. 7(2), now repealed.
136. The latest review of air quality objectives was carried out during the period mid-2016 to end of 2018, and a review report was submitted to the Advisory Council on the Environment in February 2019. Thereafter the EPD consulted the Legislative Council (Panel on Environmental Affairs) and the public. Having completed its public consultation, the EPD submitted an amendment of Schedule 5 of the Ordinance tightening three air quality objectives: namely the 24-hour AQO for sulphur dioxide (SO2) and the annual and 24-hour AQOs for fine suspended particulates (FSP/PM2.5). The

104. The Chief Executive when he establishes air control zones and the Secretary for the Environment when he periodically reviews air quality objectives must act in consultation with the Advisory Council on the Environment.

105. The responsibility for achieving and maintaining air quality objectives is with the Authority, namely the Director of Environmental Protection. The Authority shall aim to achieve the relevant air quality objectives as soon as is reasonably practicable and thereafter to maintain the quality so achieved.[137]

106. If in the opinion of the Secretary the achievement or maintenance of any air quality objective would be better served by the exercise by the Authority in a particular manner of any of his powers under section 15(4) to impose conditions on a licence to conduct a specified process, section 17 to cancel or vary such a licence or section 22 to impose conditions on, or cancelling an exemption given to a specified process, the Secretary may give directions in writing to the Authority as to the manner in which he should exercise those powers and the Authority must comply with any such direction.[138]

107. The Air Pollution Control Ordinance provides two principal ways in which air quality objectives could be maintained: (i) issuing of abatement notices in respect of obnoxious emissions and (ii) identifying specified processes which are regulated through a licensing regime.

§6. Air Pollution Abatement Notice

108. Air pollution which threatens the maintenance of the air quality objectives is controlled principally through pollution abatement notices. An abatement notice may be issued where the Authority or an authorized officer is satisfied that the emission of air pollutants from a polluting process is causing or contributing to air pollution which exists or which is imminent.[139] An air pollution abatement notice may not be issued in respect of:

(a) air pollution emitted from a specified process which is operated under a licence issued under section 15; and

amendment bill was presented to the Legislative Council on 24 March 2021. See the Legislative Council Brief on Air Pollution Control (Amendment) Bill 2021: https://www.legco.gov.hk/yr20-21/english/bills/brief/b202103191_brf.pdf.

137. *Ibid.*, s. 8(2).

138. *Ibid.*, s. 8(3) and (4).

139. *Ibid.*, s. 10(1). See the discussion in the following paragraph.

(b) the emission of an objectionable odour from a declared offensive trade carried out under and in accordance with a licence issued under bylaws made under the Public Health and Municipal Services Ordinance (Cap. 132).[140]

109. Section 10(1) provides that an air pollution abatement notice may be served on the owner of the premises or to the person carrying out the activity requiring him: (a) to cease the emission of air pollutants from the premises or to cease the operation of the polluting process; (b) to reduce the emission of air pollutants from the premises or polluting process; (c) to take other steps to abate the emission of air pollutants from the premises or polluting process.

Section 10(2) provides that In determining whether the emission of air pollutants is causing or contributing to air pollution which exists or which is imminent, the Authority and an authorized officer may take into account: (a) a Technical Memorandum; (b) research material results or publications which indicate that the type of emission may have adverse health effects; (c) the advice of a medical practitioner; (d) the advice of the Director-General of Civil Aviation; (e) the relative location of the emission source and the place affected; (f) the locality of the place affected; (g) the time, duration and frequency of the emission; (h) any of the following effects which, in the opinion of the Authority or the authorized officer, is caused by or contributed to by the emission: (i) the deposit of dust, grit or particles of any kind; (ii) an objectionable odour; (iii) the staining of, corrosion or damage to, a building, plant, equipment or other material; (iv) the irritation of the eye, nose or skin or any other sensory discomfort; (v) the disturbance of normal activities by the colour or opacity of the emission; (vi) an effect which in the opinion of the Authority or an authorized officer may affect public safety; or (vii) any other effect which in the opinion of the Authority or an authorized officer is unreasonable for a member of the public to suffer.

I. Serving Abatement Notices

110. An abatement notice may be served by the Authority or an authorized officer if he is satisfied that the emission of air pollutants[141] from a polluting process[142] is causing or contributing to air pollution[143] which exists or which is

140. Declaration of Offensive Trades Notice (Cap 132AV) contains a list of offensive trades, which includes trade, business, process or manufacture relating to boiling, burning, crushing and storing of bones; cleaning storing or processing of feathers; dressing and tanning of leather; and processing of shark's fins.
141. 'Air pollutant' means any solid particulate, liquid, vapour, objectionable odour or gaseous substance emitted into the atmosphere: Air Pollution Control Ordinance, s. 2.
142. 'Polluting process' includes an activity, process or the operation of a chimney, relevant plant, machinery and equipment that evolves air pollutants: Air Pollution Control Ordinance, s. 2. A polluting process does not necessarily have to involve an activity. *See Teng Fuk Co Ltd v Air Pollution Control Appeal Board* [2001] 3 HKLRD 304 (CA) where the polluting process involved was storing shark's fin in a shop.
143. 'Air pollution' means any emission of air pollutant which either alone or with another emission of air pollutant: (1) is prejudicial to health; (2) is a nuisance (a nuisance includes an event which is obnoxious and which results in any of the effects set out in *ibid.*, s. 10(2)(h)); (3) imperils or is

imminent.[144] *Asia Dyeing Co Ltd v The Authority*[145] is a case where an abatement notice had been issued in respect of air pollution caused by a polluting process, decided before the amendment of the Air Pollution Control Ordinance in 1993. Section 30(1) of the Ordinance, before its amendment in 1993, provided that a notice could be served where it appears to the Authority that any chimney or relevant plant is by reason of: (a) unsuitable design, defective construction or maintenance; (b) excessive wear and tear; (c) the use of unsuitable fuel or other material; or (d) any other cause, 'emitting a greater quantity of air pollutant than need be'. It was argued that the Authority is empowered to make a value judgment as to whether the quantity of pollutant being emitted is greater than need be, that is to say, in excess of what the Authority considers acceptable. The Authority acknowledged that it had originally approved the installation of the chimneys and associated plant and the use of heavy fuel in them. The Authority argued that what may have been an acceptable fuel or level of emission of pollutant at the time of installation may subsequently have become unacceptable in view of technological advances or because of the deterioration of the quality of the air in the vicinity of the chimneys. It was contended that the Authority should not be inhibited from acting under section 30 to safeguard the public interest. Rejecting this view which gives wide powers of assessing the seriousness of the emission, it was held that whether a chimney or relevant plant was emitting air pollutants 'than need be' was not a matter to be judged subjectively by the Authority. The words simply meant that there would be more emittance than need be if the owner had failed to construct, maintain or operate the chimney or to use unsuitable fuel: The words 'than need be' were governed by paragraphs (a)–(d), which are given above, and not by the subjective view of the Authority. Since the applicants' chimneys were designed for use with heavy fuel it was not unsuitable for use with them and while they emitted pollutant it was not more than was necessary having regard to the nature of the plant and the use of the fuel for which the plant was designed. The Authority was not empowered to set out a value judgment on the acceptable level of air pollutant and to issue statutory notices to those that contravened it.[146] Section 30 was amended in 1993 removing the words 'emitting a greater quantity of air pollutant than need be'. Section 30 as amended now uses the words, 'where it appears to the Authority that any chimney, relevant plant or other machinery or equipment may evolve any air pollutant by reason of … .'. It appears from the decisions of the Appeal Board that officers of the Environmental Protection Department resort to abatement notices as a last resort. They proactively advise persons engaged in potentially harmful processes on appropriate measures to prevent harmful emissions. An administrative practice has evolved whereby officers of the Environmental Protection Department serve a non-statutory warning letter to the owner of the premises or the person carrying out the activity

---

likely to imperil the safety of or otherwise interferes with the normal operation of aircraft; or (4) is determined to be air pollution under a Technical Memorandum: Air Pollution Control Ordinance, s. 2.

144. Air Pollution Control Ordinance, s. 10(1). Air pollution is 'imminent' if it could reasonably have been anticipated on the basis of existing facts that the mischief was foreseeable: *Teng Fuk Co Ltd v Air Pollution Control Appeal Board* [2001] 3 HKLRD 304 (CA).
145. [1989] HKEC 822 (CFI). Affirmed by the Court of Appeal [1990] 1 HKLR 263 (CA).
146. *Ibid.*, [15], [17].

advising him to take measures to prevent the objectionable emissions. A statutory abatement notice is issued where there has been no compliance with such warning letter.

II. What Is an Abatement Notice Aimed At?

111. An abatement notice may be served in relation to emission of air pollutants contributing to air pollution which 'which exists or which is imminent'. In *Asia Dyeing Co Ltd v Air Pollution Control Authority*,[147] the question was whether an abatement notice was invalid if it failed to specify explicitly whether the Authority was asserting existing or imminent pollution. The Court of Appeal was dealing with an earlier, and now replaced, version of the section on air pollution control abatement notices. The relevant part of the air pollution abatement notice in question was as follows: 'Notice is hereby given to you under section 9(1) of the Air Pollution Control Ordinance that your chimney ... is in the opinion of the Authority, by the emission of an air pollutant namely sulphur dioxide, contributing to the existence or imminence of an air pollutant nuisance which is prejudicial to health.'

112. The Court of Appeal held that it is not mandatory for the Authority to specify clearly whether the notice related to 'existence' or 'imminence'. The reason is the difficulty in distinguishing clearly between existing and imminent contribution to air pollution. The Court explained the situation as follows:

> As a matter of common sense there must from time to time be situations where it is difficult to distinguish, especially on a particular day, whether a nuisance is in existence or merely imminent. This, we think, explains why the overall scheme of the relevant provisions in the Ordinance does not provide for legal consequences flowing from the distinction between the assertion in the [air pollution abatement] notification of either the existence or the imminence of an air pollutant nuisance. It does not make sense to provide that the efficacy of the Authority's measures to protect public health by abating existing or imminent air pollution should depend on whether or not the Authority has accurately assessed by reference to one day whether or not the [air pollution] nuisance is existing or merely imminent.[148]

The Court of Appeal was of the opinion that the objection to the notice on the ground that the notice did not expressly state whether the air pollution nuisance was imminent or existing. Delivering the judgment of the court, Clough JA said: 'We therefore feel constrained to adopt an interpretation of the relevant provisions which seems to us to be consistent with the underlying intendment of this legislation and to conclude that the requirement in s. 9(1) that the Authority shall identify in the notification the existence or imminence of the nuisance is directory and not mandatory in the sense that non-compliance

147. [1990] 1 HKLR 263 (CA).
148. *Ibid.*, pp. 272–273.

would vitiate the notification. Likewise, we conclude that s. 10(2) is to be interpreted as it is actually expressed, so as to indicate that what matters in a prosecution is whether either existence or imminence of the nuisance can be proved.'

113. Where the Authority is satisfied that there is imminence of air pollution, but has no evidence of existing air pollution, an abatement notice can clearly be issued in relation to imminence of air pollution. *Teng Fuk Co Ltd v Air Pollution Control Authority*[149] concerned storage of large quantities of dried shark's fins in a shop, which was open to the street. The shark's fins were for distribution and would have necessitated unpacking of the sacks of dried shark's fins, inspecting contents and delivering them to customers. The air pollution abatement notice stated that authorized officers on a visit to the premises found that the emission of air pollutant from the storage of dried seafood, in the form of objectionable odour, caused the imminence of air pollution. They found that such emission would cause discomfort when inhaled by the nearby members of the public and hence air pollution was imminent. The judge said:

> As can be seen, this notice did not notify the applicant that the odour constituted air pollution. It was only imminent. What was envisaged was that in certain circumstances, the odour would become more pervasive and then become air pollution. There were three circumstances when this might occur. The first was if a greater quantity of shark's fins was stored at the premises than was there when the inspections were undertaken. In this connection there was additional storage space. The second would arise on the onset of warmer or hot weather and the third was if the volume of business increased.

The Court of Appeal rejected the argument that 'imminent' only meant 'immediate' and held that air pollution was 'imminent' if it could reasonably have been anticipated on the basis of existing facts that the mischief was foreseeable.

III. Contents of an Abatement Notice

114. An abatement notice may be given, verbally or in writing, to the owner of the premises or to the person carrying out the activity, requiring him to: (i) cease the emission of air pollutants from the premises or to cease the operation of the polluting process; (ii) reduce the emission of air pollutants from the premises or polluting process; (iii) take other steps to abate the emission from the premises or polluting process.

149. [2001] 3 HKLRD 304 (CA).

IV. Determining the Impact on Air Quality

115. Section 10(2) provides that in determining whether the emission of air pollutants is causing or contributing to air pollution which exists or which is imminent, the Authority and an authorized officer may take into account: (a) a Technical Memorandum (other than a Technical Memorandum issued under section 26G); (b) research material results or publications which indicate that the type of emission may have adverse health effects; (c) the advice of a medical practitioner; (d) the advice of the Director-General of Civil Aviation; (e) the relative location of the emission source and the place affected; (f) the locality of the place affected; (g) the time, duration and frequency of the emission.

116. The Authority or the authorized officer may also take into account any of the following effects which, in his opinion, is caused by or contributed to by the emission: the deposit of dust, grit or particles of any kind; an objectionable odour; the staining of, corrosion or damage to, a building, plant, equipment or other materials; the irritation of the eye, nose or skin or any other sensory discomfort; the disturbance of normal activities by the colour or opacity of the emission; an effect which in the opinion of the Authority or an authorized officer may affect public safety; or any other effect which in the opinion of the Authority or an authorized officer is unreasonable for a member of the public to suffer.[150]

V. The Life Span of an Abatement Notice

117. An air pollution abatement notice may require compliance with it immediately or within a specified period of time. The notice remains in force until it is withdrawn or expires. The withdrawal of a notice must be in writing. It is an offence punishable by imprisonment and fine for a person not to comply with an air pollution abatement notice served on him.[151]

VI. Appeals Against Abatement Notices

118. A person who is aggrieved by an abatement notice may appeal to the Appeal Board, which has the power to confirm, vary or reverse the abatement notice. The decisions of the Appeal Board are not published, but the author has had access to some past decisions. They dealt with objectionable odour from a polluting process: operation of a chimney serving a pig roasting furnace,[152] and from a shop used to store dried shark's fin for the purpose of exhibition, sale and distribution.[153] The decision of the Appeal Board is final, but such a decision may be challenged by

150. Air Pollution Control Ordinance, s. 10(2).
151. *Ibid.*, s. 10(7).
152. Air Pollution Control Appeal Board decision in Case No. 1 of 1997.
153. Air Pollution Control Appeal Board decision in Case No. 1 of 2000 and in Case No. 2 of 1997.

way of judicial review.[154] Judicial review of administrative action is concerned with legality of administrative action, but does not afford a second opportunity for the applicant to have his application considered afresh on merit.

§7. Controlling Specified Processes Through Licensing

119. Processes which are especially likely to cause serious pollution control have been identified for a special control regime. Schedule 1 of the Air Pollution Control Ordinance contains a list of thirty-one specified processes, such as certain processes in gas, electricity, aluminium, petrochemical, mineral and chlorine works.

120. Processes which are listed in Schedule 1 of the Ordinance as 'Specified Processes' must bear certain characteristics and must be above a certain magnitude. For example, for the purpose of 'specified process' electricity works are works in which fossil fuel is burnt either wholly or as part of the process of electricity generation where the installed generation capacity of such works exceeds 5 megawatts. Gas works are works in which: (a) coal, coke, oil, carbonaceous material or any mixtures or derivatives of such materials or any waste materials are handled or prepared for carbonization or gasification and in which such materials are carbonized or gasified; or (b) natural gas is reformed, refined or odorized. Asbestos works are works in which: (a) raw asbestos is milled, ground, opened or blended prior to use in a manufacturing operation; or (b) asbestos or any material containing asbestos is used in the manufacture of asbestos cement or asbestos cement pipes, or asbestos insulating board, or asbestos textiles, or asbestos jointing or packaging materials, or asbestos brake or clutch materials, or asbestos floor coverings, or fillers or reinforcements.

121. The owner of any premises used for the conduct of any specified process (including a person carrying on a specified process in or on the premises) must use the best practicable means[155] for preventing the emission of noxious or offensive emissions from such premises and for rendering such emissions, where discharged, harmless and inoffensive.[156]

154. *See Asia Dyeing Co Ltd v Air Pollution Control Authority* [1990] 1 HKLR 263 (CA) and *Teng Fuk Co Ltd v Air Pollution Control Appeal Board* [2001] 3 HKLRD 304 (CA), which are discussed above. Both these challenges were unsuccessful.

155. Where the phrase 'Best practicable means' is used with respect to the emission from a premises of an air pollutant, it has reference not only to the provision and the efficient maintenance of appliances adequate for preventing such emission, but also to the manner in which such appliances are used and to the proper supervision by the owner of the premises of any operation in which such an air pollutant is evolved: Air Pollution Control Ordinance, s. 2. The Environmental Protection Department has issued several guidance notes on best practicable means for specified purposes which include guidance notes on Aluminium (Secondary) Works, Cement Works (Cement Depot) and Ceramic Works.

156. Air Pollution Control Ordinance, s. 12(1). Air Pollution Control (Specified Processes) Regulations (Cap 311 sub leg F) have designated certain noxious or offensive emissions, such as acrylates, asbestos, fumes or vapours from gas works, hydrocarbons, smoke, grit and dust which the Ordinance seeks to prevent and control.

I. Exempting Specified Processes

122. A specified process may be carried out only with a licence, except in exempted premises. The Ordinance provides for the exemption of premises from the need to be licensed to conduct a specified process, and variation or cancellation of an exemption once granted. Provision is made for the procedure to be followed in each of these instances, right of appeal and compensation to affected owners of premises where a specified process is conducted.

123. The Secretary for the Environment may, having considered all relevant information, exempt any premises from the requirement of licensing, and the exemption status continues so long as it is conducted in accordance with the information that had been submitted to the Secretary for the Environment for the purpose of obtaining an exemption.[157] Where the owner had submitted inaccurate information and had been convicted of an offence of providing such inaccurate information, the exemption ceases to be effective.[158]

124. Where the Authority considers that it is necessary to do so in the public interest, he may remove an exemption or impose further terms and conditions on his own if he is of the opinion that the continuation of the process would of itself be prejudicial to health. If he does not form such an opinion, he must obtain the prior approval of the Chief Executive in Council or the agreement of the owner of the premises for cancellation or variation of an exemption. Where the Authority cancels or varies an exemption of his own motion there is no obligation to compensate the owner of the affected premises.[159]

125. The Authority may vary or cancel any term or condition of an exemption at the application of the owner of the premises, on such terms and condition as he thinks fit. He must give publicity to such an application and consider any public objections to the application. In determining the application, he must take into account the same consideration that he ought to take into account when considering an application for a specified process. A refusal to vary or cancel terms must be accompanied by reasons.[160]

126. Where the Authority, in the public interest, cancels or varies an exemption so as to impose additional obligations on the owner of the premises used for the conduct of the specified process to which the exemption relates, the Authority is liable to pay compensation to the owner of the premises whose exemption is cancelled or varied if such cancellation or variation was effected with the prior approval of the Chief Executive pursuant to section 22(2).[161]

---

157. *Ibid.*, ss 20 and 21(1).
158. *Ibid.*, s. 20A.
159. *Ibid.*, s. 22. *See also* below para. 126
160. *Ibid.*, s. 23.
161. *Ibid.*, s. 25.

II. Licensing Specified Processes

127. The Ordinance provides for the grant or refusal of an application for a licence to conduct a specified process, and variation or cancellation or transfer of a licence once granted. A specified process means a process specified in Schedule I of the Ordinance. Specified processes listed in Schedule 1 include: acrylates works; aluminium works, cement works, ceramic works, copper works, electricity works, gas works, iron and steel works, metal recovery works, incinerators, petrochemical works, petroleum works, asbestos works and glass works, where these processes are of a scale exceeding the limits specified in relation to each kind of process. Provision is made for the procedure to be followed in each of these instances, right of appeal and compensation to affected owners of premises where a specified process is conducted. The aim of the Ordinance is to control and monitor air pollution caused by industries that may have a significant adverse impact on the air quality. Through the terms and conditions of the licence, the owners of the premises used for the conduct of specified processes are required to use the best practicable means to prevent air pollution.[162]

A. *Making an Application*

128. An application for a licence to conduct a specified process must be submitted to the Authority, namely the Director of Environmental Protection. The Authority may require an applicant to submit an air pollution control plan, which he will take into consideration in determining whether or not to grant a licence.[163] He may require the applicant to include information, such as the following, in an air pollution control plan: (i) a description and technical particulars of a chimney or other plant or equipment that may evolve an air pollutant; (ii) a description and technical particulars of air pollution control equipment or measure proposed to be used to comply with the requirement to use the best practicable means of controlling air pollution; (iii) an assessment of the resulting air quality and risk to human health in the vicinity; (iv) a plan for, or scheme of, monitoring the emission at source or the ambient concentration of any air pollutant.[164]

B. *Public Consultation*

129. An application to conduct a specified process must go through public consultation. The first step of the process is the publication of the application, including in newspapers. Within thirty days of such publication in a newspaper, any member of the public may object to the grant of such a licence, on the grounds that the conduct of such specified process would inhibit the attainment or maintenance of the applicable air quality objectives or that any omissions from the proposed

162. *See* https://www.epd.gov.hk/epd/english/application_for_licences/guidance/ia_321.html.
163. *Ibid.*, s. 14A(1).
164. *Ibid.*, s. 14A(2).

specified process would be prejudicial to public health.[165] The Authority must consider such objections affording a hearing to both the applicant and objectors. Section 38 provides that the Authority may hear the applicant and any objector if he considers it expedient for the purpose of obtaining information relevant to any question to be decided and that the procedure to be followed at, or for the purpose of convening, any such hearing shall be determined by the Authority.

C. Grant of Licences

130. The Authority may, not earlier than forty days after the last notice is published in a newspaper, either grant or refuse to grant a licence. If he refuses to grant a licence the Authority must notify the applicant in writing of his refusal and must inform him of his reasons therefor. In the exercise of his discretion to grant or refuse to grant a licence, the Authority must have regard to the capability of the applicant to provide and maintain the best practicable means for the prevention of the emission from his premises of any air pollutant; have as his purpose the attainment and maintenance of any relevant air quality objective; and have regard to whether the emission of noxious or offensive emissions would be, or be likely to be, prejudicial to health.[166] An applicant who is aggrieved by the refusal of an application or the imposition of terms and conditions on a licence may appeal to the Appeal Board.[167]

D. Life Span of a Licence

131. A licence may be granted for a reasonable period of not less than two years and, without prejudice to any term or condition imposed for the purpose the attainment and maintenance of any relevant air quality objective, may be subject to such terms and conditions (including terms and conditions relating to the matters set out in Schedule 2)[168] as the Authority thinks fit; and where the licence concerned is for electricity works subject also to such terms and conditions as may be set out in Schedule 2A.[169]

165. *Ibid.*, s. 14(1)–(4).
166. *Ibid.*, s. 15.
167. *Ibid.*, s. 31.
168. Schedule 2 provides that the terms and conditions that may be imposed are any matters relating to the operation of Part IVB 'Specified Licences' of the Ordinance and, in relation to a licence for electricity works, matters set out in Sch. 2A in the Ordinance.
169. Air Pollution Control Ordinance, s. 15(4). Sch. 2A provides that 'the specified licence holder shall ensure that the actual emission of a type of specified pollutant from the licensed premises in an emission year is not greater than the allowed emission of that type of pollutant as applicable to the specified licence in respect of the emission year'.

E. Renewal of a Licence

132. The Ordinance provides for the renewal of a licence. There is no publication of the application for licence renewal and public consultation, unless the Secretary for the Environment directs the Authority to conduct a public consultation as in the case of an application for a new licence. The considerations that the Authority must take into account in determining a renewal licence are the same as those applicable to the grant of a new licence.[170]

F. Variation of a Licence

133. A licence may be varied by the Authority at the request of the licensee. Where a licensee has applied for a variation of the licence, the application must go through public consultation as in the case of a licence for a new application. In determining a variation application, the Authority must take into account the same considerations that he would in determining an application for a new licence. The Authority may permit a variation subject to such terms and condition as he thinks fit, and if he refuses the application, reasons must be given for the refusal.[171] There is a right of appeal to the Appeal Board against the refusal of the application.[172]

G. Cancellation or Variation of a Licence

134. The Authority, of his own motion, may cancel or vary a licence if he considers that the continuation of the specified process would be prejudicial to health. Unless he is able to form such opinion, he may exercise the powers of cancellation or variation of a licence only with the prior approval of the Chief Executive in Council or if he has obtained the consent of the licence holder. The licence holder has a right to make written submissions on why the licence should not be revoked or varied, and the Authority must consider such submissions when making his determination.[173] There is a right of appeal to the Appeal Board against the refusal of the application.[174]

H. Transfer of a Licence

135. The Authority may allow the transfer of a licence to conduct a specified process. For this purpose, both the licence holder and the proposed transferee must

170. For the procedure for renewal of a licence, *see* s. 16 of the Air Pollution Control Ordinance.
171. For variation of a licence, upon application by licence holder, *see* s. 18 of the Air Pollution Control Ordinance.
172. Air Pollution Control Ordinance, s. 31.
173. For cancellation or variation of a licence by the Authority, *see* s. 18 of the Air Pollution Control Ordinance.
174. Air Pollution Control Ordinance, s. 31.

make a joint application. The Authority determines such application, without any public consultation, unless he is directed by the Secretary for the Environment to follow the public consultation process as if it were an application for a new licence. The Authority is required to take into account the same considerations that he must take into account in determining whether or not to grant a new application. An applicant who is aggrieved by the refusal of a transfer application may appeal to the Appeal Board.[175]

I. Compensation for Licensing Decisions

136. Compensation must be paid to a licence holder for cancellation or imposition of additional obligations on him by varying the licence in the following situations: (i) such cancellation or variation was effected with the prior approval of the Governor in Council pursuant to section 17(2); or (ii) where the licence is cancelled or varied because the Authority considers that the continuation of the specified process to which the licence relates would be, or be likely to be, prejudicial to health, the possibility of such prejudice to health was known, or could with reasonable foresight have been known, to the Authority at the time the licence was granted or renewed; or (iii) the prejudice to health mentioned in paragraph (ii) is a consequence of the fact of licences having been granted or renewed after the grant (or, where a licence has been renewed, the last renewal) of the licence which is cancelled or varied.[176]

J. Allocation of Emission Allowances

137. An important development in relation to licensing of specified processes is the addition in 2008 of a new Part IVB to the Air Pollution Control Ordinance, which introduced a system of emission allowances, operated by the Secretary for the Environment. Emission allowances are allocated to electrical works in which fossil fuel is burnt either wholly or as part of a process of electricity generation where the installed generation capacity exceeds 5 megawatts. A licence for the operation of a specified process of electrical works is referred to in the Ordinance as a 'specified licence'. Such a specified licence sets out the upper limit of emissions permitted. The allocation is done by way of a Technical Memorandum. The first Technical Memorandum for Allocation of Emission Allowances in Respect of Specified Licences was gazetted in 2008, followed by seven further technical

175. For transfer of licence procedure, *see* s. 18(A) of the Air Pollution Control Ordinance.
176. Air Pollution Control Ordinance (Cap 311) s. 24. Section 26(1) provides as follows: 'The manner of determining the amount of compensation payable ... , the factors to be taken into account or disregarded and the principles to be applied in determining that amount shall be such as may be prescribed in regulations made under section 43.' Section 26(2) provides that, in addition, Sch. 4 of the Ordinance is also relevant to determining compensation.

memoranda to update the original one, implementing the government policy to review the emission allowances once every two years.[177]

138. In allocating a quantity of emission allowances for each type of specified pollutant in respect of each specified licence, the Secretary must: (a) have regard to the best practicable means for preventing the emission of that type of pollutant; (b) have as his purpose the attainment and maintenance of any relevant air quality objective; and (c) have regard to whether the emission of that type of pollutant would be, or would be likely to be, prejudicial to health.[178] The Secretary may increase the allowance for an emission year if there was a surplus in the previous year.[179] He may also, at the request of the licence holder, increase a particular emission allowance if there had been an unexpected emission as a result of a special event which was beyond the control of the licence holder.[180] There must also be evidence that the event could not reasonably have been foreseen and if the event could have been reasonably foreseen the licence holder exercised all due diligence to prevent its occurrence.[181]

139. A person who contravenes any term or condition of a specified licence that requires him, as a specified licence holder, to ensure that the actual emission of a type of specified pollutant from the licensed premises in an emission year is not greater than the allowed emission of that type of pollutant as applicable to the licence in respect of the emission year commits an offence.[182]

K. Contravention of a Licence

140. A licence holder who contravenes any term or condition of a licence commits a punishable offence. Enhanced punishments apply to a person who contravenes any term or condition of a licence that requires him, as a specified licence holder (i.e., an electricity works licence holder) to ensure that the actual emission of a type of specified pollutant from the licensed premises in an emission year is not greater than the allowed emission of that type of pollutant.[183]

§8. Other Specific Measures to Protect Air Quality in Hong Kong

141. Air Pollution Control Ordinance provides for a specific regime of control for premises that are used for 'specific processes'. It also provides for the control of

177. They prescribe the quantity of emission allowances for each type of specified pollutant allocated in respect of each specified licence and set out the allocation principles and determination method of the quantity of emission allowances to be allocated each year. *See* s. 26H of the Ordinance.
178. Air Pollution Control Ordinance, s. 26G(2).
179. *Ibid.*, s. 26J.
180. *Ibid.*, s. 26K(1).
181. *Ibid.*, s. 26K(2).
182. *Ibid.*, s. 30B(1).
183. *Ibid.*, ss 30A and 30.

harmful emissions from activities, which are not as potentially serious as specific processes. This, it does through several Regulations designed to control emission of harmful smokes and girt from furnaces, ovens and industrial plants as well as dust and grit emanating from construction worksites.

I. Control of Emission of Dust, Grit and Smoke

142. Air Pollution Control (Dust and Grit) Regulations (sub leg B) are intended to control emission of dust and grit from furnaces, ovens or industrial plants which use liquid fuels. Regulation 5 provides that:

(1) Except with the written permission of the Authority, no person shall use or cause or permit to be used in a burner of a furnace, oven or industrial plant a liquid fuel with a viscosity when delivered to the burner tip or point of ignition exceeding thirty centistokes or an equivalent viscosity.
(2) The Authority shall not grant permission under paragraph (1) to use a liquid fuel unless he is satisfied that the use of that fuel in a burner of a furnace, oven or industrial plant will not result in the emission of dark smoke from that furnace, oven or industrial plant.
(3) Any person who contravenes paragraph (1) shall be guilty of an offence.

143. The Authority, namely the Director of Environmental Protection, has the power to take samples of dust and grit from a furnace, oven or industrial plant to determine the concentration of dust and grit and take samples of the liquid fuel to determine whether it exceeds the limits of viscosity set out in Regulation 5.[184]

A. Emissions as Offences

144. If dust or grit is emitted from any furnace, oven, chimney, flue or industrial plant in excess of the limits set out in the Ordinance, the occupier of the premises upon which the furnace, oven, chimney, flue or industrial plant is situated shall be guilty of a punishable offence.[185]

B. Prohibition of the Use of Certain Fuels

145. Air Pollution Control (Fuel Restriction) Regulations (sub leg I) prohibit the use of certain fuels to control sulphur content in fuels used in commercial and industrial processes to reduce sulphur dioxide emissions. For the application of these controls, a geographical distinction is drawn between Shatin restriction area, which historically had serious emission problems from industrial processes, and the rest of

184. Sub leg B, reg. 6, etc.
185. Sub leg B, reg. 10.

Hong Kong. In Shatin restriction area, the use of liquid or solid fuel is almost completely banned, whereas in the rest of Hong Kong such fuels may be used subject to compliance with certain standards.

146. Regulation 4 of Air Pollution Control (Fuel Restriction) Regulations provides that no person shall use liquid fuel or solid fuel in any furnace, engine, oven or industrial plant in the Shatin fuel restriction area, other than restricted liquid fuel in any furnace, engine, oven or industrial plant that is used or operated only on a construction site; or is used or operated, or intended for use or operation, only during an emergency.

147. Regulation 4A of Air Pollution Control (Fuel Restriction) Regulations provides that no person shall use restricted liquid fuel in any furnace, engine, oven or industrial plant outside the Shatin fuel restriction area, without prior authorization. Regulation 4C requires the operation of a plant with permitted liquid fuel to be compliant with the conditions of the permission. Regulation 4D provides that no person shall use conventional solid fuel that has a sulphur content of more than 1% by weight in any furnace, engine, oven or industrial plant outside the Shatin fuel restriction area. These provisions are enforced through creation of criminal offences.[186]

C. *Controlling Dark Smoke*

148. Air Pollution Control (Smoke) Regulation (sub leg C) is directed at controlling the emission of dark smoke. Regulation 3 provides that an owner of any premises who operates any chimney, furnace, engine, oven or industrial plant in such a manner that any dark smoke[187] is emitted for more than six minutes in any period of four hours or for more than three minutes continuously at any one time, commits an offence.

D. *Controlling Smoke Emissions*

149. Air Pollution Control (Furnaces, Ovens and chimneys) (Installation and Alteration) Regulations (sub leg A) make supportive provision to control emission of smoke from furnaces, ovens or chimneys. Regulation 4 provides as follows:

(1) The occupier of any premises on which work is intended to be carried out in relation to: (a) the installation on the premises of a furnace, oven, chimney or flue; (b) the alteration or modification of a furnace, oven or chimney existing on the premises; or (c) alteration or modification of a flue between a furnace

186. *See* reg. 5.

187. Smoke includes: (a) dust or fumes; and (b) soot, ash, grit or gritty particles emitted in smoke or steam and what is dark is determined in accordance with the Rigelmann Chart: Cap 311 sub leg C, Reg. 2.

and chimney or between an oven and chimney existing on the premises, shall, not less than twenty-eight days prior to the commencement of such work, submit to the Authority for his approval plans showing the elevations and plan views of the furnace, oven, chimney or flue which is to be installed, altered or modified, together with specifications of the same.

(2) Any plans and specifications submitted to the Authority in pursuance of an application under section 14 (licence to carry out a specific process), section 16 (renewal of such licence), section 18 (variation of such licence) or section 23 (permission to alter an exempted premises) of the Air Pollution Control Ordinance shall be deemed to have been submitted also for the purposes of paragraph (1) if those plans and specifications include the plans and specifications of any furnace, oven, chimney or flue.

150. In considering an application for such installation or alteration, the Authority must not refuse it without giving an opportunity to the applicant to address any concerns that it has concerning any possible contravention of the Ordinance or contribution to air pollution.[188]

151. Regulation 11 of Air Pollution Control (Furnaces, Ovens and chimneys) (Installation and Alteration) Regulations (sub leg A) provides that no occupier shall carry out or cause or permit to be carried out any work in relation to installation, alteration or modification of any furnace, oven, chimney or flue on his premises unless approval in respect of all the plans and specifications of the same is obtained in accordance with these regulations. Contravention of Regulation 11 is a punishable offence.[189]

152. An occupier does not only refer to the person who is in actual physical occupation of land: An occupier also means a person who has control over the land. This is supported by the interpretation in section 2, the interpretation section of the Regulations: 'Occupier means (a) the occupier of premises on which a furnace, oven, chimney or flue is to be installed, altered or modified; and (b) the person having the management or control or receiving the profits of the business carried on in such premises.' Thus, it may cover a landowner who puts a contractor in occupation of his land to carry out work for his benefit. The landowner would be liable, as such, for any contravention of the regulation by the contractor.[190]

---

188. *See Kam Kong Dyeing Factory v Air Pollution Control Authority* [1987] HKLY 481.

189. Cap 311 sub leg A, r 12.

190. *R v Cabot Plastics Hong Kong Ltd* [1992] 1 HKC 465, [1992–1993] CPR 111, [1992] HKEC 524. Dismissing the appeal against the conviction in the Magistrate's Court, the High Court held that: (1) the Regulations had to be construed in a common-sense manner and looked at as a whole; the mischief aimed at was the prevention of air pollution caused by the operation of furnaces, chimneys, etc.; (2) D had caused to be erected a chimney which it intended should be used for its business. D may well have been the occupier at the time of the contravention even though it was the building contractor who was carrying out the construction; (3) even if this were wrong, the construction of reg. 2(b) of the Regulations permitted two situations: (a) where the manager of the business was actually running the business when the contravening chimney was erected; and (b) where he was intending to utilize the contravening chimney in the future. When D came to operate its

E. Control of Construction Dust

153. Air Pollution Control (Construction Dust) Regulation (sub leg R) aims to control generation of dust from construction sites. A contractor responsible for a construction site where any notifiable work[191] is proposed to be carried out must, before the proposed work is carried out, give notice to the Authority of the proposal to carry out the work. If there is any change in the particulars given in the notice, the contractor must give notice of it to the Authority before the proposed change takes effect. Failure to comply with this requirement is a punishable offence.[192]

154. Any person carrying out notifiable work or regulatory work must carry out such work in accordance with the requirements of the Ordinance, failure to comply being a punishable offence.[193] Any person carrying out excluded work must ensure that dusty materials intended to be used for such work or produced as a result of such work being carried out is safely stored and handled, failure to comply being an offence.[194] The Schedule of the Ordinance provides specific requirements that have to be met in relation to notifiable and regulatory work. It also set out some requirements which are generally applicable such as that every main haul road of the construction site should be sprayed with water or a dust suppression chemical so as to maintain the entire road surface wet. *HKSAR v China State Construction Engineering (Hong Kong) Ltd*[195] is a case of an unsuccessful appeal against a conviction in the Magistrate's Court for failure to keep the main haul road (meaning any road inside a construction site having a vehicle passing rate of higher than four in any thirty minutes) wet to prevent emanation of dust.

F. The Nature of the Offences

155. The offences created by sections 4, 5 and 6 are strict liability offences, since no *mens rea* needs to be proved, but are subject to the proof of the statutory defence

---

factory it would have been in contravention of the Regulations; (4) accordingly, D could have been convicted as 'occupier' under either limb of the definition.

191. Notifiable work means reclamation: (a) demolition of a building; (b) work carried out in any part of a tunnel that is within 100 m of any exit to the open air; (c) construction of the foundation of a building; (d) construction of the superstructure of a building; or (e) road construction work, but does not include any emergency work, excluded work (such as renovation, maintenance and alteration work carried out entirely within the external walls and under the roof of a building and work carried out exclusively for asbestos investigation, abatement and removal) or regulatory work (such as road opening or resurfacing work and slope stabilization work): Section 2.

192. Cap 311 sub leg R, s. 3.

193. Regulation R, ss 4 and 5. Regulatory work includes renovation carried out on the outer surface of the external wall or the upper surface of the roof of a building; road opening or resurfacing work; and slope stabilization work.

194. Regulation R, s. 6. Excluded work includes renovation, maintenance and alteration work carried out entirely within the external walls and under the roof of a building; work carried out exclusively for asbestos investigation, abatement and removal; and (c) any specified process.

195. [2005] HKEC 381.

set out in section 7.[196] Section 7 of the regulations provides a due diligence defence: It is a defence for a person charged with such an offence to prove that: (a) interruptions or contingencies in the supply of necessary materials, water and equipment; (b) weather conditions prevailing at the time of the offence; (c) a threat or an imminent threat to human life or building safety; (d) the physical constraints of the construction site; or (e) other circumstances beyond his control prevented him from complying with the relevant section and that he exercised due diligence to avoid the commission of the offence.[197]

G. *Open Burning*

156. Air Pollution Control (Open Burning) Regulation (sub leg O) applies more particularly to construction sites. Open burning for the following purposes is strictly prohibited: (a) the disposal of construction waste; (b) the clearance of a site in preparation for construction work; (c) the disposal of tyres; and (d) the salvage of metal. Any contravention of this regulation is a punishable offence. Open burning, other than small scale open burning such as burning of candles or cooking for human consumption, may be carried out only with a permit, provided that no such permit may be issued for construction site-related open burning which is strictly prohibited. A permit for the purpose of open burning may be issued by the Authority valid for no longer than one year and subject to any conditions that the Authority may deem fit, and such a permit may be renewed, revoked or replaced with a new permit. Any person who: (a) without a permit carries out open burning for which a permit is required; or (b) being a permit-holder contravenes any condition to which the permit is subject, commits a punishable offence.[198]

§9. Control of Motor Vehicle Emissions

157. Air Pollution Control Ordinance (Cap 311) and Road Traffic Ordinance (Cap 374) along with regulations that are made under them, provide the legislative framework for the regulation of motor vehicle emissions. The regulatory provisions are enforced through creation of offences relating to motor vehicle emissions.

---

196. *See HKSAR v Kwan On Construction Ltd* [2009] HKEC 926. It is a question of interpretation whether the availability of a statutory defence excludes the common law defence of honest and reasonable belief. *See HKSAR v Gammon Construction Ltd* [2020] 4 HKLRD 670 (CA) and cases cited therein, including *Hin Lin Yee v HKSAR* (2010) 13 HKCFAR 142 (CFA) and *HKSAR v Gammon Construction Ltd* (2015) 18 HKCFAR 110 (CFA).

197. For a discussion of these defences, *see HKSAR v China State Construction Engineering (Hong Kong) Ltd* [2005] HKEC 381, where the conviction was upheld.

198. *Ibid.*, ss 4, 5, 6, 7.

I. Legislative Framework

158. The Air Pollution Ordinance, when first enacted was intended to apply to emissions from stationary sources. In 1991, the Ordinance was amended removing the words 'with particular reference to stationary sources' from its long title. The amendments introduced provisions relating to emissions from motor vehicles. The Road Traffic Ordinance which was passed in the same year made additional provisions in relation to control of motor vehicle emissions. Regulations made under these two ordinances make detailed provisions in order to prevent excessive motor vehicle emissions, by setting out emission standards and emission limits as well as encouraging the use of petrol and diesel of high quality. The enforcement of these regulations is through the creation of criminal offences.

159. In order to enforce these new regulatory measures, the above two ordinances provide for several powers of inspection. Section 66(1) of the Road Traffic Ordinance provides that a police officer in uniform of the rank of sergeant or above who has reason to believe that an offence relating to the emission of smoke or visible vapour is being or has been committed in respect of a motor vehicle which is on a road or in any public place may stop and examine the vehicle. He may measure the emission of smoke or visible vapour from the vehicle.

160. Section 66(2) of the Road Traffic Ordinance provides that a police officer of the rank of sergeant and above, who has reason to believe that an offence against the Road Traffic Ordinance relating to the emission of smoke or visible vapour has been committed within the preceding fourteen days, may by notice require production of the vehicle at a vehicle examination centre. Section 77B provides that the Commissioner for Transport may, for the purpose of ascertaining whether a motor vehicle complies with vehicle emission standards, require the vehicle to be tested at a vehicle emission testing centre. Section 77C provides that for this purpose the Commissioner has the power to designate any place, including a car testing centre or a vehicle examination centre, as a vehicle emission testing centre.

161. For the purposes of Part VIIIA of the Road Traffic Ordinance, which deals with testing of motor vehicle emissions, the Commissioner for Transport may issue a Code of Practice setting out vehicle emission standards and the practice and procedure to be followed and specifying the equipment to be used for the testing of motor vehicles at vehicles emission testing centres.

A. Regulations Made under the Air Pollution Control Ordinance

162. Section 43 of the Air Pollution Control Ordinance, as amended in 1991, provides that the Secretary for the Environment may make regulations for matters including the following, which relate to motor vehicles:

– the application of standards (including vehicle design standards), specifications, descriptions, methods, procedures, requirements or tests laid down in documents (whether or not published or produced in Hong Kong) not forming part of the regulations and relating to the prevention or reduction of the emission of air pollutants including the application of such standards, specifications, descriptions, methods, procedures, requirements or tests in relation to the prohibition or control of the emission of air pollutants from motor vehicles;

- the inspection, examination, measurement or testing of motor vehicles and motor vehicle engines in relation to the prohibition or control of the emission of air pollutants therefrom and the fuels used or intended to be used therein, and the methods, equipment and procedures to be used or followed for such inspection, examination, measurement or testing;
- the fitting or installation of any apparatus or device to motor vehicles to prevent or reduce the emission of air pollutants therefrom;
- the prohibition or control of any material, lubricants or liquids that may evolve air pollutants if added to any fuel;
- the prohibition or control of the removal, replacement, modification, adaptation or alteration of any apparatus or device fitted to or installed in any motor vehicle or motor vehicle engine and so fitted or installed to prevent or reduce the emission of air pollutants therefrom;
- the prohibition or control of the use of any motor vehicle modified, adapted, altered, maintained or operated in contravention of any requirement imposed under this Ordinance;
- the prohibition of control of the removal, replacement, modification, adaptation or alteration of any motor vehicle or motor vehicle engine that has the effect or intended effect of increasing the emission of air pollutants therefrom;
- the imposition of requirements as to the design, construction, maintenance, adjustment, repair or operation of any motor vehicle or motor vehicle engine in order to prevent or reduce the emission of air pollutants therefrom;
- the prohibition or control of the modification, adaptation or alteration of any fuel pump or other equipment and fittings used for or in connection with the dispensing of fuel, and the prohibition or control of the removal, alteration or defacement of any information required to be displayed in respect of such fuel pump or other equipment and fittings;
- the prohibition or control of the use of any fuel pump or other equipment and fittings used for or in connection with the dispensing of fuel modified, adapted, altered or operated in contravention of this Ordinance.[199]

163. Two relevant regulations have been enacted pursuant to section 43 (r)–(ri) of Air Pollution Control Ordinance, namely the Air Pollution Control (Vehicle Design Standards) (Emission) Regulations (sub leg J) and the Air Pollution Control (Motor Vehicle Fuel) Regulations (sub leg L).

---

199. Cap 311, s. 43(r)–(ri).

1. The Air Pollution Control (Vehicle Design Standards) (Emission) Regulations

164. The Air Pollution Control (Vehicle Design Standards) (Emission) Regulations (Cap 311 sub leg J) set out specific emission standards that different types of vehicles must conform to. Section 4A of the Regulations provides as follows:

(1) Every motor vehicle registered on or after 1 April 1995 which is equipped with a compression-ignition engine shall be so constructed that no excessive smoke is emitted from the vehicle.
(2) For the purpose of sub-regulation (1), smoke shall be deemed excessive if the smoke emitted from the vehicle measured by means of the test procedure specified in the first column of Schedule 1 exceeds the maximum permitted smoke level specified in the second column of that Schedule or the maximum permitted smoke level in absolute units of light absorption specified in the third column of that Schedule.
(3) The provisions of this regulation are in addition to, and not in substitution for, Regulation 31 of the Road Traffic (Construction and Maintenance of Vehicles) Regulations (Cap 374 sub leg A).

2. The Air Pollution Control (Motor Vehicle Fuel) Regulation

165. The Air Pollution Control (Motor Vehicle Fuel) Regulation (Cap 311 sub leg L) is aimed at ensuring the uninterrupted availability of unleaded petrol and genuine motor vehicle diesel. The central provision is found in Regulations 3 together with 7, 8 and 9.

166. Regulation 3 provides that any petrol supplier who knowingly supplies, distributes, sells or offers for sale leaded petrol commits an offence. For the purposes of any proceedings in relation to such an offence, the petrol supplier charged shall, unless there is evidence to the contrary, be presumed to have known that the petrol the supplier supplied, distributed, sold or offered for sale was leaded petrol. A petrol retailer does not commit an offence of selling or offering to sell if the retailer proves that: (a) he purchased, or otherwise obtained, the petrol with a warranty or other written evidence from the petrol supplier who supplied or distributed the petrol that the petrol was unleaded petrol; and (b) at the time of the alleged offence, the petrol was in the same state that it was in at the time of delivery.

167. Regulation 7 replicates Regulation 3 in relation to supply, distribution and sale of any substance (which is not motor vehicle diesel) as motor vehicle diesel. Regulation 8 replicates Regulation 3 in relation to supply, distribution and sale of any fuel additive containing any amount of lead whatsoever. Regulation 9 replicates Regulation 3 in respect of any person who knowingly pours, places, discharges or adds any fuel additive containing any amount of lead whatsoever into the fuel tank, the fuel supply system, or the combustion space of the engine of a motor vehicle.

B. Regulations Made under the Road Traffic Ordinance

168. Section 9 of the Road Traffic Ordinance (Cap 374) enables the Secretary for Transport to make regulations generally as to the construction and maintenance of vehicles and their equipment. It goes on to specify several matters in relation to which regulations could be made and the list includes 'the emission by vehicles of smoke, fumes vapour, sparks and grit'.

169. The only directly relevant regulation made under the Road Traffic Ordinance is the Motor Traffic (Construction and Maintenance) Regulations (sub leg A), which make provision in relation to motor vehicle emissions. Regulation 31 provides as follows:

> (1) Every motor vehicle shall be so constructed and maintained that (a) no excessive smoke or visible vapour is emitted therefrom; (b) so far as is reasonably practicable, the products of combustion, ashes, steam, cinders, petrol, water or oil are not discharged on the road or in such manner as to be likely to cause damage to property or injury or danger or loss of amenity or annoyance to persons.
> (2) For the purposes of paragraph (1)(a), smoke or visible vapour shall be deemed to be excessive if the smoke or visible vapour emitted from the vehicle measured by means of any one of the apparatuses specified by the Commissioner from time to time by notice published in the Gazette exceeds the maximum permitted smoke or visible vapour level specified in column 1 of Part I of the Fourth Schedule or the maximum permitted smoke or visible vapour level in absolute units of light absorption specified in column 2 of that Part.
> (2A) For the avoidance of doubt, a notice under paragraph (2) is not subsidiary legislation.
> (3) Every motor vehicle using solid fuel shall be fitted with an efficient appliance for the purpose of preventing the emission of sparks or grit.
> (4) It shall be a good defence in any proceedings in respect of a contravention of this regulation to prove that the emission or discharge was due to some temporary or accidental cause which could not be prevented by the exercise of reasonable care.

170. Regulation 31A provides that without limiting Regulation 31 every motor vehicle (other than a motorcycle or a motor tricycle) manufactured after 1975 and equipped with a positive ignition and uses unleaded petrol as fuel or equipped with a positive ignition engine and uses liquefied petroleum gas as fuel should be so constructed and maintained that its exhaust emission is not excessive. Criteria to determine whether exhaust emissions are excessive were set out in the Fourth Schedule of the regulation.

171. Regulation 121 provides that any person who uses or causes or permits to be used on any road any vehicle which does not comply in all respects with the provisions of the regulations, and any person who contravenes or fails to comply with any requirement under the regulations commits an offence. Regulation 31A(7) provides that it shall be a defence in any proceedings in respect of a contravention of that regulation to prove that the excessive exhaust emission was due to some temporary or accidental cause which could not be prevented by the exercise of reasonable care.

§10. Control of Harmful Effects of Asbestos

I. Legislative Framework

172. Provision to eliminate or minimize harmful effects of asbestos is found in the Air Pollution Control Ordinance which makes comprehensive provision to eliminate as far as possible Hong Kong's reliance on asbestos materials. The Ordinance adopts several strategies for this purpose: It bans the import and sale of two kinds of harmful asbestos which are known as amosite or crocidolite; regulates asbestos-related activities; and provides for safety measures to protect workers from exposure to harmful asbestos. The Air Pollution Control (Asbestos) (Administration) Regulation (sub leg P) deals with qualifications of asbestos personnel. The other relevant statutory source is the Factories and Industrial Undertaking (Asbestos) Regulation (sub leg AD) which is intended to protect workers from harmful exposure to asbestos.

II. Prohibition of Importation or Sale of Asbestos

173. The Ordinance makes it an offence to use, supply, import or tranship asbestos or asbestos-containing material or cause or permit the use, supply, import or transhipment of asbestos or asbestos-containing material (section 80(1)). This prohibition is subject to the following exceptions: (i) Section 81(1) provides that section 80 does not prohibit a person from importing or transhipping, or causing or permitting the import or transhipment of, asbestos or asbestos-containing material that is goods in transit; (ii) Section 81(3) provides that section 80 does not prohibit a person from supplying, importing or transhipping, or causing or permitting the supply, import or transhipment of, asbestos-containing material that is proprietary Chinese medicine, which registered or exempted under the Chinese Medicines Ordinance (Cap 549); (iii) Section 81(5) provides that section 80 does not prohibit a person from using asbestos or asbestos-containing material in work carried out in an industrial undertaking. Section 83 provides that the Authority may exempt a person from a prohibition imposed by section 80(1) if the Authority considers that the exemption is warranted and would be unlikely to lead to a health risk to the community.

III. Regulation of Asbestos-Related Activities

174. Statutory provisions relating to the control of harmful use of asbestos are set out in the Air Pollution Control Ordinance in Part VIII 'Control of Environmental Asbestos' and Part IX 'Asbestos Control Work'. Part VIII of the Ordinance deals with the registration and regulation of asbestos personnel. Part IX of the Air Pollution Control Ordinance provides for investigation to determine if there is any hazard of asbestos-containing material[200] in any premises or a ship; preparation of an asbestos management plan either to manage any asbestos which does not require to be removed or to abate any asbestos work; and to manage asbestos abatement work.[201]

175. Four codes of practice have been made to provide guidance on asbestos control. These are the Preparation of Asbestos Investigation Report, Asbestos Management Plan and Asbestos Abatement Plan; Asbestos Work Using Full Containment or Mini Containment Method; Safe Handling of Low Risk Asbestos Containing Material; and Asbestos Work Using Glove Bag Method. The Environmental Protection Department has also issued a non-statutory Practice Note on 'Handling of Asbestos Containing Materials in Buildings'.

IV. Registration of Persons and Institutions Who May Carry Out Asbestos-Related Work

176. The first step in relation to control of asbestos-related works is to ensure that such work is undertaken by qualified persons only. For this purpose, the Ordinance provides that the Authority shall keep registers of: (a) asbestos consultants for natural persons who are qualified to perform the duties and functions of a registered asbestos consultant; (b) asbestos contractors for natural persons, companies and other bodies corporate which are qualified to perform the duties and functions of a registered asbestos contractor; (c) asbestos supervisors for natural persons who are qualified to perform the duties and functions of a registered asbestos supervisor; (d) asbestos laboratories for all laboratories which are qualified to perform the duties and functions of a registered asbestos laboratory together with details of the natural persons, companies and other bodies corporate that have an interest in a registered asbestos laboratory.[202]

---

200. Asbestos-containing material means any material, substance or product which is made with or contains as determined by a method approved by the Secretary: Cap 311, s. 2.

201. Asbestos abatement work means any work or a procedure to control fibre release from asbestos-containing material, and includes the removal and transport of asbestos-containing material: Air Pollution Control Ordinance, s. 2.

202. Air Pollution Control Ordinance, s. 51(1). Subs. (2) provides that the Authority shall maintain a copy of the registers for inspection by the public free of charge during business hours.

V. Advisory Role of the Asbestos Administration Committee

177. To assist the Authority in the task of regulating persons and institutions (namely asbestos consultants, asbestos contractors, asbestos supervisors and asbestos laboratories) that may be involved in asbestos-related work, the Ordinance authorizes the Authority to appoint an Asbestos Administration Committee.[203] The committee is chaired by the Director of Environmental Protection and consists of representatives from relevant government departments, persons nominated by their professional bodies to represent engineers, architects and surveyors and three persons who are not civil servants.[204] The functions of the Administration Committee are: (a) to assist the Authority in processing applications for entry in the registers as set out in this Part VIII 'Control of Environmental Asbestos'; (b) hear complaints of a disciplinary nature against persons whose names are on any of the registers and make recommendations that it sees fit in accordance with this Part; and (c) carry out other functions and duties of the Authority relating to asbestos, its use and disposal that the Authority may delegate in writing to it.[205]

178. Applications to be entered in the register must be made to the Secretary of the Asbestos Administration Committee, and the Authority must not enter the name of a person, company, body corporate or laboratory in a register unless the Authority is satisfied that the person is qualified to perform the duties and functions required of a person entered in the register.[206] It is the duty of the Asbestos Administration Committee to assist the Authority in considering applications for inclusion in the registers by: (a) examining the qualifications of an applicant; (b) making enquiries and conducting tests that the Administration Committee considers necessary to ascertain whether an applicant has the appropriate experience; (c) conducting a professional interview, if the Administration Committee considers it necessary, with an applicant; and (d) advising the Authority as to the acceptance, deferral or rejection of an application for entry on the registers.[207]

179. Where it appears to the Authority or a member of the Administration Committee that: (a) a registered asbestos consultant, registered asbestos contractor, registered asbestos supervisor or registered asbestos laboratory; or (b) a director, partner or owner of a registered asbestos contractor or registered asbestos laboratory, has committed neglect or misconduct that renders the person, company, body corporate or laboratory unfit to continue to be entered on the relevant register; or

---

203. *Ibid.*, s. 52.
204. *See* http://www.epd.gov.hk/epd/english/boards/asbestos/maincontent.html.
205. Air Pollution Control Ordinance, s. 53.
206. *Ibid.*, s. 55.
207. *Ibid.*, s. 57.

makes further entry of the person, company, body corporate or laboratory on the relevant register prejudicial to the administration of this Ordinance; or renders the person, company, body corporate or laboratory deserving of censure, the Authority or the member may refer the matter to the Administration Committee which may conduct an enquiry.[208]

180. Provision has been made to ensure that the Administration Committee conducts an independent and impartial disciplinary enquiry including the safeguard that the registered person who is the subject of a hearing, and the directors, partners and proprietors of a registered asbestos contractor or registered asbestos laboratory, are entitled to hear and to have access to all evidence produced at the hearing and to cross-examine witnesses adducing the evidence.[209] The Committee has been given extensive powers for the conduct of its disciplinary proceedings, including power call witnesses and to inspect premises.[210] The Administration Committee may, if upon the conclusion of the enquiry finds a proved misconduct or negligence, recommend an appropriate penalty. The Authority may, on receiving the recommendation of the Administration Committee, order: (a) that the name of the person, company, body corporate or laboratory be removed, either permanently or for a specified period, from the relevant register; (b) that the person, company, body corporate or laboratory be reprimanded; (c) that a shareholder, director or other officer of a company or body corporate be reprimanded; (d) the findings and order be published in the Gazette.[211]

VI. Investigation of Premises for Asbestos-Containing Material

181. The owner of premises which contain or may reasonably be suspected of containing asbestos-containing material must engage a registered asbestos consultant to carry out an investigation on any asbestos-containing material which may be in the premises. He must after such investigation submit an asbestos investigation report. And, if asbestos-containing material is found in the premises, an asbestos abatement plan must be prepared, at least twenty-eight days before he carries out any intended asbestos abatement work or work which involves the use or handling of any asbestos-containing material. An owner is not required to submit an asbestos investigation report or an asbestos abatement plan if the asbestos abatement work or work involving the use or handling of asbestos-containing material is of a class specified by the Secretary. The Secretary shall publish notice in the Gazette of a class of work specified for this purpose.[212]

208. *Ibid.*, s. 62.
209. *Ibid.*, ss 63, 64 and 65.
210. *Ibid.*, s. 68.
211. *Ibid.*, s. 67. The Authority may make an order as to costs.
212. *Ibid.*, s. 69(1) and (2).

A. Carrying Out an Investigation

182. The owner of premises specified by the Authority shall, unless the premises have been certified in writing by the Director of Architectural Services or a public officer authorized by the Secretary as being free of asbestos-containing material, engage a registered asbestos consultant to carry out an investigation on any asbestos-containing material which may be present in the premises.[213] Premises that may be specified by the Secretary for the Environment are such as hospitals or schools which could reasonably be suspected of having asbestos-containing material. An asbestos investigation would be compulsory for such premises, except where such premises have been certified to be free of asbestos-containing material.[214]

B. Asbestos Management Plan

183. An asbestos management plan must include: (a) an operation and maintenance plan for asbestos-containing material not requiring asbestos removal work; and (b) an asbestos abatement plan for any asbestos abatement work or work which involves the use or handling of any asbestos-containing material.[215]

184. A registered asbestos consultant must sign the asbestos management plan in which he must include the following information: (a) a detailed description of the premises or ship; (b) the names, positions and structure of the organization of people in charge of the implementation of the plan; (c) the location and type of all the identified asbestos-containing material; (d) the physical condition of the identified asbestos-containing material; (e) a statement of reasons why any asbestos-containing material should not be removed; (f) the method of labelling of all asbestos-containing material; (g) the method of informing all people who may be affected about the existence and the location of the asbestos-containing material; (h) a surveillance scheme; (i) a record-keeping scheme; (j) the methods by which the disturbance of asbestos-containing material can be avoided; and (k) the actions to be taken in case the condition of the asbestos-containing material is found to be deteriorating.[216] After receiving the asbestos management plan, the Authority may require the owner of the premises or ship to submit further plans and specifications within the period specified by the Authority.[217] The Authority may, by notice in writing to the owner of premises or a ship, require additional measures or impose conditions as he considers necessary to be included in an asbestos management plan.[218]

213. *Ibid.*, s. 69(4).
214. *See* the clarification made by the Secretary in the Legislative Council: Hong Kong Hansard of 8 November 1995 at p. 88.
215. Air Pollution Control Ordinance, s. 71(1).
216. *Ibid.*, s. 71(2).
217. *Ibid.*, s. 71(4).
218. *Ibid.*, s. 72(1).

C. Asbestos Abatement Plan

185. An asbestos abatement plan must be prepared by an asbestos consultant, and must contain the following information: (a) a detailed description of the premises or ship; (b) the names of the registered asbestos consultant, registered asbestos contractor, and registered asbestos laboratory; (c) a statement of reasons why any asbestos-containing material should not be removed; (d) a programme for asbestos abatement work; (e) descriptions of methods, measures and steps for checking the performance of the asbestos control measures before, during and after the asbestos abatement work or work which involves the use or handling of asbestos-containing material; (f) the amount of asbestos waste and the method of disposal; and (g) any emergency procedures and contingency measures which may be required.[219]

186. After receiving the asbestos abatement plan, the Authority may require the owner of the premises or ship to submit further plans and specifications within the period specified by the Authority.[220] The Authority may, by notice in writing to the owner of premises or a ship, require additional measures or impose conditions as he considers necessary to be included in an asbestos abatement plan.[221]

D. Asbestos Abatement Work

187. The owner of premises must give not less than twenty-eight days' written notice to the Authority of the date on which the asbestos abatement work or work involving the use or handling of asbestos-containing material is to be commenced. A person who fails to comply with this requirement commits a punishable offence.[222]

1. Asbestos-Related Work Must Be Supervised by a Registered Asbestos Consultant

188. The implementation of an asbestos management plan or an asbestos abatement plan must be supervised by a registered asbestos consultant. The registered asbestos consultant so appointed by the owner of the premises must: (a) supervise the carrying out of the asbestos management plan or an asbestos abatement plan and the conduct of any asbestos abatement work; (b) notify the Authority of any modification of the content of the asbestos management plan or an asbestos abatement plan before implementing the modification; and (c) notify the Authority of any contravention of a requirement under the Air Pollution Control Ordinance or in respect

219. *Ibid.*, s. 71(3).
220. *Ibid.*, s. 71(4).
221. *Ibid.*, s. 72(1).
222. *Ibid.*, s. 73.

of a step, measure, requirement and condition in an asbestos management plan or an asbestos abatement plan, or required by the Authority.[223]

2. Asbestos-Related Work Must Be Carried Out by a Registered Asbestos Contractor

189. The registered owner of premises who implements an asbestos abatement plan or carries out work which involves the use or handling of asbestos-containing material in the premises must appoint a registered asbestos contractor to carry out the work. A registered asbestos contractor so appointed must give continuous supervision through registered asbestos supervisors stationed continuously at the asbestos abatement area to supervise the carrying out of the asbestos abatement plan, asbestos abatement work or work which involves the use or handling of any asbestos-containing material and any related work.[224] An owner is not required to appoint a registered asbestos contractor to carry out any work which involves the use or handling of any asbestos-containing material in premises if the work is of a class specified by the Secretary. The Secretary is required to publish notice in the Gazette of a class of work so specified.[225]

3. Engagement of a Registered Asbestos Laboratory

190. A registered asbestos library must be engaged to carry our sampling, measurement or analysis where the owner of premises is required to carry out sampling, measurement or analysis of a substance containing, or suspected to contain, asbestos-containing material in the premises to comply with an asbestos management plan or an asbestos abatement plan or otherwise to comply with Part IX of the Air Pollution Control Ordinance.[226]

4. Compliance with Requirements Relating to Asbestos-Related Work

191. Compliance with the provisions contained in Part IX of the Air Pollution Control Ordinance is enforced through criminal sanction. Section 77 of the Air Pollution Control Ordinance provides as follows: A person who implements or causes the implementation of an asbestos management plan or asbestos abatement plan contrary to section 74 commits an offence. A person who implements or causes the implementation of an asbestos management plan or carries out or causes the carrying out of work involving the use or handling of asbestos-containing material contrary to section 75 commits an offence. A person who carries out or causes the carrying out of the sampling, measurement or analysis of a substance containing or

223. *Ibid.*, s. 74.
224. *Ibid.*, s. 75(1) and (3).
225. *Ibid.*, s. 75(4) and (5).
226. *Ibid.*, s. 76.

suspected to contain asbestos-containing material contrary to section 76 commits an offence. A person who does not follow the specifications, steps or measures specified in an asbestos management plan or an asbestos abatement plan and any additional measures or steps stipulated by the Authority and any conditions imposed on the plan by the Authority commits an offence. In *HKSAR v Wing Lok Construction & Engineering Co Ltd*,[227] the owner of a demolition site was found guilty in the Magistrate's Court of causing the carrying out of work involving the handling of asbestos-containing material, without appointing a registered asbestos contractor to carry out such work, in breach of section 75 of the Air Pollution Control Ordinance (Cap 311). In determining the liability of the construction site owner, the central issue was whether he 'caused' the carrying out of such work. Beeson J referred to the following interpretation of the word 'cause' given in the Australian case of *O'Sullivan v Truth and Sportsman Ltd*,[228] which was adopted by the Privy Council in *Attorney General v Tse Hung Li*:[229] 'When it is made an offence by or under a statute for one man to "cause" the doing of a prohibited act by another, the provision is not to be understood as referring to any description of antecedent event or condition produced by the first man which contributed to the determination of the will of the second man to do the prohibited act. It should be interpreted as confined to cases where the prohibited act is done on the actual authority, express or implied, of the party said to have caused it or in consequence of his exerting some capacity which he possesses in fact or in law to control or influence the acts of the other. He must moreover contemplate or desire that the prohibited act will ensue.' Beeson J adopted that test in the circumstances of the instant case which were as follows: The site owners appointed a registered asbestos contractor to remove asbestos-containing material which were known to be present in the construction site; they also engaged contractors to remove general rubbish from the site; and during the general cleaning of the site, some asbestos-containing equipment went missing. The defendant-appellant submitted that they might have been either stolen by thieves or removed by the workers negligently or with the intention of stealing. In finding the site owner not guilty of the offence of 'causing', Beason J said: 'What is required is a positive application of either the appellant's authority, or its exertion of some capacity to control or influence the act of the workers. Thus, although the appellant, when securing the site, might have taken inadequate steps to prevent the theft of items and a workman seeing the unguarded items might have decided to steal them, it cannot be said that the appellant "caused" the theft. Counsel for the appellant submitted that to find otherwise would mean that a householder who failed to lock his door could be blamed for any burglary that resulted.' Beeson J concluded: 'Here the appellant did not want the items removed by anyone but the specialist contractor hired for that purpose. The appellant did not want the items to be stolen nor was there any indication that their less than adequate anti-theft measures were intended to benefit prospective thieves. If it was a possibility that the items had been stolen, which on the facts it was, the appellant could not be held to have "caused" their removal.' Compare the case of *HKSAR v Sunley Engineering and Construction Co*

227. [2014] 2 HKLRD 669; [2014] HKEC 444.
228. (1957) 96 CLR 220.
229. [1986] AC 876 (PC).

Ltd,[230] which is discussed in paragraphs 308–310 below, where Beeson J seems to have taken a more stringent view of the liability of a construction contractor for a breach of licence conditions, which had been committed by his employees.

192. Section 78 sets out the following defences: A person does not commit an offence under section 77 if he adduces evidence that shows: (a) he carried out the work, or caused or permitted the work to be carried out, in an emergency situation that did not permit him to comply with that section without risk to human life or serious disruption to a public service; or (b) he did not know and could not have reasonably known of the presence of asbestos or asbestos-containing material at the time when he carried out the work, or caused or permitted the work to be carried.

E. Asbestos Abatement Notice

193. An asbestos abatement notice enables the Authority to require any owner of premises to carry out asbestos-related investigation and remedial work.

1. Issuing an Abatement Notice

194. If in the opinion of the Authority, any premises, relevant plant or activity contains, or is believed may release, any asbestos, the Authority or an authorized officer may issue an asbestos abatement notice either verbally or in writing. Such notice may require the person to whom the notice is given to do any of the following: (a) to take measures or steps and within the time as specified to prevent, control, reduce or eliminate the release of asbestos; (b) to hire a registered asbestos consultant to prepare an investigation report and to prepare an asbestos management plan; (c) to hire a registered asbestos contractor to implement an asbestos management plan and to carry out any asbestos abatement work or work involving the use of handling of any asbestos-containing material; and (d) to hire a registered asbestos laboratory to carry out sampling and measurement to assess fibre concentration.[231]

2. What the Notice May Require to Do

195. The Authority or an authorized officer may by notice require the owner of premises to suspend immediately the operation of a relevant plant or activity until the Authority or the authorized officer is satisfied that sufficient measures have been taken to prevent the release of asbestos, if: (a) the premises or activity releases any visible asbestos-containing material in any form of dust, debris, effluent or contaminated item; or (b) any visible dust, debris, untreated effluent or contaminated item is observed to be originating from a containment in which asbestos abatement work

230. [2001] 2 HKC 318, [2001] HKLRD (Yrbk) 322.
231. *Ibid.*, s. 79(1).

or work involving the use of handling of asbestos-containing material is being carried out; or (c) the premises or activity causes or contributes to a concentration of asbestos of more than 0.01 fibres per millilitre in ambient air at any time as determined by a method approved by the Secretary.[232] A person who fails to comply with any of the requirements of a notice given to him under subsection (1) or (2) commits an offence, punishable by imprisonment and fine.[233]

VII. Protecting Workers from Harmful Exposure to Asbestos

196. The Factories and Industrial Undertakings (Asbestos) Regulation (Cap 59 sub leg AD) which applies to all industrial undertakings in which any work with asbestos is carried out (*see* section 3), provides for the protection of workers in factories and industrial undertakings from harmful exposure to asbestos.

A. *Risk Assessment*

197. A proprietor must, before carrying out any work which exposes or is liable to expose any workman to asbestos, ensure that an adequate assessment of exposure or the likely exposure has been made by a person who by reason of his training and experience is competent to make that assessment. The assessment must identify the type of asbestos to which any workman is or is liable to be exposed; or assume that the asbestos involved is not chrysotile alone; determine the nature and degree of exposure or the likely exposure; and set out the steps that may be taken to prevent the exposure or to reduce it to the lowest level reasonably practicable. A proprietor must ensure that a further such assessment is made when there is reason to suspect that the existing assessment is no longer valid; or there is a significant change in the work to which the existing assessment relates.[234]

1. Measures to Reduce Exposure to Asbestos

198. A proprietor must prevent the exposure of any workman to asbestos; or where it is not reasonably practicable to prevent exposure, reduce the exposure of any workman to asbestos to the lowest level reasonably practicable by measures other than the use of respiratory protective equipment. A proprietor must in all circumstances provide every workman who is or is liable to be exposed to asbestos with approved respiratory protective equipment that is suitable for the circumstances; and ensure the full and proper use by each workman of the respiratory protective equipment. A proprietor must take such measures as may be necessary to prevent or, where this is not reasonably practicable, reduce to the lowest level reasonably practicable, the spread of the asbestos from any place where work with

232. *Ibid.*, s. 79(2).
233. *Ibid.*, s. 79(7).
234. The Factories and Industrial Undertakings (Asbestos) Regulation (Cap 59 sub leg AD), s. 5.

asbestos is carried out, including providing in cases where there is risk of spread of asbestos dust in the use of changing and washing facilities, separate facilities for washing and changing of personal protective clothing, of personal clothing and of respiratory protective equipment.[235]

2. Duty to Keep the Work Place Clean

199. A proprietor who carries out work with asbestos must ensure that the premises or those parts of the premises where the work is carried out and the plant used in connection with the work are kept in a clean state and as far as possible free from asbestos and, in particular, where work with asbestos has been completed the premises or those parts of the premises and the plant used in connection with the work are thoroughly cleaned. A proprietor must provide adequate and suitable protective clothing for use by any workman who is exposed to asbestos unless no asbestos is liable to be deposited on the body or personal clothing of the workman. A proprietor who provides any such control measure, personal protective equipment or other thing or facility must ensure so far as is reasonably practicable that it is properly used or applied, as the case may be; and ensure that it is maintained in an efficient state, in efficient working order and in good repair.[236]

3. Duty to Provide Protective Equipment

200. A proprietor must designate any area where work with asbestos is being carried out as a protective equipment zone.[237] In respect of the protective equipment zone, a proprietor must ensure that the area is clearly demarcated and identified by notices indicating that it is a protective equipment zone, that entry into it is limited to persons authorized by the proprietor and that any person who enters the area must wear suitable approved respiratory protective equipment and suitable protective clothing; provide suitable approved respiratory protective equipment and suitable protective clothing for the use of every workman in the protective equipment zone; and ensure that no person enters or remains in a protective equipment zone unless he is wearing suitable approved respiratory protective equipment and suitable protective clothing.[238]

4. Duty to Take Preventive Measures

201. A proprietor must ensure that the exposure of any workman in an industrial undertaking to asbestos in the air is monitored by means of an approved method

235. *Ibid.*, ss 7 and 8.
236. *Ibid.*, ss 9, 10 and 11.
237. *Ibid.*, s. 12(1).
238. *Ibid.*, s. 12(1).

where such monitoring is appropriate for the protection of the health of the workman and whenever there is a substantial change in the working conditions rendering the findings of the previous air monitoring no longer valid.[239] A proprietor must give every workman who is or is liable to be exposed to asbestos adequate information about risks of asbestos and the precautions that should be observed; ensure that every workman who works with asbestos is trained and instructed in safety precautions for working with asbestos; and the purpose, proper use and limitations of any control measure, personal protective equipment or other things or facility provided in pursuance of this Regulation.[240] A proprietor must take all reasonable steps to ensure that no workman eats, drinks or smokes in an area where work with asbestos is being carried out.[241]

5. Duty to Provide Medical Surveillance

202. A proprietor must not employ any person in working with asbestos unless that person has within the four months immediately preceding the commencement of such employment undergone a radiographic examination of his chest and is certified by a registered medical practitioner to be fit to do such work. A proprietor shall ensure that at intervals of not more than twelve months, every person employed in working with asbestos undergoes a radiographic examination of his chest; and is certified by a registered medical practitioner to be fit to continue to do such work.[242]

6. Prohibition Against Certain Uses of Asbestos

203. No proprietor may undertake asbestos spraying; use asbestos insulation for the purpose of thermal, acoustic or other insulations (including fire protection); and use amphibole asbestos in any process, except that process for the removal and disposal of such kind of asbestos which was in use before coming into effect of this Regulation are exempted.[243]

B. Enforcement of Proprietor's Duties

204. The duties of a proprietor are enforced through criminal sanctions, failure by a proprietor to comply with the above statutory requirement being a punishable offence.[244] Likewise, the regulations impose a duty on the workmen to cooperate in

239. *Ibid.*, s. 15.
240. *Ibid.*, s. 16.
241. *Ibid.*, s. 13.
242. *Ibid.*, s. 17(1) and (2).
243. *Ibid.*, ss 21A, 21B and 21C.
244. *Ibid.*, s. 23.

the implementation of the safeguards against and protection from exposure to asbestos.[245] Section 24 provides that any workman who fails to comply with section 10(4) or 22(1) commits an offence. Section 22(1) provides that any workman in an industrial undertaking where work with asbestos is carried out must: (a) observe the safety precautions and the procedures set by the proprietor in respect of the asbestos work which have been made known to him in the industrial undertaking; (b) make full and proper use of any control measure, personal protective equipment or other things or facility provided in pursuance of this Regulation which have been made known to him in the industrial undertaking; and (c) report forthwith to the proprietor any fault or defect in any such control measure, personal protective equipment or other thing or facility as provided in pursuance of this Regulation. Section 10(4) provides that where, as a result of failure or improper use of the protective clothing, asbestos is deposited on the personal clothing of a workman, such clothing must forthwith be handed over by the workman to the proprietor for safe disposal.

§11. Marine Pollution

205. Three Ordinances contain provision relating to control of marine air pollution: Shipping and Port Control Ordinance (Cap 313) Merchant Shipping (Local Vessels) Ordinance (Cap 548) and Merchant Shipping (Prevention of Air Pollution) Ordinance (Cap 413)

I. Shipping and Port Control Ordinance

206. Section 51(1) of Shipping and Port Control Ordinance (Cap 313) provides that no vessel in the waters of Hong Kong shall emit smoke in such quantity as to be a nuisance, except in circumstances affecting the safety of life or of the vessel. The owner and master of the vessel may be prosecuted for such prohibited smoke emissions. The Ordinance provides that the Chief Executive in Council may make regulations for all or any of the following purposes: (a) specifying periods during which emission of smoke from vessels may be permitted in any class of case and subject to limitations; (b) the adoption of precautions against the emission of smoke from vessels; and generally for effectively controlling the emission of smoke from vessels (section 51(1)). No regulations have been made for this purpose.

II. Merchant Shipping (Local Vessels) Ordinance

207. Section 51 of Merchant Shipping (Local Vessels) Ordinance (Cap 548) provides that no local vessel in the waters of Hong Kong shall emit smoke in such quantity as to be a nuisance except in circumstances affecting the safety of life or of

245. *Ibid.*, Part VI 'Duties of Workmen and Other Persons'.

the vessel. Contravention of this provision is a punishable offence for which the owner of the vessel, his agent and the coxswain of the vessel may be prosecuted.

III. Merchant Shipping (Prevention of Air Pollution) Regulation

208. Merchant Shipping (Prevention of Air Pollution) Regulation (sub leg M) made under the Merchant Shipping Ordinance also contains some comprehensive provisions. Section 25 provides that a specified ship is not to be engaged in deliberate emissions of ozone-depleting substances. Section 26 provides that new installations on a specified ship must not contain ozone-depleting substances. Sections 27 and 33 deal with controlling the emission of nitrogen oxide from diesel engines and for the control of fuel oil quality.

§12. Implementation of the Air Pollution Control Regime

209. The regulatory framework for air pollution control relies on the setting up of standards, licensing and compliance notices known as abatement notices. Failure to comply with such standards and requirements is a criminal offence. In order to strike the right balance between public interest in protecting the environment and the primacy of individual rights, the Ordinance provides a system of appeals against unfavourable decisions, compensation for financial loss, and defences when a person is prosecuted for a criminal offence.

I. Enforcement

210. Part V of the Air Pollution Control Ordinance deals with enforcement. In order to ensure that compliance with the air pollution control regime, the Air Pollution Control Ordinance grants extensive powers to the relevant authority, the Director of Environmental Protection, such as those relating to entry and inspection, and modification of chimneys and plants. The Authority may, by notice in writing to any person, require him to furnish any information that the Authority may reasonably require for the purpose of exercising and performing his functions, duties and powers. Failure to comply with such a request, or the supply of incorrect information, is a punishable offence. The person who is required to furnish such information may appeal to the Appeal Board against such requirement.

A. Power to Gather Information

211. The Air Pollution Control Ordinance provides that the Authority may, by notice in writing to any person, require him to furnish to the Authority, within such time and in such form as is specified in the notice, any information specified in the notice which the Authority may reasonably require for the purpose of exercising and performing his functions, duties and powers under the Ordinance. A person, who fails without reasonable excuse to comply with any of the requirements of such a notice or in compliance or purported compliance with such a notice, makes any statement which he knows to be incorrect in a material respect or recklessly makes any statement which is incorrect in a material respect or knowingly omits any material particular, commits a punishable offence.[246]

B. Powers of Entry and Inspection

212. Powers of entry and inspection that the Authority or any authorized officer may exercise are set out in section 28: For the purpose of: (a) determining the position of any apparatus or device or sampling point to be used for the measurement of any air pollutant emitted from any polluting process or passing through any chimney; (b) determining the composition, concentration, quantity, quality or density of any air pollutant emitted from any polluting process or passing through any chimney; (c) determining the composition of any fuel, or other materials, or viscosity of any liquid fuel used in any polluting process; (d) observing and recording any process or procedure used in or in connection with the operation of any polluting process, or, the conduct of any specified process; (e) ascertaining the source of any air pollutant; (f) ascertaining whether there is or has been on or in connection with any premises, ship or motor vehicle any contravention of any of the requirements of this Ordinance; or (g) establishing any other matter in connection with paragraphs (a) to (f), the Authority or an authorized officer may exercise a variety of powers including the power to inspect any polluting process; inspect any motor vehicle; inspect any premises, place or facility in which fuel is stored, supplied, distributed, sold or offered for sale. They may make such examination and enquiry as may be necessary to ascertain whether the requirements of the Ordinance are complied with, and seize, remove and detain anything which may appear to be evidence of an offence against the Ordinance.

C. Failure to Assist in the Exercise of Entry and Inspection Powers

213. Section 29 makes it an offence to fail to assist an officer acting under section 28 or hindering an officer acting under section 28. Any person, who: (a) wilfully resists, obstructs or delays any officer; (b) fails without reasonable excuse to comply with any requirement duly made by an officer; (c) in compliance or purported compliance with any such requirement produces any drawing, record or document which he knows to be incorrect or inaccurate in a material respect or does not believe to be correct or accurate; or (d) wilfully or recklessly gives information which is incorrect in a material respect or withholds information as to any of the matters in respect of which information is required to be given, commits a punishable offence.

246. Air Pollution Control Ordinance, s. 27.

D. Power to Require Remedial Work to Be Carried Out

214. Where it appears to the Authority that a chimney, relevant plant or other machinery or equipment may evolve any air pollutant by reason of: (a) unsuitable design, defective construction or lack of maintenance; (b) excessive wear and tear; (c) the use of unsuitable fuel or other material; or (d) improper operation, the Authority may serve a notice on the owner of the premises in which the chimney, relevant plant or other machinery or equipment is found. Such a notice may require him, giving his reasonable time: (i) to modify, replace, clean or repair the chimney, relevant plant or other machinery or equipment specified in the notice or to take any other steps specified in the notice; (ii) to instal control equipment or a control system or additional control equipment or an additional control system specified in the notice;(iii) to operate the chimney, relevant plant or other machinery or equipment in the manner specified in the notice; (iv) not to use or permit the use the fuel, or other material, or mixture of fuels, or other materials specified in the notice. Such notice must give the owner of the premises 'a reasonable time specified in the notice' to comply with the notice. In a prosecution against the owner of premises for failure to comply with such notice, the prosecution must prove to the satisfaction of the court that the time allowed for compliance was reasonable. If the time permitted for compliance appears to be inadequate, the Authority has no power to extend such period. The notice is invalid for failure to grant a reasonable time for compliance. In *R v Boon Wai*,[247] the notice required the appellant company to replace its oil-fired ovens with gas-fired ovens, within 60 days, which was found to be inadequate. The Director informally agreed to grant an extension for compliance. It was held that the Director had no authority to grant an extension and therefore the notice was invalid. 'Any owner who fails, without reasonable excuse, to comply with any of the requirements of a notice duly served upon him commits an offence and is liable to a fine of $100,000 on conviction for a first offence and $200,000 and imprisonment for 6 months for a second or subsequent offence and in addition, if the offence is a continuing offence, to a fine of $20,000 for each day during which it is proved to the satisfaction of the court that the offence has continued.'[248]

E. Offences

215. The Air Pollution Control Ordinance creates several offences such as for causing emissions, import or sale of prohibited materials, failure to comply with an abatement notice, contravention of a licence, or failure to comply with a reasonable request made by the Authority or an authorized officer. The offences under the Ordinance are punishable, depending on the degree of seriousness of the offence, by fine, and in some instances by fine and imprisonment.

247. [1995] 1 HKC 483.
248. *Ibid.*, s. 30.

216. Some offences created by the Ordinance observe the rule of the common law that no offence is committed without *mens rea* or a guilty mind. There are other offences where no mental element is specified. They create absolute offences or, where a statutory or common law defence is available, strict liability offences.

1. Fault-Based Offences

217. Some offences require a specified *mens rea*. For instance, section 19(3) provides that:

> Any owner who in any notice under subsection (1) makes any statement or gives any particular or information which he knows to be incorrect in a material respect or who recklessly makes any statement or gives any particular or information which is incorrect in a material respect or knowingly omits any material particular therefrom commits an offence and is liable to a fine of \$50000.[249]

2. Absolute Liability Offences

218. Many offences created by the Air Pollution Control Ordinance make no explicit reference to the need to prove any mental element, and do not provide any statutory defences. These are presumably offences of absolute liability. For instance, section 10(7) provides that 'a person who fails to comply with an air pollution abatement notice given to him under subsection (1) commits an offence' without any reference to a mental element or any statutory defences. This section appears to create an absolute offence. The following offences too appear to belong to that category: failure to take best practicable means to prevent noxious or offensive emissions from premises used for a specified process (section 12(1)); using premises for a specified process without a licence (section 13(2)); failure to provide requisite information regarding an existing specified process (section 19(2)); contravention of a licence (section 30(A)).

3. Strict Liability Offences

219. Some provisions of the Ordinance create an offence without reference to any mental element but go on to provide statutory defences. These offences may be

249. For similar offences, where both the requisite *actus reus* and *mens rea* are specified, *see* s. 21(3) 'Any owner who, without reasonable excuse, fails to [apply for a licence to carry out a specified process where the exemption has come to an end]'; s. 27(2) 'any person who fails without reasonable excuse to comply with any of the requirements of a notice duly served on [to provide information]'; s. 29(a) 'Any person who wilfully resists, obstructs or delays any officer in the exercise of any power [of entry and inspection] under section 28'; s. 30(2) 'Any owner who fails, without reasonable excuse, to comply with any of the requirements of a notice [for modification of a chimney or other relevant plant].'

regarded as strict liability offences. For instance, section 77 provides that a person who implements or causes the implementation of an asbestos management plan or asbestos abatement plan contrary to section 74 commits an offence. Section 78 provides that a person does not commit an offence under section 77 if he adduces evidence that shows: (a) he carried out the work, or caused or permitted the work to be carried out, in an emergency situation that did not permit him to comply with that section without risk to human life or serious disruption to a public service; or (b) he did not know and could not have reasonably known of the presence of asbestos or asbestos-containing material at the time when he carried out the work, or caused or permitted the work to be carried.

220. While offences under the Ordinance relating to the emission of an air pollutant may have been defined without reference to any mental element, section 48 provides certain defences:

> It shall be a defence to prove the contravention complained of was (a) solely due to the lighting up of a relevant plant which was cold and that the best practicable means had been taken to prevent or minimise the emission of the air pollutant; or (b) solely due to some failure of a chimney or relevant plant or of an apparatus used in connection with a chimney or relevant plant and that the failure could not have reasonably been foreseen, or if foreseen, could not reasonably have been provided against; (ii) the contravention could not reasonably have been prevented by action taken after the failure occurred; and (iii) as soon as was reasonably practicable after the occurrence of the failure the Authority was informed thereof in writing.

221. Section 41 is an example of a situation where an offence is created without an accompanying mental element but provides exceptions to liability in specified circumstances. Section 41(1) provides that:

> A person commits an offence who, except in the circumstances provided for in subsection (2), discloses or gives to another person any information or document concerning a trade, business or manufactory secret which has come to his knowledge or into his possession in the course of the exercise or performance of his powers, functions or duties under this Ordinance.

Subsection (2) provides the exceptions as follows:

> A person does not commit an offence under subsection (1) if he discloses or gives any information or document to another person (a) for the purpose of the exercise or performance of his functions, duties or powers under this Ordinance or proceedings connected therewith; (b) pursuant to an order of a court under subsection (3); (c) with the consent in writing of all such persons as appear to him, after reasonable inquiry, to be interested in the confidentiality of the information or document.

4. Corporate Liability

222. Where a person convicted of an offence under the Ordinance is a body corporate and it is proved that the offence was committed with the consent or connivance of, or was attributable to any neglect or omission on the part of, a director, manager, secretary or other person concerned in the management of the body corporate, the director, manager, secretary or other person also commits the offence. Where a person convicted of an offence under the Ordinance is a partner in a partnership and it is proved that the offence was committed with the consent or connivance of, or was attributable to any neglect or omission on the part of, any other partner or any person concerned in the management of the partnership, the partner or the person concerned in the management also commits the offence.[250]

5. Institution of Prosecutions

223. A Prosecution may be brought only within the time limits. A prosecution may be brought in respect of an offence under the Ordinance within six months from the time when the commission of the offence first came to the knowledge of the Authority or an authorized officer or one year from the time of the commission of the offence, whichever is the earlier.[251] Prosecutions for offences against the Ordinance may be brought in the name of the Authority, and may be commenced and conducted by any public officer appointed under section 13 of the Magistrates Ordinance. This is subject to the powers of the Secretary for Justice in relation to the prosecution of offences.[252]

6. Appeals Against Adverse Decisions

224. In order to balance the powers of the administration with the rights of individuals, the Ordinance provides a system of appeals. A right of appeal is available in the following circumstances: A person may appeal to the Appeal Board if he is aggrieved by a decision, requirement or specification of a public officer requiring the abatement of air pollution; refusing to grant a licence; fixing terms and conditions of licence; refusing to renew a licence; imposing new or amended terms or conditions for continuance of a licence; cancelling a licence; revoking, amending or adding to a notice or substituting a new notice; refusing to vary a licence; fixing terms and conditions for variation of a licence; refusing to transfer a licence; fixing terms and conditions on transfer of a licence; cancelling an exemption; amending or adding to a notice or substituting a new notice; amending or adding to a notice or substituting a new notice; refusing to vary or cancel terms or conditions subject to which an exemption may continue in force; refusing to increase a quantity of allocated allowances upon occurrence of a special event or failure to acquire emission

250. Air Pollution Control Ordinance, s. 47A.
251. *Ibid.*, s. 46(1).
252. *Ibid.*, s. 47(1).

credits; refusing to grant an approval for the purposes of section 26M(2); imposing terms and conditions upon granting an approval for the purposes of section 26M(2); requiring information to be furnished; requiring the modification, replacing, cleaning or repair of or other steps to be taken relating to, a chimney, relevant plant or other machinery or equipment; requiring the installation of control equipment or systems; requiring the operation of a chimney, relevant plant or other machinery or equipment in a specified manner; prohibiting the use of specified fuels or other materials; refusing to withhold information from public notification or other public access; refusal to enter or deferral of entry of an applicant's name in the relevant register; ordering the suspension or removal of registered asbestos persons from the relevant register; requiring the owner to comply with conditions set by the Authority in an asbestos management plan or an asbestos abatement plan; requiring the owner to comply with requirements set by the Authority in an asbestos abatement notice.[253]

225. An appeal may be entertained by the Board only if (a) a decision, requirement or specification is not justified; or has some material error in content or material defect in administrative procedure; (b) the opinion of the Authority or an authorized officer that air pollution which is caused or contributed to by an emission is unreasonable; (c) the opinion of the Authority or the authorized officer that the air pollution is prejudicial to health is unreasonable; or (d) a disciplinary order or order for costs against a registered asbestos consultant, supervisor, contractor or laboratory is unjustifiable.[254]

226. An Appeal Board may receive evidence on oath; admit or take into account any statement, document, information or matter whether or not it would be admissible as evidence in a court of law; and by notice in writing summon any person to appear before it to produce any document or to give evidence that may reasonably be required.[255] On any appeal, an Appeal Board may confirm, reverse or vary the decision, requirement or specification appealed from.[256] The Appeal Board's decision is final and there is no further administrative review or appeal. A decision of the Appeal Board may be questioned in a court of law by way of judicial review.[257]

7. Protecting the Ozone Layer

227. Being a signatory to 1985 Vienna Convention for the Protection of the Ozone Layer and the 1987 Montreal Protocol on Substances that Deplete the Ozone

253. *Ibid.*, s. 31(1).
254. *Ibid.*, s. 31(5).
255. *Ibid.*, s. 33(5).
256. *Ibid.*, s. 33(2).
257. Administrative decisions are amenable to judicial review. *See*, for instance, *Teng Fuk Co Ltd v Air Pollution Control Appeal Board* [2001] 3 HKLRD 304. *Asia Dyeing Co Ltd v Air Pollution Control Authority* [1989] HKEC 822, affirmed by the Court of Appeal: *Asia Dyeing Co Ltd v Air Pollution Control Authority* [1990] 1 HKLR 263 (CA), concerned a decision of the Air Pollution Control Authority to issue an air pollution abatement notice.

Layer, Hong Kong enacted the Ozone Layer Protection Ordinance (Cap 403) in pursuance of its international obligation under these agreements.

II. Legislative Framework

228. The purpose of the Ordinance is to prohibit the manufacture of, and to control the importation and exportation of, and to conserve the resources of, substances that deplete the ozone layer and of products containing or made with those substances; and to provide for related matters.[258] The Secretary for the Environment has the power to make regulations, after consultation with the Advisory Council on the Environment, to give effect to the provisions of the Ozone Layer Protection Ordinance.[259] Regulations may make it an offence to contravene any regulation.[260] The following regulations have been made:

(1) the Ozone Layer Protection (Fees) Regulations (sub leg A) which sets out prescribed fees for the purpose of registration or licensing;
(2) the Ozone Layer Protection (Controlled Refrigerants) Regulation (sub leg B) which prohibits the releasing or recycling of controlled refrigerants;
(3) the Ozone Layer Protection (Products Containing Scheduled Substances) (Import Banning) Regulation (sub leg C), which makes it an offence to import a controlled product, such as air conditioners, refrigerators and aerosol products, that contain any scheduled substance; and
(4) the Ozone Layer Protection (fees) Regulation (sub leg A).

A. *Offences under the Ordinance and Its Regulations*

1. Manufacture of Scheduled Substances

229. A person who manufactures a scheduled substance[261] commits an offence. This prohibition does not apply where the scheduled substance is manufactured solely for the purpose of research or academic instruction and the person manufactures no more than 1 kg of the substance in any twelve-month period.[262]

258. The Ozone Layer Protection Ordinance (Cap 403), Long Title.
259. *Ibid.*, s. 16(1).
260. *Ibid.*, s. 16(2).
261. A 'scheduled substance' means a substance listed in the Schedule, whether existing alone or in a mixture: s. 2. They include, for instance, Chlorofluorocarbons (CFCs), Halons, other fully halogenated Chlorofluorocarbons, Methyl Chloroform, Methyl Bromide.
262. The Ozone Layer Protection Ordinance, s. 3.

2. Importing or Exporting Scheduled Substances

230. A person who imports or exports a scheduled substance without a licence commits an offence.[263] This prohibition does not apply in relation to a scheduled substance that is air transhipment cargo. However, if at any time between its being brought into and taken out of Hong Kong such scheduled substance is removed from the cargo transhipment area of Hong Kong International Airport, the scheduled substance is deemed to be imported at the time of such removal and the person who brought the scheduled substance, or caused it to be brought, into Hong Kong as air transhipment cargo is deemed to be the person who imports the scheduled substance at the time of its removal.[264]

231. Where it is necessary for the prosecution to prove that, at any time between its being brought into and taken out of Hong Kong, the scheduled substance was removed from the cargo transhipment area of Hong Kong International Airport, it is a defence for the person to show that he took all reasonable steps and exercised reasonable diligence to avoid such removal occurring or that he reasonably believed that such removal had not occurred, as the case may be.[265]

3. Improper Handling of Controlled Refrigerants

232. The Ozone Layer Protection (Controlled Refrigerants) Regulation (sub leg B) prohibits the use of controlled refrigerants in refrigeration or motor vehicle air conditioner equipment. It is a punishable offence for a person to allows or cause any controlled refrigerant[266] used or intended for use in refrigeration equipment or motor vehicle air conditioner to escape into the atmosphere. It is a defence to prove that:

(a) the escape occurred in the course of transferring the controlled refrigerant to a container designed for the purpose of storing refrigerants; or recycling the controlled refrigerant; or transferring the controlled refrigerant into refrigeration equipment or into a motor vehicle air conditioner; or disposing of the controlled refrigerant by a method approved by the Director; and that he took all reasonable precautions and exercised all due diligence to prevent the escape to occur;

263. *Ibid.*, s. 4. For the purpose of this section and s. 6, a 'scheduled substance' does not include a substance listed in the Schedule that is: (i) in a manufactured product (other than one used solely for the transportation or storage of the substance) and the substance is used in the operation of the product or the mere dispensing of the contents of the product constitutes the intended use of the substance; or (ii) part of a manufactured product solely because the substance was used in the process of manufacturing the product.

264. *Ibid.*, s. 4A(1).

265. *Ibid.*, s. 4A(3).

266. A controlled refrigerant means a scheduled substance which the Director has by notice in the Gazette, declared to be a controlled refrigerant: Cap 403 sub leg B, s. 2.

(b) the escape occurred by reason of an accident or other cause beyond his control and that he took all reasonable precautions and exercised all due diligence to prevent the escape to occur; or

(c) it was necessary to allow the escape to occur by reason of an emergency and in order to prevent danger to the health or safety of any person.[267]

233. It is a punishable offence for any person to recover, recycle or otherwise treat or cause or allow to be recovered, recycled or otherwise treated a controlled refrigerant unless the refrigerant recycling equipment is approved by the Director and is used in accordance with the manufacturer's instructions and in a manner specified by the Director.[268]

4. Importing Controlled Products

234. Ozone Layer Protection (Products Containing Scheduled Substances) (Import Banning) Regulation (sub leg C) is designed to control the importation of certain products containing certain scheduled substances. It is a punishable offence to import a controlled product[269] from any country or place, whether or not the country or place is bound by the terms of the 1987 Montreal Protocol on Substances that Deplete the Ozone Layer.[270]

B. Licensing Import or Export of Scheduled Substances

235. As noted above, it is an offence to import or export scheduled substances without a licence. In this regard, the Ordinance provides for registration of importers and exporters and for licensing them. Registration is given for a limited or unlimited period. A registered person who wishes to export or import a consignment of scheduled substances must obtain a licence for such specified consignment.

C. Registration of Importers and Exporter of Scheduled Substances

236. The Director of Environmental Protection is the Authority to grant registration. There are two types of persons who may apply for registration: (i) A person, who the Director is satisfied, was before the commencement of the Ozone Layer

267. Cap 403 sub leg B, s. 5.
268. *Ibid.*, s. 6.
269. 'Controlled product' means any air conditioner or heat pump designed to cool a motor vehicle, any refrigeration equipment or air conditioning or heat pump equipment, an aerosol product, an insulation panel, insulation board or insulation pipe cover, or a prepolymer which contains a scheduled substance: Cap 403 sub leg C, s. 2.
270. Cap 403 sub leg C, s. 3.

Protraction Ordinance on 1 July 1989 an importer or exporter of scheduled substances; (ii) A person who bona fide intends to import or export scheduled substances if granted a licence.[271]

1. Conditions of Registration

237. It is a condition of continued registration that the registrant bona fide intends to import or export scheduled substances if granted a licence.[272] Apart from this mandatory condition, the Director may, at the time of registration or at any time after giving written notice to a registrant, impose conditions of registration that are reasonably related to Hong Kong's international obligations under the 1985 Vienna Convention for the Protection of the Ozone Layer and the 1987 Montreal Protocol on Substances that Deplete the Ozone Layer.[273] Such conditions may be stricter than required under such international obligations.[274]

2. Grant or Refusal of Registration

238. The Director, if he has agreed to register a person, must issue a certificate of registration to a person who is registered in which he must set out the conditions of registration.[275] A registered person who contravenes a condition of registration commits an offence.[276] Where the Director specifies an expiry date in a certificate of registration, the registration ceases to have effect after that date.[277] If the Director refuses to register an applicant, the Director shall serve on the applicant, by personal service or by post, a notice stating the reasons for his refusal.[278]

3. Cancelling a Registration

239. The Director may at any time cancel a registration where he considers that a condition of the registration has been contravened or that the registration was issued as a result of an error or an unlawful act of the applicant or a false representation of a fact made by him.[279] The Ozone Layer Protection Ordinance envisages that the applicant will be given an opportunity to be heard before cancellation of a registration. Where notice of cancellation has been served without giving the registrant an opportunity to be heard before his registration is cancelled, he may

271. Ozone Layer Protection Ordinance, s. 5(1).
272. *Ibid.*, 35(2).
273. *Ibid.*, s. 5(3) read with s. 6(4)(a).
274. *Ibid.*, s. 5(3) read with s. 6(4).
275. *Ibid.*, s. 5(5).
276. *Ibid.*, s. 5(8).
277. *Ibid.*, s. 35(6).
278. *Ibid.*, s. 5(7).
279. *Ibid.*, s. 7(1).

apply to the Director to review his decision and the Director may, after hearing the applicant, reinstate the registration, subject to any conditions he may impose.[280]

4. Right of Appeal

240. A person aggrieved by a decision of the Director in relation to registration may apply to the Administrative Appeals Board.[281] The Director shall take such action as is necessary to give effect to the Administrative Appeals Board's decision.[282]

D. Licence to Import or Export a Specific Consignment of Scheduled Substances

241. A registered person may, while his registration is in operation, apply for a licence to import or export a specified consignment of scheduled substances.[283] Licences are issued in the exercise of the Director's discretion and the fact that a person is a registered person does not mean that he would be entitled to a licence.[284] The Director may issue a licence in respect of a specified consignment of a scheduled substance, which may be: (i) an import licence, i.e., a licence to import the scheduled substance; (ii) an export licence, i.e., a licence to export the scheduled substance; or (iii) an import and export licence, i.e., a licence to import and export the scheduled substance.[285]

1. Imposition of Conditions on a Licence

242. A licence may be subject to any conditions that the Director may impose.[286] In imposing conditions, the Director must take into account the need to give effect to Hong Kong's international obligations under the relevant conventions and protocols. He may in his discretion impose conditions which are harsher than those required by Hong Kong's such international obligations.[287] The Director has the power to vary the conditions of a licence, at the request of the licensee.[288]

280. *Ibid.*, s. 7(4).
281. *Ibid.*, s. 8(1). *See* Administrative Appeals Board Ordinance (Cap 442).
282. *Ibid.*, s. 8(2).
283. *Ibid.*, s. 6(1).
284. *Ibid.*, s. 5(4).
285. *Ibid.*, s. 6(1).
286. *Ibid.*, s. 6(1).
287. *Ibid.*, s. 6(4).
288. *Ibid.*, s. 6(2).

2. Cancelling a Licence

243. The Director may at any time cancel a licence where he considers that a condition of the licence has been contravened or that the licence was issued as a result of an error or an unlawful act of the applicant or a false representation of a fact made by him.[289] The Ozone Layer Protection Ordinance envisages that the applicant will be given an opportunity to be heard before refusal to vary a licence or cancellation of a licence. Where a notice of cancellation has been served without giving the applicant an opportunity to be heard before his licence is cancelled, he may apply to the Director to review his decision and the Director may, after hearing the applicant, reinstate the licence, subject to any conditions he may impose.[290] A licence holder aggrieved by a licensing decision of the Director may appeal to the Administrative Appeal Board.[291] The Director shall take such action as is necessary to give effect to the Administrative Appeals Board's decision.[292]

E. Enforcement

244. The Director of Environmental Protection has power to enforce the Ordinance and for that purpose may appoint authorized officers to assist him.[293]

1. Special Powers of Authorized Officers

245. The following are the special powers of entry, search and seizure that are conferred on authorized officers: (i) An authorized officer may enter and search any place or premises (other than domestic premises) if he reasonably suspects that there is in or on that place or premises anything in respect of which an offence has been committed under the Ordinance or which is, or contains, evidence of the commission of such offence; (ii) An authorized officer may seize anything, other than an aircraft, vessel or vehicle in respect of which he reasonably suspects that an offence has been committed under the Ordinance; or which he reasonably suspects to be, or to contain, evidence of the commission of such an offence; (iii) An authorized officer may enter and search any premises (other than domestic premises) or place connected with the manufacture, processing, production, storage, distribution or sale of anything in respect of which a licence has been issued under the Ordinance.[294]

289. *Ibid.*, s. 7(1).
290. *Ibid.*, s. 37(4).
291. *Ibid.*, s. 8(1).
292. *Ibid.*, s. 8(2).
293. *Ibid.*, s. 9.
294. *Ibid.*, s. 11.

2. General Powers of Authorized Officers

246. In addition to the above special powers, authorized officers have many general powers. They include:

- The power to enter at any reasonable time and search: (a) any premises (other than domestic premises) occupied by a registrant or a licensee; (b) any premises (other than domestic premises) in which there is a machine or machinery designed to cool or freeze anything or to function as a heat pump; (c) any premises (other than domestic premises) occupied by a person who carries on the business of, or any business that includes servicing, repairing or decommissioning air conditioners or heat pumps; or (d) any premises (other than domestic premises) occupied by a person who carries on the business of, or any business that includes the recovery or recycling of scheduled substances.
- Power to inspect licences or registrations, documents which may relate to the commission of an offence.
- To examine anything that may be necessary to determine compliance with a registration or a licence.
- Take samples, inspect premises operations or measurements.[295]

3. Obstructing Authorized Officers

247. A person who: (a) wilfully resists, obstructs or delays any authorized officer in the exercise of his powers; (b) fails without reasonable excuse to comply with any requirement made by an authorized officer; (c) in compliance or purported compliance with any such requirement produces a record or document which is incorrect or inaccurate in a material respect and which he knows to be incorrect or inaccurate or does not believe to be correct or accurate; or (d) wilfully or recklessly gives information which is incorrect or inaccurate in a material respect or withholds information as to any of the matters in respect of which information is required to be given, commits a punishable offence.[296]

4. Immunity of Authorized Officers

248. The Ordinance grants immunity to authorized officers. Section 15A provides that a public officer shall not be personally liable in respect of any act or omission of his if it was done or made by him in the honest belief that it was required or authorized in the exercise of any function, duty or power of his under the Ozone Layer Protection Ordinance. It also provides that the protection conferred on public officers does not in any way affect any liability of the government in tort for an act or omission of such officers.

295. *Ibid.*, s. 10.
296. *Ibid.*, s. 13.

F. Prosecutions and the Role of the Judiciary

249. Prosecutions under the Ordinance may be brought in the name of the Director or the Commissioner of Customs and Excise.[297] A complaint or information in respect of an offence under this Ordinance shall be made or laid within six months after the time the matter of the complaint or information first came to the knowledge of the Director, the Commissioner of Customs and Excise or an authorized officer.[298] It has been judicially recognized in *R v Tsui Chit-fan* that it is the duty of the courts to ensure that prosecutions are as effective as permissible and that penalties imposed under the Ozone Layer Protection Ordinance reflect the community's determination to observe its international obligations under the various environmental protection agreements.[299]

250. *R v Tsui Chit-fan* was an appeal against the fines imposed by the magistrate on the appellants who were convicted of offences under the Ozone Layer Protection Ordinance. At the outset, the judge of the High Court before whom the appeal had been listed suggested to the appellants' counsel that in his view the penalties imposed by the magistrate were woefully inadequate, and the appellants withdrew their appeal. The judge increased the fines and gave reasons for his decision.

251. Daffy J said that it was:

> incumbent upon the courts of Hong Kong to ensure that the message of the Ozone Layer Protection Ordinance is clearly and without equivocation brought home to all those who are involved commercially or otherwise with substances which endanger our environment. It was … the deliberate policy of our legislature to enact that the penalty for each offence could be one million dollars and two years' imprisonment. The courts … must ensure that the penalties that they impose adequately reflect the community's determination to protect its own environment, and to observe its international obligations under the various environmental protection agreements, and they must ensure that these penalties are a real deterrent against those whose priorities list profit above our ecological well-being.[300]

252. In relation to the appropriate fines that ought to be imposed on the appellants, Duffy J said:

> It is clearly not appropriate to have regard to the commercial gain which the appellants have derived from this enterprise when assessing the proper level of fines. The seriousness of the offences speaks for itself and is reflected in the maximum penalties available. The level of fines should in my view be governed by the amount of damage that can result from the indiscriminate use of

297. *Ibid.*, s. 15(1).
298. *Ibid.*, s. 15(2).
299. *R v Tsui Chit-fan* [1994] 2 HKCLR 273 at 274.
300. *Ibid.*, at 273.

the offending substances, the amount of the substances involved, the frequency of the breaches of the legislation, the degree of deceit involved, and the number of countries to which these offending goods had been exported. Eventually a body of jurisprudence will be built up to assist sentencing courts when dealing with these offences. For the moment, I simply say that taking the factors I have set out into account, the total fines I would have imposed in the present case would have been at least double the total fines of $703,500 imposed by the learned magistrate. Offences against environmental protection legislation are, in my view, of significantly greater seriousness than offences against ordinances which protect Hong Kong's commercial credibility. The former can cause irreversible damage.[301]

G. *Managing Information*

253. The administration of the air pollution control regulatory system involves receipt and disclosure of information. The Ordinance makes special provision to ensure that the authorities are effective in receiving requisite information, that such information is used only for lawful purposes and that any information so received is treated in confidence.

1. Register of Information

254. Section 39(1) of the Air Pollution Control Ordinance requires the Authority to cause to be kept, in such form as the Secretary may determine, a register containing details of: (a) applications required to be entered any licensing applications made under section 14(3)(a); (b) the particulars and information contained in notices given to the Authority in relation to specified processes pursuant to section 19(1); (c) any exemption from licensing requirements under section 20; (d) all licences and (e) such other matters as may be required by regulations made under section 43 to be recorded in the register. Subsection (2) requires such register to be made available for inspection by the public and to supply a certified copy of any entry in the register to any person upon payment of the prescribed fee.

255. There is provision to limit public access to entries in the register. Section 40(1) provides that any person may apply to the Secretary to withhold from public notification or other public access any information concerning a specified process, whether appearing in a licence or an application therefor or in any notice, return or other document. Section 40(1A) provides that any person may apply to the Secretary to withhold from public notification or other public access under this Ordinance any information relating to the design, construction, modification or adaptation of any motor vehicle, fuel pump, equipment used for the storage of fuel or other similar apparatus or any petrol delivery vehicle, whether appearing in a

301. *Ibid.*, 274–275.

licence or an application or in any notice, return, drawing, record or other document, if the release of that information would otherwise reveal to a competitor of that person vehicle designs, manufacturing techniques or strategy or other details of a confidential nature known only to the applicant, his employees or his professional advisers or consultants. Section 40(1B) provides that any person may apply to the Secretary to withhold from public notification or other public access under this Ordinance any information concerning measures taken to prevent air pollution caused or contributed to by emissions from motor vehicles, whether appearing in a licence or an application or in any notice, return, drawing, record or other document, if the release of that information would otherwise reveal to a competitor of that person vehicle designs, manufacturing techniques or strategy or other details of a confidential nature known only to the applicant, his employees or his professional advisers or consultants.

256. The right to withhold information from the public is not absolute. Section 40(2) provides that any such application to withhold information may be granted by the Secretary to the extent that he is satisfied that public notification or other public access to the information would: (a) be contrary to the applicant's private interest to an unreasonable degree; or (b) be contrary to the public interest. Section 40(3) provides that where an application to withhold information is refused by the Secretary, whether in whole or in part (a) notice of the refusal and of the reasons therefor must be given in writing by the Secretary to the applicant; and that (b) the information shall not be publicly notified or otherwise made accessible to the public until the time for appeal under section 31(2) has expired, or, if notice of appeal is lodged before that time, until determination or withdrawal of the appeal.

2. Confidentiality of Information

257. Section 41 of the Ordinance seeks to protect information that public officers receive by way of creating offences punishable by fine and imprisonment. Subsection (1) provides that a person commits an offence who discloses or gives to another person any information or document concerning a trade, business or manufactory secret which has come to his knowledge or into his possession in the course of the exercise or performance of his powers, functions or duties under this Ordinance. Subsection (2) provides some exceptions to that offence. It provides that a person does not commit an offence under subsection (1) if he discloses or gives any information or document to another person for the purpose of the exercise or performance of his functions, duties or powers under this Ordinance or proceedings connected therewith; or with the consent in writing of all such persons as appear to him, after reasonable enquiry, to be interested in the confidentiality of the information or document. Subsection (3) provides a further exception when it provides that where in any proceedings a court considers that the justice of the case so requires, the court may order the disclosure of any information or the giving of any document referred to in subsection (1).

Chapter 2. Water Pollution Control

§1. Introduction

258. Hong Kong's water pollutants come from human and industrial sources and livestock farms. Hong Kong's water quality has somewhat improved in recent years, but an expected growth in population will put added pressure on water quality. It will be useful to review the role played by the Environmental Protection Department, and the following relies on its publicly available information.[302]

259. The Environmental Protection Department has an extensive and successful programme for cleaning Hong Kong's waters. The number of gazetted beaches meeting the Water Quality Objective for bathing water increased from twenty-six in 1997 to forty-one in 2010. The number of river monitoring stations with bad or very bad water quality has dropped, from 52% in 1988 to less than 15% in recent years.

260. The Environmental Protection Department controls waste water discharges through the Water Pollution Control Ordinance (Cap 358). Operators are required to ensure their discharges meet the standards which are specified in licences allowing them to discharge their waste water into receiving water bodies. It regularly inspects operators, responds to complaints and will prosecute offenders.

261. The Ordinance mandates that all sewage should be discharged into sewers, not storm water drains which are only meant to carry rainwater into the sea. The Environmental Protection Department will extend the public sewer networks in the new territories and new development areas. The department prepares sewerage master plans and the works are carried out by the Drainage Services Department. The plans are revised to take into account a projected population increase of about 2 million by 2016.

262. Hong Kong shares its waters with Guangdong. In 2000, agreement was reached on a fifteen-year plan to clean Deep Bay and to reduce pollution from existing sources and control future pollution. At the end of 2007, Hong Kong and Shenzhen completed a review of the plan and at the same time agreed on a new set of water pollution reduction targets and the next phase of collaboration to improve the Deep Bay water quality. The two sides also undertook a review of the regional water quality control strategy for Mirs Bay in 2008. Necessary additional measures for protecting the Mirs Bay water environment and meeting the sustainable development objectives will be recommended.

263. In addition, the Guangdong Environmental Protection Bureau and the Hong Kong Environmental Protection Department successfully developed an advanced numerical water quality model for the Pearl River Estuary region in 2008. The model is capable of simulating the complicated flow dynamics and water quality

302. *See* http://www.epd.gov.hk/epd/english/environmentinhk/water/water_maincontent.html.

processes in both the river network and the coastal region, and provides a scientific analytical tool for the formulation of regional water quality management and pollution control plans.

§2. Legislative Framework

264. The principal statute relating to water pollution control is the Water Pollution Control Ordinance which was designed to control the pollution of the waters of Hong Kong. Another important statute is the Waste Disposal Ordinance which controls polluting discharges into the waters of Hong Kong. There are two other statutory sources of water pollution control law, namely Dumping at Sea Ordinance (Cap 466), and Merchant Shipping (Prevention and Control of Pollution) Ordinance (Cap 413).

§3. Water Pollution Control Ordinance

265. The Water Pollution Control Ordinance (Cap 358) was enacted to control the pollution of the waters of Hong Kong. It operates in relation to areas which have been designated by the Chief Executive as water control zones, for each of which the Secretary for the Environment has to establish water quality objectives. The Authority has the duty of achieving the relevant water quality objectives, acting under the direction of the Secretary. In order to control and regulate discharges and deposits into water, the Ordinance has set up a licensing system. Unlicensed discharging of polluting matters into water is prohibited under penalty. The Ordinance provides for the restoration of polluted waters by offenders or by the Authority, as the case may be.

266. When the Water Pollution Control Ordinance was enacted in 1981 it was not intended to take immediate effect, the reason being that the regulatory framework of the Ordinance envisaged the establishment of water control zones for which water quality objectives would be set, which would be implemented through a system of licensing and criminal prosecutions for prohibited discharges in water control zones. The coming into effect was delayed until administrative arrangements could be in place for these purposes. The Ordinance also provided amnesty to any discharges that would exist at the time a water control zone came into effect. Subsequently, in 1990, the Ordinance was amended to remove such amnesty from water control zones that might be declared thereafter. Provision was also made requiring any discharges that existed in 1990 to be licensed.

267. The Authority has extensive powers of enforcement to ensure compliance with the provisions of the Ordinance. Such enforcement powers may be exercised by authorized officers on behalf of the Authority. There is a right of appeal to an Appeal Board against certain decisions taken by the Secretary or the Authority. Certain decisions of the Appeal Board are reviewable by the Chief Executive in Council.

268. The provisions in the Ordinances are supplemented by subsidiary legislative provisions which may be made by way of Regulations. Technical Memoranda, which are subsidiary legislation, also supplement the provisions in the Ordinance. There is no provision in the Ordinance for the making of Codes of Practice, but there exist some non-statutory guidance notes and guidelines which facilitate the implementation of the regulatory regime of the Ordinance.

269. The regulatory regime for water pollution control confers important legislative or administrative powers on the Chief Executive, the Chief Secretary for Administration, the Secretary in charge of the environment, the Water Pollution Control Authority and the Appeal Board.

I. Regulations

270. Section 46 of the Ordinance provides for the making of regulations by the Chief Executive. Subsection (1) provides the matters in relation to which regulations may be made, after consultation with the Advisory Council on the Environment. They are:

(a) the control and maintenance of wastewater treatment facilities, including the requirement that only persons registered under the regulations may operate and maintain a wastewater treatment facility;
(b) the form and contents of licensing applications;
(c) the period within which a licensee has to make an application for a renewal of the licence, and the circumstances in which a licence may continue in force pending the determination of any such application;
(d) the particulars to be entered in the register;
(e) the particulars to be contained in a notice of licence applications;
(f) the manner in which objections may be made to an application for a licence;
(g) the manner of determining the amount of compensation payable for cancellation or variation of a licence, the factors to be taken into account or disregarded and the principles to be applied in determining that amount;
(h) the forms to be used and the procedure to be followed for the purpose of appeals under Part VI of the Ordinance;
(i) fees and charges which may be imposed in relation to licensed discharges and on persons making any licensing application;
(j) matters about which information may be obtained under section 35(1);
(k) the manner in which notices required or authorized by the Water Pollution Control Ordinance may be given or sent to the person to whom they are addressed;
(l) the inclusion of a lake, pool or pond or any description of lake, pool or pond within the definition of 'inland waters' in section 2;
(m) prescribing anything (including any fee) which is to be or may be prescribed by regulations;
(n) generally for the better carrying out of the provisions and purposes of the Ordinance.

271. Subsection 2 provides that the Chief Executive may also exercise some administrative powers, by regulation. The purposes for which he may exercise such power, after consultation with the Advisory Council on the Environment, are to:

(a) provide for the construction, maintenance, repair and demolition of sewerage;
(b) require an owner or occupier of property to construct works to convey waste-water from the property to a place for connection to sewerage;
(c) authorize the Authority to: (i) construct the works referred to in paragraph (b) if the owner or occupier fails to do so and to recover the costs from the owner or occupier; and (ii) connect the works to sewerage;
(d) require an owner or occupier of property to maintain the works and connection referred to in paragraphs (b) to (c);
(e) authorize the Authority to maintain the works and connection referred to in paragraphs (b) and (c) if the owner or occupier fails to do so and to recover the costs from the owner or occupier;
(f) require an owner or occupier of property on which a wastewater treatment facility has become redundant as a result of providing a sewerage connection to the property to carry out works to fill in or demolish the wastewater treatment facility and to fill in or demolish redundant drainage facilities;
(g) authorize the Authority to carry out the works referred to in paragraph (f) if the owner or occupier fails to do so and to recover the costs from the owner or occupier;
(h) authorize the Authority to require the owner of a wastewater treatment facility in a water control zone to construct works, effect repairs or modify or carry out operations as he specifies in order to ensure the effective operation of the facility;
(i) authorize the Authority to do the things referred to in paragraph (h) if the owner fails to do so and to recover the costs from the owner;
(j) authorize the Authority, if there is more than one owner of the facility referred to in paragraph (h) and they fail to do the things referred to in that paragraph, to take over the operation of the facility and to recover the costs from the owners;
(k) provide for compensation for damage that may be caused by the Authority during entry onto property or the carrying out or construction of works under this subsection;
(l) provide for appeals to an Appeal Board from decisions of the Authority under regulations made under this subsection; and
(m) apply any or all of the provisions of the Roads (Works, Use and Compensation) Ordinance (Cap 370), with any modifications or additions as are considered necessary or desirable, for any purposes of the Air Pollution Control Ordinance relating directly or indirectly to the carrying out of works or the construction, maintenance, repair and demolition of works.

272. Three regulations have been made under the Ordinance. They are Regulation C 'Water Pollution Control (Appeal Board) Regulations', Regulation D 'Water Pollution Control (General) Regulations', and Regulation AL 'Water Pollution Control (Sewerage) Regulation'. The Appeal Board Regulation provides for the appeals procedure. The General Regulations make supplementary provisions in relation to statutory public notices, procedures in relation to licences, assessment of compensation and other miscellaneous matters. The Sewerage Regulation makes supplementary provisions in relation to construction of sewerage, wastewater treatment facilities, the Authority's power to undertake sewerage works, and compensation payments.

II. Technical Memoranda

273. Technical Memoranda made under the Water Pollution Control Ordinance are subject to Legislative Council Approval.[303] While Technical Memoranda do not have to be approved by an affirmative or positive resolution in the Legislative Council, if the Legislative Council resolves that a Technical Memorandum must be amended, the Secretary must amend it before it can take effect.[304]

274. Only one Technical Memorandum has been published under the Water Pollution Control Ordinance, namely the Technical Memorandum on 'Standards for Effluents Discharged into Drainage and Sewage Systems, Inland and Coastal Waters' (Cap 358 AK). This Technical Memorandum on Effluent Standards is a guide to the Authority under the Ordinance. It sets the limits that make effluents acceptable into foul sewers, storm water drains, inland and coastal waters. The limits control the physical, chemical and microbial quality of effluents. The standards are enforced through licences. The Authority, namely the Director of Environmental Protection, must consult this memorandum when fixing the conditions that he will include in a licence. Unless there is good reason to so, he will not impose conditions that are more stringent than those in the memorandum.

III. Non-statutory Guidance Notes and Guidelines

275. In the absence of any statutory provisions for the making of Codes of Practice, as under the Air Pollution Control Ordinance, the Environmental Protection Department has issued some non-statutory guidance notes and guidelines. Among them are Guidance Notes on Discharges from Village Houses, Guidelines for the Design of Small Sewage Treatment Plants, and Guidelines for Estimating Sewage Flows for Sewage Infrastructure Planning.

303. It is not clear whether Technical Memoranda made under the Water Pollution Control Ordinance are subsidiary legislation, or instruments simply analogous to subsidiary legislation and therefore are subject to Legislative Council Control as if they are subsidiary legislation. Some ordinances specifically provide that Technical Memoranda made under them, while they have to go through Legislative Council scrutiny, are not subsidiary legislation. *See*, for instance, s. 37B(6) of the Air Pollution Control Ordinance, s. 16(12) of the Environment Impact Assessment Ordinance and s. 14(6) of the Dumping at Sea Ordinance.

304. Water Pollution Control Ordinance, s. 21(5).

§4. The Application of the Water Pollution Control Ordinance

I. The Impact of the Ordinance on the Government

276. Water Pollution Control Ordinance, like other environmental statutes, binds the government subject to specified qualifications. In relation to discharges into waters of Hong Kong, its internal waters or into communal sewers and communal drains the Ordinance provides as follows:

- The Ordinance grants some immunity to the government. Sections 8 and 9, which deal with prohibited discharges, do not have effect to permit proceedings to be taken against, or to impose any criminal liability on, the government or on any person who makes any discharge or deposit which he is required to make in the course of carrying out his duties in the service of the government.[305]
- If it appears to the Authority that any discharge or deposit is being, or has been, made in contravention of section 8(1) or (1A) or 9(1) by any person in the course of carrying out his duties in the service of the government, he must, if the contravention is not forthwith terminated to the satisfaction of the Authority, report the matter to the Chief Secretary for Administration.[306]
- On receipt of such a report, the Chief Secretary for Administration must enquire into the circumstances and, if his enquiry shows that a contravention of section 8(1) or (1A) or 9(1) is continuing or likely to recur, he must ensure that the best practicable steps are taken to terminate the contravention or avoid the recurrence.[307]
- No compensation is payable under section 25 in respect of any discharge or deposit made by or on behalf of the Crown.[308]
- No fee or charge prescribed for the purposes of the Water Pollution Control Ordinance is payable by the Crown.[309]

277. In relation to grant of licences for discharges, section 45 provides as follows:

(a) No liability shall rest on the government or upon any public officer by reason of the fact that any licence is granted or continued under the Ordinance for the discharge or deposit of any matter into the waters of Hong Kong or into inland waters or into a communal sewer or communal drain.
(b) A public officer may be held personally liable in respect of any act or omission of his if it was done or made by him in the honest belief that it was required or authorized in the exercise of any power, function or duty of his under the Water Pollution Control Ordinance.

305. *Ibid.*, s. 47(2).
306. *Ibid.*, s. 47(3).
307. *Ibid.*, s. 47(4).
308. *Ibid.*, s. 47(7).
309. *Ibid.*, s. 47(8).

(c) Such protection conferred on public officers in respect of any act or omission does not in any way affect any liability of the government in tort for that act or omission.

II. The Key Personnel

278. The key persons involved in the administration of the Ordinance are the Chief Executive, the Chief Secretary for Administration, the Secretary in charge of the environment, the Water Pollution Control Authority and Appeal Board.

A. *The Chief Executive*

279. The Chief Executive of Hong Kong exercises an important subsidiary legislative power when he makes regulations. He may also exercise some administrative powers through regulations, as seen above in paragraphs 270 and 271. He also has an important advisory function, by way of giving directions as he thinks fit, either generally or in any particular case, with respect to the exercise or performance by the Secretary or the Authority of any powers, functions or duties under this Ordinance. Section 3 provides that the Secretary and the Authority must, in the exercise or performance of their respective powers, functions and duties under this Ordinance, comply with any such directions. Section 4(1) provides that the Chief Executive may by order publish in the Gazette, after consultation with the Advisory Council on the Environment, declare any part of Hong Kong to be a water control zone for the purposes of the Ordinance. Section 30 provides that where the Authority exercises his power to cancel or vary a licence in circumstances where certain conditions are not satisfied, he may exercise such power only with the prior approval of the Chief Executive, as to both the exercise and the manner of the exercise of the power, or with the agreement of the person who is making the discharge or deposit.[310] The Chief Executive appoints the Chairman and members of the Appeal Board.

280. An important power that the Chief Executive exercises is the power of review. The Secretary for the Environment or the Authority may in some special circumstances, set out in section 33, apply to the Chief Executive in Council to review a decision of the Appeal Board.

310. *Ibid.*, s. 24(2).

B. The Chief Secretary for Administration

281. The Chief Secretary for Administration performs two functions under the Water Pollution Control Ordinance: (1) If a question arises regarding the membership of the Advisory Council on the Environment, such questions must be determined by him; (2) The Hong Kong government or its officers not being criminally liable for any prohibited discharges, the Authority must bring to the attention of the Chief Secretary any such discharges. The Chief Secretary must take measures to ensure that the best practicable steps are taken to terminate the contravention or avoid the recurrence.

C. The Secretary for Environment

282. The following are the powers and functions of the Secretary for Environment in relation to water pollution control:

(a) It is the Secretary for Environment who establishes water quality objectives for water control zones. The Secretary has the power to give directions to the Authority regarding the implementation of such water quality objectives through licensing decisions.
(b) The Secretary for Environment has the power to issue a Technical Memorandum setting out permissible limits of the physical characteristics and chemical components of discharges and deposits in a water control zone. The Secretary may issue different technical memorandums in respect of different locations in Hong Kong or in respect of different parts of the environment, or both.
(c) The Secretary for Environment has the power to order the withholding of information that has been submitted to the Authority. Any person may apply to the Secretary to withhold from public notification or other public access under the Ordinance any specified information concerning a discharge or deposit, whether appearing in a licence or an application therefor or in any notice, return or other document. Such a request will be granted only if the Secretary is satisfied that the publication of such information is: (a) contrary to the applicant's private interest to an unreasonable degree or (b) is contrary to the public interest.

D. The Water Pollution Control Authority

283. The principal responsibility of the Authority, namely the Director of Environmental Protection, is to achieve and maintain the water quality objectives. Section 6(3) provides that the Authority must exercise and perform his powers, functions and duties under this Ordinance with the aim of achieving the relevant water quality objectives as soon as is reasonably practicable and thereafter maintaining the quality so achieved. The Authority is the licensing authority for licensing of discharges under the Ordinance. In granting a licence, the Authority must take various factors into account such as adverse impact of granting the licence on public health, or sewage or on drainage systems.[311]

E. The Appeal Board

284. The Appeal Board hears and determines appeals against certain decisions taken by the Secretary for Environment or the Authority, which are listed in section 29. The members of the Appeal Board are appointed by the Chief Executive for a renewable term of not more than three years. Its members are drawn from among public officers and other persons who are suitable to be appointed as Board members. An Appeal Board may: (a) receive evidence on oath; (b) admit or take into account any statement, document, information or matter whether or not it would be admissible as evidence in a court of law; and (c) by notice in writing summon any person to appear before it to produce any document or to give evidence.[312]

285. The Appeal Board has been given wide powers to enable it to carry out an effective examination of the matters on appeal by receiving evidence, admitting documents and summoning persons to appear before it.[313] Appeal hearings are conducted in public.[314] Parties have the right to legal representation.[315]

286. The Appeal Board may at the conclusion of its proceedings confirm, reverse or vary the decision or requirement that has been appealed against.[316] The Appeal Board's decision is final, except that the respondent (the Secretary or the Authority as the case may be) may make an application to the Chief Executive in Council to review the decision of the Appeal Board on the ground that the respondent considers that exceptional circumstances require the review of the Appeal Board's decision in the public interest.[317]

§5. Maintaining Water Quality in Water Control Zones

287. The Water Pollution Control Ordinance envisaged the establishment of water pollution control zones and the prescription of water quality objectives for those water control zones. With the creation of fourteen water control zones nearly all waters of Hong Kong have been brought under the water quality objective

311. *Ibid.*, s. 15.
312. *Ibid.*, s. 31(5).
313. *Ibid.*, s. 31(4).
314. Water Pollution Control (Appeal Board) Regulations, Cap 358 sub leg C, reg. 6.
315. *Ibid.*, reg. 7.
316. Water Pollution Control Ordinance, s. 31(2).
317. *Ibid.*, s. 33(1).

regime. It is the Chief Executive who has been given the responsibility of declaring water control zones, on the advice of the Advisory Council on the Environment.[318]

I. Making and Maintaining Water Quality Objectives

A. Establishing Water Quality Objectives

288. Water quality objectives are targets that the government aims to maintain. Section 5(2) says that the water quality objective for any particular waters shall be the quality which, in the opinion of the Secretary, should be achieved and maintained in order to promote the conservation and best use of those waters in the public interest. The Secretary for the Environment has the responsibility of establishing water quality objectives, who may after consultation with the Advisory Council on the Environment set water quality objectives for each water control zone or different objectives for different parts of a zone. Any water quality objective may be amended from time to time by the Secretary, after consultation with the Advisory Council on the Environment. A statement of every water quality objective so established and all subsequent amendments have to be published in the Gazette and be made available for inspection by the public free of charge.[319]

B. Achieving Water Quality Objectives

289. Once the Secretary has established the water quality objectives, it is the duty of the Water Pollution Control Authority to ensure that such objectives are achieved. The Water Pollution Control Ordinance provides that the Secretary must notify the Authority of all water quality objectives and of any subsequent amendments and that the Authority must exercise and perform his powers, functions and duties under the Water Pollution Control Ordinance with the aim of achieving the relevant water quality objectives as soon as is reasonably practicable and thereafter maintaining the quality so achieved.[320]

II. Licensing of Discharges

290. The objective of licensing of discharges is to regulate discharges that may be made into waters of Hong Kong such as the sea, internal waters, communal sewers and communal drains. Licensing provisions of the Ordinance relate to existing discharges and new discharges.

318. *Ibid.*, s. 4(1) provides that 'after consultation with the Advisory Council on the Environment' the Chief Executive may declare any part of Hong Kong to be a water control zone for the purposes of the Ordinance.
319. *Ibid.*, s. 5.
320. *Ibid.*, s. 6(2) and (3).

A. *Licensing of Existing Discharges*

291. As shown above, when the Water Pollution Ordinance came into effect an amnesty was granted to existing discharges, namely discharges that existed when a water control zones was declared and established. The Ordinance was amended in 1990 in order to bring to an end the regime of permitted existing discharges.[321] It provided that all existing discharges in water control zones that had already been established had to be regularized by obtaining a licence within two years; and that existing discharge would not be immune when any new control zone was established in the future.[322] The exemption given to existing discharges came to an end in 1992, when the grace period given by the 1990 Amendment Ordinance expired.

B. *Licensing of New Discharges*

292. Since 1992, any discharge which is otherwise a prohibited discharge may be authorized by a licence. The following is an example of such a provision: 'Bypass of treatment facilities shall be prohibited unless it is unavoidable to prevent loss of life, personal injury or severe property damage or no feasible alternative exists and the licensee shall inform the authority thereof in writing and prove to the authority.'[323] It is a defence to a charge of prohibited discharge under section 8 or 9 of the Water Pollution Control Ordinance that the discharge was made pursuant to or in accordance with a licence.

1. Making an Application for a Licence

293. The licensing authority is the Director of Environmental Protection who functions as the Water Pollution Control Authority. The Authority is not required to consider an application for the purpose of making a discharge into waters of Hong Kong or internal waters under section 8 or into communal sewers or communal drains under section 9 unless it is made by the person who makes or authorizes the discharge or deposit or the owner or occupier of the premises from which the discharge or deposit is made.[324]

---

321. *See Hong Kong Hansard* of 25 June 1980, pp. 911–913.
322. *See* Water Pollution Control (Amendment) Ordinance No. 67 of 1990.
323. In *HKSAR v Vibro (HK) Ltd* [2001] HKEC 1155. a licence to discharge liquids provided that 'bypass of treatment facilities shall be prohibited unless it is unavoidable to prevent loss of life, personal injury or severe property damage or no feasible alternative exists and the licensee shall inform the authority thereof in writing and prove to the authority'. The defendant failed in their appeal against conviction because they were not able to bring them within the exception.
324. Water Pollution Control Ordinance, s. 19(2).

2. Publication of the Application

294. The Authority must enter particulars of the licence in the register that he keeps of all discharges covered by licences. He must also cause a notice of the particulars of the application to be published in newspapers. Arrangements must be made for the public to inspect the applications.[325] The particulars that the Authority is required to notify to the public include: (a) the type of discharge or deposit, specifying whether it is from industrial premises or from a domestic sewage treatment plant or where it is from any other source, specifying such source; (b) the receiving waters, specifying: (i) in the case of discharge to or deposit in the waters of Hong Kong, the name of the water control zone and of the subzone, if any, within which the waters lie and (ii) in the case of discharge to or deposit in a communal drain or communal sewer flowing into the waters of Hong Kong, the name of the water control zone and subzone, if any, within which those waters lie; and (c) a statement of any method proposed by the applicant for treating the discharge or deposit before it reaches the discharge point.[326]

3. Objections to an Application

295. Within thirty days of such public notification any person may, in such manner as may be prescribed, object to the granting of the application on the ground that it would tend to inhibit the attainment or maintenance of the relevant water quality objective. Where any objection to the grant of the application is made to the Authority, he may hear the applicant and any objector if he considers it expedient for the purpose of obtaining information relevant to any question to be decided. The Authority may determine the procedure to be followed at, or for the purpose of convening, such a hearing.[327]

4. Determination

296. The Secretary for the Environment may give directions to the Authority in relation to his licensing powers. The Authority must comply with any such direction given by the Secretary and such direction overrides any discretion that the Authority would otherwise have in relation to his licensing powers. If in the opinion of the Secretary the achievement or maintenance of any water quality objective would be better served by the exercise by the Authority of any of his powers to grant, revoke or vary a licence for discharges, the Secretary may give directions in writing to the Authority as to the manner in which he shall exercise those powers; and, in the case of a direction which relates to revocation or variation of a licence

325. *Ibid.*, s. 19(3).
326. *See* Water Pollution Control (General Regulations, Regulation 5).
327. *Ibid.*, s. 41.

for discharges, any such direction may be of a general nature or relate to a particular case or particular cases. The Secretary shall not give any direction under subsection (4) as to the manner in which the Authority shall exercise the powers in section 24 in relation to a discharge or deposit unless he considers that any part of the waters of Hong Kong are in such a condition as to constitute a danger to the health of the public, or a section of the public, and the exercise of the powers in relation to that discharge or deposit would tend to lessen the danger; or in the case of a licence for discharges into communal sewers or communal drains, the discharge or deposit may be harmful to the operation of any sewage treatment plant.[328]

297. The Authority must make a decision to grant or not to grant a licence not earlier than forty days after the public notification of the application, giving time for public objections to be raised within the first thirty days and at least ten days for the Authority to consider the application. After consideration of the application the Authority may grant the application with or without any conditions, or may refuse to grant it.[329]

298. The Authority may refuse to grant a licence if, in relation to the discharge or deposit, there has been a breach of any of the terms or conditions of a licence granted under sections 15, 16 or 23A or a person has been convicted of an offence under the Ordinance in relation to the discharge or deposit.[330] If he refuses to grant a licence under this section, the Authority must notify the applicant in writing of his refusal and in the notice state his reasons therefor.[331]

5. Imposition of Conditions

299. A licence may be granted in such terms and on such conditions as he thinks fit including terms and conditions relating to the matters set out in the First Schedule.[332] The Authority must not grant a licence where he considers that, even by imposing terms or conditions, the discharge or deposit will endanger or is likely to endanger public health; the discharge or deposit will be or is likely to be harmful to the health or safety of any person engaged in the operation or maintenance of a drainage or sewerage system; the discharge or deposit will be or is likely to be

328. *Ibid.*, s. 6(5).
329. *Ibid.*, s. 20(1).
330. *Ibid.*, s. 20(3A).
331. *Ibid.*, s. 20(2).
332. *Ibid.*, s. 20(4). The particulars prescribed in the First Schedule include: place and times or periods at or during which the discharge or deposit may be made; the design and construction of any plant or equipment used in making the discharge or deposit; the treatment of matter before it is discharged or deposited and the plant and equipment to be provided, maintained and used therefor; the equipment and facilities to be provided for inspecting, sampling or measuring the discharge or deposit or any constituent thereof; and, precautions to be taken against matter discharged or deposited entering any specified part of the waters of Hong Kong or any communal drain or communal sewer.

harmful to a drainage or sewerage system; or the attainment and maintenance of water quality objectives will not be or is not likely to be achieved.[333]

6. Life Span of a Licence

300. The Authority may grant a licence for a period of not less than two years.[334] A licensee may make an application for renewal of licence not earlier than four months and not less than two months before the expiry of the existing licence.[335] Where an application made less than two months before the expiry of the licence, the application will still be considered. However, if the renewal is not approved before the expiry of the existing licence, any discharges between the expiry of licence and approval of the renewal licence will constitute prohibited discharges. An application for renewal received after the expiry of the existing licence will be rejected.[336] Applications for renewal of a licence attract the provisions that apply to applications for licences in relation to publication, consideration and determination.

7. Cancellation or Variation of Licences

301. A licensee may apply for the variation of a licence and such application must be considered following the notification to the public procedure that applies to licence applications. The Authority has the power to cancel or vary a licence, on his own initiative, where he considers that: (a) any part of the waters of Hong Kong are in such a condition as to constitute a danger to the health of the public, or a section of the public and the exercise of the power in relation to the discharge or deposit would tend to lessen that danger; (b) in the case of a licence for discharges into communal sewers or communal drains, the discharge or deposit may be harmful to the drainage or sewerage system or to the health or safety of any person engaged in the operation thereof; or (c) it is necessary in order to achieve a new water quality objective.[337]

302. Where none of the above requirements are present, the Authority may nevertheless exercise his powers of revocation or variation of a licence with the prior approval of the Chief Executive, as to both the exercise and the manner of the exercise of the power, or with the agreement of the person who is making the discharge or deposit.[338]

333. *Ibid.*, s. 20(3).
334. *Ibid.*, s. 20(5).
335. *Ibid.*, s. 23(1).
336. Water Pollution control (General) Regulations, Reg. 10.
337. Water Pollution Control Ordinance, s. 24(1).
338. *Ibid.*, s. 24(2).

303. Powers that the Authority has of cancellation and variation are spelt out in section 24(3). They are: (i) to impose new or amended terms and conditions subject to the observance of which, as from a specified date, the licence will continue in force; (ii) to declare the licence liable to cancellation at any time the person fails to observe any such term or condition; (iii) to cancel the licence as from a specified date if the person fails to observe any such term or condition; (iv) to cancel the licence as from a specified date; (v) to amend or add to any notice previously given under this section, or any part of such notice, or to substitute a new notice for it.

304. The conditions that the Authority may impose include a condition requiring the person to restrict or from time to time to suspend the discharge or deposit and a condition relating to the matters set out in the First Schedule, such as the place where and the times during which a discharge or deposit may be made and the design and construction of any plant or equipment used in making the discharge or deposit.[339]

8. Compensation for Cancellation or Imposition of New and Harsher Conditions

305. Where during the first two years of validity a licence is cancelled or varied by imposing additional obligations, compensation is payable if: (a) the possibility of danger to health or harm to the drainage or sewerage system or to the health or safety of any person engaged in the operation thereof or the establishment of a new water quality objective was known or could with reasonable foresight have been known to the Authority at the time the licence was granted or renewed; or (b) the danger, harm or new water quality objective mentioned in paragraph (a) is a consequence of licences granted or renewed after the grant, or, where a licence has been renewed, the last renewal of the licence which is cancelled or varied.[340] Where the cancellation or variation of the licence, imposing additional obligations, was done with the approval of the Chief Executive, the above two conditions need not be satisfied.[341]

306. The factors to be taken into account or disregarded and the principle to be applied in determining the amount of compensation are set out in Part IV of the Water Pollution Control (General) Regulations. After setting out the factors that may be considered, the Regulations proceed to prohibit the taking of any other factor into account.

307. The Second Schedule of the Water Pollution Control Ordinance sets out the procedure for the handling of compensation claims and enables the Authority refer any claim to the Lands Tribunal if parties cannot agree on amount payable as compensation payment.

339. *Ibid.*, s. 24(4).
340. *Ibid.*, s. 25(1) and (2).
341. *Ibid.*, s. 26.

9. Contravention of Licensing Provisions

308. Contravention of any licence provision is a criminal offence.[342] Regulation 17B(1) provides as follows: 'A person who contravenes any of the provisions of a licence granted under the Ordinance as are specified in subregulation (2) commits an offence and is liable to a fine of $200,000 and to imprisonment for 6 months.' That provision refers to no requisite mental element and the regulation does not provide for any statutory defences. However, the defendant could have pleaded a defence: '… there was a positive duty on the licensee to take all possible steps to ensure that breaches did not occur. It was not sufficient to hold the appropriate licence; it was necessary also that any deposit or discharge was made in accordance with its provisions. The licensee would have a defence by establishing on the balance of probabilities that it had taken all reasonable steps to prevent a discharge of sub-standard effluent, or that it had a reasonable, if mistaken, belief that proper preventative steps had been taken to comply with the conditions of the licence'. In view of the availability of such possible defences, contravention of a licence was not an absolute offence. The court rightly held that just as the offence of prohibited discharge is a strict liability offence,[343] breach of a licence condition in the form of a prohibited discharge is also a strict liability offence. As Beeson J explained in *HKSAR v Sunley Engineering and Construction Co Ltd*:

> The offence was not one which could be regarded as truly criminal in character. It was 'clearly or by necessary implication the effect of the statute' that the presumption of *mens rea* could be displaced. The licensing provisions existed to deal with an issue of social concern, to prevent contractors who were carrying out development or construction work from uncontrolledly discharging from construction sites effluent containing solids which might damage the drainage system; affect the water table; or pollute streams, rivers and harbours. It could be shown in such circumstances that the creation of strict liability was effective to promote the object of the legislation, by encouraging greater vigilance to prevent the commission of the prohibited act or acts. The legislature, by setting up the licensing system, intended to control the discharge of effluent and to that end intended that proof of knowledge of breaches of the licence was not necessary.[344]

309. Where a contravention of a licence provision has occurred, the licensee may be held liable for such contravention without the need for the prosecution to establish the identity of the person responsible for such contravention. All that the prosecution has to establish is to prove that a contravention of licence has taken place.[345] The legislative framework makes it clear that there is an obligation on the

342. Water Pollution Control (general) Regulations, Cap 358 sub leg D, reg. 17B.
343. *See* below under 'Criminalizing Prohibited Discharges'.
344. *HKSAR v Sunley Engineering and Construction Co Ltd* [2001] 2 HKC 318, [2001] HKLRD (Yrbk) 322.
345. *Ibid.*

licensee to ensure that the provisions of the licence are not breached. If the prosecution was required to establish precisely who had caused the discharge, that would place an impossible burden on them and render nugatory the purpose for which the licence was issued.[346]

310. 'There was no point in having a licensing system, unless the licensee could be made to bear the responsibility for breaches of it. If all the licensee needed to do to escape liability for breaches was to point the finger at unknown persons as having caused the discharge, no one could ever be held responsible for breaches of the licence.'[347] Beeson J went on to say:

> The Magistrate was correct in holding that there was a positive duty on the licensee to take all possible steps to ensure that breaches did not occur. It was not sufficient to hold the appropriate licence; it was necessary also that any deposit or discharge was made in accordance with its provisions. The licensee would have a defence by establishing on the balance of probabilities that it had taken all reasonable steps to prevent a discharge of sub-standard effluent, or that it had a reasonable, if mistaken, belief that proper preventative steps had been taken to comply with the conditions of the licence.[348]

III. Criminalizing Prohibited Discharges

A. *Criminal Offences*

311. Sections 8 and 9 create offences of prohibited discharges into the waters of Hong Kong or inland waters in any water control zone or into communal sewers and communal drains. Section 8 provides that it is an offence to discharge: (a) any waste or polluting matter into the waters of Hong Kong, unless permitted under a licence; or (b) any matter into any inland waters which tends to impede the proper flow of the water in a manner leading or likely to lead to a substantial aggravation of pollution, unless permitted under a licence, or (c) any poisonous or noxious matter into the waters of Hong Kong.[349] Section 9 prohibits discharging any matter into a communal sewer or Communal drain in a water control zone, unless permitted under a licence. Both these sections provide some exceptions to these prohibitions.

---

346. In *HKSAR v Sunley Engineering and Construction Co Ltd* [2001] 2 HKC 318, [2001] HKLRD (Yrbk) 322 the defendant licensee, the registered building contractor of a construction site, was prosecuted under s. 8 for a prohibited discharge, namely muddy effluent from their construction site into a sedimentation tank from which it was discharged to a surface channel outside the site.

347. *Ibid.*, per Beeson J.

348. *Ibid.*

349. 'The ordinance does not carry within it definitions of waste matter, polluting matter or of poisonous or noxious matter. But they are ordinary words and their meaning can be determined from ordinary usage.' *Secretary of Justice v Flame Construction co Ltd* [2002] 2 HKC 305; [2001] HKEC 1544,[18]. Deputy Judge McMahon.

Discharges are lawful if: (i) they are licensed under the Waste Disposal Ordinance or (ii) they comply with the Waste Disposal (Livestock Waste) Regulations.[350]

1. Persons Who May Be Held Liable

312. Criminal liability for an offence under section 8 or 9 may be imposed not only on the persons who are responsible for the offence. The occupier of the premises or the person in command of the vessel from where the prohibited discharge into Hong Kong waters originated may also be held criminally responsible.[351] Similarly, the occupier of the premises from where prohibited discharges into a communal sewer or a communal drain originated may also be prosecuted.[352] Where a person convicted of an offence is a body corporate and it is proved that the offence was committed with the consent or connivance of, or was attributable to any neglect or omission on the part of, any director, manager, secretary or other person concerned in the management of the body corporate, the director, manager, secretary or other person also commits the offence.[353] Where a person convicted of an offence is a partner in a partnership and it is proved that the offence was committed with the consent or connivance of, or was attributable to any neglect or omission on the part of, any other partner or any person concerned in the management of the partnership, the partner or the person concerned in the management also commits the offence.[354]

2. What Must Be Proved?

313. The prosecution has to establish that a discharge has occurred in a way that is prohibited by either section 8 or 9. In *HKSAR v VSL Hong Kong Ltd and Kaden Construction Ltd*,[355] the prosecution failed because although it had established that there was a discharge it was unable to establish further that the discharge was not made by way of a communal drain.

314. It has also been judicially held that what the prosecution has to establish is that a prohibited discharge has occurred. It is not necessary to establish further what adverse effect the discharge had on the waters. In *Secretary of Justice v Flame Construction co Ltd,* Deputy Judge McMahon said that the Water Pollution Control Ordinance simply prohibits:

> certain sorts of matter being discharged into protected waterways. It does not, in its terms, expressly require that the prohibited matter discharged be proven

350. Water Pollution Control Ordinance, s. 12(1B).
351. *Ibid.*, s. 8(2).
352. *Ibid.*, s. 9(2).
353. *Ibid.*, s. 10A(1).
354. *Ibid.*, s. 10A(2).
355. [2012] HKEC 2472.

> to have had in fact a polluting, poisonous or noxious effect. Its language is addressed to the nature of the discharged matter rather than the effect of the discharged matter upon the waterway. … If it were otherwise, one would expect the legislation to be expressed in simple terms of prohibiting the actual pollution or poisoning of a waterway or of the rendering of that waterway noxious. Instead, the legislation is directed at prohibiting a discharge of a particular nature into a waterway or waters. … It may well be that to establish the nature of the matter in question some evidence is required of the general properties of the matter to prove that that it is in fact, in its properties, noxious or poisonous or a pollutant. But the legislation does not require that it be shown to have in fact harmed, poisoned or polluted the particular waterway the subject of the charged offence. … In my view all that has to be proven is that so far as a protected waterway or Hong Kong waters are concerned the matter alleged to be polluting has the intrinsic property of dirtying or befouling other substances in the terms of the definition of polluting I have referred to and for the reasons that I have given that there does not have to be any proof that the particular water way was in fact polluted. Indeed, it may be that the particular waterway is already so polluted and noxious that the additional polluting matter has no measurably adverse effect upon it. That does not matter. The legislation is not designed to excuse the discharge of polluting noxious or poisonous matter simply because the receiving water has already been polluted, poisoned or rendered noxious by previous offences.[356]

315. However, Deputy Judge McMahon went on to observe that especially where it is not obvious that what was discharged was polluting, poisonous or noxious:

> Some matter may be more ambiguous in its characteristics and be able to be established as poisonous or noxious or polluting in its nature only upon proof of further matters such as the quantity of matter involved. It may well be that in the majority of cases brought under this legislation the prosecution will lead evidence that the waterway was in fact harmed, or life in it was poisoned, or that its natural quality was degraded in some way. Such proof would be one factor, often perhaps the most important factor, bearing on the question whether the nature of the matter or substances discharged was in fact poisonous, noxious or polluting. Equally, whether matter was 'waste' matter would also often depend upon proof of the origin as well as the composition of the material. But such evidence is not required as a matter of law, and there may well be cases where the composition of the discharge without more is such as to allow an inference to be drawn that, as a matter of fact, the discharged material was noxious or poisonous or polluting matter or waste matter. In short assuming the application of the proper definition of waste, polluting, noxious or poisonous matter, any finding whether the substance discharged was waste,

356. [2002] 2 HKC 305, [2001] HKEC 1544, [19], [23], [24], [35].

noxious, poisonous or polluting matter is a finding of fact. And as with all such findings the evidence sufficient to establish that fact will vary from case to case.[357]

316. HKSAR v Kwan On,[358] another case involving discharges from a construction site, affirms that where a licence condition has been breached, it is not necessary to establish the effect of the discharge on the waters. Judge Saw said:

> The water that was discharged was unclean water. It was discoloured because of the suspended solids in it. I am satisfied that in the circumstances of this case once what is discharged contains that which the licence says it should not (in this case suspended particles in excess of 30 mg/L of suspended solids) ... it is not incumbent upon the prosecution to establish the effect of or the nature of the suspended particles in the discharge. It suffices that the discharge is in excess of that which the appellant is permitted by its licence to discharge.[359]

3. Liability Is Strict

317. Once the prosecution has established beyond reasonable doubt that a prohibited discharge has taken place, there is no requirement that the prosecution must also establish the presence of *mens rea*. In fact, section 10 explicitly states that:

> In any proceedings for an offence under section 8(1), 8(1A), 8(2), 9(1) or 9(2) in which it is alleged that the defendant caused matter to enter the waters of Hong Kong or inland waters or a communal sewer or communal drain or caused matter to be deposited as provided in section 2(3) it shall not be necessary for the prosecution to prove that the acts or omissions in question were accompanied by any intention, knowledge or negligence on the part of the defendant as to any element of the offence.

The offences created by sections 8 and 9 are thus strict liability offences.[360]

318. While the prosecution does not have to establish any mental element in a charge in respect of a discharge prohibited by section 8 or 9, a defendant may set up certain statutory defences. For instance, the defendant may set up the defence that: (a) the discharge or deposit was made in an emergency in order to avoid danger to life or property[361] and as soon as was reasonably practicable he informed the

357. *Ibid.*, [27]–[29].
358. [2009] HKEC 978.
359. *Ibid.*, [28].
360. For s. 8 *see Secretary of Justice v Flame Construction co Ltd* [2002] 2 HKC 305, [2001] HKEC 1544, [18]; For s. 9 *see HKSAR v Sunley Engineering and Construction Co Ltd* [2001] 2 HKC 318, [2001] HKLRD (Yrbk) 322; and *HKSAR v Sims Trading Co Ltd* [2002] HKCU 658; [2002] HKLRD (Yrbk) 437.
361. In *HKSAR v Sims Trading* [2002] HKCU 658; [2002] HKLRD (Yrbk) 437 there was an accidental spillage of a large amount of salad dressing on a warehouse floor. On the manager's instructions

Authority thereof in writing; or (b) he acted under instructions given to him by his employer and he exercised the care and took the steps that the court, having regard to his position as an employee, considers reasonable in the circumstances to avoid the occurrence of the prohibited discharge or deposit.[362]

B. Remedial Measures Where Prohibited Discharges Have Occurred

1. Notice May Be Served Requiring Restoration of the Waters

319. The primary responsibility of taking remedial measures by way of restoring waters is on the person who is convicted of an offence of prohibited discharge. Where any person has been convicted of an offence of prohibited discharge under section 8 or section 9, the Authority may, if he is of the opinion that: (a) any part of the waters of Hong Kong suffered continuing damage as a direct result of the commission of the offence; and (b) it is reasonably practicable to restore or partially restore that part to the condition it was in before the commission of the offence, by notice in writing require the person so convicted to carry out such work as is specified in the notice to effect such restoration or partial restoration.[363] The notice may specify the manner in which the work is to be carried out and must stipulate the time before which the work must be commenced and the time by which it must be completed.[364]

2. The Authority May Take Remedial Measures to Restore the Waters

320. If a person fails to comply with such a notice, the Authority may, without further notice, carry out or cause to be carried out the work or the remaining work specified in the notice and recover from that person the cost of so doing as a civil debt due to the government.[365]

3. The Authority's Exceptional Power to Take Urgent Remedial Action

321. The Authority also has exceptional powers to take urgent remedial action to restore or partially restore waters without waiting for prosecution or conviction of any person of an offence of prohibited discharge. The Authority may exercise such power if: (a) any part of the waters of Hong Kong is suffering continuing damage as a direct result of the commission of the alleged offence; (b) it is reasonably

---

the floor workers removed most of the spillage and used a water hose to flush it out. The polluted water entered a communal drain. Upon a prosecution under s. 9, the warehouse pleaded that the discharge was made in an emergency in order to avoid danger to life or property. The defence failed because the facts were woefully inadequate to establish an imminent danger to life or property.

362. Water Pollution Control Ordinance, s. 12(1A).

363. *Ibid.*, s. 13(1).

364. *Ibid.*, s. 13(2).

365. *Ibid.*, s. 13(3).

practicable to restore or partially restore that part to the condition it was in before the commission of the alleged offence; and (c) the damage is so severe that work to restore or partially restore the waters should start before any person has been charged or convicted. Following completion of the work, the Authority must reinstate any land that it entered to carry out such restorative work, as far as it is practicable to do so, to the condition it was in before the entry.[366]

322. All costs incurred by the Authority in carrying out such work, including any compensation paid by the Authority under the regulations to a third party, are recoverable from any person who is responsible for the damage to the waters of Hong Kong, regardless of whether or not the person has been convicted of an offence of prohibited discharge.[367]

§6. Appeals

323. Any person aggrieved by an appealable requirement or decision of the Authority or the Secretary for the Environment may appeal to the Appeal Board, except where the requirement of the Authority has been made with the prior approval of the Chief Executive in Council.

I. Appealable Decisions

324. The decisions or requirements against which an appeal lies are listed in section 29(1). They are:

(1) requiring a convicted person to restore waters;
(2) respecting the responsibility for damage and the reasonableness of the costs incurred by the Authority in restoring waters;
(3) refusing to consider an application for a licence in respect of an existing discharge or deposit;
(4) refusing to grant such a licence;
(5) fixing terms and conditions of such a licence;
(6) cancelling a temporary licence in respect of an exempted discharge;
(7) granting or fixing terms and conditions of a new licence replacing such a temporary licence;
(8) refusing to consider an application for a licence in respect of a discharge or deposit;
(9) refusing to grant a licence;
(10) fixing terms and conditions of such a licence;
(11) fixing the period of such a licence;
(12) refusing to renew a licence;
(13) refusing to renew a temporary licence in respect of an exempt discharge;

366. *Ibid.*, s. 13A.
367. *Ibid.*, s. 13A(3).

(14) fixing terms and conditions of a renewed licence;
(15) fixing the period of a renewed licence;
(16) imposing new or amended terms or conditions for continuance of a licence;
(17) cancelling a licence;
(18) amending or adding to a notice or substituting a new notice;
(19) refusing to vary a licence at the request of a licensee;
(20) requiring information to be furnished for enforcement purposes;
(21) refusing an application requesting that certain information concerning a discharge or deposit must be withheld from public disclosure.

II. Making an Appeal

325. An appeal must be lodged within twenty-one days after receiving notice of such decision or requirement. Notice of appeal must be given to the Chairman and must set out the grounds of the appeal and a copy of the notice of appeal must be served on the respondent. Where the decision or requirement appealed against had been made under certain provisions, the notice of such decision or requirement remains suspended from the date on which notice of appeal is given until the disposal, abandonment or withdrawal of the appeal.[368]

III. Appeal Hearing

326. When the Chairman receives notice of appeal, he must set up an Appeal Board to hear an appeal and must fix the date, time and place of the hearing of the appeal, giving notice to the appellant and the respondent at least fourteen days in advance.[369]

327. Appeal Board proceedings must generally be held in public and the parties are entitled to legal representation. If the appellant fails to attend or be represented at the appeal hearing, the Appeal Board may conduct the hearing in the absence of the appellant or dismiss the appeal without a hearing. The Appeal Board may, however, postpone or adjourn the meeting if the appellant's failure to attend or be represented is due to a reasonable cause. Where an appeal has been dismissed without a hearing because of the failure of the appellant to be present or be represented at the hearing, the appellant may, within thirty days, apply to the Board to review its decision. If the appellant satisfies the Board that his absence was due to a reasonable cause, the Appeal Board may set aside the order for dismissal and set a date for the hearing of the appeal.[370]

---

368. *Ibid.*, s. 29(4).
369. Water Pollution Control (Appeal Board) Regulations (Cap 358 sub leg C), reg. 4.
370. *Ibid.*, regs 6, 7, 8, 9 and 10.

328. Section 36 of the Water Pollution Control Ordinance provides that an Appeal Board may receive evidence on oath; admit or take into account any statement, document, information or matter even if it would be inadmissible as evidence in a court of law; and summon any person before it to produce any document or to give evidence. The Chairman has the power to determine any form or matter of practice or procedure in so far as no provision is found in the Ordinance.

IV. Appeal Board's Determination

329. The Appeal Board may confirm, reverse or vary the decision or requirement of the Authority or the Secretary for the Environment. Every question before the Appeal Board is determined by the opinion of the majority of the members of the Appeal Board. The Chairman has both an original vote and a casting vote. Any question of law is determined by the Chairman, but he may refer a question of law to the Court of Appeal by way of case stated.[371]

V. Review of Appeal Board Decisions

330. An application to review a decision of the Appeal Board may be made by the Authority or Secretary for the Environment, within fourteen days of being notified of the decision of the Appeal Board. A review application may be made if: (1) the Appeal Board has reversed or varied a decision or requirement of the Authority or Secretary; and (2) the Authority or Secretary considers that exceptional circumstances require the review of the Board's decision in the public interest. The Authority or Secretary must notify the appellant of the reference for review together with the reasons for such reference so as to enable him to submit written representations concerning the review to the Chief Executive in Council. Any such representations must be made by the appellant within fourteen days of receiving notice of the reference for review. The Chief Executive in Council may review the case, consider any representations made by the appellant and may confirm, reverse or vary the decision of the Appeal Board.[372]

§7. The Enforcement of the Water Pollution Control Ordinance

331. The Water Pollution Control Ordinance, which relies on a system of establishing and monitoring water quality objectives through licensing and creation of criminal offences to effectively control water pollution, makes provision for a system to support enforcement. The Ordinance empowers the Authority to obtain information necessary for the effective carrying out of his duties; empowers him to

371. Water Pollution Control Ordinance, ss 31 and 34.
372. *Ibid.*, s. 33.

appoint authorized officers to assist him; confers special powers of authorized officers; and grants them protection by creating criminal offences relating to obstructing them in the performance of their duties.

I. Power to Gather Information

332. The Authority may by notice in writing to any person require him to furnish to the Authority, within a period and in a form stipulated in the notice, any information specified in the notice being information which he is authorized to obtain by regulations or which the Authority may reasonably require for the purpose of exercising and performing his powers, functions and duties.[373] Water Pollution Control (General) Regulations authorize the Authority to require a person to supply information relating to: (a) any matter in relation to which particulars are required to be supplied in support of an application for a licence or renewal of a licence; and (b) any discharge or deposit, including but not limited to periods or times during which the discharge or deposit is made and particulars of any process, plant or equipment involved in making the discharge or deposit.[374]

333. A person who: (a) fails without reasonable excuse to comply with the requirements of a notice served on him; or (b) in compliance or purported compliance with such a notice, makes any statement which he knows to be false in a material particular or recklessly makes any statement which is false in a material particular or knowingly omits any material particular, commits an offence.[375] A person who in an application under this Ordinance makes a statement or gives an estimate which he knows to be false in a material particular or who recklessly makes a statement or gives an estimate which is false in a material particular or knowingly omits a material particular from the application commits an offence and is liable to a similar fine.[376]

A. *Special Provisions Relating to Information Gathering*

334. Public officers gather information for different purposes of the Ordinance, such as licensing and enforcement. There is a duty on the public officers to make available any information that the Ordinance requires to be made public and to desist from disclosing private information that they are not authorized to disclose.

335. The Authority is required to make the following information public by maintaining information in a register: (a) particulars of all discharges and deposits for which a licence is in force; (b) applications for licences; (c) other applications;

---

373. *Ibid.*, s. 35(1).
374. Water Pollution Control (General) Regulations, reg. 17A.
375. Water Pollution Control Ordinance, s. 35(2).
376. *Ibid.*, s. 35(3).

and (d) any notices relating to such applications.[377] Water Pollution Control (General) Regulations prescribe particulars that must be entered in the register in respect of licensing applications.

B. *Disclosure and Withholding of Information*

336. While such information is required to be made public, any person may apply to the Secretary for the Environment to withhold any such information from the register. Such an application will be granted only if the disclosure is contrary to the applicant's private interest to an unreasonable degree or is contrary to public interest.[378]

337. The disclosure of information must not compromise trade or business secrets. It is an offence for anyone to disclose any information concerning a trade or business secret that came to his knowledge in the course of exercising any powers under the Ordinance. Such information may be released only upon a court order or with the consent of the affected person [379]

II. Power of Authorized Officers

338. Authorized officers have been given extensive powers. The first such power is to enter premises. An authorized officer may, for the purposes of the Ordinance, without a warrant enter any place or premises or stop and board any vessel: (a) from or on which he has reason to suspect that matter has been or is being discharged or deposited into the waters of Hong Kong or inland waters, or any communal sewer or communal drain; (b) from or on which matter is being so discharged or deposited pursuant to a licence, whether or not the discharge is a suspected contravention of section 8 or 9; (c) on which he has reason to believe there is anything likely to be, or to contain, evidence of an offence against the Ordinance.[380]

339. Where an authorized officer or authorized agent has reasonable grounds for believing that it is necessary for the purpose of carrying out any restoration work to do so, he may without warrant enter any place or premises on which any inspection, survey or work is to be carried out or through which access is needed for that purpose.[381]

340. The power to enter premises without a warrant does not apply in relation to domestic premises (other than that part of such premises on which there is a private

377. *Ibid.*, s. 4291.
378. *Ibid.*, s. 43.
379. *Ibid.*, s. 44.
380. *Ibid.*, s. 37(1).
381. *Ibid.*, s. 37(3A).

wastewater treatment facility) or any vessel used wholly or principally for dwelling purposes.[382] A warrant to enter such premises has to be obtained from a magistrate.[383]

341. Authorized officers may, in the exercise of their powers to enter and search, do certain specified things. They may, for instance: (a) inspect any plant or equipment or observe any process or procedure which he has reason to suspect is being, or has been, or is intended to be, used in connection with: (i) a discharge or deposit which is being, or has been, made contrary to section 8(1) or (1A) or 9(1), or is made pursuant to a licence; (ii) the treatment of any matter which is being, or is intended to be, discharged or deposited into the waters of Hong Kong or inland waters or into any communal sewer or communal drain and require any person in charge of the place, premises or vessel to do anything which the officer reasonably considers to be necessary for facilitating the inspection or observation;[384] and (b) seize, remove and detain any drawing, record or document relating to any plant or equipment referred to in section 38(b) or any other article or thing if he has reason to suspect that it is, or contains, evidence of an offence.[385]

342. A person who: (a) wilfully obstructs an authorized officer in the exercise of any statutory powers referred to above; or (b) fails without reasonable excuse to comply with any requirement duly made by an officer; or (c) in compliance or purported compliance with any such requirement produces any drawing, document or record which he knows to be incorrect or inaccurate in a material particular or does not believe to be correct and accurate, commits an offence.[386]

§8. Supplementary Legislation

I. Dumping at Sea Ordinance

343. The aim of Dumping at Sea Ordinance (Cap 466) is to control the disposal of substances and articles at sea and the dumping of substances and articles in the sea and under the seabed.[387] The Ordinance envisages the grant of permits for any disposals at sea and provides for the serving of marine abatement notices. The Authority may issue a Technical Memorandum setting out principles, procedures, guidelines, standards and limits: (a) used to predict, measure, assess or determine whether marine pollution is caused by, or contributed to by, or may be imminent by reason of, a process referred to in section 12(1), such as marine construction work and land reclamation; (b) for the issue of marine pollution abatement notices for the abatement of pollution; (c) used to determine whether or not a marine pollution

---

382. *Ibid.*, ss 37(2), 37(3A).
383. *Ibid.*, ss 37(3), 37(3C).
384. *Ibid.*, s. 38(a).
385. *Ibid.*, s. 38(b) and (c).
386. *Ibid.*, s. 40.
387. Dumping at Sea Ordinance (Cap 466), Long Title.

abatement notice is being complied with (section 13). The Ordinance creates several offences including contravention of permit requirements and non-compliance with a marine pollution abatement notice (section 25). A person charged with an offence under the Ordinance has a defence if he proves that he took all reasonable precautions and exercised all due diligence to avoid the commission of the offence (section 26).

Authorized officers are given extensive enforcement powers in order to implement the Ordinance effectively (*see* Part VI of the Ordinance).

A. Application of the Ordinance

344. The Dumping at Sea Ordinance binds the government. However, an authorized officer is not liable in civil or criminal proceedings for anything he does or omits to do in the purported performance of his functions under the Ordinance if the court is satisfied that it was done or omitted in good faith. This protection conferred on public officers for an act or omission does not affect any liability of the government for the act or omission.[388]

345. If the Authority considers that a public officer, in carrying out his duties in the service of the government, has done or omitted to do something that contravenes the Ordinance, the Authority must, if the act or omission is not immediately terminated to his satisfaction, report the matter to the Chief Secretary for Administration. On receiving a report, the Chief Secretary for Administration must enquire into the matter and, if his enquiry shows that a public officer is continuing to contravene the Ordinance or is likely to contravene the Ordinance again, the Chief Secretary for Administration must ensure that the best practicable steps are taken to stop the contravention or avoid the recurrence.[389]

B. Technical Memorandum

346. The Authority may issue a Technical Memorandum setting out principles, procedures, guidelines, standards and limits: (a) used to predict, measure, assess or determine whether marine pollution is caused by, or contributed to by, or may be imminent by reason of, a process referred to in section 12(1); (b) for the issue of marine pollution abatement notices for the pollution; (c) used to determine whether or not a marine pollution abatement notice is being complied with.[390]

347. A Technical Memorandum is not subsidiary legislation.[391] However, a Technical Memorandum has to be placed before the Legislative Council for its scrutiny. A Technical Memorandum takes effect: (a) if the Legislative Council does not

388. *Ibid.*, s. 22.
389. *Ibid.*, s. 2.
390. *Ibid.*, s. 13(1).
391. *Ibid.*, s. 3(2).

pass a resolution amending the Technical Memorandum, upon the expiry of the period or the period as extended, as the case may be, for passing an amending resolution; and (b) if the Legislative Council passes a resolution amending the Technical Memorandum, at the beginning of the day of the publication in the Gazette of the resolution.[392]

C. Declaration of Marine Dumping Areas

348. The regulatory regime has as its starting point the declaration of marine dumping areas. The Ordinance empowers the Authority, namely the Director of Environmental Protection, to designate areas within Hong Kong waters as marine dumping areas. It provides that in determining the suitability of an area for designation as a marine dumping area, the Authority must have regard to: (a) the need to protect the marine environment, the living resources which it supports, and human health; (b) the need to prevent interference with other legitimate uses of the sea; and (c) the proposed quantity and type of material to be dumped.[393]

D. Permits

349. Certain operations may be carried out in marine dumping areas only with a permit. These operations listed in section 8(1) include, for instance:

(a) dumping substances or articles within the waters of Hong Kong, either in the sea or under the seabed: (i) from an aircraft, vehicle, vessel or marine structure; (ii) from a container floating in the sea; or (iii) from a structure on land constructed or adapted wholly or mainly for the purpose of dumping solids in the sea;
(b) dumping substances or articles anywhere in the sea or under the seabed: (i) from a Hong Kong aircraft, Hong Kong vessel or other Hong Kong marine structures; or (ii) from a container floating in the sea, if the dumping is controlled from a Hong Kong aircraft, Hong Kong vessel or other Hong Kong marine structures;
(c) scuttling a vessel, aircraft or marine structure: (i) in the waters of Hong Kong; or (ii) anywhere at sea, if the scuttling is controlled from a Hong Kong aircraft, Hong Kong vessel or other Hong Kong marine structures.

350. A permit is required for incinerating substances or articles on a vessel or marine structure: (i) in the waters of Hong Kong; or (ii) anywhere at sea if the incineration takes place on a Hong Kong vessel or other Hong Kong marine structures.[394]

---

392. *Ibid.*, s. 14.
393. *Ibid.*, s. 7.
394. *Ibid.*, s. 9.

351. In determining whether to issue a permit, the Authority: (a) must have regard to the need: (i) to protect the marine environment, the living resources which it supports, and human health; and (ii) to prevent interference with other legitimate uses of the sea; and (b) may have regard to such other matters as the Authority considers relevant, such as the proposed specific water pollution avoidance measures.[395] The Authority may prescribe conditions including those in order to protect the marine environment, the living resources which it supports, and human health.[396]

352. A person who: (a) except under and in accordance with a permit, does anything for which a permit is needed; or (b) except under and in accordance with a permit, causes or allows another person to do anything for which a permit is needed, commits an offence.[397] Such a person has a defence if he proves: (a) that the operation was reasonably carried out to secure the safety of an aircraft, vessel or marine structure or to save life; (b) that the necessity for the operation was not due to his fault; and (c) that he took steps within a reasonable time to inform the Authority: (i) of the operation; (ii) of the locality and circumstances in which it took place; and (iii) of the substances or articles concerned (*see* section 26).

353. A person who, to procure the issue of a permit: (a) makes a statement which he knows to be false in a material particular; (b) recklessly makes a statement which is false in a material particular; or (c) intentionally fails to disclose a material particular, commits an offence.[398] A person who, in purporting to comply with a condition imposed on him under a permit: (a) makes a statement which he knows to be false in a material particular; (b) recklessly makes a statement which is false in a material particular; or (c) intentionally fails to disclose a material particular, commits an offence.[399]

E. Marine Pollution Abatement Notices

354. Where the Authority is satisfied that: (a) marine construction work; (b) dredging; (c) marine borrowing; (d) land reclamation; or (e) stock piling on the seabed, is causing or contributing to marine pollution which exists or which is imminent, the Authority may serve a marine pollution abatement notice. Such a notice may be served on: (i) the master of a vessel or commander of an aircraft; (ii) the person in charge of a vehicle or marine structure; or (iii) the person, carrying out the activity or responsible for the activity.[400]

---

395. *Ibid.*, s. 10.
396. *Ibid.*, s. 10(4).
397. *Ibid.*, s. 25(1).
398. *Ibid.*, s. 25(2).
399. *Ibid.*, s. 25(3).
400. *Ibid.*, s. 12(1).

355. The Authority may require a person served with a marine pollution abatement notice: (a) to cease dumping marine pollutants; (b) to cease the dumping activity; (c) to take other steps to abate the dumping of marine pollutants from the activity; (d) to undertake the activity so that it does not cause the quality of the water in the vicinity of the activity to exceed the levels set out in the notice; (e) to provide, operate and maintain a facility to measure characteristics and constituents of sea water and the discharge.[401] The Authority may, in serving a marine pollution abatement notice, either: (a) require that the notice be complied with immediately; or (b) state a time by which the person served with the notice shall comply with the notice.[402] A person who fails to comply with a marine pollution abatement notice served on him under section 12 commits an offence.[403]

F. Appeals

356. The Dumping at Sea Appeal Board may hear appeals from persons aggrieved by a decision or direction of the Authority. The appealable decisions, as listed in section 27, are: (a) designation of an area as a dumping area under section 7, (b) issuing of a permit under section 10, (c) issuing of a marine pollution abatement notice, and (d) taking remedial action under section 23 to protect the marine environment, the living resources which it supports, and human health, and to prevent interference with other legitimate uses of the sea. An Appeal Board may: (a) receive evidence on oath; (b) take into account a statement, document, information or matter whether or not it would be admissible as evidence in a court of law; (c) by notice in writing, summon a person to appear before it to produce a document or to give evidence; and (d) award such amount for costs in an appeal as is just and equitable in the circumstances of the case.[404] On an appeal an Appeal Board may confirm, reverse or vary the decision or direction appealed from.[405]

G. Enforcement

357. Where the Authority is satisfied that dumping or incineration at sea has been done otherwise than under and in accordance with a permit, the Authority may do anything reasonably necessary to protect the marine environment, the living resources which it supports, and human health, and to prevent interference with other legitimate uses of the sea. If the Authority acts in the exercise of these powers, he is entitled to recover the expenses reasonably incurred by him in carrying

401. *Ibid.*, s. 12(2).
402. *Ibid.*, s. 12(3).
403. *Ibid.*, s. 25(6).
404. *Ibid.*, s. 29(7).
405. *Ibid.*, s. 29(3).

out his actions from a person who has been convicted of an offence in consequence of the act or omission which made it appear to the Authority to be necessary or expedient to take remedial action.[406]

358. Part VI of the Ordinance confers extensive powers on authorized officers, who assist the Authority in the enforcement of the Ordinance. An authorized officer may enter: (a) land and vehicles in Hong Kong; (b) aircraft, vessels and other marine structures, other than Hong Kong aircraft, Hong Kong vessels and other Hong Kong marine structures, where they are in Hong Kong or the waters of Hong Kong; (c) Hong Kong aircraft, Hong Kong vessels and other Hong Kong marine structures, wherever they are. These powers may be exercised if he: (i) has reason to believe that substances or articles to be dumped in the sea or under the seabed or incinerated on a vessel or marine structure at sea are or have been present there; or (ii) is giving or enforcing a marine pollution abatement notice.[407] An authorized officer may require a person: (a) to give details of substances or articles on board an aircraft, vessel or marine structure; and (b) to give information concerning substances or articles lost or dumped from an aircraft, vessel or marine structure.[408]

359. Without limiting the powers of an authorized officer, an authorized officer may: (a) open a container; (b) carry out searches, inspections, measurements and tests; (c) take samples; (d) require the production of documents, books and records; and (e) photograph or copy anything, in performing his duties under the Ordinance.[409]

360. A person who: (a) intentionally obstructs the Authority or an authorized officer in the performance of his functions under the Ordinance; (b) fails without reasonable excuse to comply with a requirement made or direction given by the Authority or an authorized officer in the performance of his functions under the Ordinance; or (c) in purporting to give information required by the Authority or an authorized officer for the performance of his functions under the Ordinance: (i) makes a statement which the person knows to be false in a material particular; (ii) recklessly makes a statement which is false in a material particular; or (iii) intentionally fails to disclose a material particular, commits an offence.[410]

H. Offences

361. The Ordinance has created several offences such as: (a) except under and in accordance with a permit, doing anything for which a permit is needed, (b) securing a permit by making false or misleading statements or by withholding material information, (c) failure to comply with a marine pollution abatement notice, (d)

406. *Ibid.*, s. 23.
407. *Ibid.*, s. 15(2).
408. *Ibid.*, s. 15(4).
409. *Ibid.*, s. 18.
410. *Ibid.*, s. 25(7).

obstructing a public officer. These offences generally require some mental element for liability, or are subject to defences. For instance, where the offence is non-compliance with a request for information by a public officer liability attaches if the person makes a statement which he knows to be false in a material particular. In relation to the offence of acting without a permit, it is a defence if the operation was reasonably carried out to secure the safety of an aircraft, vessel or marine structure or to save life. The defence of due diligence applies to all offences under the Ordinance. Section 26 provides as follows: 'A person charged with an offence under this Ordinance has a defence if he proves that he took all reasonable precautions and exercised all due diligence to avoid the commission of the offence.' Without limiting the general nature of that defence, a person establishes the defence if he proves: (a) he acted under instructions from his employer; or (b) he relied on information supplied by another person without reason to believe that the information was false or misleading, and in either case that he took all steps reasonably open to him to ensure that an offence would not be committed.[411] If a person wishes to rely on a defence involving an allegation: (a) that the commission of the offence was due to an act by or omission of another person (other than acting on the instructions of his employer); or (b) that he relied on information supplied by another person, he is not entitled, without leave of the court, to rely on the defence unless seven clear days before the hearing, he has served on the prosecutor a notice giving all information he then had that identifies or assists in identifying the other person.[412]

§9. Shipping and Port Control Ordinance

362. The aim of this Ordinance is to provide for the regulation and control of ports and of vessels in Hong Kong or in the waters of Hong Kong, the regulation and control of repairs and breaking up of vessels, cargo handling on vessels and pollution caused by vessels in the waters of Hong Kong, the regulation for and control of construction or reclamation works in which vessels are used and for other matters affecting vessels, navigation and the safety of vessels at sea (whether within or beyond the waters of Hong Kong).[413]

363. This Ordinance which is primarily aimed at regulation of Hong Kong ports contains a section on pollution of water, namely Part VI. Section 46 makes it an offence to discharge any oil or mixture containing oil into the waters of Hong Kong. It is a defence to prove that the discharge was carried out to: (a) secure the safety of the vessel; (b) prevent damage to the vessel or its cargo; or (c) save life, unless the court is satisfied that the discharge of the oil or mixture containing oil was not necessary for that purpose or was not a reasonable step to take in the circumstances.[414] It is also a defence to prove: (a) that the oil or mixture containing oil escaped in consequence of damage to the vessel and that as soon as practicable after

411. *Ibid.*, s. 26(2).
412. *Ibid.*, s. 26(3).
413. Shipping and Port Control Ordinance Cap 313, Long Title.
414. *Ibid.*, s. 47(1).

the damage occurred all reasonable steps were taken for preventing, or (if it could not be prevented) for stopping or reducing, the escape of the oil or mixture containing oil; or (b) that the oil or mixture containing oil escaped by reason of leakage, that neither the leakage nor any delay in discovering it was due to want of reasonable care, and that as soon as practicable after the escape was discovered all reasonable steps were taken for stopping or reducing it.[415] No offence is committed by, and no obligation arises under section 48 to report a discharge on the part of, any person who makes a discharge or deposit of oil or a mixture containing oil under and in accordance with a licence for the purposes of the Water Pollution Control Ordinance.[416]

§10. Oil Pollution (Land Use and Requisition) Ordinance

364. The aim of this Ordinance is to empower appropriate measures to be taken to prevent, mitigate and repair pollution of and damage to the waters, foreshore and adjoining areas of Hong Kong arising from oil spillage, and for matters incidental thereto and connected therewith.[417]

365. A competent authority and any public officer authorized in that behalf by a competent authority in writing may, if and for so long as it appears to him to be necessary or expedient for a specified purpose: (a) requisition any property, other than land, vessels registered outside Hong Kong and aircraft; (b) give such directions and take such steps as appear to him to be necessary to secure effective use or possession of the requisitioned property; and (c) use and deal with any such property as if he were the owner thereof. All property so requisitioned must as far and as soon as practicable be returned to the owner or person from whom it was requisitioned,[418] subject to the payment of compensation for any damage or loss caused by such requisition as is just having regard to all the circumstances of the case.[419]

366. The owner of a vessel from which any oil is discharged or escapes into the waters of Hong Kong is liable to the government for the costs of all measures taken under the Ordinance or otherwise reasonably taken by the government for a specified purpose in relation to the discharge or escape of oil, including the amount of any compensation reasonably paid for land requisition. The owner of any installation or container, whether on land or in or on water, from which any oil is discharged or escapes into the waters of Hong Kong is liable to the government for the costs of all measures taken under the Ordinance or otherwise reasonably taken by

415. *Ibid.*, s. 47(2).
416. *Ibid.*, s. 48A.
417. Oil Pollution (Land Use and Requisition) Ordinance Cap 247, Long Title.
418. *Ibid.*, s. 6.
419. *Ibid.*, s. 7.

the government for a specified purpose in relation to the discharge or escape of oil, including the amount of any compensation reasonably paid for requisition of property.[420]

§11. Mining Ordinance

367. The Mining Ordinance (Cap 285) contains some relevant provisions. It provides, for instance, that every person who uses water in connection with mining operations, whether for the generation of power or for the removal of mineral substances or for concentrating, milling or otherwise, must make such provision as will ensure that all water so used shall not contain any injurious substance in quantities likely to prove detrimental to human, animal or vegetable life when it leaves the mining area in which it has been so used.[421] The holder of a mining licence must take care not to pollute, or permit to become polluted, any water, or in any way render such water unfit for the purpose for which it is being used.[422] No offence under section 27 or 28 is committed by a person who makes a discharge or deposit under and in accordance with a licence under the Water Pollution Control Ordinance.[423]

§12. The Summary Offences Ordinance

368. The Summary Offences Ordinance (Cap 228) contains some relevant provisions. For instance, section 4(1) provides that any person who without lawful authority or excuse throws or lays, or causes or knowingly permits to be thrown or laid, any carrion, dirt, soil, straw or dung, or any other filth, rubbish or noisome or offensive matter whatsoever … into any well, stream, watercourse, ford or reservoir, or into any drain or sewer; or permits or suffers any such noisome or offensive substance as aforesaid to remain exposed in any drain, sewer or elsewhere, opposite to or in the immediate neighbourhood of his house; or allows any accumulation of filth or offensive substances within the premises occupied by him, or in any manner defiles or pollutes any well, stream or watercourse used by any of the inhabitants of Hong Kong or for the supplying with water of ships resorting thereto.

369. Any person who without lawful authority or excuse deposits or causes or permits to be deposited any litter into the waters of Hong Kong or in any place (not being a place in respect of which management or control is vested in a public officer or public body) from which it is likely that the litter will be swept by the tide into the waters of Hong Kong commits an offence.[424]

420. *Ibid.*, s. 10(1) and (2).
421. The Mining Ordinance Cap 285, s. 28.
422. *Ibid.*, s. 27.
423. *Ibid.*, s. 28A.
424. Summary Offences Ordinance Cap 228, s. 4D.

370. Where such an offence is committed from any vessel, or from any place or premises (not being a place or premises in respect of which management or control is vested in a public officer or public body) the owner or master of the vessel or the proprietor or occupier of the place or premises, or the part thereof from which the offence was committed shall be guilty of an offence. It shall be no defence to a charge against the owner or master of a vessel or the proprietor or occupier of any place or premises that the person who committed the offence has not been prosecuted or that the litter was deposited without his knowledge or consent, but he shall not be convicted if he proves that the commission of the offence was due to an accident or some other cause beyond his control and that he took all reasonable precautions and exercised all due diligence to prevent the commission of the offence.[425]

§13. Country Parks and Special Areas Regulations

371. Country Parks and Special Areas Regulations contain one relevant provision which enacts that any person who wilfully or negligently obstructs or pollutes in any way any stream, water course, pool or body of water, except where he makes a discharge or deposit under and in accordance with a licence under the Water Pollution Control Ordinance, commits an offence.[426]

425. *Ibid.*, s. S4D(2) and (3).
426. Country Parks and Special Areas Regulation Cap 208, sub leg A, Reg 12(1) (b) and (2).

Chapter 3. Waste Management

§1. Introduction

372. Urbanization together with the rise of construction, manufacturing, industrial and commercial activities inevitably leads to production of waste which calls for special control measures. Hong Kong, with its huge population and a rapidly increasing tourist influx, is facing an unmanageable waste disposal problem, accentuated by relentless construction work and increasing use of chemicals and disposable clinical instruments. As in other similarly placed developed countries, Hong Kong has resorted and continues to resort to various methods to control the mountains of waste. Hong Kong government has in recent years taken the lead in waste reduction and management.

373. In 1998 the government published its Waste Reduction Framework Plan setting out various initiates for waste reduction.[427] A review of the plan conducted in 2001 considered that while some progress had been made much remained to be done and set out targets to (i) raise the municipal solid waste (MSW) rate; (ii) raise the domestic waste recovery rate; and (iii) reduce the rate of construction and demolition waste going to landfills. While this plan was being implemented, the government realizing the importance of a comprehensive plan, in 2005 published a Policy Framework for MSW 2005–2014, based on the polluter pays principle through charges on disposal of MSW and producer responsibility schemes. The government implemented the producer responsibility scheme through the Product Eco-Responsibility Ordinance (Cap 603) enacted in 2009. The first charge introduced by this Ordinance is the levy on plastic shopping bags which now applies to all retail outlets. This scheme was extended to waste electrical and electronic equipment (WEET) and construction of a WEET treatment and recycling facility commenced in January 2016.[428] In 2013, the government published the 'Hong Kong Blueprint for Sustainable Use of Resources 2013-2022', which aims at further reducing the rate of MSW. The Environmental Protection Department (EPD) is currently working on legislative scheme to impose charges on MSW, to come into effect in 2019–2020.[429]

374. The two leading measures that Hong Kong relies on are landfills and incineration. Various facilities for collecting, transferring, treating and disposing of a variety of waste types. Since 1989 the EPD has overseen the establishment of a chemical waste treatment centre, three strategic landfills and a network of refuse

427. The contents of this paragraph has been taken mainly from EPD website: http://www.epd.gov.hk/epd/english/environmentinhk/waste/waste_maincontent.html.

428. *See* EPD website on the progress of the scheme as at 1 March 2017. https://www.wastereduction.gov.hk/en/workplace/weee_intro.htm.

429. *See* the discussion paper of 27 March 2017 presented to the Legislative Council. http://www.legco.gov.hk/yr16-17/english/panels/ea/papers/ea20170327cb1-697-1-e.pdf. *See also* 'Hong Kong's proposed household waste charging scheme means "dump less, save more"' South China Morning Post, 31 March 2017 http://www.scmp.com/special-reports/property/topics/weekend-property/article/2083716/hong-kongs-proposed-household-waste.

transfer stations. While the landfills were intended to go out of operation in 2020, the indications are that they will not be phased out for several more years.[430]

375. In order to reduce the weight placed on waste disposal, the Hong Kong government encourages reducing, reusing and recycling waste. It also encourages biological reprocessing of waste. Where waste disposal through landfills is inevitable, the government ensures that new methods are followed to ensure that the landfills are managed to minimize adverse impacts on health and safety of the people, and encourages energy recovery from landfill sites.[431]

376. Wastes that Hong Kong produces may be classified, according to how they may be regulated and disposed of, as follows: municipal waste, food waste, construction waste, chemical waste, clinical waste and special wastes such as livestock waste and radioactive substances. The Waste Disposal Ordinance (Cap 354) provides the legal framework for the disposal and management of these different types of waste. MSW comprises solid waste from households, commercial and industrial sources (excluding construction waste, chemical waste, clinical waste and other special waste). MSW is disposed of at landfills. Food waste, a major constituent of MSW, comprises waste produced during food production, processing, wholesale, retail and preparation, as well as after meal leftovers and expired foods. It is highly degradable which can easily cause odour and hygiene problems. Construction waste includes waste arising from construction work such as construction, renovation, demolition, land excavation and road works. Through waste sorting and separation, inert material is used as fill in reclamation sites, when available. The non-inert portion of the waste still goes to landfills. Chemical waste comprises substances specified under the Waste Disposal (Chemical Waste) (General) Regulation as posing a possible risk to health and/or the environment. Clinical waste consists of waste generated from various healthcare, laboratory and research practices as defined in section 2 and Schedule 8 of the Waste Disposal Ordinance. It should be managed properly so as to minimize danger to public health or risk of pollution to the environment. Special wastes include animal carcasses, livestock waste, radioactive waste, grease trap waste, sewage sludge and waterworks sludge. These wastes need to be treated separately. Arrangements are being developed for the proper treatment and disposal of these wastes, but more time is needed to address community concerns about such facilities.[432]

I. Historical Background to Modern Day Waste Disposal Control

377. In the early years, before the introduction of specifically drafted legislation, waste disposal was controlled by penal legislation. The first waste disposal offence was created by the Summary Offences Ordinance first enacted in 1845 and

430. *See* http://www.epd.gov.hk/epd/english/environmentinhk/waste/waste_maincontent.html.
431. *See* http://www.epd.gov.hk/epd/english/environmentinhk/waste/waste_maincontent.html.
432. *See* http://www.epd.gov.hk/epd/english/environmentinhk/waste/waste_maincontent.html.

currently appears as section 4 in re-enactment of the Ordinance in 1932, which described the punishable offence as follows:

> Any person who without lawful authority or excuse (1) throws or lays, or causes or knowingly permits to be thrown or laid, any carrion, dirt, soil, straw or dung, or any other filth, rubbish or noisome or offensive matter whatsoever, on any public place, or on any Government property unless with the consent of a public officer, or on any private property unless with the consent of the owner and of the occupier (if any) of such private property; or into any well, stream, watercourse, ford or reservoir, or into any drain or sewer; or permits or suffers any such noisome or offensive substance as aforesaid to remain exposed in any drain, sewer or elsewhere, opposite to or in the immediate neighbourhood of his house; or allows any accumulation of filth or offensive substances within the premises occupied by him, or in any manner defiles or pollutes any well, stream or watercourse used by any of the inhabitants of Hong Kong or for the supplying with water of ships resorting thereto.

378. Section 4D(1) of the Summary Offences Ordinance dealt with disposal of waste into waters of Hong Kong:

> Any person who without lawful authority or excuse deposits or causes or permits to be deposited any litter into the waters of Hong Kong or in any place (not being a place in respect of which management or control is vested in a public officer or public body) from which it is likely that the litter will be swept by the tide into the waters of Hong Kong commits an offence.

379. Section 32(1) of Summary Offences Ordinance provided for remedial action to be taken and to recover costs from the offender:

> It shall be lawful for the Commissioner of Police to require any person whose duty it may be to remove any filth or obstruction, or to do any other matter or thing required to be done by this Ordinance, to do so within a certain time to be then fixed by the said officer, and, in default of such requisition being complied with, the officer shall cause to be removed such filth or obstruction or do or cause to be done such other matter or thing as aforesaid.

380. Provision for collection of waste predates the Waste Disposal Ordinance. The Public Health and Urban Services Ordinance (Cap 132) was the main pre-existing legislation. Sections 16–19 of that Ordinance have now been repealed and incorporated into the Waste Disposal Ordinance.

II. Current Situation

381. Today, the principal legislation dealing with waste management is the Waste Disposal Ordinance, Cap 354, first enacted in 1980. Several other statutes contain provision relating to waste management in specific contexts. For instance,

Dumping at Sea Ordinance (Cap 466) provides for controlled disposal of dredged mud and excavated materials at designated marine disposal sites. The Public Health and Municipal Services Ordinance (Cap 132) makes provision to control discharging of hazardous materials into sewers. Provisions relating to handling and disposal of waste or harmful substances are also found in statutes such as the Dangerous Goods Ordinance (Cap 295), the Radiation Ordinance (Cap 303), the Pharmacy and Poisons Ordinance (Cap 138) and Pesticides Ordinance (Cap 133).

§2. WASTE DISPOSAL ORDINANCE

I. Introduction

382. The objective of the Waste Disposal Ordinance is to provide for the control and regulation of the production, storage, collection and disposal, including the treatment, reprocessing and recycling of waste of any class or description, the licensing and registration of places and persons connected with any such activity, the protection and safety of the public in relation to any such activity and to provide for matters incidental thereto.[433] In respect of disposal of waste, the Ordinance provides a system of licensing for the waste collection and waste disposal facilities, with special provision made for the regulation of the production, storage, transportation and disposal of chemical and clinical waste. It makes special provision for the regulation of livestock keeping and discharge of livestock waste. Provision has also been made to control the import and export of many types of waste such as those containing metal, glass, plastic or paper.[434]

383. The Product Eco Responsibility Ordinance of 2009 (Cap 603) enables the government to control the disposal of various products such as plastic shopping bags, vehicle tyres, electrical and electronic equipment, packaging materials, beverage containers and rechargeable batteries by introducing charging schemes based on the 'polluter pays' principle requiring manufacturers, importers, wholesalers, retailers, consumers or any other parties to share the responsibility for the reduction in the use, or the recovery, recycling or proper disposal, of those products.[435]

II. Policies That Guide Waste Disposal

384. The Waste Disposal Ordinance provides for the preparation by the Secretary for the Environment, after consultation with the Advisory Council on the Environment, of a draft waste disposal plan which is a plan showing: (a) the arrangements made or proposed to be made for the collection and disposal of all

433. Cap 354, Long Title.
434. Schedule 6 of the Ordinance lists the types of waste whose import or export is regulated.
435. Cap 603, s. 2. The first, and the only, such levy was introduced by the Product Eco Responsibility (Plastic Shopping Bags) Regulation in 2009.

solid and semi-solid wastes other than those which may be discharged into the atmosphere as particulates or discharged into water as solids suspended in effluents and such other wastes, or classes of waste, as may be prescribed; and (b) all existing and proposed waste disposal sites and the methods of waste disposal used or to be used at each site.[436]

385. A draft waste disposal plan, once it is prepared by the Secretary for the Environment, is required to go through public consultation and submitted to the Chief Executive in Council for approval.[437] Once adopted, the plan may be revised from time to time.[438] In discharging their duties and functions under this Ordinance, the collection authorities and the waste disposal authorities must have regard to the waste disposal plan.[439] In order to facilitate due observance of the plan, it must be available for public inspection free of charge.[440]

386. As will be shown below in paragraph 391, the waste disposal plan of 1989[441] concerned the disposal of waste and has not been revised or updated. Instead, the government has resorted to adopting non-statutory documents to provide the way forward in waste management, with emphasis on reduction and reuse of waste, in order to decrease the inevitable reliance on waste disposal through incineration, landfills, exporting or dumping at sea. Reference may also be made to the 'A Policy Framework for the Management of Municipal Solid Waste', of 2005 and the Environment Bureau's 2013 framework for managing waste entitled 'Hong Kong: Blueprint for Sustainable Use of Resources 2013-2022', which are discussed below in paragraphs 387–389.

III. Government Strategy for Waste Management

387. The first such non-statutory strategy is the Waste Reduction Framework Plan for 1998–2007. The objectives of this plan were to extend the useful life of strategic landfills; to minimize the amount of waste produced that required disposal; to help conserve non-renewable resources; to increase the waste recycling rate; to identify the true costs of waste management to ensure maximum efficiency and minimum costs of collection, treatment and disposal of wastes; and improve the institutional arrangements.

388. In 2005, the government introduced 'A Policy Framework for the Management of Municipal Solid Waste', which set up three targets: (1) Waste avoidance and minimization – to reduce the amount of MSW generated in Hong Kong by 1% per

436. Cap 354, s. 391.
437. Cap 354, ss 4 and 5.
438. Cap 354, s. 7.
439. Cap 354, s. 8.
440. Cap 354, s. 6(3). Also *see* s. 3(4).
441. The Waste Disposal Plan may be found at: http://www.epd.gov.hk/epd/sites/default/files/epd/english/environmentinhk/waste/prob_solutions/files/WDP.pdf.

annum up to the year 2014; (2) Reuse, recovery and recycling – to increase the overall recovery rate of MSW to 45% by 2009 and 50% by 2014; and (3) Bulk reduction and disposal of unavoidable waste – to reduce the total MSW disposed of in landfills to less than 25% by 2014.

389. In May 2013, the Environment Bureau published a framework for managing waste entitled 'Hong Kong: Blueprint for Sustainable Use of Resources 2013-2022'. The Blueprint maps out a comprehensive strategy, targets, policies and action plans for waste management for the coming decade. The Blueprint aims at reducing the per capita disposal of MSW (generally referred to as household waste) by 40% by 2022, primarily by raising an environmental awareness in the community. The government's educational plan will see waste reduction campaigns, such as on food waste reduction and recycling. To discourage disposal of household waste, the government plans to use MSW charging and producer responsibility schemes. The government also plans to greatly improve the waste-related infrastructure, including organic waste treatment facilities, waste-to-energy integrated waste management facilities and landfill extensions. The aim of the government is to ensure that by 2022 waste recycling will account for 55%, reducing the reliance on incineration and landfill disposal to 23% and 22%.[442]

IV. Waste Disposal Plan

390. In 1986, the Hong Kong government published a Waste Disposal Plan, principally aimed at MSW,[443] which set out strategies that it would pursue in order to reduce, recycle or effectively dispose of different types of waste through disposal at sea and at landfills or through incineration.

391. The 1989 waste disposal plan, which according to the Waste Disposal Ordinance, is intended to deal with disposal of waste at waste disposal sites or through marine dumping, was not ever formally revised. Instead, the government has resorted to non-statutory statements to plan and implement waste management strategies concentrating more on the reduction of waste production, resource recovery and improving the disposal methods using the latest technology and methods.

442. Information on environmental initiatives and their periodic assessment by the Hong Kong government provides useful information. The following latest document refers to all relevant past documents: 'Updated background brief on management of municipal solid waste in Hong Kong prepared by the Legislative Council Secretariat (Position as at 21 Mar. 2012)', LC Paper No. CB(1) 1369/11-12(02) which was presented to the Panel on Environmental Affairs at its meeting on 26 March 2012. *See* http://www.legco.gov.hk/yr11-12/english/panels/ea/papers/ea0326cb1-1369-2-e.pdf.

443. Municipal solid waste consists of (1) Domestic solid waste, which comes from households and public areas, including waste collected from residential buildings, litter bins, streets, marine areas and country parks; (2) Commercial solid waste, which comes from shops, restaurants, hotels, offices and markets in private housing estates; and (3) Industrial solid waste, which is generated by all industries, but does not include construction and demolition waste, chemical waste or other special waste. *See* 'Municipal Solid Waste' http://www.gov.hk/en/residents/environment/waste/msw.htm.

V. Regulations

392. Section 33 of the Waste Disposal Ordinance empowers the Chief Executive in Council to make regulations in consultation with the Advisory Council on the Environment to provide for various matters including the precautions to be taken to guard against dangers to public health or risks of pollution arising from waste; the registration of persons producing or causing to be produced any waste, the keeping of a register or registers by the Director for that purpose and the particulars to be entered in any such register or registers; the authorization of any person to provide services for the collection or removal of chemical waste or clinical waste without a licence for that purpose; the collection, removal, transportation, transfer, reception, import or export or disposal, including treatment, reprocessing and recycling of any waste including in particular the equipment to be used, the arrangements to be made and the procedure to be observed in relation to such activities; the storage of any waste, the places, manner and conditions in which it is to be stored; prohibitions against producing or causing to be produced any waste by an unregistered person and the invalidity of the transfer of any registration; different requirements in relation to wastes of different classes or descriptions; the procedure for appeals; and generally carrying into effect the provisions of the Ordinance.

393. A regulation may empower the Director to do several things specified in section 33(1A). He may, for instance, issue any document, in such form as he may determine, to be used in relation to the production, possession, collection, transportation, transfer, reception, import or export or disposal, including treatment, reprocessing or recycling of any waste; require the removal from any place of any waste which in his opinion is a threat to the health or safety of any person or constitutes a risk of pollution to the environment; or grant exemptions, with or without conditions, from the regulations or any specified provision of the regulations.

394. A regulation may provide that a contravention of any regulation, or to knowingly or recklessly provide incorrect or misleading information or omit material particulars or information or knowingly or recklessly certify as correct anything which is incorrect, in relation to any requirement in the regulations, shall be an offence.[444]

395. The following regulations have been made and are currently in force:

- Waste Disposal (Appeal Board) Regulation (sub leg B), which makes supplementary provision for the appeal procedure.
- Waste Disposal (Livestock Waste) Regulations (sub leg A), which makes supplementary provision for the regulation of livestock waste disposal.
- Waste Disposal (Permits, Authorizations and Licences) (Fees) Regulation (sub leg D).
- Waste Disposal (Designated Waste Disposal Facility) Regulation (sub leg L) which makes supplementary provision for waste disposal facilities.

---

444. Cap 354, s. 33(2).

- Waste Disposal (Refuse Transfer Station) Regulation (sub leg M), which makes supplementary provision for transfer stations.
- Waste Disposal (Chemical Waste) (General) Regulation (sub leg C), which makes supplementary provision relating to collection and storage of chemical waste.
- Waste Disposal (Charges for Disposal of Chemical Waste) Regulation (sub leg J).
- Waste Disposal (Charges for Disposal of Construction Waste) Regulation (sub leg N, which makes supplementary provision for the regulation of disposal of construction waste).
- Waste Disposal (Clinical Waste) (General) Regulation (sub leg O) which makes supplementary provision for the regulation of disposal of clinical waste.
- Waste Disposal (Charges for Disposal of Clinical Waste) Regulation (sub leg P).

VI. Codes of Practice and Guidance Notes

396. The Secretary for the Environment may, after consultation with the Advisory Council on the Environment, prepare and revise Codes of Practice giving guidance and directions as to the collection, storage, treatment, transportation and disposal of waste.[445] A failure on the part of any person to observe any such Code of Practice shall not of itself render that person liable to criminal proceedings of any kind but any such failure may, in any proceedings whether civil or criminal and including proceedings for an offence under the Ordinance, be relied upon as tending to establish or to negative any liability which is in question in those proceedings.[446] Several Codes of Practice have been issued such as the Code of Practice on Livestock Management, Code of Practice on the Handling, Transportation and Disposal of Asbestos Waste, Code of Practice on the Operation of Refuse Collection Vehicles and the Code of Practice on Packaging, Labelling and Storage of Chemical Waste.

397. In addition to such statutory Codes of Practice, several non-statutory publications have been published to provide guidance. Such non-statutory guidelines made by the Environmental Protection Department include Guidelines on Litter Bedding Method for the Treatment of Livestock Waste, Guidance Note for Contaminated Land Assessment and Remediation and the Guidelines for the Management of Livestock Waste Arising from Free-Range Poultry Keeping. The EPD has also published several guides such as A Guide to the Registration of Chemical Waste Producers, A Guide to the Registration of Chemical Waste Producers and Practice Guide for Investigation and Remediation of Contaminated Land.

445. Cap 354, s. 35(1).
446. Cap 354, s. 35(2).

§3. The Application of the Ordinance

I. The Impact of the Ordinance on the Government

398. The Waste Disposal Ordinance applies to the Hong Kong Government[447] subject to the following exception: Section 16 which prohibits unauthorized disposal of waste, section 17 which requires notice to be given of prescribed wastes (namely chemical wastes), section 19 which requires information as to waste delivered for disposal and section 20 which relates to movement of waste into and out of Hong Kong[448] shall not have effect to permit proceedings to be taken against, or to impose any criminal liability on, the government or any person who does any act which he is required to do in the course of carrying out his duties in the service of the government.[449]

399. While the public officers are exempt from criminal liability, if any pollution is caused by an act or omission on the part of a public officer, the Ordinance has a system in place to effect remedial measures. Where a contravention of any of the above provisions is brought to the notice of the Director of Environmental Protection he is expected to ensure that such contravention is brought to an end forthwith.[450] If the contravention is not forthwith terminated, the Director is required to report the matter to the Chief Secretary for Administration, who must enquire into the circumstances of the case and, if the contravention is likely to continue or recur, ensure that best practicable steps are taken to terminate the contravention or prevent recurrence.[451]

II. Key Personnel

A. The Chief Executive

400. The Chief Executive participates in waste management policy formulation, in that when a waste disposal plan prepared by the Secretary for the Environment is referred to him, he may approve the draft plan, refuse to approve it or refer it back to the Secretary for further consideration and amendment.[452] The Chief Executive exercises these powers in relation to the waste disposal plan with the agreement of the Executive Council. He has certain powers of a legislative nature: As under other environmental legislations, he has power to make regulations.[453] He also has power

447. Cap 354, s. 36(1).
448. Section 20 was repealed by Ordinance No. 14 of 1995 and its place is taken by Part IVA which now deals with movement of waste into and out of Hong Kong. Arguably the exemption that the government enjoys in relation to s. 20 has to be understood as an exemption from Part IVA of the Ordinance.
449. Cap 354, s. 36(2).
450. Cap 354, s. 36(3).
451. Cap 354, s. 36(4).
452. Cap 354, s. 6.
453. Cap 354, s. 33.

to amend, by notice published in the Gazette, any of the following schedules of the Ordinance, namely Schedule 1 (Livestock Prohibition Areas), Schedule 2 (Livestock Waste Control Areas), Schedule 3 (Enlarged Waste Prohibition/Control Areas), Schedule 4 (Exempt Persons), Schedule 5 (Livestock Waste Restriction Areas), and Schedule 8 (Groups of Clinical Waste).[454] The Chief Executive carries out a supervisory function when he gives directions, generally or in a particular case, to a public officer with respect to the exercise or performance of any powers, functions and duties under the Ordinance.[455] A public officer must comply with any such directions.[456] The Chief Executive exercises some administrative powers such as when he makes appointments to the Appeal Board.

B. The Chief Secretary for Administration

401. The Chief Secretary has two important supervisory functions under the Waste Disposal Ordinance. First, where the Director of Environmental Protection has reported a contravention of sections 16, 17, 19 or 20 of the Ordinance by a public officer, the Chief Secretary must enquire into the circumstances and, if his enquiry shows that such a contravention is continuing or likely to recur, he must ensure that the best practicable steps are taken to terminate the contravention or avoid the recurrence.[457] Second, if a question arises as to who the current members of the Advisory Council on the Environment are, the Chief Secretary must determine such question.[458]

C. The Secretary for the Environment

402. The Secretary for the Environment has three powers of a legislative nature: (1) he has the power to prepare a waste disposal plan to be submitted to the Chief Executive in Council for his approval and to revise it from time to time; (2) he has the power to promulgate Codes of Practice, which he may revise from time to time; (3) he may amend the relevant dates specified in Schedule 1 (Livestock Prohibition Areas), Schedule 2 (Livestock Waste Control Areas), Schedule 5 (Livestock Waste Restriction Areas) and Schedule 9 (application of the Basel Convention relating to transboundary movement and disposal of hazardous waste); and (4) subject to the approval of the Financial Secretary, the Secretary may, by notice published in the Gazette, amend Schedule 12 (privately managed waste disposal facilities).

---

454. Cap 354, s. 37(1).
455. Cap 354, s. 30(1).
456. Cap 354, s. 30(2).
457. Cap 354, s. 36(4).
458. Cap 354, s. 34.

D. *The Waste Disposal Authority*

403. The Director of Environmental Protection is the waste disposal authority.[459] In that capacity, he exercises regulatory and supervisory functions of an administrative nature, some of which are given here. A permit issued by him is required for the import into or export from Hong Kong of any waste of a kind specified in the Seventh Schedule and the Sixth Schedule of the Ordinance. His approval is necessary for keeping livestock in a livestock waste restriction area, and he has the power to seize livestock that is kept without authorization in such an area.[460] He may order taking of remedial or preventive action if there is in his opinion any environmental pollution caused by livestock keeping.[461] He exercises supervisory powers in his capacity as the collection authority in relation to chemical and clinical waste.[462] He is the Waste Disposal Authority in relation to all classes of Waste.[463] He has some powers of a legislative nature: He may specify certain wastes as wastes that belong to Group 6 of Schedule 8[464] and amend the list of pathogens listed in Group 4 of Schedule 8 and Schedules 10 and 11.[465]

E. *The Waste Collection Authority*

404. The Director of Food and Environmental Hygiene is the collection authority in relation to all classes of waste other than chemical and clinical waste, the collection authority for chemical and clinical waste being the Director of Environmental Protection. The collection authority has the responsibility, in relation to classes of waste within his authority, to collect waste and to license waste collectors to carry out collection work on his behalf.[466]

F. *The Appeal Board*

405. The Waste Disposal Ordinance has introduced an Appeal Board to hear appeals as provided for in the Ordinance. For the purpose of constituting an Appeal Board to hear an appeal, the Chief Executive must appoint a Chairman and members of an Appeal Board Panel.[467] The Chairman must be 'qualified in law'[468] meaning that he must be qualified to be appointed as a District Judge.[469] The members

459. Cap 354, s. 2.
460. Cap 354, ss 15AA(1) and 15D.
461. Cap 354, s. 15G.
462. Cap 354, s. 2. In relation to any other waste, collection authority means the Director of Food and Environmental Hygiene and the Director of Environmental Protection.
463. Cap 354, s. 2.
464. Cap 354, s. 37(2).
465. Cap 354, s. 37(2A).
466. Cap 354, ss 9 and 10.
467. Cap 354, s. 25(2) and (4).
468. Cap 354, s. 25(2).
469. Cap 354, s. 25(6).

must be persons who the Chief Executive considers to be suitable for appointment as members of the Appeal Board.[470] While public officers may be appointed to the panel and serve as members of an Appeal Board, at no time should an Appeal Board consist of a majority of public officers.[471] The Chairman and members are appointed for a renewable term of three years.[472] The Chairman decides on how many members should hear an appeal under his chairmanship and appoint the Appeal Board members.

406. A person who is aggrieved by a decision or direction of a public officer or a collection authority or waste disposal authority or the Director given under certain specified provisions of the Waste Disposal Ordinance may appeal to the Appeal Board. Those provisions which are listed in section 24 are:

(1) section 15F (refusing to grant or revocation of written authorization);
(2) section 15G (directions as to livestock waste pollution);
(3) section 17(1) (directions as to disposal of waste);[473]
(4) section 20A(3) and 20B(3) (refusing to issue a permit for the import of waste into or the export of waste from Hong Kong or fixing the conditions of such a permit (including any condition deemed to apply by virtue of section 20D));[474]
(5) section 20C(1)(a) (varying, suspending or revoking a permit); section 20C(1)(b) (revoking the suspension of a permit);
(6) section 20DA(4)(a) (fixing the conditions of an authorization for disposal of imported waste);
(7) section 20DA(4)(b) (refusing to grant an authorization for disposal of imported waste);
(8) sections 21(4) and 21A (refusing to grant a licence); section 23(1) (fixing terms and conditions of licence);
(9) section 23(1) (fixing terms and conditions of a licence);
(10) section 23(3)(a)(i) (imposing new or amended terms or conditions for continuance of licence);
(11) section 23(3)(a)(ii) and 23(3)(b) (cancelling a licence); and
(12) section 23(3)(c) (revoking, amending or adding to a notice).

407. A person who is aggrieved by a decision or direction of the Director may appeal to the Appeal Board, and such appeal must be made within twenty-one days

470. Cap 354, s. 25(4).
471. Cap 354, s. 26(4).
472. Cap 354, s. 25(3) and (4A).
473. However, no appeal lies against: (a) the Director's decision whether or not to accept any waste at a designated waste disposal facility; (b) the Director's decision whether or not a charge is to be imposed in respect of any waste or class of waste accepted for disposal at a waste disposal facility as may be prescribed by regulations made under s. 33. *See* s. 24(1B).
474. Subject to this provision, a person who is aggrieved by a decision or direction of the Director made pursuant to regulations made under s. 33 may also appeal to the Appeal Board established under s. 25.

after the receipt of notice of such decision or direction.[475] Where the decision appealed from imposed new or amended terms or conditions for the continuance of a licence, or cancelled a licence, or revoked, amended or added to a notice, such decision stands suspended until the appeal is disposed of withdrawn or abandoned.[476] An Appeal Board may: (a) receive evidence on oath; (b) admit or take into account any statement, document, information or matter whether or not it would be admissible as evidence in a court of law; and (c) by notice in writing summon any person to appear before it to produce any document or to give evidence.[477] The Chairman may determine any form or matter of practice or procedure in so far as no provision is made therefor in the Ordinance.[478]

408. On any appeal an Appeal Board may confirm, reverse or vary the decision or direction appealed from.[479] Every question before an Appeal Board shall be determined by the opinion of the majority of the Chairman and the members hearing the appeal except a question of law which shall be determined by the Chairman; in the event of an equality of votes the Chairman shall have a casting vote.[480]

§4. Managing Livestock Waste

409. Keeping of Livestock, meaning pigs and poultry (chickens, ducks, geese, pigeons and quail),[481] is regulated mainly by the Waste Disposal Ordinance, supplemented by the Public Health (Animals and Birds) Ordinance which contains provision relating to prevention of disease among animals and birds.[482] The application of the provisions relating to livestock waste in Waste Disposal Ordinance depends on the demarcation of areas where livestock activity takes place, namely livestock prohibition areas, livestock restriction areas and livestock control areas:

– A livestock waste prohibition area is an area where there is an absolute prohibition on keeping livestock except by an exempt person, such as a person managing a slaughterhouse.[483]

475. Cap 354, s. 24(2).
476. Cap 354, s. 24(3).
477. Cap 354, s. 26(5).
478. Cap 354, s. 26(6).
479. Cap 354, s. 26(2).
480. Cap 354, s. 26(3).
481. Cap 354, s. 2.
482. Cap 139.
483. Cap 354, s. 15. Sch. 4 contains a list of exempt persons. In that list are the following representative categories. Any person who owns, leases or manages any abattoir or slaughter house in which livestock is kept; any person who owns, leases or manages any part of any wholesale market or retail market in which livestock is kept; any person who holds a valid licence or permit granted under the Public Health (Animals and Birds) Ordinance (Cap 139) in respect of holding of exhibition of animals or birds; any person who keeps poultry pursuant to a valid exemption permit issued under s. 9A of the Public Health (Animals and Birds) (Licensing of Livestock Keeping) Regulation (Cap 139 sub leg L); any person who owns or manages a school or other educational institution providing kindergarten, primary, secondary, post-secondary or tertiary education in which livestock is kept for the purpose of education.

- A livestock waste restriction area is an area where livestock keeping is restricted to pre-existing livestock keeping. In such areas existing livestock keeping may be continued in compliance with the relevant regulations made under the Waste Disposal Ordinance[484] in relation to the collection, storage, treatment and disposal of livestock waste generated or produced in or on livestock premises.[485]
- A livestock waste control area is an area where a person may keep livestock only if he is licensed under the Public Health (Animals and Birds) (Licensing of Livestock keeping) Regulation (Cap 139 sub leg L) or exempt.[486] The Director may grant a licence only if he is satisfied that it is a pre-existing livestock keeping and that no ex gratia payment has not been made to the livestock keeper for him to cease livestock keeping activities.[487]

A licensed person must comply with regulations in relation to the collection, storage, treatment and disposal of livestock waste generated or produced in or on livestock premises.[488] The Livestock Control Scheme introduced by the Environmental Protection Department in 1987 was amended in 1994 to enable converting of some control areas to prohibition areas and restriction areas so that no new livestock keeping would be permitted there, as a means of phasing our livestock keeping activities.

I. Regulatory Provisions

410. Regulation of livestock waste is mainly through prohibition, restriction or control of livestock keeping in the areas which have been created for these purposes. As shown above, no livestock keeping is permitted in livestock waste prohibition areas and any person who keeps livestock in such an area commits an offence. In livestock waste control areas, it is an offence to keep livestock without a licence or obtaining an exemption. In livestock waste restriction areas, any livestock keeping which existed at the time the Ordinance came into effect is tolerated, in the sense that such livestock keeping may be continued if authorization has been obtained.

411. Where livestock keeping is authorized, licensed or exempted, regulatory provisions relating to livestock waste disposal have to be complied with. These provisions are found in the Waste Disposal Ordinance (Cap 354), Waste Disposal

484. The relevant regulation is Waste Disposal (Livestock Waste) Regulations, Cap 354 (sub leg A).
485. Cap 354, s. 15A.
486. Cap 354, s. 15AA. Exemptions may be granted under the Public Health (Animals and Birds) (Licensing of Livestock keeping) Regulation (Cap 139 sub leg L), s. 9 which provides that the Director may exempt any person from applying for or from holding a licence if he is satisfied that the person keeps or intends to keep livestock solely for the purpose of exhibition. Those listed in Sch. 4 of the Waste Disposal Ordinance are also exempt.
487. Cap 139 sub leg L, reg. 4.
488. Cap 354, s. 15AA(1). The relevant regulation is Waste Disposal (Livestock Waste) Regulations (sub leg A).

(Livestock Waste) Regulations (Cap 354 sub leg A) and the Public Health (Animals and Birds) (Licensing of Livestock Keeping) Regulation (Cap 139, sub leg L).

A. *Waste Disposal (Livestock Waste) Regulations*

412. Waste Disposal (Livestock Waste) Regulations[489] provide that a livestock keeper must ensure that every storage container or storage bag used or intended for use in or on his livestock premises in a livestock waste restriction area or livestock waste control area is properly constructed and in particular is designed to prevent so far as is practicable: (a) the spillage, leakage or escape of any livestock waste contained therein; and (b) any nuisance or annoyance to any person whether arising from odours, insects, vermin or from any other cause in connection with that waste.[490] Similar provision has been made in respect of containers used outside any livestock premises in a livestock waste control area or livestock waste restriction area.[491] It is the duty of the livestock keeper to ensure that such storage containers are kept in good order and repair and free from breaks, cracks, holes or any other defects.[492] Such containers must be used solely for the storage of livestock waste.[493]

413. Where a livestock keeper intends to store in the premises and solid animal waste for use as fertilizer or soil conditioner in landscaping schemes, agriculture, horticulture, forestry or for the production of animal feedstuffs or fishmeal, he must ensure that they are kept in specially constructed enclosures in such manner as not to cause any nuisance or annoyance to any person whether arising from odours, insects, vermin or from any other cause in connection with that waste, until such time as that waste is removed from those premises.[494]

414. Any liquid waste from livestock premises has to be removed from the premises or directed to liquid waste disposal facilities, in compliance with the regulations.[495] Any liquid livestock waste generated or produced in or on livestock premises in a livestock waste control area or livestock waste restriction area and treated in a livestock waste treatment plant situated in or on those premises may be discharged into communal sewer or a water course.[496] Where free-range livestock keeping is practised, the livestock keeper must cause to be constructed permanent and impermeable barriers to prevent the escape of liquid livestock waste from the livestock premises.[497]

---

489. Cap 354 sub leg A.
490. *Ibid.*, reg. 3.
491. *Ibid.*, reg. 4(2).
492. *Ibid.*, reg. 5.
493. *Ibid.*, reg. 6.
494. *Ibid.*, reg. 7.
495. *Ibid.*, reg. 8.
496. *Ibid.*, reg. 8.
497. *Ibid.*, reg. 9A.

415. Failure to comply with any of the provisions regulating the storage and disposal of animal waste is a publishable offence.[498] In any proceedings for an offence in relation to discharge of waste into a communal sewer or a watercourse in contravention of the regulatory provisions, it is a defence for the defendant: (i) that the commission of the offence was due to the breakdown of a livestock waste treatment plant caused by circumstances beyond the control of that person; (ii) that the breakdown was reported to the Director within a period of forty-eight hours; and (iii) that the person charged or any other person under his control took all reasonable measures and exercised all due diligence to repair that plant and to bring it back into operation. In any proceeding for any other offence, it is a defence for the defendant: (i) that the commission of the offence was due to some cause beyond his control; and (ii) that he took all reasonable precautions and exercised all due diligence to avoid the commission of such an offence by himself or any other person under his control.[499]

B. Public Health (Animals and Birds) (Licensing of Livestock Keeping) Regulation

416. Public Health (Animals and Birds) (Licensing of Livestock Keeping) Regulation[500] provides as follows: No person shall keep livestock in or on any premises within a livestock waste control area unless he is an exempt person or has been exempted under section 9; or he does so under and in accordance with a licence issued by the Director. Any person who contravenes this provision commits a punishable offence.[501] Upon application, the Director may grant a licence to the applicant to keep livestock in or on premises in respect of which the licence is granted within a livestock waste restriction area or a livestock waste control area.[502] *Lin Kai Yuen v Director of Agriculture Fisheries and Conservation*[503] concerned a judicial review application challenging the refusal of the Director to grant the applicant a livestock keeping licence for the purpose of keeping more than 20 racing pigeons in his premises. The Public Health (Animals and Birds) (Licensing of Livestock Keeping) Regulation (Cap 139L) prohibits the keeping of livestock in or on any premises within a 'livestock restriction area' unless he holds a licence for the purpose. The refusal of the Director was on the following grounds: (1) because of the serious threat of avian influenza paused by poultry farms, it is the established policy of the government not to grant any new applications, and the applicant has not shown that a departure from such policy was justified in the present case; and (2) the application did not satisfy the standard licensing conditions. Regulation 4(2) provides that the Director shall not grant a licence unless the applicant is able to

498. *Ibid.*, reg. 10.
499. *Ibid.*, reg. 11.
500. Cap 139 sub leg L.
501. *Ibid.*, reg. 3.
502. *Ibid.*, reg. 4.
503. [2011] HKEC 231.

satisfy two statutory requirements, which the applicant had failed to do. It was held that the Director has no discretionary power to grant a licence if all the statutory requirements are satisfied.

II. Enforcement

A. Notification of Livestock Waste Pollution

417. Where in the opinion of the Director, pollution to the environment by livestock waste generated or produced in or on livestock premises exists or is imminent, the Director may notify in writing the livestock keeper of the livestock premises of the existence or imminence of such pollution. The Director may, in such a notice, direct the livestock keeper to do any of the following in a specified period: (a) comply with any standard or limit contained in any relevant Code of Practice; (b) cease the use of or remove any plant, machinery, vehicle, or equipment which in the opinion of the Director is used in an improper manner or improper for the collection, storage, treatment, transportation or disposal of waste, and to implement any remedial measures as may be specified in the notice; (c) restore the proper operation of any plant, machinery, vehicle, equipment or process for the collection, storage, treatment, transportation or disposal of waste, or maintain such plant, machinery, vehicle or equipment, in a proper manner as specified in the notice; (d) acquire and use proper and sufficient plant, machinery, vehicles or equipment for the collection, storage, treatment, transportation or disposal of waste as specified in the notice; (e) cease any procedure used for the collection, storage, treatment, transportation or disposal of waste as specified in the notice; and (f) take such other appropriate measures for the purpose of preventing or mitigating pollution as are specified in the notice.[504] Any person who without reasonable excuse fails to comply with the directions of such a notice commits a punishable offence.[505]

B. Power to Seize Unauthorized Livestock

418. The Director of Environmental Protection has the power to clear any livestock keeping in contravention of the regulatory provisions of the Waste Disposal Ordinance. The Director may seize, detain and dispose of any livestock that he has reasonable cause to suspect is being kept in contravention of section 15 (keeping livestock in a livestock prohibition area), 15A (keeping livestock in a livestock waste control area without complying with the provisions in relation to collection, storage, treatment and disposal of livestock waste generated or produced in or on livestock premises) or 15AA (keeping livestock in a livestock restriction area without authorization or a licence).[506] Where livestock is seized under subsection (1), the livestock may be sold by the Director, whether or not any person is prosecuted

504. Waste Disposal Ordinance (Cap 354) s. 15G.
505. *Ibid.*
506. *Ibid.*, s. 15D.

for, or convicted of, an offence under section 15, 15A or 15AA.[507] The Director must, after deducting the costs of sale, pay the proceeds of such sale to the person who owns such livestock.[508] Where livestock so seized is of no commercial value or the sale of the livestock is for any reason not considered by the Director to be practicable, the Director may order the livestock to be destroyed or otherwise disposed of.[509]

419. Where the livestock keeping that the Director wishes to seize is in a livestock restriction area, he may not exercise the power of seizure without a warrant issued by a magistrate. A magistrate may issue a warrant to the Director to seize livestock that the Director has reasonable cause to suspect is being kept in contravention of section 15A(1) or 15AA if the magistrate is satisfied by information on oath that there are reasonable grounds for seizing that livestock.[510]

C. Compensation for Seizure of Livestock

420. Where any livestock is seized in respect of an alleged contravention of section 15A(1) or 15AA and no person is subsequently convicted of an offence under that section in relation to that livestock, the livestock keeper is entitled to compensation. Similarly, if the Director seizes livestock in a livestock restriction area without a warrant, the livestock owner may obtain compensation.[511] The right to compensation exists even where the Director has returned the seized livestock to the owner. An application for compensation must be made to the District Court or the Court of First Instance. An award of compensation by the court must be an award of such sum, if any, as is just and equitable in all the circumstances of the case, including the conduct and comparative blameworthiness of: (a) the owner of the livestock; (b) the livestock keeper (other than the owner); (c) the person in charge of the livestock premises in or on which the livestock was kept at the time of seizure; and (d) the Director and any authorized officers concerned.[512]

D. Prosecutions and Court-Ordered Forfeitures

421. A person who fails to comply with any relevant statutory provision may be prosecuted, if non-compliance has been made an offence. A court which convicts any person of an offence under section 15, 15A or 15AA may, in addition to any other order that it makes, order the forfeiture of any livestock in respect of which the offence is committed.[513]

507. *Ibid.*, s. 15D(2).
508. *Ibid.*, s. 15D(3).
509. *Ibid.*, s. 15D(4).
510. *Ibid.*, s. 15E.
511. *Ibid.*, s. 15B.
512. *Ibid.*
513. *Ibid.*, s. 15C.

§5. Waste Collection and Waste Disposal Licences

I. Licensing

A. Application for a Licence

422. A person who wishes to apply for a waste collection licence or a waste disposal licence must apply to the collection authority or the disposal authority.[514] The waste disposal authority for all classes of waste is the Director of Environmental Protection. The collection authority for chemical and clinical wastes is the Director of Environmental Protection, while the collection authority for wastes other than chemical wastes is the Director of Food and Hygiene.

B. Determination of a Licence Application

423. The licensing authority may either grant or refuse to grant a licence. If he refuses to grant a licence, the licensing authority shall within thirty days of such refusal notify the applicant in writing of his refusal and shall inform him of his reasons therefor. The licensing authority shall not grant a collection or disposal licence where he considers that, notwithstanding any terms and conditions that might be included in a licence:

(a) the waste collection or disposal operation will not be able to achieve all the limits, and requirements, and quality standards and quality objectives prescribed in the Air Pollution Control Ordinance (Cap 311); the Water Pollution Control Ordinance (Cap 358); and the Noise Control Ordinance (Cap 400); or
(b) any emission or discharge arising from the waste collection or disposal operation would be, or would be likely to be, a danger to public health, a source of pollution to the environment or a source of nuisance to the neighbouring area.

C. Imposition of Terms and Conditions on a Licence

424. A licence may be issued for such period and may be subject to such terms and conditions as the licensing authority thinks fit. Without limiting the general nature of the terms and conditions which the Authority may include in a waste collection licence, he may include terms and conditions relating to the matters set out in Schedule 10.[515] The matters listed in Schedule 10 include: the types, quantities and sources of waste which may be collected or received; the places, or facilities provided by the collection authority or the waste disposal authority, to which waste may be delivered for repackaging, storage, recovery, disposal or export, and times or periods at or during which waste may be so delivered; the methods of temporary

514. *Ibid.*, s. 21(1).
515. *Ibid.*, s. 23(1A).

storage of waste if it cannot be delivered to the waste disposal facility within the specified time limit; and precautions to be taken to prevent the release of any substance that may cause air pollution or land or water contamination.

425. Without limiting the general nature of the terms and conditions which the Authority may include in a waste disposal licence, he may include terms and conditions relating to the matters set out in Schedule 11.[516] The matters set out in Schedule 11 include: the management and maintenance of the site and its surrounding areas and associated structures, communication equipment and facilities on the site; the places, times or periods at or during which the emission of air pollutants may take place or the discharge or deposit of matters may be made; the rate of discharge or deposit of any pollutants, or any constituent of the pollutants, into the air, the waters, a public sewer or public drain or the total amount in relation to the matter discharged or deposited.

D. Power to Amend or Cancel a Licence

426. Where a licence is in force and the Authority by whom it was issued considers it necessary in the public interest, the Authority may, by notice in writing, to the holder of the licence impose new or amended terms or conditions subject to the observance of which, as from a specified date, the licence shall continue in force; cancel the licence as from a specified date if the holder fails to observe any such term or condition; cancel the licence as from a specified date; or revoke or amend or add to any notice previously given under this subsection, or any part of such notice.[517] The licensing authority is required to give notice of his intention to amend or revoke a licence enabling the licence holder to make representations.[518] Upon consideration of such representation the Authority may withdraw the notice of amendment or cancellation.[519] The requirement of giving notice to the licence holder does not apply where the licensing authority is of the view that the continuation of the activities to which the licence relates would cause a danger to public health or would be so seriously detrimental to the amenities of the area affected by the activities that the continuation of them ought not to be permitted.[520]

II. Collection and Disposal of Waste

A. Regulating Waste Collection

427. The collection authority may provide services for: (a) the removal and disposal of household waste, street waste, trade waste, livestock waste and animal

516. *Ibid.*, s. 23(1B).
517. *Ibid.*, s. 23(3).
518. *Ibid.*, s. 23(4).
519. *Ibid.*, s. 23(6) and (7).
520. *Ibid.*, s. 23(5).

waste; (b) the cleansing and emptying of pail latrines; (c) the desludging of aqua privies and septic tanks; and (d) the removal and disposal of excretal matter from such latrines, privies and tanks.[521] The collection authority may, by licence, permit any person to provide services for all or any of such matters.[522] It is an offence for anyone, other than a licensed collector, to provide such collection services.[523] However, an occupier of any building, or any person responsible for the management of any building, may remove household waste from any building if the collection authority or any person holding a waste collection licence neglects or fails for a period of forty-eight hours to remove household waste for any building in respect of which the Authority or person provides that service; or no such service for the removal of household waste is provided by a collection authority or a person holding a waste collection licence.[524]

B. Regulating Waste Disposal

428. For the purpose of disposal and management of waste, twenty-five designated waste disposal facilities have been established. They include strategic landfills, refuse transfer facilities, construction waste sorting facilities and special waste facilities such as a chemical waste treatment centre.[525] These facilities may be operated by the government or by private facility operators under contract.[526]

429. The Director may exercise several powers for purposes such as ensuring the safety of all personnel present at any designated waste disposal facility; avoiding any nuisance or any danger to health or the environment arising from the carrying on of any activity in any designated waste disposal facility; preventing disruption to the operation of any designated waste disposal facility or the carrying out of any relevant activity in the designated waste disposal facility; and preventing or deterring the commission of any offence against the Ordinance in or in relation to any designated waste disposal facility.[527]

430. Waste Disposal (Refuse Transfer Stations) Regulation, sub leg M makes provision to facilitate the working of refuse transfer stations. Disposal of waste at refuse transfer stations may be undertaken by registered persons.[528] Applications for registration must be made to the Director. Where the Director is satisfied that the applicant is a fit and proper person to be registered as a registered account-holder of refuse transfer stations and that the vehicle or vehicles specified in his application are suitable for disposing of waste at refuse transfer stations, he may register the

521. *Ibid.*, s. 9.
522. *Ibid.*, s. 10.
523. *Ibid.*, s. 11(1).
524. *Ibid.*, s. 12.
525. *See* Waste Disposal (Designated Waste Disposal Facility) Regulation (Cap 354L) and http://www.epd.gov.hk/epd/english/environmentinhk/waste/prob_solutions/iwdp.html.
526. The Waste Disposal (Designated Waste Disposal Facility) Regulation, Cap 354, sub leg L, s. 2.
527. *Ibid.*, s. 4.
528. Waste Disposal (Refuse Transfer Stations) Regulation (Cap 354, sub leg M), ss 4 and 5.

applicant as a registered account-holder at specified refuse transfer stations, and the vehicle or vehicles as registered in his name. Such registration may be issued subject to such terms and conditions as the Director thinks fit and may from time to time revoke or vary any such term or impose new terms.[529] The Director may revoke any registration, for instance, where he is satisfied that unacceptable waste has been disposed of from a vehicle registered under the name of the registered person at a refuse transfer station or any person has attempted to dispose of unacceptable waste from such vehicle at such station; any damage has been caused to any refuse transfer station by such vehicle or any person involved with such vehicle has attempted to cause any damage to such station; or the continued registration of that person as a registered account-holder is, in the opinion of the Director, prejudicial to the operation of any refuse transfer station.[530]

431. The Ordinance prohibits the use of any land or premises for the disposal of waste without a licence from the Director to use the land or premises for that purpose.[531] Certain disposals of waste are not within this prohibition. These exempted disposals include: the disposal of household waste from a private dwelling if the disposal takes place within the curtilage of that dwelling; the disposal of waste if the land is used for tipping by the Civil Engineering and Development Department or such use is authorized by the Director; and the deposit of any substance (other than chemical waste or clinical waste) which is being used in the course of agricultural or horticultural operations.[532] Unauthorized disposal of waste is a punishable offence.[533]

C. Offences in Respect of Waste Disposal

432. A person commits an offence if he deposits or causes or permits to be deposited waste in any place except with lawful authority or excuse, or except with the permission of any owner or lawful occupier of the place. If waste is deposited from a vehicle that is not being used as a public transport carrier, the following persons are regarded as causing the waste to be deposited: the driver of the vehicle at the time when the waste is deposited from it; and any person employing that driver to drive the vehicle at that time.[534] A person charged with such offence has a defence if he proves that he took all reasonable precautions and exercised all due diligence to avoid the commission of the offence.[535] Without limiting the general nature of the defence, a person may establish the defence if he proves: (a) that he acted under instructions from his employer or that he relied on information supplied

529. *Ibid.*, ss 5 and 6.
530. *Ibid.*, s. 13.
531. Waste Disposal Ordinance (Cap 354), s. 16(1).
532. *Ibid.*, s. 16(2).
533. *Ibid.*, s. 16(3).
534. *Ibid.*, s. 16A(1).
535. *Ibid.*, s. 16A(3).

by another person and had no reason to believe that the information was false or misleading; and (b) that in either case he had no reason to believe that an offence would be committed.[536]

It is an offence to deposit or cause to deposit construction waste on private land without the valid permission of the sole owner or of all the owners of the land. Such permission is valid only if it is given in a form prescribed by the Director for that purpose under section 16C(2)(a) which bears an acknowledgement by the Director.[537] The Director may affix an acknowledgement on the form only if it is submitted to him 21 days before the planned activity. The form must be completed by the applicant with the requisite information. Before affixing the acknowledgement, the Director must be satisfied that the form is signed by all the owners and that they are in fact the owners of the land. The person who deposits construction waste on a private lot must, at all times during the depositing activity, display in a conspicuous place on the land a copy of the acknowledgement form. *Lucien Masset v Secretary for Justice (for Director of Environmental Protection)*[538] is a case where an environmental activist challenged the decision of the Director to affix the acknowledgement on a form in connection with depositing construction waste on private land situate within a coastal protection area and close to an area of rich biodiversity and natural beauty. The applicant argued that the Director who had received comments from the relevant departments suggesting that the proposed depositing of construction waste was not in line with the planning intention for the area and other environmental considerations, should have exercised his discretion and withheld his approval. The Director submitted that the words 'may affix' in section 16(3) did not mean that there was any residuary discretionary power if the requirements of that section are satisfied. The judge carefully considered all the relevant material, including a 'Proposal to further enhance the regulation of depositing of abandoned construction and demolition materials on private land', a consultation paper prepared by the Environmental Protection Department in 2010, which led to the amendment of the Waste Disposal Ordinance by adding sections 16B and 16C. The purpose of these two sections was to collect information in advance of such depositing activities, so the relevant government departments could take necessary enforcement action, if need be. Section 16(3)(c) was intended only to ensure that no construction waste is deposited in private land without proper authorization of the landowners.

D. Disposal of Chemical Waste

433. It is an offence for a person to produce or cause to be produced chemical waste unless he is a registered waste producer.[539] The Director of Environmental Protection may maintain a register of chemical waste producers, which should be open for public inspection.[540] Disposal of chemical wastes may be undertaken only

536. *Ibid.*, s. 16A(4).
537. *Ibid.*, s. 16B(3) and (5).
538. [2018] 5 HKLRD 55.
539. Waste Disposal (chemical Waste) (General) Regulation, Cap 354 sub leg C, s. 6(1) and (6).
540. *Ibid.*, s. 7.

by a person who has been licensed for that purpose.[541] A person who intends to dispose of chemical wastes must notify the Director of Environmental Protection about such disposal and where the waste is of a hazardous nature, the Director may give directions to ensure that such disposal will be handled with special care.[542] Failure to give notice of intended disposal of chemical wastes and failure to comply with directions given by the Director are punishable offences.[543]

434. Any waste producer who does not possess a chemical waste disposal licence must deliver the chemical waste to a licensed chemical disposal facility.[544] Storage of chemical wastes, before their disposal, is regulated by the Waste Disposal (Chemical Waste) (General) Regulation.[545] The removal and transportation of chemical must be carried out by a licensed waste collector, who must ensure safe collection, transportation and delivery of such waste.[546] Supplementary guidance is contained in the Code of Practice on Packaging, Labelling and Storage of Chemical Wastes.

435. Statutory provisions relating to disposal of chemical wastes are supplemented by three codes of practice. They are The Code of Practice on the Packaging, Labelling and Storage of Chemical Wastes; the Code of Practice on Handling, Transportation and Disposal of PCB (polychlorinated biphenyls) Waste and the Code of Practice on the Handling, Transportation and Disposal of Asbestos Waste.

E. Disposal of Clinical Waste

436. The Waste Disposal Ordinance provides that clinical waste collection and disposal must be carried out by licensed collectors and disposal facility operators. It also provides for the setting up of a clinical waste treatment centre.[547] Clinical waste may be collected only by a licensed waste collector, who is authorized to remove clinical waste.[548] Similarly, clinical waste disposal may be carried out only by a person licensed for that purpose.[549]

437. Waste Disposal (Clinical Waste) (General) Regulations supplement the Ordinance with provisions such as those relating to the safe disposal of clinical

541. Waste Disposal Ordinance (Cap 354), s. 21(4) and s. 33 of the Waste Disposal (chemical Waste) (General) Regulation, Cap 354 sub leg C.
542. *Ibid.*, s. 17(1) and (2).
543. *Ibid.*, s. 17(4).
544. Waste Disposal (Chemical Waste) (General) Regulation, s. 8(1).
545. *Ibid.*, ss 9–11.
546. *Ibid.*, ss 21, 22–28.
547. Clinical waste means waste from medical premises or laboratories that have potential to cause disease: Waste Disposal Ordinance, Cap 354, s. 2.
548. Waste Disposal Ordinance, Cap 354, s. 10(5).
549. *Ibid.*, s. 21, 21A.

waste, removal of improperly stored clinical waste by the Director of Environmental Protection, and removal of clinical waste in an emergency otherwise than by a licence holder.[550]

III. Import and Export of Waste

438. Waste may be imported into or exported from Hong Kong only as permitted by the Director of Environmental Protection. A permit to import or export waste is required for wastes specified in the Sixth and Seventh Schedules. However, any waste described in the Sixth Schedule may be imported or exported without a permit where such waste is uncontaminated and is imported or exported for the purpose of reprocessing, recycling or recovery operation or the rescue of the waste.[551]

439. In granting a waste import permit, the Director must be satisfied that there is a valid justification for importation of waste and that the waste will be managed in Hong Kong lawfully and in an environmentally sound manner.[552] In granting a waste export permit, the Director must be satisfied that there is a valid reason to export (such as non-availability of suitable disposal facilities), and that the waste will be managed lawfully and in an environmentally sound manner.[553] The Director may impose conditions on a waste import or export permit.[554] He may vary, suspend or revoke a permit in case of a breach of permit.[555] He may issue directions in respect of import and export of waste.[556]

440. It is an offence to import or export waste without a permit.[557] Where a person is convicted of an offence in respect of import or export of any waste, the Director of Environmental Protection may seize and dispose of the waste, or by notice order the exportation of unlawfully imported waste or importation of the unlawfully exported waste, or order the disposal of waste in an environmentally sound manner.[558] Failure to comply with such a notice is a punishable offence. Where a person is convicted of such non-compliance, the Director has the power to seize and dispose of the waste and recover the cost of such operation from the convicted exporter or importer.[559]

---

550. Waste disposal (Clinical Waste) (General) Regulations, Cap 354 sub leg O.
551. Cap 354, s. 20A, 20B.
552. *Ibid.*, s. 20A.
553. *Ibid.*, s. 20B.
554. *Ibid.*, s. 20A(3), 20B(3).
555. *Ibid.*, s. 20C.
556. *Ibid.*, s. 20D.
557. *Ibid.*, s. 20E.
558. *Ibid.*, s. 20F.
559. *Ibid.*

§6. APPEALS

441. A person who is aggrieved by a decision or direction of a public officer, collection authority, a waste disposal authority or the Director of Environmental Protection may appeal to the Appeal Board. The decisions and directions which are appealable have been referred to in paragraph 406 above.

I. Making an Appeal

442. Notice of appeal must be submitted to the Appeal Board within twenty-one days after the person aggrieved has received notice of the decision or direction, with copy to the Authority. The notice must state the grounds of the appeal with sufficient particulars. Any party to the appeal may obtain further particulars or any documents from the other party. Where the Appeal Board is satisfied that the appellant has failed: (1) to serve a copy of the notice of appeal on the Authority; (2) to furnish a statement of particulars to the Authority and the Chairman; or (3) to furnish further particulars without reasonable cause to the Authority, the Appeal Board may dismiss the appeal. Where a party has failed without reasonable justification to comply with a request by the other party to produce a document for inspection, such document is inadmissible in evidence (*see* Waste Disposal (Appeal Board) Regulations, sections 3–6).

II. Appeal Hearing

443. Upon receiving notice of appeal, the Chairman of the Appeal Board must fix the date of appeal hearing as soon as reasonably practicable, giving at least twenty-eight days' notice to the appellant and the Authority. The hearing of the appeal must normally be conducted in public and the parties are entitled to legal representation. If the appellant fails to attend the appeal hearing, the Appeal Board may proceed to hear the appeal or dismiss the appeal, but if there is a reasonable excuse for such absence, the Appeal Board may postpone or adjourn the hearing for such period as it thinks fit. Where the Appeal Board dismisses an appeal for failure of the appellant to appear, the appellant may request the Appeal Board to review that decision, and if the Appeal Board is satisfied that the appellant had a valid reason to absent himself, it may fix a new date for the appeal hearing. The Appeal Board may receive evidence on oath; admit or take into account any statement, document, information or matter whether or not it would be admissible in a court of law; and summon any person to appear before it to produce any document or to give evidence (*see* Waste Disposal Ordinance section 26 and Waste Disposal (Appeal Board) Regulations, sections 7–15).

III. Determination of the Appeal

444. The Appeal Board takes decisions by majority opinion, with the Chairman having a casting vote. Any question of law which will be determined by the Chairman who may refer any question of law to the Court of Appeal by way of case stated. The Chairman may determine any form or matter of practice or procedure in so far as no provision is made there for in the Waste Disposal Ordinance. The Appeal Board may confirm, reverse or vary the decision or direction appealed from (Waste Disposal Ordinance, section 26).

§7. Enforcement

445. We have seen above that the Ordinance relies on criminal prosecutions to prevent breaches of regulatory provisions, such as the requirement of a licence or permit. An important aspect of enforcement is the Director's power to seize and dispose of waste. The Ordinance makes provision to facilitate the effective exercise of such powers by empowering authorized officers to enter and search premises and during such entry to inspect any waste treatment plant and observe any process used in connection with collection, storage, treatment, transportation or disposal of any waste.[560] The waste collection authority and the waste disposal authority may require any person to provide information which may be reasonably required for the exercise of its functions.[561] Failure to comply with a notice requiring information or providing incorrect or misleading information is a punishable offence. Similarly, failure to comply with any requirement made by a collection authority, disposal authority or an authorized officer is a punishable offence. It is an offence to obstruct any such officer in the exercise of their powers.[562]

I. Criminal Offences

446. The offences created by Waste Disposal Ordinance are of varied character. The first category of offences concerns the commission of prohibited acts, such as depositing waste without lawful authority, excuse or landowner's permission,[563] or provision of waste collection services without a licence.[564] The second category of offences deals with failure to comply with a notice, for instance, a notice to remove livestock waste,[565] or failure to comply with a direction, such as a direction to take remedial measures in respect of eminent or existing pollution by livestock waste.[566] The third category of offences relates to failure to provide information or giving

560. *Ibid.*, s. 23C.
561. *Ibid.*, s. 23B.
562. *Ibid.*, s. 23F.
563. Waste Disposal Ordinance, s. 16A(1).
564. *Ibid.*, s. 11.
565. *Ibid.*, s. 13(3).
566. *Ibid.*, s. 15G(6).

misleading information, for instance, failure of a person to give notice as required by law relating to waste in his possession,[567] or giving misleading information to a public officer.[568]

A. *Offences of Absolute Liability*

447. Some offences created by the Waste Disposal Ordinance are silent on any required mental element and do not refer to any defences. They must therefore be treated as offences of absolute liability. Section 11 which prohibits the provision of waste disposal services without a licence and section 15 which prohibits keeping of livestock in a livestock prohibition area are good examples. Section 31 provides as follows: 'In any proceedings for an offence under sections 11, 15, 15A, 15AA, 16, 16A, 17, 18A, 20E or 23 it shall not be necessary for the prosecution to prove that the acts or omissions in question were accompanied by any intention, knowledge or negligence on the part of the defendant as to any element of the offence.' Interestingly the offence created by section 13, namely failure to comply with a notice to remove livestock waste, which makes no reference to a mental element, is not governed by section 31.

B. *Fault-Based Offences*

448. Some offences created by the Waste Disposal Ordinance explicitly refer to the required mental element. For instance, section 20E(1) refers to a person who '(a) makes a statement which he knows to be false in a material particular; or (b) recklessly makes a statement which is false in a material particular, in order to obtain an authorization for disposal of waste' to obtain a permit or authorization. Section 23(2)(b) refers to a person who 'in purported compliance with such a notice, makes any statement to the authority which he knows to be incorrect in a material respect or recklessly makes any statement to the authority which is incorrect in a material respect or knowingly omits any material particular'. Some sections make reference to a higher or objective standard of knowledge. For instance, section 21(8)(B) refers to providing information 'which he knows or reasonably ought to know is false or misleading in such particular'.

449. Some offences provide a mental element by way of absence of lawful authority or excuse. Section 15G(6) refers to 'any person who without reasonable excuse fails to comply with the directions of a notice' to eliminate an eminent or existent pollution by livestock waste. Section 16A (1) provides another example: 'A person commits an offence if he deposits or causes or permits to be deposited waste in any place except with lawful authority or excuse, or except with the permission of any owner or lawful occupier of the place.'

---

567. *Ibid.*, s. 17.
568. *Ibid.*, s. 23B.

C. Defences

450. Section 16A(3) additionally provides the defence of diligence to a person who is charged with an offence under section 16(A)(1): 'A person charged with an offence under subsection (1) has a defence if he proves that he took all reasonable precautions and exercised all due diligence to avoid the commission of the offence.' Section 20G(1) extends the defence of due diligence to offences relating to control of waste into and out of Hong Kong: 'A person charged with an offence under this Part [relating to control of waste into and out of Hong Kong] has a defence if he proves that he took all reasonable precautions and exercised all due diligence to avoid the commission of the offence.' Both sections 16(A) and 20(G) go on to explain the scope of the defence. Section 20G provides as follows:

> Without limiting the general nature of subsection (1), a person establishes the defence under that subsection if he proves (a) that he acted under instructions from his employer; or (b) that he relied on information supplied by another person without reason to believe that the information was false or misleading, and that in either case that he took all steps reasonably open to him to ensure that an offence would not be committed.

451. Another defence that might be available relates to acting out of necessity, tending to exonerate the defendant. Section 18(2) provides:

> A person does not commit an offence under section 16 [unauthorized disposal of waste], 16A [unlawful depositing waste] or 17 [requirement to give notice of possession of prescribed wastes] if he proves that the waste was disposed of in an emergency to avoid danger to the public and as soon as was reasonably practicable he informed the Director thereof in writing.

452. It is a defence for a person to plead that the alleged wrong complied with statutory requirements: What is permitted by law cannot be an offence. Similarly, if the defendant can prove that he acted in accordance with any statutory guidance, directions given by a public officer, or any non-statutory guidance, he would be able to escape liability. While failure to comply with a statutory provision may lead to criminal liability, the failure to comply with statutory or non-statutory guidelines do not necessarily lead to unlawful action. Section 35(2) provides:

> A failure on the part of any person to observe any Code of Practice shall not of itself render that person liable to criminal proceedings of any kind but any such failure may, in any proceedings whether civil or criminal and including proceedings for an offence under this Ordinance, be relied upon as tending to establish or to negative any liability which is in question in those proceedings.

§8. PUBLIC ACCESS TO INFORMATION

453. The Waste Disposal Ordinance does not require a register of information to be maintained for public information. Licence applications do not have to be made public and members of the public have non-statutory right to object to the grant of a licence. While public officers, in the discharge of their duties, may gather information, there is no provision which prohibits them from divulging such information to other persons.

§9. OTHER RELEVANT LEGISLATION

454. Several other ordinances contain provision relating to waste disposal, chief among them being the Dumping at Sea Ordinance, the Shipping and Port Control Ordinance and the Merchant Shipping (Prevention and Control of Pollution) Ordinance.

I. Dumping at Sea Ordinance

455. This Ordinance implements the London Convention on the Prevention of Marine Pollution by the Dumping of Wastes at Sea. The Director of Environmental Protection may designate any area within Hong Kong waters as a marine dumping area, where no dumping of waste is allowed without a permit. He may issue a permit having regard to the need to protect the marine environment and to prevent interference with other legitimate uses of the sea.[569] The Director may issue a marine pollution abatement notice in respect of marine pollution caused by reclamation or marine construction and such similar activities.[570]

456. The Director has been given enforcement powers, such as powers of entry and search and the power to take remedial action, which he may delegate to authorized officers.[571] Criminal offences have been introduced in order to secure compliance with the Ordinance.[572]

II. Merchant Shipping (Prevention and Control of Pollution) Ordinance

457. The Merchant Shipping (Prevention and Control of Pollution) Ordinance was enacted to prevent and control pollution from ships.[573] The Ordinance seeks to give effect, through regulations made under the Ordinance, to the International Convention for the Prevention of Pollution from Ships and other relevant international

569. Dumping at Sea Ordinance, Cap 466, s. 10.
570. *Ibid.*, s. 12.
571. *Ibid.*, ss 23–26.
572. *Ibid.*, s. 25.
573. Merchant Shipping (Prevention and Control of Pollution) Ordinance (Cap 413), Long Title.

agreements and relating, *inter alia*, to the prevention or control of pollution of the sea or other waters by oil, or any substance other than oil, from ships.[574] The following relevant regulations have been made: the Merchant Shipping (Prevention of Oil Pollution) Regulations (sub leg A); the Merchant Shipping (Control of Pollution by Noxious Liquid Substances in Bulk) Regulations (sub leg B); the Merchant Shipping (Reporting of Pollution Incidents) Regulations (sub leg C); the Merchant Shipping (Safety) (Dangerous Goods and Marine Pollutants) Regulation (sub leg H); the Merchant Shipping (Prevention and Control of Pollution) (Charges for Discharge of Polluting Waste) Regulation (sub leg I); the Merchant Shipping (Prevention of Pollution by Garbage) Regulation (sub leg J).

458. Where an accident has occurred to or in a ship and, in the opinion of the Director of Marine, oil or other substance may cause pollution on a large scale in Hong Kong or in the Hong Kong waters, he may give directions to the owner or master or salvor of the ship for the purpose of preventing or reducing pollution.[575] Failure to comply with such a direction is a punishable offence.[576] Where a fine imposed in proceedings against the owner or master of a ship is not paid at the time ordered by the court or magistrate, the court or magistrate, as the case may be, shall, in addition to any other powers for enforcing payment, have power to direct the amount remaining unpaid to be levied by distress and sale of the ship and its equipment.[577]

III. Radiation Ordinance

459. The Radiation Ordinance was enacted to control the import, export, possession and use of radioactive substances,[578] and has for the purposes of the Ordinance created a Radiation Board, which may in particular: (a) grant or refuse to grant licences and to impose conditions on any licence so granted; (b) to cancel, suspend or renew licences; (c) to handle any other matter which under this Ordinance may be referred to it.[579]

460. The Board may make regulations to provide for, for instance: (a) precautions to be taken to prevent injury being caused by ionizing radiations to the health of persons employed in places where radioactive substances are manufactured, produced, treated, stored, or used, or where irradiating apparatus is used, or of other persons likely to be exposed to harmful radiation; (b) methods of disposing of radioactive waste products from any source whatever; (c) the structural requirements of buildings where any radioactive substance is manufactured, produced, treated, used, or stored, or where irradiating apparatus is used; (d) precautions to be taken to prevent injury being caused by the transport of radioactive substances to the health of

574. *Ibid.*, s. 3(2).
575. *Ibid.*, s. 6.
576. *Ibid.*, s. 8.
577. *Ibid.*, s. 10.
578. Radiation Ordinance (Cap 303), Long Title.
579. *Ibid.*, ss 3 and 4.

persons engaged therein and other persons; and (e) the method of packing any radioactive substance.[580] Two regulations have been made: The Radiation (Control of Radioactive Substances) Regulations (sub leg A) and the Radiation (Control of Irradiating Apparatus) Regulations (sub leg B).

461. Through licensing, the Ordinance provides for the control of manufacture, sale and possession of radioactive substances and irradiating apparatus and for the control of prospecting for and mining radioactive minerals.[581] The Radiation Board has the power to grant, cancel or suspend a licence.[582] The Board may from time to time issue recommendations for protection from radiation hazards for the guidance of licensees and persons engaged in radiation work.[583]

462. The Ordinance has created offences to ensure the compliance with licensing requirements. A person who is proved to have committed an offence under the Ordinance is liable unless he proves that the offence was committed without his knowledge and that he had exercised all due diligence to prevent the commission of the offence.[584] A magistrate may order to be forfeited to the government any radioactive substance or irradiating apparatus in respect of which an offence against the Ordinance has been committed, whether any person has been charged with such offence or not.[585]

463. The Board may appoint inspectors for the purposes of the Ordinance, who have the power to enter and inspect any premises, vehicle, vessel or aircraft in which there is any radioactive substance or irradiating apparatus. Inspectors may take samples, carry out tests, and seize anything that may be linked to an offence under the Ordinance.[586]

IV. Miscellaneous Legislation

464. The Dangerous Goods Ordinance (Cap 295) regulates the storage and removal of dangerous goods. The Dangerous Drugs Ordinance (Cap 134) provides for the authorized disposal of dangerous drugs. The Pharmacy and Poisons Ordinance (Cap 138) provides for the control and disposal of approved medicines and poisons. The Summary Offences Ordinance (Cap 228) creates some littering offences. Regulations made under the Country Parks Ordinance (Cap 208) and the Marine Parks Ordinance (Cap 476) contain provisions to control littering and waste disposal. The Public Health and Municipal Services Ordinance (Cap 132), which we have already seen at the start of this chapter, contains several provisions which are aimed at prohibiting waste disposal. For instance, the Authority may prosecute any

580. *Ibid.*, s. 13.
581. *Ibid.*, ss 7 and 8.
582. *Ibid.*, ss 9 and 10.
583. *Ibid.*, s. 14.
584. *Ibid.*, s. 22(1).
585. *Ibid.*, s. 21(1).
586. *Ibid.*, s. 16.

person who throws any solid matter, mud or waste, or discharges any chemical, oils or trade wastes into public sewers or drains.[587] The Authority may take action to have any waste or litter removed from any place.[588] An important feature of this Ordinance is that it makes use of nuisance abatement notices, with attendant prosecutions for breach. The Ordinance also provides for remedial work to be carried out and costs recovered from the offender.[589]

587. The Public Health and Municipal Services Ordinance (Cap 132), s. 6.
588. *Ibid.*, s. 20.
589. *Ibid.*, ss 127 and 13.

Chapter 4. Noise Control

§1. Introduction

465. Hong Kong being a congested small city state, noise on the streets, in public places and at work place is a matter of considerable environmental concern. In order to appreciate the nature and seriousness of the situation, it will be useful to examine the role of the Environmental Protection Department in alleviating noise pollution. The following account relies on information available on the department's website.[590]

466. Hong Kong's environmental authorities are well aware that traffic noise, which affects more than 1 million people, is the city state's biggest noise problem. Poor land-use planning in the past, leading to cramped residential and commercial developments quite often right along busy high roads, is blamed for much of the present problems. The growth in the economy during the 1980s and 1990s, which accelerated building construction leading to increased vehicular traffic, worsened the situation. No better than street-level noise is excessive noise from building construction sites, ventilation systems and intruder alarm systems. Hong Kong people live in high-rise buildings, and thus neighbourhood noise can be a much more serious problem than in a place where people live in their detached, semi-detached or terraced houses in different degrees of privacy.

467. Noise is a common subject of complaint in Hong Kong, and reducing it has been a priority for the Environmental Protection Department since the department was established in 1986. Controls are imposed on construction noise, noise from commercial and industrial premises and neighbourhood noise, and much effort has gone into preventing noise. Most forms of environmental noise are under statutory control. Legislative controls cover noise from construction activities, commercial and industrial activities, motor vehicle noise, noisy products, and noise from domestic premises and in public places. The Environmental Protection Department seeks to control noise through its participation in planning and policymaking processes and through implementation of noise abatement measures.

I. Traffic Noise

468. The Environmental Protection Department is addressing two sources of traffic noise. One is from new roads and the other, from existing roads. Since 1990, more than 30 km of noise barriers and screens have been erected along new roads, benefiting some 120,000 people.[591] Another measure to control road noise is the use

590. *See* http://www.epd.gov.hk/epd/english/environmentinhk/noise/noise_maincontent.html. Generally, see on the Noise Control Ordinance *Environmental Noise* (Environmental Protection Department). https://www.epd.gov.hk/epd/noise_education/web/ENG_EPD_HTML/m1/index.html.

591. *See*, Environmental Protection Department and Highways Department, *Guidance on Designs of Noise Barriers* (2nd ed , 2003). *See* http://www.epd.gov.hk/epd/english/environmentinhk/noise/

of low-noise surfaces.[592] The Environmental Protection Department also advises on the design of new roads and buildings to reduce noise. As a last resort, insulation may be provided. Noise from existing roads is more difficult to tackle. Some 600 roads generate noise greater than seventy decibels. Noise barriers could be built in some forty identified road sections for implementation under the Public Works Programme. Other solutions are being investigated for the remainder, such as traffic management and alternatives to motor vehicles.

469. The Environmental Protection Department liaises with other government departments during the planning stage of road construction to minimize noise impacts. The alignment of new roads must be in such a way as to minimize exposure of people to traffic noise. An adequate buffer distance between a proposed road and buildings, or where that is impracticable screening structures, such as roadside barriers, is most desirable. Where neither is possible, building insulation may be the last resort. Insulation usually involves upgrading the electrical supply, improving windows and installing new air conditioning units.[593]

II. Construction Noise

470. Construction noise is an important target for noise pollution control. The Environmental Protection Department publishes guidance notes for construction industry, and has adopted technical standards to regulate emission of noise, and issues construction noise permits based on technical standards it has adopted. The enforcement of noise level controls is through the creation of criminal offences of causing prohibited noisy activities or contravening noise control permit.[594]

III. Aircraft and Other Noise

471. Aircraft noise is controlled by the Civil Aviation Department, which monitors the noise and requires quieter practices such as noise abatement procedures during take-off.[595] The problem of aircraft noise was greatly reduced when the airport moved from Kai Tak to Chek Lap Kok in 1998. The Kai Tak airport was surrounded by congested residential development and, according to the Environmental

---

guide_ref/files/barrier_leaflet.pdf. This booklet provides guidelines in the detailed design of roadside noise barriers including vertical & crank-top barriers, semi-enclosures, full enclosures and deck over. These roadside noise barriers are in general termed as Direct Technical Remedies. Their locations, dimensions, types and shapes are normally determined and defined in statutory Environmental Impact Assessment studies or other non-statutory Noise Impact Assessment (NIA) studies, etc. *Ibid.*, '1. Introduction'.

592. *See* Research and Development Division of the Highways Department, *Guidance Notes on Low Noise Road Surfacing* (RD/GN/011C: November 2016, replacing RD/GN/011B of July 2001). *See* https://www.hyd.gov.hk/en/publications_and_publicity/publications/technical_document/guidance_notes/pdf/gn011c.pdf.

593. *See* http://www.epd.gov.hk/epd/english/environmentinhk/noise/prob_solutions/new_road.html.

594. *See* http://www.gov.hk/en/residents/environment/noise/constructionnoise.htm.

595. *See* http://www.cad.gov.hk/english/ac_noise.html.

Protection Department about 380,000 people were affected by the noise, whereas only about 200 people are directly affected by noise from Chek Lap Kok.

472. Factories and commercial operators, such as restaurants, generate noise often from their ventilation systems. Their noise is controlled under the Noise Control Ordinance, as is neighbourhood noise, noise from intruder alarms and noisy products. The regulatory framework also envisages measures to control noise from domestic premises and public places, noise from industrial, commercial trading or business places, etc. Factories and Industrial Undertakings Ordinance makes provision to ensure that workers are not exposed to harmful levels of noise at workplace.

§2. Legislative Framework

473. Noise Control Ordinance[596] is the principal statute which seeks to control noise pollution. Supplementary provision may be found in Industrial Undertakings Ordinance[597] which contains provision relating to noise in factories and industrial undertakings, Road Traffic Ordinance which has provision relating to noise from motor vehicles and the Civil Aviation (Aircraft Noise) Ordinance[598] which relates to noise from aircraft. Provisions in these statutes are supplemented by subsidiary legislation, Technical Memoranda and practice notes.

474. Noise Control Ordinance deals with the following types of noises: (1) noise emanating from domestic premises and public places, which are controlled through creation of criminal offences; (2) noise from construction sites, which are controlled by creation of criminal offences and control through a noise permit system. Certain activities such as use of mechanical equipment are limited to certain hours of the day and any breach of these restrictions is an offence. Construction noise permits play an important part as the Authority is able to prescribe noise levels for a specific construction site, guided by general criteria set out in the relevant Technical Memorandum, failure to comply with a construction permit being an offence; (3) noise from places such as industrial, commercial and business premises is controlled through the service and enforcement of noise abatement notices.

475. The Ordinance also makes provision relating to the following: (1) noise emission from intruder alarms, which is controlled through the creation of criminal offences; (2) noise from handheld percussive breakers and air compressors, which are controlled through regulation of their importation, manufacture, supply and sale supported by creation of criminal offences.

476. Factories and Industrial Undertakings Ordinance (Cap 59) provides for the control of workplace noise as a matter of health and safety measure. The Ordinance

596. Cap 400.
597. Cap 59.
598. Cap 312.

together with its specialized regulation provides for protective and preventive measures against workmen's exposure to harmful noise levels. Compliance with these requirements is enforced through criminal prosecutions.

477. Civil Aviation (Aircraft Noise) Ordinance (Cap 312) makes provision for the control of noise emanating from aircraft. To enforce the requirements of the Ordinance, the Director of Aviation has been given the power to prohibit aircraft which fail to comply with the requirements of the Ordinance from landing in Hong Kong, or to limit the number of times it may land in or take-off from an airport in Hong Kong.

478. Noise from motor vehicles is controlled by the Air Pollution Control Ordinance as well as the Road Traffic Ordinance. The control of vehicle noise emissions is accomplished through the imposition of acceptable noise standards. Vehicles that do not conform to the specified standards are not permitted to be imported to Hong Kong.

479. Just as other environmental statutes, the Noise Control Ordinance provides for appeals to an Appeal Board and confers powers of enforcement on public officers. Provision is made for public access to information counterbalanced by the need to respect confidentiality of sensitive information.

§3. Noise Control Ordinance

480. The Noise Control Ordinance which was enacted in 1988 provides for the prevention, minimizing and abatement of noise; the appointment of a Noise Control Authority; the powers and duties of the Noise Control Authority relating to the control of noise; the creation of offences; and for connected purposes.[599]

I. Legislative Framework

481. Part II of the Ordinance deals with noisy activities and is aimed at: (i) general neighbourhood noise emanating from domestic premises and in public places (ii) noise generated by construction work and (iii) noise from places not covered by (i) and (ii), such as restaurants, shops and schools. Part II also contains provision relating to noise from intruder alarms.

482. General neighbourhood noises are controlled solely through the creation of criminal offences. Noise from construction sites is regulated through construction noise permits, with the power given to the Authority to cancel or vary a permit. There is provision for criminal prosecution for contravention of permits. Noises from places other than domestic premises, public places and construction sites are controlled principally through noise abatement notices, failure to comply with

599. Noise Control Ordinance (Cap 400), Long Title.

which is a criminal offence. Intruder alarm systems have to comply with some noise control requirements. Failure to comply with such requirements is a criminal offence.

483. Part III of the Noise Control Ordinance deals with prescribed noisy products, namely air compressors and handheld percussive breakers and aims to control the importation, manufacturer, sale or use of such noisy products. Noisy products are controlled through a system of noise labelling. Importation, manufacture or sale of unlabelled products is a criminal offence.

484. Section 27 of the Noise Control Ordinance provides that regulations made under that statutory provision may deal with the control of noise emissions from motor vehicles.[600] These regulations rely on prescribed emission standards.

A. Regulations

485. The Secretary for the Environment has the power to make regulations in consultation with the Advisory Council on the Environment. Regulations may prescribe anything required or permitted to be prescribed under the Ordinance; regulate appeals and the practice and procedure of the Appeal Board; generally, provide for the better carrying into effect of the provisions and purposes of the Ordinance.[601] The following regulations have been made: Noise Control (General) Regulation,[602] Noise Control (Appeal Board) Regulation,[603] Noise Control (Air Compressors) Regulation,[604] Noise Control (Handheld Percussive Breakers) Regulation,[605] Noise Control (Construction Work) Regulation,[606] and Noise Control (Motor Vehicles) Regulation.[607]

B. Technical Memoranda

486. Technical Memoranda are made by the Secretary for the Environment and are subjected to a negative resolution procedure in the Legislative Council. Technical Memoranda may be made to operate in relation to regulation of: (1) noise from construction sites through noise permits and (2) noise from places other than construction sites, domestic premises and public places through noise abatement notices.

600. *Ibid.*, s. 27(3A).
601. *Ibid.*, s. 27(1).
602. Cap 400, sub leg A.
603. Cap 400, sub leg B.
604. Cap 400, sub leg C.
605. Cap 400, sub leg D.
606. Cap 400, sub leg G.
607. Cap 400, sub leg I.

487. Technical Memoranda in relation to construction sites are intended to set out principles, procedures, guidelines, standards and limits for: (a) the prediction, measurement and assessment of noise emanating from a construction site; (b) the issuing of construction noise permits; (c) the imposition and variation of conditions in relation to construction noise permits; (d) the determination of whether or not the conditions of a construction noise permit are being complied with.[608] Such a Technical Memorandum may set out different principles, procedures, guidelines, standards and limits in respect of different types of percussive device that may be used in percussive piling.[609] The Authority must be guided by the relevant Technical Memoranda when carrying out his functions in respect of noise emanating from a construction site.[610] A Technical Memorandum may require or authorize the Authority, in any particular case, to follow the advice of the Secretary in relation to issuing of noise permits and imposing conditions on the grant of a noise permit.[611]

488. Technical Memoranda relating to noise emanating from places other than domestic premises, public places or construction sites are intended to set out principles, procedures, guidelines, standards and limits for: (a) the measurement and assessment of noise emanating from any place other than domestic premises, a public place or a construction site; (b) the issuing of noise abatement notices in respect of such noise; (c) the determination of whether or not a noise abatement notice is being complied with.[612] The Authority must be guided by such Technical Memoranda when undertaking any measurement or assessment to determine if a noise abatement notice should be served.[613]

489. Four technical memoranda have been issued: (1) The Technical Memorandum on Noise from Construction Work in Designated Areas; (2) The Technical Memorandum on Noise from Percussive Piling; (3) The Technical Memorandum on Noise from Construction Sites other than Percussive Piling; and (4) The Technical Memorandum for the Assessment of Noise from Places Other Than Domestic Premises, Public Places or Construction Sites.[614]

C. Codes of Practice

490. The Noise Control Ordinance empowers the Authority to issue Codes of Practice containing such practical guidance as he thinks fit for the purpose of providing industries with good management practice in order that a director or other officer of a corporate body on whom personal liability may be imposed is able to prove in defence that he took reasonable precautions and exercised due diligence to

608. Noise Control Ordinance, s. 9(1).
609. *Ibid.*, s. 9(1A).
610. *Ibid.*, s. 9(2).
611. *Ibid.*, s. 9(1).
612. *Ibid.*, s. 10(1).
613. *Ibid.*, s. 10(2).
614. *See* https://www.epd.gov.hk/epd/english/envir_standards/statutory/esg_stat.html.

prevent the commission of the offence by the body corporate.[615] The Authority may from time to time revise the whole or any part of any such Code of Practice by revoking, varying or adding to its provisions or requirements.[616] A Code of Practice or any revision to a Code of Practice must be published in the Gazette.[617] A Code of Practice or any revision to a Code of Practice commences at the beginning of the day on which it is published.[618] Two codes of practice have been issued. They are: 'Code of Practice on Good Management Practice to Prevent Violation of the Noise Control Ordinance (for Construction Industry)' and 'Code of Practice on Good Management Practice to Prevent Violation of the Noise Control Ordinance (for Industrial/Commercial Operations)'.[619]

D. Non-statutory Guidance

491. Several non-statutory practice notes have been issued, including 'Good Practices on Noise Abatement for Karaokes, Discos and Bars', 'Good Practices on Pumping System' and 'Good Practices on Ventilation System Noise Control' 'Guidelines on Design of Noise Barriers' and 'Noise Control Guidelines for Cargo Handling Activities'.

§4. Application of the Noise Control Ordinance

I. The Impact of the Ordinance on the Government

492. The Noise Control Ordinance, just as the other environmental statutes, binds the government.[620] Those provisions in the Ordinance relating to criminal liability do not have effect to permit proceedings to be taken against, or to impose any criminal liability on, the government or on any public officer who causes or permits to be made any noise in the course of carrying out his duties in the service of the government.[621] As an alternative to criminal prosecution, an administrative arrangement has been put in place to prevent contraventions of the Ordinance. If it appears to the Authority that any noise is being or has been made in contravention of any section imposing criminal liability by any public officer, in the course of carrying out his duties in the service of the government, the Authority is required to, if the contravention is not forthwith terminated to his satisfaction, report the matter to the Chief Secretary for Administration.[622] On receipt of a report under subsection (3), the Chief Secretary for Administration must enquire into the circumstances and,

615. *Ibid.*, s. 28C(1).
616. *Ibid.*, s. 28C(2).
617. *Ibid.*, s. 28C(3).
618. *Ibid.*, s. 28C(4).
619. *See* https://www.epd.gov.hk/epd/english/envir_standards/statutory/esg_stat.html.
620. Noise Control Ordinance, s. 38(1).
621. *Ibid.*, s. 38(2).
622. *Ibid.*, s. 38(3).

if his enquiry shows that a contravention of such section of the Ordinance is continuing or likely to recur, he must ensure that the best practicable steps are taken to terminate the contravention or avoid the recurrence.[623] The application of the Ordinance has been restricted wholly or partly in certain specified circumstances. They are:

(a) The Ordinance will not apply to any place or activity if so directed by the Chief Executive. Such exemption may be full or partial. The Chief Executive may by order published in the Gazette exempt any area, place, premises or activity from all or any of the provisions of the Ordinance. An exemption order may: (a) be made subject to such conditions or limitations; (b) have effect for such period of time; or (c) have such partial operation, as may be specified in the order.[624]
(b) The Ordinance does not apply to certain specified noises. Nothing in sections 4 and 5 shall apply to noise caused by: (a) a tram; (b) a vehicle of the North-west Railway within the meaning of the Kowloon-Canton Railway Corporation Ordinance (Cap 372); or (c) any other vehicle travelling in a public place, whether or not mechanically propelled, which is constructed or adapted for use on roads.[625] The Ordinance does not apply to noise caused by aircraft,[626] for which special legislation has been enacted.[627]
(c) Provision in section 13 on noise abatement notices applies to the Mass Transit Railway (MTR) Corporation Limited and the Kowloon-Canton Railway Corporation only so far as is practicable and compatible with the discharge of any function or the exercise of any power or duty conferred or imposed upon them according to law.[628]

II. Key Personnel

493. As in other environmental legislation, the key personnel are the Chief Executive, the Chief Secretary for Administration, the Secretary for the Environment, the Authority and the Appeal Board.

623. *Ibid.*, s. 38(4).
624. *Ibid.*, s. 35. Four orders have so far been promulgated. The Noise Control Ordinance (Exemption from s. 6(1) and (2)) (Chek Lap Kok) Order of I June 1997, which was made to exempt construction work relating to reclamation and preparation of land for the construction of Hong Kong's new international airport (Cap 400E); Noise Control Ordinance (Exemption from s. 6(1) and (2)) (Lantau Fixed Crossing) Order of 30 June 1997 to exempt construction work relating to the construction of the Lantau Fixed Crossing (Cap 400 F); the Noise Control Ordinance (Exemption from s. 6(1) and (2)) (Chek Lap Kok Airport) Order of 1 June 1997, which was made to exempt construction work relating to the construction of Hong Kong's new international airport (Cap 400J); and Noise Control Ordinance (Exemption from ss 4, 5 and 13) (Millennium Celebrations) Order of 1999 in connection with the millennium celebrations.
625. Noise Control Ordinance, s. 5A.
626. *Ibid.*, s. 36.
627. Namely, the Civil Aviation (Aircraft Noise) Ordinance, Cap 312. This will be examined later in this chapter. *See* paras 543 to 546 below.
628. Noise Control Ordinance, s. 37.

A. The Chief Executive

494. The Chief Executive has the power to appoint the Noise Control Authority and the members of the Appeal Board, including its Chairman. The Chief Executive in Council has the power to exempt any area, place, premises or activity from all or any of the provisions of this Ordinance. Four Exemption Orders have so far been made. They are Noise Control (Exemption from section 6(1) and (2) Chek Lap Kok Airport) Order,[629] Noise Control (Exemption from section 6(1) and (2) Chek Lap Kok) Order,[630] Noise Control (Exemption from section 6(1) and (2) Lantau Fixed Crossing) Order,[631] Noise Control (Exemption from sections 4, 5 and 13 Millennium Celebrations) Order.[632]

B. The Chief Secretary for Administration

495. The Chief Secretary for Administration has two functions under the Noise Control Ordinance: (1) if a question arises as to who are members of the Advisory Council on the Environment, it will be resolved by him;[633] and (2) if a question arises as to which government department is responsible for a noise emission, it will be resolved by him.[634]

C. The Secretary for the Environment

496. The Secretary for the Environment has several tasks: (1) he establishes designated areas where more stringent controls apply in relation to construction noise. He has specified several highly populated areas as designated areas by promulgating the Noise Control (Construction Work Designated Areas) Notice;[635] (2) he has the power to issue Technical Memoranda; (3) he has the power to make regulations to give effect to the Ordinance; and (4) he may amend the relevant provisions of the Ordinance by way of altering the time that an intruder alarm may sound before automatically stopping.

D. Noise Control Authority

497. The Director of Environmental Protection has been appointed as the Noise Control Authority. He exercises the following important powers: the power to issue

629. Cap 400, sub leg E.
630. Cap 400, sub leg J.
631. Cap 400, sub leg F.
632. Cap 400, sub leg K.
633. Noise Control Ordinance, s. 3C.
634. *Ibid.*, s. 38(6).
635. Cap 400, sub leg L. This notice is now spent.

noise permits, which he may subsequently vary or cancel;[636] the power to issue noise abatement notices, which he may subsequently cancel or amend;[637] the power to certify copies of noise permits and noise abatement notices;[638] the power to order that any noisy product as defined under the Ordinance be tested;[639] the power to issue directions regarding the use of noisy products as prescribed under the Ordinance;[640] and the power of bringing criminal charges under the Ordinance;[641]

E. The Noise Control Appeal Board

498. Appeals lie against: (1) refusal of Authority to issue a construction noise permit, to impose condition on a permit, or to cancel a permit[642] and (2) service of a noise abatement notice or a notice to produce any noisy product for testing.[643]

499. The Chief Executive has the power to appoint a Noise Control Appeal Panel and a Chairman of the Panel.[644] An Appeal Board to hear an appeal will consist of a Chairman, who must be qualified to be appointed a District Judge,[645] and such other number of members as the Chairman may appoint from the panel.[646]

500. In hearing an appeal under this part, the Appeal Board may: (a) receive evidence on oath; (b) admit or take into account any statement, document, information or matter whether or not it would be admissible in a court of law; (c) by notice in writing summon any person to appear before it to produce any document or to give evidence; (d) confirm, reverse or vary the decision or requirement appealed against; and (e) make an award of such sum, if any, in respect of the costs involved in the appeal as is just and equitable in all the circumstances of the case.[647] The Appeal Board may, before an appeal is determined, refer any question of law arising in the appeal to the Court of Appeal for determination by way of case stated. On the hearing of the case, the Court of Appeal may amend the case or order it to be sent back to the Appeal Board for amendment.[648]

501. Elaborate provision has been made regarding the appeal procedure in Noise Control (Appeal Board) Regulations.[649]

636. Noise Control Ordinance, s. 8.
637. *Ibid.*, s. 13.
638. *Ibid.*, s. 34.
639. *Ibid.*, s. 16.
640. *Ibid.*, s. 17A.
641. *Ibid.*, s. 32.
642. *Ibid.*, s. 18.
643. *Ibid.*, s. 19.
644. *Ibid.*, s. 20(4).
645. *Ibid.*, s. 20(2).
646. *Ibid.*, s. 21(1).
647. *Ibid.*, s. 21(6).
648. *Ibid.*, s. 23.
649. Cap 400, sub leg B.

§5. CONTROL OF GENERAL NEIGHBOURHOOD NOISE

502. Sections 4 and 5 deal with noise from public places and domestic premises, commonly referred to as neighbourhood noise. Noise from domestic premises or public places includes noise which is produced in domestic premises by sources such as television sets, air conditioners or dogs, and noise produced in public places by sources such as radios, hawkers or loudspeakers. Where there is a mix of uses in a building such as commercial, residential and industrial, it is only the residential units of such building which are considered 'domestic premises'. Noise from the non-residential parts of such buildings is controlled through noise abatement notices issued under section 13 of the Ordinance.[650]

I. Noise During Night or on General Holidays

503. Section 4 deals with noise during the night or on a general holiday causing annoyance. That section provides as follows: Any person who between the hours of 11.00 pm and 7.00 am or at any time on a general holiday in any domestic premises[651] or public place makes or causes to be made any noise which is a source of annoyance to any person commits an offence. Any person being the owner, tenant, occupier or person in charge of any domestic premises who between the hours of 11.00 pm and 7.00 am or at any time on a general holiday knowingly permits or suffers noise which is a source of annoyance to any person to emanate from those domestic premises commits an offence. Any person who commits an offence under this section is liable to a fine of HKD 10,000.

II. Noise Causing a Nuisance

504. Section 5 deals with certain types of noise in domestic premises or in a public place causing annoyance. It provides as follows: Any person, who at any time in any domestic premises or public place: (a) plays or operates any musical or other instrument, including any record or cassette player or radio or television apparatus; (b) uses any loudspeaker, megaphone, or other device or instrument for magnifying sound; (c) plays any game or engages in any pastime; or (d) carries on a trade or business, the noise of which is a source of annoyance to any person, commits an offence. Any person, who at any time in any domestic premises operates, or causes or permits to be operated, any air conditioning or ventilating system or part thereof, the noise of which is a source of annoyance to any person, commits an offence. Any

650. *See* generally *A Concise Guide to the Noise Control Ordinance*, issued by the Department of Environmental Protection (2006). https://www.epd.gov.hk/epd/sites/default/files/epd/english/environmentinhk/noise/guide_ref/files/CG_E-06n.pdf.

651. *A Concise Guide to the Noise Control Ordinance* clarifies that the term 'domestic premises' applies to individual dwellings or household units and not to an entire building, which may have mixed commercial and residential uses or even industrial activities on lower floors. Noise from the non-residential parts of such buildings is controlled by provisions in section 13 of the Ordinance, which provides for the service and enforcement of noise abatement notices.

person, who at any time in any domestic premises or public place keeps any animal or bird that makes any noise which is a source of annoyance to any person, commits an offence. Any person, who at any time in or near any public place, for the purpose of attracting attention to his goods, wares or trade, makes any noise which is a source of annoyance to any person, commits an offence.

505. Sections 4 and 5 do not apply to noise caused by: (a) a tram; (b) a vehicle of the north-west Railway within the meaning of the Kowloon-Canton Railway Corporation Ordinance (Cap 372); or (c) any other vehicle travelling in a public place, whether or not mechanically propelled, which is constructed or adapted for use on roads.[652]

A. *The Meaning of Annoyance*

506. There are judicial decisions which define the meaning of 'annoyance' in relation to these two sections. The first case *HKSAR v Woo Carrie*[653] was an appeal against a criminal conviction for breach of section 4(1) in relation to playing loud music in the night. Section 4(1) provides as follows: 'Any person who between the hours of 11.00 pm and 7.00 am, or at any time on a general holiday, in any domestic premises or public place makes or causes to be made any noise which is a source of annoyance to any person commits an offence.' The issue on the unsuccessful appeal was whether the playing of loud music caused an annoyance to the complainant. The complainant's evidence was corroborated by two police officers who had arrived on the scene on two different occasions on the same night. The magistrate had considered that the main issue was whether the noise, in the form of music and shouting by the defendant-appellant, was made or caused by the appellant such as to cause annoyance to the complainant. She had also ruled that it was not necessary for the prosecution to lead scientific evidence with reference to noise levels. Deputy Judge Wright agreed that so long as the magistrate was satisfied on the evidence that the defendant was responsible for making noises which caused an annoyance to the complainant, there was no merit in the appeal.

507. This decision finds support in section 2 of the Noise Control Ordinance which defines 'annoyance' as 'annoyance that would not be tolerated by a reasonable person'. *HKSAR v Woo Carrie* was followed in *HKSAR v Chan Oi Chun,*[654] an appeal from under section 5(3) which provides that 'any person who at any time in any domestic premises or public place keeps any animal or bird that makes any noise which is a source of annoyance to any person commits an offence'. There, a case concerning incessant loud barking by a dog in the defendant's premises, the magistrate had identified the relevant issues to be as follows: (a) Did any animal which was kept by anyone make any disturbing noise? (b) Did such noise emanate

652. Noise Control Ordinance, s. 5A.
653. [2005] HKEC 12.
654. [2011] 5 HKLRD 799.

from the defendant-appellant's residence? (c) Did the complainant suffer any annoyance? (d) Was the disturbing noise the source of annoyance to the complainant? and (e) Was the annoyance of such nature and extent that it would not be tolerated by a reasonable person? Louis Tong J at ([32]) agreed with the magistrate and said: 'In my judgment, a reasonable person will find such non-stop barking intolerable. The absence of complaints from other people cannot militate from the fact that the complainant was annoyed by the noises.'

508. *The Concise Guide to the Noise Control Ordinance*, published by the Environmental Protection Department, states that the nature of the noise sources covered by sections 4 and 5 of the Ordinance is such that it is not possible to specify what are acceptable noise levels or noise measurement procedures to be used in assessing the acceptability of the noise. Noise from domestic premises and in public places must be responsively dealt with by the police on a reasonableness approach.[655]

B. Meaning of Annoyance in English Law

509. This approach finds support in English case law. In *Hampstead & Suburban Properties Ltd. v Diomedous,*[656] Megarry J observed that words 'nuisance or annoyance' in a restrictive covenant cannot be said to be uncertain and said: 'I have no doubt that what is a nuisance or annoyance will continue to be determined by the courts according to robust and common-sense standards.'[657] Megarry J referred to the 1888 case of *Tod-Heatley v Benham*[658] where Lindley LJ (at page 96) described annoyance as 'that which annoys, that which raises objections and unpleasant feelings. Anything which raises an objection in the minds of reasonable men may be an annoyance'. Bowen LJ expressed a similar sentiment when he said at page 98:

> 'Annoyance' is a wider term than nuisance, and if you find a thing which reasonably troubles the mind and pleasure, not of a fanciful person or of a skilled person who knows the truth, but of the ordinary sensible English inhabitant of a house – if you find there is anything which disturbs his reasonable peace of mind, that seems to me to be an annoyance, although it may not appear to amount to physical detriment to comfort.

---

655. *A Concise Guide to the Noise Control Ordinance*, issued by the Department of Environmental Protection (2006). http://www.epd.gov.hk/epd/english/environmentinhk/noise/guide_ref/files/CG_E-06n.pdf.
656. [1969] 1 Ch. 248.
657. It has been held in England that a noise which exceeds the prescribed noise levels (in this case night time noise levels recommended by the WHO) may nevertheless not be regarded as a nuisance, if the interference was not unreasonable. Conversely a level of noise which does not breach the prescribed standards might amount to a nuisance if the making of the noise was unreasonable. *See Murdoch v Glacier Metals* [1998] Env LR 732 (CA).
658. (1888) 40 Ch. D 80.

§6. CONTROL OF CONSTRUCTION NOISE

510. Noise from construction sites is controlled through the creation of criminal offences and the issuance of construction noise permits. Certain construction activities are absolutely prohibited, for instance, carrying out percussive piling during restricted hours, namely between 7.00 pm and 7.00 pm and any time during a general holiday. Some construction activities may be carried out with a valid construction noise permit, for instance, carrying out percussive piling outside restricted hours, namely between 7.00 am and 7.00 pm any day not being a general holiday.

I. Construction Noise Permits

511. Certain noisy activities may be carried out in connection with construction work only in accordance with a construction noise permit. They are: carrying out percussive piling between 7.00 am and 7.00 pm on any day (not being a general holiday);[659] use of any powered mechanical equipment, other than for percussive piling, between 7.00 pm and 7.00 am or any time on a general holiday;[660] and carrying out of prescribed construction work (such as hammering or scaffolding work) within designated areas (which are predominantly populated built-up areas) between 7.00 pm and 7.00 am or any time on a general holiday.[661]

A. Applications for Construction Noise Permits

512. An application for a construction noise permit must be made in the appropriate prescribed form[662] and submitted to the Noise Control Authority for determination. In considering an application for a permit, the Authority is guided by any Technical Memorandum in operation and the Authority may refuse to issue a construction noise permit if the issue of a permit would be contrary to any principle, procedure, guideline, standard or limit set out in such Technical Memorandum.[663]

B. The Grant of a Construction Noise Permit

513. Where the Noise Control Authority decides to grant a construction noise permit, he may impose any conditions he thinks fit. Where the Authority issues a construction noise permit, the Authority must serve written notice of that decision on the applicant and, in the case of a permit subject to conditions issued in respect

659. Noise Control Ordinance, s. 6(4).
660. *Ibid.*, s. 6(1).
661. *Ibid.*, s. 6(2).
662. The forms are prescribed in the Noise Control (General) Regulation, Cap 400 sub leg A.
663. Noise Control Ordinance, s. 8(3) and 8(5). The relevant technical memoranda are: The Technical Memorandum on Noise from Percussive Piling, the Technical Memorandum on Noise from Construction Work other than Percussive Piling and the Technical Memorandum on Noise from Construction Work in Designated Areas.

of percussive piling, must adequately state in the notice the reasons for the imposition of those conditions.[664] Where the Authority refuses to issue a construction noise permit, the Authority shall serve written notice of that decision on the applicant and shall adequately state in the notice the reasons for such refusal.[665]

514. A construction noise permit is valid for the period for which it is granted and is renewable.[666] Any grant of extension may be subject to the imposition of new conditions or variation of existing conditions.[667]

C. Amendment, Variation and Cancellation of a Construction Noise Permit

515. The Authority may amend a permit or impose new conditions on it where: (a) a condition of the construction noise permit has been contravened; (b) the construction noise permit was issued in consequence of misleading, false, wrong or incomplete information furnished by the applicant in connection with the application; or (c) except where the construction noise permit is in respect of any percussive piling, the public interest so requires.[668]

516. The Authority may cancel a permit: (a) if the person to whom the construction noise permit was issued requests the cancellation thereof; (b) if the Authority is satisfied that a condition of the construction noise permit has been contravened or the construction noise permit was issued in consequence of misleading, false, wrong or incomplete information furnished by the applicant in connection with the application or except where the construction noise permit is in respect of any percussive piling, the public interest so requires.[669]

D. Appeals Against Adverse Decisions

517. An applicant for a construction noise permit may appeal against an adverse decision only in the following situation: If any person who applies for a construction noise permit under section 8 to carry out percussive piling between the hours of 7.00 am and 7.00 pm on any day, not being a general holiday, is aggrieved:

(a) where the Authority refuses to issue the construction noise permit, by that refusal;
(b) where the Authority issues the construction noise permit subject to any condition, or amends or varies any such condition or imposes a new condition, by that imposition, amendment or variation; or

664. *Ibid.*, s. 8(1) and 8(6).
665. *Ibid.*, s. 8(7).
666. *Ibid.*, s. 8(1), (3) and (5).
667. *Ibid.*, s. 8(9)(c).
668. *Ibid.*, s. 8(10).
669. *Ibid.*, s. 8(11).

(c) where the Authority issues the construction noise permit and subsequently cancels the permit, by that cancellation.[670]

518. No appeal shall be made under this section except on the following grounds:

(a) that the refusal to issue a construction noise permit is not justified by the terms of the Ordinance or the applicable Technical Memoranda;
(b) that the conditions imposed, amended or varied in relation to a construction noise permit are not justified by the terms of the Ordinance or the applicable Technical Memoranda;
(c) that the refusal to issue a construction noise permit or compliance with the conditions imposed in relation to a construction noise permit or the cancellation of a construction noise permit would cause the appellant economic hardship seriously prejudicial to the conduct of his business; or
(d) that the cancellation of a construction noise permit is not justified by the terms of the Ordinance or the applicable Technical Memoranda.

E. *Offence of Contravention of Construction Noise Permit Requirement*

519. It is an offence to carry out any construction activities for which a construction noise permit is required, without a valid permit or in contravention of such a permit.[671] The nature of this offence is discussed below.

II. Criminal Offences

520. Section 6 of the Ordinance identifies four situations where criminal liability may be imposed:

(a) Use of any powered mechanical equipment for the purpose of carrying out any construction work other than percussive piling between the hours of 7.00 pm and 7.00 am, or at any time on a general holiday: (a) in respect of which a construction noise permit is not in force; or (b) otherwise than in accordance with the conditions of a construction noise permit in force in respect thereof.
(b) Carrying out any prescribed construction work[672] within a designated area between the hours of 7.00 pm and 7.00 am, or at any time on a general holiday:

---

670. *Ibid.*, s. 18(1).
671. *Ibid.*, s. 6(1), (2) and (4). *See HKSAR v Hip Hing Construction Co Ltd* [2000] HKEC 1384, an unsuccessful appeal against a criminal conviction for causing construction work to be carried out other than in accordance with a construction noise permit Contrary to s. 6(2B) and s. 6(5).
672. The Schedule of the Noise Control (Construction work) Regulation (sub leg G) sets out 'prescribed construction work' as follows: (1) erection or dismantling of formwork or scaffolding; (2) loading, unloading or handling of rubble, wooden boards, steel bars, wood or scaffolding material; (3) hammering.

(a) in respect of which a construction noise permit is not in force; or (b) otherwise than in accordance with the conditions of a construction noise permit in force in respect thereof.

(c) Carrying out any percussive piling between the hours of 7.00 am and 7.00 pm on any day, not being a general holiday: (a) in respect of which a construction noise permit is not in force; or (b) otherwise than in accordance with the conditions of a construction noise permit in force in respect thereof.

(d) Carrying out any percussive piling person between the hours of 7.00 pm and 7.00 am or at any time on a general holiday.

A. *Categories of Construction Work Offences*

521. These four offences may be placed into three categories depending on whether construction work is 'prescribed work' carried out in a designated area, whether construction work involves percussive piling, and whether construction work is carried out during or outside restricted hours (meaning between 7.00 pm and 7.00 am or at any time during a general holiday), as follows:

(a) percussive piling, which is prohibited during restricted hours and which may be carried out with a construction noise permit outside restricted hours;

(b) use of mechanical equipment (other than percussive piling) which may be carried out any time outside the restricted hours but may be carried out only with a construction noise permit during restricted hours; and

(c) prescribed construction work which may be carried out any time, but may be carried out in a designated area only with a construction noise permit during restricted hours.

B. *Exemptions*

522. The above restrictions on construction work do not affect situations where the owner, tenant or occupier of domestic premises carries out construction work without a construction noise permit thereof provided that: (a) the construction work is performed only by the owner, tenant or occupier, as the case may be; (b) the only powered mechanical equipment used for the construction work is portable and designed for operation while held by hand without any other form of support; and (c) only one item of powered mechanical equipment is in use in the premises at any one time.[673]

673. Noise Control Ordinance, s. 6(6).

C. The Nature of Criminal Liability

523. The offences created by section 6 in relation to construction noise do not refer to any mental element such as 'wilfully', 'negligently' or 'knowingly'. Courts have construed this absence to mean that the legislative intention was to create strict liability offences.[674] These are, however, not offences of absolute liability because a defendant may plead any of the defences enumerated in section 35, including the defence that the offence was caused: (i) in pursuance of the purpose of the prevention of injury to any person or the saving of the life of any person; (ii) in pursuance of the purpose of the prevention of damage to property where the circumstances placing the property in danger of being damaged could not reasonably have been foreseen by the person charged with the offence; or (iii) in pursuance of the purpose of the prevention of serious interruption or disruption to any public transport system where the circumstances which would otherwise cause such an interruption or disruption could not reasonably have been foreseen by the person charged with the offence.[675]

D. Who Can Be Held Liable

524. These offences may be committed by any person 'who carries out, or causes or permits to be carried out' the prohibited acts. In *HKSAR v Paul Y-ITC Construction Ltd,*[676] it was held that the principal contractor in charge of a construction site may be said to have caused an offence under section 6, where the contravention of the Ordinance was carried out by workers employed by a subcontractor. Stuart-Moore JA held that the word 'cause' must be given its ordinary and common-sense meaning and that whether the defendant caused the breach of law was a matter for the magistrate to decide. He said that the defendant-appellant, the principal contractor, 'had the same responsibility as if it had done the work itself. This could not be delegated or the main contractor would always escape liability by contracting out the work to others. The main contractor initiated the work; it was responsible for the whole site and had a financial interest in the work being carried out. It had contracted out the work to other sub-contractors. The workers committed the offences, but the Appellant caused the offences to be committed by employing the sub-contractors, and thereby the workers, to do the work. There was a direct link between the [defendant] and those who were carrying out the work'.[677]

674. *See HKSAR v Paul Y-ITC Construction Ltd* [1998] 2 HKLRD 35, [1998] 3 HKC 189 (CA).

675. On the difference between absolute liability offences and strict liability offences, *see* Anton Cooray, *Environmental Offences,* in *Archbold Hong Kong 2017* (Sweet and Maxwell), Chapter 40. *See* especially, 'the nature of environmental offences' pp. 2211–2214.

676. [1998] 2 HKLRD 35, [1998] 3 HKC 189 (CA).

677. *Ibid.*, [45], per Stuart-Moore, JA.

§7. Noise Other Than Neighbourhood Noise and Construction Noise

525. These provisions deal with noise emanating from places such as industrial, commercial, trade or business premises. Noise from these places is controlled by means of noise abatement notices which may be served on owners or occupiers of premises if the noise emitted: (a) does not comply with objective technical criteria in the form of Acceptable Noise Levels as set out in the Technical Memorandum for the Assessment of Noise from Places other than Domestic Premises, Public Places or Construction Sites; (b) is a source of annoyance to any person (other than a person in the place from which the noise is emanating) in any place considered to be a noise sensitive receiver (NSR);[678] or (c) does not comply with any standard or limit which may be prescribed by Regulation (although so far no regulation has been made for this purpose).[679]

I. Noise Abatement Notices

526. Section 13(1) of the Noise Control Ordinance provides that where the Authority is satisfied that noise is emanating from any place other than domestic premises, a public place or a construction site and that such noise, whether on its own or together with noise emanating from any other place other than domestic premises, a public place or a construction site, is a source of annoyance to any person (other than a person in the place from which the noise is emanating) in any place considered to be a NSR in any Technical Memorandum issued under section 10; does not comply with any standard or limit prescribed for the purposes of this section;[680] or does not comply with any standard or limit contained in Technical Memoranda, the Authority may serve a noise abatement notice in the prescribed form on any or all of the following: the person making the noise or causing or permitting the noise to be made; the owner, tenant, occupier or person in charge of the place from which the noise is emanating.[681] The Authority may, by notice in the prescribed from served on any person on whom a noise abatement notice has been served, cancel the noise abatement notice or vary any requirements therein.[682]

678. The term 'Noise Sensitive Receiver' refers to premises that is used for purposes sensitive to noise and requires protection. Examples of noise sensitive receivers are domestic premises, hotels and hostels, educational institutions and hospitals and clinics. Non-NSRs (or noise tolerant uses) include multistorey car parks and markets, godowns, community uses such as sports complexes and commercial centres or premises. https://www.epd.gov.hk/epd/noise_education/web/ENG_EPD_HTML/m2/types_5.html.

679. *See A Concise Guide to the Noise Control Ordinance* (2006: Environmental Protection Department).

680. Section 13(1)(b) which enables a noise abatement notice to be issued in respect of any noise 'that does not comply with any standard or limit prescribed for this section' is not yet in operation.

681. Cap 400, s. 13(1). *See* for a recent examination of the noise abatement notice procedure *Serge Berthier v Noise Control Appeal Board* [2011] HKCU 1432.

682. Cap 400, s. 13(4).

A. The Relevance of Technical Memoranda

527. The Secretary may issue from time to time Technical Memoranda setting out principles, procedures, guidelines, standards and limits for: (a) the measurement and assessment of noise emanating from any place other than domestic premises, a public place or a construction site; (b) the issuing of noise abatement notices in respect of such noise; (c) the determination of whether or not a noise abatement notice is being complied with.[683] The Authority shall be guided by Technical Memoranda when undertaking any measurement or assessment to determine if a noise abatement notice should be served.[684]

B. Technical Memoranda Are Only for Guidance

528. There may be situations where the Authority will be within its power to prescribe a limit below the tolerable noise limit set out in the Technical Memorandum, if, for instance, the noise emanating from the premises in question together with noise emanating neighbouring sources may exceed the prescribed noise level. In *Secretary for Justice v Tak Yue Restaurant Ltd,*[685] the court upheld the noise level of sixty-two decibels that the Authority had set as the upper noise level, which was below the level prescribed in the Technical Memorandum sixty-five decibels. Hon Leong J said: 'The Notice cannot be invalid by reason only of the Authority in the exercise of its discretion specifying therein noise limits which are more harsh than those specified in the Technical Memorandum. In any case, the acceptable noise levels in the Technical Memorandum are the noise levels registered by a noise sensitive receiver indicating the general level of noise in the area where the NSR is located and that is the aggregate of several noise sources. The noise limits in the Notice are directed to the Respondent's restaurant and … in order to achieve the acceptable noise levels in the area, the individual noise sources which together make up the acceptable noise levels in question, must be more strictly controlled or the purpose cannot be achieved.'

529. In *Noise Control Authority v Step In Ltd,*[686] the Court of Final Appeal decided that the Authority is not restricted to adopting noise levels scientifically fixed but may adopt commonly understood standards such as 'not audible in the night'. Brennan SPJ said: 'Application of the not audible' requirement does not produce a uniform quantifiable measurement but it does produce an objective standard or limit. It forbids the making of a noise which can be heard at the assessment point during the night hours. So construed, the requirement achieves a similar meaning to the meaning which the English Court of Appeal in *Tod-Heatley v Benham* (1889) 40 Ch D 80 at pp. 93–94, attributed to 'annoyance' in a covenant as 'an annoyance to reasonable people'. Once the objectivity of the 'not audible' requirement appears,

683. Noise Control Ordinance, s. 10(1).
684. *Ibid.*, s. 10(2).
685. [1997] HKEC561.
686. [2005] HKCU 407, [2005] 1 HKLRD 702, CFA.

the objection of uncertainty fails. So construed, the requirement is clearly within the power conferred by section 13(2)(a) ['ensure that the noise emanating from such place does not exceed any limit or standard specified in the notice'].[687] The Court of Final Appeal observed at [48]–[49]: 'The principle of legal certainty requires that a law must be sufficiently precise to enable a citizen to foresee, to a degree that is reasonable in the circumstances, the consequences that a given action may entail. The principle of legal certainty is not offended by the terms of the noise abatement notice. The person to whom the noise abatement notice is directed knows precisely what is forbidden, namely, the emission of music and other noise from [the premises] which is audible in the flat above.'

C. What a Noise Abatement Notice May Require to Be Done

530. A noise abatement notice may require the person on whom it is served to abate the noise within the period specified therein[688] and to do all things as may be necessary for that purpose, and may require the person on whom it is served to: (a) ensure that the noise emanating from such place does not exceed any limit or standard specified in the notice; (b) where the noise is emanating from such place by reason of the operation of any plant, machinery, vehicle, equipment or process, ensure that any such plant, machinery, vehicle, equipment or process is operated in accordance with any condition specified in the notice; and (c) notify the Authority in writing within the period specified in the notice that any requirement referred to in paragraph (a) or (b) and specified in the notice has been complied with.[689]

D. Life Span of a Noise Abatement Notice

531. A noise abatement notice or any notice varying a requirement in a noise abatement notice shall not take effect until a date specified in any such notice, being a date not less than 21 days after the day on which the notice is served.[690] The Ordinance requires compliance with the notice within a prescribed period of time in calculating which the Authority must have regard to the nature, difficulty and complexity of complying with any requirement in the noise abatement notice.[691]

687. *Ibid.*, [47].

688. 'In specifying a period … within which noise is to be abated, the Authority shall have regard to the nature, difficulty and complexity of complying with any requirement in the noise abatement notice' (s. 13(2)). Unless the defendant is able to satisfy the court that the Authority did not pay heed to this requirement the court is justified in presuming that there was due compliance: *HKSAR v Hop Shing Loong Lighting Ltd* [1998] HKEC 1134, [7], where it was observed that ' … the maxim *omnia praesumuntur rite et solemniter esse acta donec probetur in contrariam* applies. The prosecution does not have to prove the validity of the notice; it is presumed valid until the contrary is proved'.

689. Noise Control Ordinance, s. 13(2).

690. *Ibid.*, s. 13(5).

691. *Ibid.*, s. 13(3). In *HKSAR v Hop Shing Loong Lighting Ltd* [1998] HKEC 1134, [9] Deputy Judge Muttrie explained how a recipient of notice may challenge the validity of the prescribed period as follows: 'Of course, the recipient of a notice cannot directly appeal [to the Appeal Board] under s.

Any person who, having been served with a noise abatement notice or a notice of variation, fails to comply with any requirement therein commits an offence.[692] Courts have construed section 13 to mean that once the notice has been complied with within that period, the notice ceases to be effective. An abatement notice does not have perpetual validity. If there is any new contravention of permissible noise levels, a new noise abatement notice must be issued.[693]

E. *Failure to Comply with a Noise Abatement Notice*

532. Any person who, having been served with a noise abatement notice, fails to comply with any requirement therein commits an offence.[694] While this offence does not refer to any accompanying mental element that must be established by the prosecution, section 33 sets out certain defences that the defendant may rely on:

> '[i]t shall be a defence to show that the circumstances constituting or leading to the commission of the offence arose':

19 on the ground that the Authority has not complied with s. 13(3). The recipient will not know the matters to which the Authority has or has not had regard. But he can appeal under s. 19(2)(c) on the grounds that the requirements of the notice are unreasonable or unnecessary or under s. 19(2)(d) on the ground that compliance will cause economic hardship seriously prejudicial to the conduct of his business. An appeal on either ground, but particularly the first, would, it seems to me, require the appellate body to consider whether the Authority had complied with s. 13(3). He can also take judicial review proceedings against the Authority and such proceedings would also inevitably entail an inquiry into whether or not the Authority had complied with s. 13(3).' For appeals to the Appeal Board *see* below '§9. Appeals under the Noise Control Ordinance'.

692. *Ibid.*, s. 13(6).

693. *See Secretary for Justice v Poly Gain Enterprises Ltd* [1998] HKEC 1110, [12]-[14], per Yeung: 'It must be remembered that the source of the noise in question was certain ventilating and refrigerating systems which, presumably, when become defective, would create excessive noise. The effect of the notice was to require Poly Gain to rectify such defect within a period which was considered to be appropriate by the authority, having regard to the nature, difficulty and complexity of complying with the requirement in the Noise Abatement Notice – that's under s. 13(3) of the Ordinance. The Ordinance does not require Poly Gain to ensure that the ventilating and refrigerating systems will never become defective again in the future. If it had been the intention of the legislation that requirement under a Noise Abatement Notice should have perpetual validity it would have been spelt out in clearer and more certain terms. As the learned Magistrate had rightly pointed out, the mere creation of excessive noise from places other than domestic premises, public places or construction sites, was not an offence. Under s. 13 of the Ordinance, an offence was committed, not by the creation of the noise but by the failure to comply with the requirement of a Noise Abatement Notice. Is it reasonable that Poly Gain should be held responsible every time there was excessive noise from the ventilating or refrigerating systems just because a Noise Abatement Notice had been served two years, or even twenty years ago when the mere creation of excessive noise is not an offence under the Ordinance? To me, the answer is clear. Quite apart from the wording of the Noise Abatement Notice in question, in my view, once the requirement under the notice had been complied with, the notice will be discharged and will not have any further legal effect. Should it be found that excessive noise are being emanated after such discharge, a fresh notice must be served, and an offence under s. 13 of the Ordinance is committed only when the requirement under the fresh notice has not been complied with.'

694. Noise Control Ordinance, s. 13(6).

a. by reason of the fact of any authorization under any licence, permit or exemption granted under any other Ordinance;
b. in pursuance of the purpose of the prevention of injury to any person or the saving of the life of any person;
c. in pursuance of the purpose of the prevention of damage to property where the circumstances placing the property in danger of being damaged could not reasonably have been foreseen by the person charged with the offence; or
d. in pursuance of the purpose of the prevention of serious interruption or disruption to any public transport system where the circumstances which would otherwise cause such an interruption or disruption could not reasonably have been foreseen by the person charged with the offence.

533. Any person who, having been required to notify the Authority in writing under subsection (2)(c) that any requirement has been complied with, makes or furnishes any statement in so notifying the Authority which to his knowledge is misleading or false in a material particular, commits an offence.[695]

II. Control of Intruder Alarm Systems

534. An intruder alarm system installed in a building must have an efficient automatic system that causes the audible signal to cease not more than fifteen minutes after the activation of the signal. Any person who controls such a system that does not comply with that requirement commits an offence.[696]

535. Where an intruder alarm system is installed in a motor vehicle, the owner of the vehicle must ensure that the system has an efficient automatic device which: (a) shall not emit any audible signal caused otherwise than by an act of direct physical contact with the vehicle; and (b) shall cause any audible signal to cease not more than five minutes after the activation of the signal. Failure to comply with this requirement is an offence [697]

III. Control of Noisy Products

536. Part III of the Ordinance deals with the control of prescribed noisy products, namely handheld percussive breakers and air compressors.[698] Any person who by way of trade or business imports, manufactures or supplies, or offers or exposes for supply, any product prescribed for the purposes of this Part which: (a) is

695. *Ibid.*, s. 13(8).
696. *Ibid.*, s. 13A.
697. *Ibid.*, s. 13B.
698. *See* Noise Control (Handheld Percussive Breakers) Regulations, sub leg D and Noise Control (Air compressors) Regulations, sub leg C.

intended for use in Hong Kong; and (b) when operated under prescribed test conditions emits noise that is not in accordance with any standard prescribed for the purposes of this section, commits an offence.[699]

537. Where it is permissible to import, supply or sell in Hong Kong any prescribed noisy product only if it is fitted or equipped with any prescribed device or prescribed equipment so as to prevent, reduce or minimize the emission of noise or fitted with a prescribed plate, label or other marking relating to noise emission, it is an offence to import, supply or sell such product without complying with such requirements.[700] Where a product is required to be supplied or sold with a plate, label or other marking, it is an offence to supply or sell them if they do not comply with any information stated on any such prescribed plate, label or other marking.[701]

538. Any person who by way of trade or business imports, manufactures or supplies, or offers or exposes for supply, any prescribed product which: (a) is intended for use in Hong Kong; and (b) when tested within the warranty period emits noise that does not comply with any prescribed standards, commits an offence.[702]

539. In order to control the use of prescribed noisy products, the Ordinance target not only those who supply such products but also those who use them: Any person who uses, or causes to be used, any prescribed product which does not comply with any prescribed requirement relating to noise emission commits an offence.[703] Any person who being the owner of any prescribed product which does not comply with any such prescribed requirement relating to noise emission knowingly permits or suffers such product to be used commits an offence.[704]

540. For the purpose of reducing excessive noise emission during usage, the Authority may give a written direction: (a) to any person who uses, or causes to be used, any prescribed product; and (b) requiring that person to use the product in accordance with such directions or instructions in respect of the manner of using the product issued by the manufacturer of the product and referred to in such direction.[705]

541. The Authority has been given the power to inspect and test prescribed products. For this purpose, the Authority may either order the production of goods for testing or inspection or order the owner, importer, manufacturer or supplier to carry

699. Noise Control Ordinance, s. 14(1). The standards are prescribed in the two regulations which are referred to in the immediately preceding footnote.
700. *Ibid.*, s. 14(3).
701. *Ibid.*, s. 14(4).
702. *Ibid.*, s. 15(1).
703. *Ibid.*, s. 17(1).
704. *Ibid.*, s. 17(2). Note under subs. (2) criminal liability may be imposed only if the user had knowledge of the requirements which he failed to observe.
705. *Ibid.*, s. 17A.

out tests or inspections.[706] There is a right of appeal to the Appeal Board against such a direction.[707] Failure to comply with a direction is a criminal offence.[708]

IV. Control of Motor Vehicle Noise

542. The control of noise emissions from motor vehicles is facilitated by Noise Control (Motor Vehicles) Regulation.[709] Regulation 4 provides that every motor vehicle or motorcycle first registered on or after 1 June 2002 must conform to the same noise emission standard as that which applies in relation to motor vehicles or motorcycles situated in the Member States of the European Union (EU) and subject to the laws of the Member States of the EU; or in relation to motor vehicles or motorcycles situated in Japan and subject to the laws of Japan.

V. Control of Aircraft Noise

543. The Civil Aviation (Aircraft Noise) Ordinance aims to control the emission of noise by aircraft.[710] It provides that an aircraft shall not land or take-off in Hong Kong unless there is in force in respect of that aircraft a noise certificate or other equivalent certification.[711] The Director lays down and publishes requirements that landing and taking off aircraft must comply with in order to limit or mitigate the effect of noise or vibration. It is an offence to fail to comply with such requirements, and the Director may order that airport facilities be withheld from any aircraft that fails to comply with the requirements.[712]

544. The Director of Civil Aviation may give to an airport manager such directions as he considers appropriate for the purpose of avoiding, limiting or mitigating the effect of noise and vibration connected with the taking off or landing of aircraft at the aerodrome and it is the duty of the airport manager to comply with the directions.[713]

545. If the Director of Civil Aviation considers it appropriate, for the purpose of avoiding, limiting or mitigating the effect of noise and vibration connected with the taking off or landing of aircraft at an aerodrome, to prohibit aircraft from taking off or landing, or to limit the number of occasions on which they may take-off or land, at an aerodrome during certain periods, he may by notice in the Gazette prohibit aircraft of descriptions specified in the notice from taking off or landing at the aerodrome (otherwise than in an emergency) during periods so specified; specify the

706. *Ibid.*, s. 16(1).
707. *Ibid.*, s. 19.
708. *Ibid.*, s. 16(6).
709. Cap 400, sub leg I.
710. The Civil Aviation (Aircraft Noise) Ordinance, Cap 312, s. 2.
711. *Ibid.*, s. 3.
712. *Ibid.*, s. 5.
713. *Ibid.*, s. 7.

maximum number of occasions on which aircraft of descriptions so specified may be permitted to take-off or land at the aerodrome (otherwise than in an emergency) during periods so specified.[714]

546. The Director may order the detention of any aircraft which is about to take-off in contravention of any restriction placed under the Civil Aviation (Aircraft Noise) Ordinance. There is provision for the Chief Executive to make regulations for several specified purposes and generally for restricting or mitigating aircraft noise and vibration. Currently no regulations are in operation.

§8. Noise in Factories and Industrial Undertakings

547. Factories and Industrial Undertakings Ordinance (Cap 59) provides that it is the duty of every proprietor of an industrial undertaking to ensure, so far as is reasonably practicable, the health and safety at work of all persons employed by him at the industrial undertaking.[715] This general duty includes the duty to provide and maintain plant and systems of work that are, so far as is reasonably practicable, safe and without risks to health and to provide such information, instruction, training and supervision as is necessary to ensure, so far as is reasonably practicable, the health and safety at work of all persons employed by him at the industrial undertaking and provide and maintain a working environment for all persons employed by him at the industrial undertaking that is, so far as is reasonably practicable, safe, and without risks to health.[716]

I. Regulations

548. To give further and detailed effect to these duties in relation to noise pollution, the Commissioner of Labour has made the Factories and Industrial Undertakings (Noise at Work) Regulations.[717] The regulations require the provision of protective measures depending on the level of noise exposure: First action level meaning a daily personal noise exposure of 85 decibels (A); second action level meaning a daily personal noise exposure of 90 decibels (A); and peak action level meaning noise reaching a peak sound pressure level of 140 decibels or peak sound pressure of 200 Pa.[718]

---

714. *Ibid.*, s. 6.
715. Factories and Industrial Undertakings Ordinance (Cap 59), s. 6A(1).
716. *Ibid.*, s. 6A(2).
717. Cap 59, sub leg T.
718. *Ibid.*, s. 2.

A. *Noise Risk Assessment*

549. Where a proprietor's employee is likely to be exposed to a first action level or above or to a peak action level or above, the proprietor shall ensure that a person who by reason of his training and experience is competent to carry out a noise assessment makes a noise assessment which is adequate for the purposes: (a) of identifying which of his employees are likely to be so exposed; and (b) of providing him with information with regard to the noise to which his employees may be exposed that will enable him to comply with his duties under sections 4 (to provide ear protection zones), 6 (to provide ear protection), 8 (to reduce exposure to noise) and 9(1) (to provide noise protection equipment).[719]

B. *Duty to Provide Ear Protectors*

550. Where an employee is likely to be exposed to a first action level or above in circumstances where the daily personal noise exposure of the employee is likely to be less than ninety decibels (A), the employee must be provided, at his request, with a suitable approved ear protector except where the wearing of the protector would likely cause risk to the safety of the employee or to any other person.[720]

551. Where an employee is likely to be exposed to a second action level or above or to a peak action level or above, the employee must be provided with a suitable approved ear protector which, when properly worn, can reasonably be expected to keep the risk of damage to that employee's hearing to below that arising from exposure to the second action level or, as the case may be, to the peak action level.[721]

C. *Designating Ear Protection Areas*

552. Where an employee is likely to be exposed to a second action level or above or to a peak action level or above, the proprietor must ensure, as far as is practicable, that the area within the industrial undertaking where the employee will likely be so exposed is demarcated and identified as an ear protection zone. Clear signs must be posted to indicate that it is an ear protection zone and that employees must wear suitable approved ear protectors while in the zone. The proprietor must also ensure that no employee enters or remains in the zone unless the employee is wearing a suitable approved ear protector.[722]

---

719. *Ibid.*, s. 3(1).
720. *Ibid.*, s. 6(1) and (2).
721. *Ibid.*, s. 6(3).
722. *Ibid.*, s. 4(2).

D. Provision of Equipment and Safety Information

553. The proprietor has a duty to ensure that noise control equipment is properly installed and maintained.[723] He must also provide his employees who are likely to be exposed to noise above level one with adequate information, instruction and training on: (a) the risk of damage to hearing that the exposure may cause; (b) the steps that the employee should take to minimize the risk; and (c) the employee's obligations under section 9(2) to properly use noise control equipment and promptly report any defect in such equipment.[724] Criminal offences have been created to ensure due compliance with these regulations by proprietors and employees.[725]

§9. Appeals under the Noise Control Ordinance

554. A person adversely affected by a decision of the Noise Control Authority may appeal to the Appeal Board.

I. Appealable Decisions

555. An applicant for a construction noise permit to carry out percussive piling outside restricted hours; a person on whom a noise abatement notice has been served in respect of noise emanating from any place other than domestic premises, a public place or a construction site; and persons who have been required to measure, inspect or test prescribed noisy products namely air compressors and hand held percussive breakers may appeal against an adverse decision.[726]

II. Grounds of Appeal

556. Where the appeals is against the issuing or varying a noise abatement notice, requiring a prescribed noise product to be produced for the Authority to inspect, measure or test it, or requiring a person to carry out inspection, measurement or testing of a prescribed product, the appellant may rely only on the following grounds, namely: (a) that the service of notice is not justified by the terms of the Noise Control Ordinance or, in the case of a noise abatement notice issued on the ground that the noise does not comply with any standard or limit contained in a Technical Memorandum, that such noise abatement notice is not justified by the terms of such Technical Memorandum; (b) that there has been some material informality, defect or error in the form or content of the notice or in connection with the service of the notice; (c) that the requirements of the notice are unreasonable in character or extent or are unnecessary; (d) that compliance with the requirements of

723. *Ibid.*, s. 9.
724. *Ibid.*, s. 10.
725. *Ibid.*, s. 12.
726. Noise Pollution Control Ordinance, s. 19(1).

the notice would cause the appellant economic hardship seriously prejudicial to the conduct of his business; or (e) that the notice should have been served on some person other than the appellant.[727]

III. Commencement of an Appeal

557. An appeal must be made in the prescribed form, and lodged with the Chairman of the Appeal Board within twenty-one days of the decision or notice to which it relates. A copy of the notice of appeal must be served on the Noise Control Authority. The appellant must at the same time submit a statement specifying the grounds of appeal, and including such particulars of the evidence to be adduced, documents to be produced, and names of witnesses to be called as may suffice to ensure that the Appeal Board and Authority are fully and fairly informed of the grounds of appeal. Any party to the appeal may, with the authorization of the Chairman of the Appeal Board, obtain further particulars from the other party. Any party to the appeal may request the other party to produce any document relating to the appeal for inspection. If the other party refuses such request, he will not be permitted to put such document in evidence unless he satisfies the Appeal Board that he had a valid reason for the failure to comply with the request.[728]

IV. The Appeal Hearing

558. An appeal hearing must be held as soon as reasonably practicable and at least twenty-eight days' notice of the hearing must be served on the parties to the appeal. Where the appellant has failed to serve a copy of the notice of the appeal on the Noise Control Authority, or to furnish a statement of particulars to the Authority and the Chairman, or to furnish further particulars to the Authority at its request, the Appeal Board may dismiss the appeal.[729]

559. If the appellant or his legal representative fails to attend the hearing, the Appeal Board may proceed to hear the appeal in his absence or dismiss the appeal or, if satisfied that the appellant's failure to attend was due to sickness or other reasonable cause, postpone or adjourn the hearing for such period as it thinks fit. Where the Appeal Board has dismissed an appeal due to the failure of the appellant to attend the hearing, the appellant may apply for a review of the decision to dismiss and if the Appeal Board is satisfied that the appellant's absence was for a reasonable cause, it may set aside the order for dismissal.[730]

727. *Ibid.*, s. 19(2).
728. *See ibid.*, Part IV 'Appeals' and Noise Control (Appeal Board) Regulations, Cap 400 sub leg B.
729. *See* the Noise Control (Appeal Board) Regulations (Cap 400 sub leg B).
730. *Ibid.*, reg. 13.

560. An appeal hearing must be conducted in the public, except where the Chairman orders all or any persons to be excluded from the whole or any part of the hearing. Parties to the appeal are entitled to be legally represented.[731]

V. The Determination of the Appeal Board

561. At the conclusion of the hearing, the Appeal Board may confirm, reverse or vary the decision or requirement appealed against; and make an award of such sum, if any, in respect of the costs involved in the appeal as is just and equitable in all the circumstances of the case.[732] In hearing an appeal, the Appeal Board may, in relation to such appeal, give directions to the Noise Control Authority with respect to the exercise of such of the functions of the Authority under the Noise Control Ordinance as are relevant to the appeal and the Authority must comply with any such direction.[733]

§10. Enforcement Powers under the Noise Control Ordinance

I. Introduction

562. The central authority to implement the provisions of the Noise Control Ordinance is the Authority who has been given important enforcement powers, which he may exercise through public officers. An authorized officer has the power to enter and search premises without a warrant, except that in case of domestic premises a warrant issued by a magistrate must be produced unless the occupier of the premises consents to entry without a warrant.[734] These powers may be exercised where he reasonably believes that an offence against the Ordinance is being committed in such place or there may be any evidence in such place suggestive of the commission of an offence against the Ordinance.[735]

563. The effective observance of the Ordinance is secured by creating a number of offences in relation to noise abatement notices and construction noise permits, which we have already seen above. In order to ensure effective enforcement of the Ordinance, several offences have been created to deter obstruction of enforcement work carried out by authorized officers, and failure to provide information or provision of inaccurate or misleading information.[736] In order to protect confidentiality of information that has been discovered during the exercise of enforcement powers, the Ordinance has created an offence of unauthorized disclosure of information.[737]

731. *Ibid.*
732. Noise Control Ordinance, s. 21(6).
733. *Ibid.*, s. 21(2).
734. Noise Control Ordinance, s. 25.
735. *Ibid.*, s. 25.
736. *Ibid.*, s. 26.
737. *Ibid.*, s. 28.

564. The Noise Control Ordinance confers various powers of enforcement on the Noise Control Authority, including the power to take measures to ensure compliance with notices and permits issued by the Authority. The powers of entry and inspection given to the Authority may be exercised by any public officer authorized by the Authority.[738]

II. Powers of Entry and Inspection

565. An authorized officer may without a warrant enter and search any place if he reasonably believes that: (1) an offence against the Noise Control Ordinance has been or is being committed in any such place; or (2) there is in any such place anything that might be evidence of an offence against the Ordinance. He may enter any place for purposes such as to serve any noise abatement notice or a notice cancelling or varying such notice; to serve any notice requiring any testing of a noisy product or a notice cancelling or varying such notice; to carry out any measurement, inspection or test to determine whether an offence has been or is being committed. However, an authorized officer may enter any domestic premises only with the consent of the occupier of the premises or with a warrant issued by a magistrate. An authorized officer exercising powers of entry and inspection may obtain the assistance of such persons as he reasonably requires for the purpose of exercising his powers of enforcement.[739]

III. Offences

566. The Ordinance creates four types of offences:

(1) Substantive offences: These include making any noise at night or on a general holiday, making certain specified noises in domestic premises or a public place and causing noises to emanate from construction sites.
(2) Offences relating to notices and decisions: Failure to comply with the requirements of: (a) a noise abatement notice; or (b) a notice requiring the testing of a noisy product is an offence. It is an offence to carry out construction work without a construction noise permit, where such is needed, or in contravention of the permit.
(3) Offences in relation to enforcement: These include: (1) wilfully resisting, obstructing or delaying any public officer in the exercise of his enforcement powers of entry and inspection; (2) failure without reasonable excuse to comply with any requirement of the public officer in the exercise of such power; (3) wilfully or recklessly giving incorrect information or withholds information.

738. *Ibid.*, Part V (ss 24–26).
739. *Ibid.*, s. 25.

(4) Offence of disclosing confidential information: It is an offence for any person to disclose any confidential information concerning a trade, business or profession, which he receives in the discharge of his duties under the Noise Control Ordinance.

A. *Nature of the Offences*

567. The majority of offences that the Ordinance has created refer only to the *actus reus* and there is no express reference to *mens rea*, while some offences require proof of *mens rea*.[740] Two sections may be cited to show the difference between these two types of case: Subsection (1) of section 4 makes no reference to a mental element while subsection (2) does. '4(1) Any person who between the hours of 11.00 pm and 7.00 am, or at any time on a general holiday in any domestic premises or public place makes or causes to be made any noise which is a source of annoyance to any person commits an offence. (2) Any person being the owner, tenant, occupier or person in charge of any domestic premises who between the hours of 11.00 pm and 7.00 am, or at any time on a general holiday knowingly permits or suffers noise which is a source of annoyance to any person to emanate from those domestic premises commits an offence.'

568. Similarly, subsection (1) of section 17 makes no reference to *mens rea* while subsection (2) does. '17 (1) Any person who uses, or causes to be used, any product prescribed for the purposes of this Part which does not comply with any requirement relating to noise emission prescribed for the purposes of this subsection commits an offence. (2) Any person who being the owner of any product prescribed for the purposes of this Part which does not comply with any requirement relating to noise emission prescribed for the purposes of subsection (1) knowingly permits or suffers such product to be used commits an offence.'

569. It must be noted that in any proceeding for an offence in respect of noise at night or on general holiday, certain types of noises at any time, noise from construction sites, noise from construction sites in contravention of noise control regulations, failure to comply with a noise abatement notice, and use of products not in compliance with noise standards, it is a defence to show that the acts were done under authorization by the Ordinance, or to prevent injury to person or property, or to prevent serious interruption or disruption to public transport.[741]

Lord Scarman explained in *Gammon (Hong Kong) Ltd & Others v A-G* the criteria that determine where the imposition of strict or absolute liability is justified:[742]

740. The first type of offences (where there is no requirement of proving *mens rea*) will be regarded as an absolute offence or, if the court considers that the offence is subject to a common law defence or similar statutory defence, as a strict liability offence.

741. Noise Control Ordinance, s. 33.

742. [1985] AC 1, 14 (PC).

(1) there is a presumption of law that *mens rea* is required before a person can be held guilty of a criminal offence;
(2) the presumption is particularly strong where the offence is 'truly criminal' in character;
(3) the presumption applies to statutory offences, and can be displaced only if this is clearly or by necessary implication the effect of the statute;
(4) the only situation in which the presumption can be displaced is where the statute is concerned with an issue of social concern; public safety is such an issue;
(5) even where a statute is concerned with such an issue, the presumption of *mens rea* stands unless it can also be shown that the creation of strict liability will be effective to promote the object of the statute by encouraging greater vigilance to prevent the commission of the prohibited act.

Lord Diplock said as follows in *Sweet v Parsley*: 'But where the subject matter of a statute is the regulation of a particular activity involving potential danger to public health, safety or morals in which citizens have a choice whether they participate or not, the court may feel driven to infer an intention of Parliament to impose, by penal sanctions, a higher duty or care on those who choose to participate and to place on them an obligation to take whatever measures may be necessary to prevent the prohibited act, without regard to those considerations of cost or business practicability which play a part in the determination of what would be required of them in order to fulfil the ordinary common law duty of care. But such an inference is not lightly to be drawn, nor is there any room for it unless there is something that the person on whom the obligation is imposed can do directly or indirectly, by supervision or inspection, by improvement of his business methods or by exhorting those whom he may be expected to influence or control, which will promote the observance of the obligation.'[743]

Courts have recognized that environmental offences cause serious harm to the society and been willing to take a strict view of the appropriate penalties in order to disincentivize construction industry from engaging in pollution causing activities for their own advantage. As the Court of Appeal observed in *HKSAR v Paul Y-ITC Construction Ltd*: 'In a society which is crying out for sensible control over pollution of whatever kind, the penalties should properly reflect society's concern.' Courts have taken into account whether the offence in question is a first or repeated offence, how profitable has it been for the offender to engage in the prohibited activity, the degree of fault of the offender (for instance, the breach of law was cause d by a mere lack of supervision or active involvement in causing the breach) and a lack of remorse.[744]

743. *Sweet v Parsley* [1969] 1 All ER 347, 362 (HL).
744. *See HKSAR v Paul Y-ITC Construction Ltd* [1998] 2 HKLRD 35, 45 (CA) and *HKSAR v Dragages Hong Kong Ltd* [2015] 2 HKLRD 1165 (CFI).

B. Prosecution

570. Proceedings for offences against the Ordinance may be instituted in the name of the Authority, and may be commenced and conducted by a public officer appointed under the Magistrates Ordinance (Cap 227), however, without prejudice to the powers of the Secretary for Justice in relation to the prosecution of offences. Criminal proceedings must be instituted within six months from the time the commission of the offence came to the knowledge of the Noise Control Authority or an authorized officer, or one year from the time of the commission of the offence, whichever is earlier.[745]

§11. PUBLIC ACCESS TO INFORMATION

571. The Noise Control Ordinance does not require any applications for a construction noise permit to be publicized and does not provide for public participation. However, where the Noise Control Authority grants a construction noise permit, he may require the construction noise permit to be displayed at specified locations. The display of the construction noise permit informs the public of the conditions that are placed on a particular construction activity and enable them to complain in case of breach of such conditions and enables them to bring to the notice of the authorities any violation of those conditions.

572. Subject to certain statutory exceptions, it is an offence to disclose or give confidential information to another, which concerns a trade, business or profession, which has come to his knowledge or into his possession in the course of the discharge of his functions under the Noise Control Ordinance.[746]

745. *Ibid.*, ss 31, 32.
746. *Ibid.*, s. 28.

Chapter 5. Environmental Impact Assessment

§1. Introduction

573. We have seen in relation to water, air and noise pollution control as well as waste management that managing and controlling pollution involves various stages. They start with the adoption of policies for prevention, regulation and control of pollution followed by the specification of technical standards for the carrying out of preventive, regulatory and controlling processes. The implementation of these processes starts with grant of permits or licences at which stage the regulators have to examine the possible impacts of proposed activities on the environment and measures that could be taken to eliminate or mitigate such adverse impacts.

574. The law provides for public consultation before granting, amending or revoking licences and permits. In order to ensure that there is sufficient compliance with the relevant standards for polluting activities, the Director of Environmental Protection has been given enforcement powers including prosecution, orders to cease polluting activities or to take remedial measures. A thorough examination of plans for a potentially polluting process before it is given permission to operate will give the regulators an opportunity to take proactive measures to ensure the carrying out of the proposed activity in an environmentally friendly way causing the least environmental harm.

I. Major Projects Need Close Scrutiny

575. Large scale projects which are likely to have major environmental impacts call for more intense scrutiny of plans before permission to proceed is granted. In relation to such projects, the law provides for a comprehensive framework of assessment of environmental impacts. Thus, Environmental Impact Assessment (EIA) may be described as a means of drawing together, in a systematic way, an assessment of the likely significant adverse environmental effects arising from a proposed development.

576. In order to provide guidance for EIAs, the environmental regulator has to adopt policies which determine what environmental interests call for protection, such as of the climate, forests and water resources. Once policies are adopted, technical standards have to be established which guide project proponents. The assessment of a project has to be based on scientifically produced information. In determining the desirability of the proposed project and if it is desirable (or tolerable) the best way of implementing the project, there must be full and open public participation: For it is in the greater public interest that the environment has to be protected, keeping in mind at the same time the need for sustainable development.

577. Once an impact assessment is completed, the task of the Authority responsible for the assessment is to determine whether the project can be carried out in compliance with environmental law, policy and standards. Failure to obtain approval of the assessment authority would virtually rule out the project because the ultimate decision-maker such as the land-use planning authority is unlikely to authorize a project which has failed the applicable environmental standards.

578. It will be useful if we provide an outline of the EIA process. The process begins with identifying the projects which attract the requirement of an EIA. Unlike in the UK where the question whether a project requires an EIA is determined at the stage of screening, where the relevant local authority decides on request by project proponents whether an EIA is necessary for consideration of the project approval, in Hong Kong the Environmental Impact Assessment Ordinance sets out what are 'designated projects' that require an EIA.[747] The Director of Environmental Protection has some discretion that he exercises in relation to determining whether a combination of projects, although each of such projects is not a designated project, may be considered a designated project.[748]

579. The proponent of a designated project must generally go through the EIA process, except in some limited circumstances where he may directly apply for an environmental permit.[749] Where an applicant does not qualify for direct application for an environmental permit, the EIA process begins with the project proponent applying to the Director for an environmental impact assessment study brief. The application must be accompanied a project profile. The purpose of a project profile is to enable the Director to consider the scope of the environmental impact assessment appropriate for the proposed project.[750] The Director then issues a study brief to guide the project proponent in preparing the environmental impact assessment report. In the environmental impact assessment report, the project proponent must identify the possible adverse impacts of the project on the environment and suggest how he proposes to eliminate them or to mitigate the harshness of unavoidable adverse impacts on the environment.[751] The Director must review the report and, when he is satisfied that it meets the requirements of the study brief and the Technical Memorandum, he must proceed to the stage of public consultation.

580. Public consultation of a project profile takes two forms: consulting the pubic directly and through the Advisory Council on the Environment. Public consultation serves an important purpose: It enables the project proponent to identify any aspects of the project which may be addressed at this early stage so that there will not remain many concerns at the stage of EIA report to address. After completion of the public consultation of the project profile, the Director must supply the project proponent with public comments and those of the Advisory Committee on the Environment for his consideration.

747. A list of designated projects are listed in Schedules 2 and 3 of the Environmental Impact Assessment Ordinance (Cap 499).
748. *See* below para. 594.
749. *See* below paras 643–644.
750. *See* below para. 645 where the relevance of Technical Memorandum as a guide to preparing a project profile and its approval is dealt with.
751. *See* below paras 646–651.

581. The Director may seek further information that he considers necessary in evaluating the environmental impact assessment report. Once the project proponent submits the environmental impact assessment report, if necessary amended or modified in response to the comments that he had received, the Director must decide whether the environmental impact assessment report complies with the relevant technical memorandum, the study brief, and adequately addresses any concerns raised by the public or the Advisory Committee on the Environment. After such consideration, the Director may approve the environmental impact assessment report, unconditionally or subject to conditions, or reject it.

582. Once the environmental impact assessment report has been approved, the project proponent may apply for an environmental permit, which authorizes him to construct or operate the designated project. The Director may, if he is satisfied that the project can be implemented without causing serious adverse impacts, grant an environmental permit, with or without conditions. A person who assumes responsibility from the original project proponent must apply for and obtain a further environmental permit. He must conduct a fresh environmental impact assessment if there are material changes to the project as originally approved. In granting such a permit, the Director must require the conduct of an environmental impact assessment if there are material changes to the already permitted project. Similarly, in an application for the amendment of an environmental permit, the Director may require a fresh environmental impact assessment to be conducted if there are material changes to the originally permitted project.

583. The Director may in his discretion cancel or vary an environmental permit if the permit was obtained by submitting incomplete, false, wrong or misleading information, or, if the project proponent or his successor is no longer able to comply with the conditions of the environmental permit. Similar powers are given to the Chief Executive of the HKSAR. There is a monitoring and auditing process in place to ensure compliance with the environmental permit in the implementation of the project. The environmental authority has powers of inspection and may order necessary remedial work to be carried out. The Authority's powers of enforcement are supported by creation of a number of offences for which the responsible persons may be prosecuted.

584. As mentioned above, it is possible for a project proponent to apply the Director for permission to implement a designated project without going through an environmental impact assessment to obtain an environmental permit, where (i) having regard to the project profile that has been received, there is already on record a previous environmental report that is still relevant to the application; (ii) having regard to the project profile submitted by the applicant, the environmental impacts of the project are not likely to be adverse to the environment; or (iii) where the application is to make a material change to an exempted project, the environmental impacts of the project are not likely to be adverse to the environment. The applicant must submit a project profile, for the Director's consideration, and it will go through public consultation and consideration by the Advisory Committee on the Environment.

II. Impact Assessment of Strategic Plans

585. The Hong Kong government conducts EIAs of strategic policies and plans that the government proposes to introduce. In relation to the adoption of policies that guide future strategic development, EIA serves more of an instructional role, in the sense that policymakers are able to make informed decisions on the way forward with environmentally sustainable developmental plans. These assessments are known as Strategic Environmental Assessments and such assessments have played an important part in the *Territorial Development Strategy Review*, the *Third Comprehensive Transport Review*, and the *Second Railway Development Study*.

586. An important outcome of these strategic reviews has been to identify the most desirable way of implementing development proposals and the adoption of appropriate environmental standards to assess the sustainability of specific projects, such as a railway development, when proposed in pursuance of the strategic plans. While the non-statutory Strategic Impact Assessment informs broad-brush development policies, statutory EIA comes into play when any specific project is proposed in pursuance of the strategic policies.[752]

587. Because of the importance of properly predicting the future impacts of planned developments and the need to balance social and economic interests, lawmakers and judges alike have emphasized the importance of the integrity of the EIA process, with special emphasis on public participation.

III. The Formative Years

588. The introduction of EIA process in Hong Kong predates the enactment of the Environmental Impact Assessment Ordinance in 1997.[753] As early as 1979, the government set in motion an administrative practice of conducting EIAs for both private and public projects. The Environmental Protection Agency, the predecessor of the present-day Environmental Protection Department, carried out EIAs looking at site selection, design, construction and operation of major development projects such as a new coal-fired 1,700 megawatt power station, the development of Tin Shui

752. Environmental impact assessment for individual projects and plans for future development is the practice, for instance, in the European Union, where environmental assessment can be undertaken for individual projects, such as a dam, motorway, airport or factory, on the basis of Directive 2011/92/EU (known as 'Environmental Impact Assessment' – EIA Directive) or for public plans or programmes on the basis of Directive 2001/42/EC (known as 'Strategic Environmental Assessment' – SEA Directive). *See* http://ec.europa.eu/environment/eia/home.htm.

753. The following historical introduction draws from information available on the Environmental Protection Department's website.

Wai new town and Chek Lap Kok Airport. Recognizing the importance of environmental considerations in the planning process, the government in 1985 introduced a set of environmental standards and guidelines into the Hong Kong Planning and Standards Guidelines.[754]

589. Until 1986 EIA took the form of an ad hoc requirement imposed on a small number of government and private infrastructure projects. In that year, a more systematic administrative procedure was proposed to be followed by proponents of all major or environmentally significant development projects, with the publication of an internal directive entitled 'Environmental Review of Major Development Projects', which set out the screening process and assessment requirements for public works. EIAs carried out under this arrangement covered a wide range of projects such as roads, sewage treatment works, major residential developments and waste disposal facilities.

590. The 1990s witnessed more frequent use of the EIA process. From 1992 to 1994, there were 239 assessments, completed or ongoing, compared to only eighty during the preceding six-year period. This reflected the more pronounced demands from the public, the Legislative Council, local government authorities and government advisory bodies for a more thorough consideration of environmental impacts of proposed development projects. During the period the EIA process was refined in three aspects. First was the facilitation of public access to environmental impact reports. The second refinement was the introduction of a mechanism to resolve disagreements. Third, and perhaps the most important refinement was the introduction of a formal system of environmental monitoring and auditing to track project performance.

591. In 1992, the government proposed a new requirement for an EIA to accompany any developmental studies submitted to the Executive Council, including the Territorial Development Strategy Review. This policy continues to be operative and as a result any policy submissions to the Executive Council must include an environmental implications section. In a similar vein, an environmental implications section must accompany any public sector project proposals for funding approval by the Public Works Sub-Committee of the Legislative Council's Finance Committee.[755]

IV. Introduction of a Statutory EIA

592. The transformation of the administrative arrangement into a statutory requirement began with the introduction of the EIA Bill in 1996 in the Legislative

754. This now appears as 'Environment' Ch. 9 in Hong Kong Planning Standards and Guidelines. *See* http://www.pland.gov.hk/pland_en/tech_doc/hkpsg/sum/index.htm.

755. *See* Environmental Protection Department *Advice Note 2 of 1992* and Practice Note for Professional Persons No. 2 of 1993 *Application of the Environmental Impact Assessment (EIA) Process to Major Development Projects*.

Council. The Environmental Impact Assessment Ordinance (Cap 499) was enacted on 4 February 1997 and the Appeal Board Regulations and the Application Fess Regulations were enacted the same year. The Ordinance which came into operation on 1 April 1998 makes an EIA mandatory for any designated projects. It is an offence to construct, operate or decommission a designated project listed in Schedule II of the Environmental Impact Assessment Ordinance without or in breach of an environmental permit. Along with the administrative practice of conducting EIAs, the Town Planning Board began to require an EIA report in respect of any major land-use developments. With the enactment of the Environmental Impact Assessment Ordinance, EIA has now become a statutory requirement.

V. Main Aspects of EIA Process

A. *Screening*

593. An important first step in the EIA process is to identify the type of processes that call for impact assessment. This can be done by mandatory assessment for projects specified in primary or subsidiary legislation, or granting discretionary power to an administrative agency to identify processes which must be submitted to an EIA. This discretionary identification process is known as screening.[756]

594. The Environmental Impact Assessment Ordinance has adopted a combination of these two methods. The Ordinance has identified the types of project or proposal which may have significant environmental impacts by listing them in Schedules 2 and 3. Projects that are listed in Schedule 2 require an environmental permit. Projects listed in schedule do not require an environmental permit and only require the submission of an EIA report. Section 4(4) of the Ordinance gives authority to the Director of Environmental Protection to specify a combination of projects as a designated project where contiguous projects which, if taken individually, do not meet the specified levels in Schedule 2 or 3 qualify as a designated project, and which are proposed by the same person or associated persons, if he is satisfied that the purpose behind the separation of the projects is to avoid the purposes of this Ordinance.

756. The European Union Directive The EIA Directive (85/337/EEC), as amended in 1997, 2003 and 2009 and codified by Directive 2011/92/EU, is in force since 1985 and applies to a wide range of defined public and private projects, which are defined in Annexes I and II:. All projects listed in Annex I are considered as having significant effects on the environment and therefore an impact assessment is mandatory (e.g., long-distance railway lines, motorways and express roads, airports with a basic runway length ≥ 2100 m, installations for the disposal of hazardous waste, installations for the disposal of non-hazardous waste > 100 tonnes/day, wastewater treatment plants > 150,000 p.e.). For projects listed in Annex II, the national authorities have to decide whether an environmental impact assessment is needed. This is done by the 'screening procedure', which determines the effects of projects on the basis of thresholds/criteria or a case-by-case examination. The criteria that national authorities must apply are set out in Annex III of the Directive. *See* http://ec.europa.eu/environment/eia/eia-legalcontext.htm.

B. Scoping

595. Scoping refers to identifying significant environmental impacts for assessment, thereby eliminating the need for extensive and peripheral documentation if all impacts, however insignificant, were to be assessed. Scoping also involves determining the level of assessment appropriate for a particular project. The Director of Environmental Protection carrying out scoping through a study brief he issues to the applicant providing guidance to prepare the EIA report.

C. Public Participation

596. Public participation is probably the most significant aspect of EIA in that it ensures that the administration takes its decisions in a fully transparent manner. In order to ensure genuine public scrutiny, it is important for the public to be given an opportunity to participate at every important stage of the EIA process.

D. Project Profile and Study Brief

597. The formal process of EIA begins with the submission by the project proponent of a project profile, which satisfies the requirements set out in the relevant Technical Memorandum. The project profile must be such as to enable the Director of Environmental Protection to determine the environmental issues that the applicant must address. The Advisory Council on the Environment and the public are consulted on the project profile before the Director makes his decision. Once the scoping has been completed, the Director issues a study brief to guide the applicant in preparing the EIA report.

E. EIA Report

598. EIA is a process to study likely impacts of the proposed project, in order to ensure that once implemented the project has no or minimum adverse impacts on the environment. The project proponent must carry out an impact assessment guided by the study brief. The report must address the potential environmental impacts, beneficial or adverse, proposed mitigation matters and plans for environmental monitoring and auditing. The resultant EIA report has to be submitted to the Director of Environmental Protection for his approval. In considering whether the report meets the requirements of the study brief and the Technical Memorandum on EIA Process, the Director is required to consult the public as well as the Council on the Environment.

F. Environmental Permit

599. The project proponent must submit an approved environmental assessment report for the Director of Environmental Protection[757] to consider the granting of an environmental permit if he is satisfied that the project can be undertaken in compliance with the relevant environmental standards. In granting or refusing an environmental permit, the Director of Environmental Protection must have regard not only to the assessment report but also to several other matters which are set out in the Ordinance such as relevant Technical Memoranda and public comments.

G. Direct Application for an Environmental Permit

600. The Director of Environmental Protection may allow a project proponent to apply directly for an environmental permit, bypassing the submission of an EIA report, if he is satisfied that the proposed designated project complies with the relevant Technical Memorandum in respect of its likely environmental impacts and proposed mitigation measures. In that event, the project proponent does not have to submit a study brief and an impact assessment report. A project proponent who wishes to apply directly for an environmental permit must submit a project profile to enable the Director to decide whether he could waive the impact assessment report stage.

H. Exempted Projects

601. Any project which is a designated project under the Ordinance, but which had been authorized before the coming into effect of the Environmental Impact Assessment Ordinance, is exempt from the provisions of the Ordinance. Such authorization might have been granted by, for instance, the Town Planning Board by way of planning permission or the Building Authority by way of consent to commence building works.

I. Monitoring Designated Projects

602. An important aspect of EIA is the provision of a monitoring mechanism to ensure that the designated project is implemented in accordance with the understanding between the Director of Environmental Protection and the project proponent. This is achieved through imposition of conditions on the environmental permit providing for the monitoring of the environmental impacts of the project. The project operators may also be required to have a system in place for continuous

757. Unless there is an earlier environmental report on the register of approved environmental reports, which the Director considers to be still valid, or where the Director has permitted the project proponent to apply directly for an environmental permit, without going through the study brief and environmental report stage: Environmental Impact Assessment Ordinance (Cap 499), s. 10(1).

auditing of the project to identify any remedial measures to address adverse environmental impacts. The Ordinance, like other environmental statutes, creates criminal offences to deter infringements of the law or conditions of the environmental permit and any failure to cooperate with law enforcement officers. The Director of Environmental Protection has been given enforcement powers such as the power to issue a cessation order if a designated project is carried out in breach of an environmental permit and to carry out remedial work, at the cost of the project operator, where environmental damage is caused by a designated project.

§2. LEGISLATIVE FRAMEWORK

603. The legislative framework is provided by the Environmental Impact Assessment Ordinance, whose objective is to provide for assessing the impact on the environment of certain projects and proposals, for protecting the environment and for incidental matters. This, the Ordinance does by introducing an EIA process for designated projects.[758]

604. Designated projects are projects which are likely to have a significant adverse impact on the environment unless properly studied and controlled. Hong Kong's EIA process involves: (a) determining what type of project is required to go through the assessment process; (b) submission of a project profile to the environmental authority; (c) preparation of a study brief by the environmental authority to guide the project proponent on what aspects of the proposed project needs elaboration; (d) the submission of an environmental report by the project proponent; and (e) the decision by the environmental authority to grant or refuse an environmental permit. Throughout this process, there is provision for consulting relevant agencies and the public.[759]

I. Regulations

605. Regulations may be made by the Secretary for the Environment for any of the following purposes: (a) to prescribe anything required or permitted to be prescribed under the Environmental Impact Assessment Ordinance; (b) to prescribe minimum qualifications and experience of persons undertaking EIA studies; (c) to

758. A designated project means a project listed in Sch. 2 or 3 of the Ordinance or specified by the Secretary under s. 4(4) as a designated project. *See* the Environmental Impact Assessment Ordinance (Cap 499), Sch. 1 'Interpretation'.

759. The environmental impact assessment procedure in the European Union may be summarized as follows: the developer may request the competent authority to say what should be covered by the environmental impact assessment information to be provided by the developer (scoping stage); the developer must provide information on the environmental impact (Environmental Impact Assessment Report); the environmental authorities and the public (and affected Member States) must be informed and consulted; the competent authority decides, taking into consideration the results of consultations. The decision of the Authority is made public. http://ec.europa.eu/environment/eia/eia-legalcontext.htm.

regulate appeals and the practice and procedure of the Appeal Board; and (d) to generally provide for the better carrying into effect of the provisions and purposes of the Ordinance.[760] A regulation may provide for payment of fees and such fees may be charged differently according to different circumstances.[761] Regulations are by their nature subsidiary legislation, which are subject to scrutiny by the Legislative Council. Although the Ordinance does not provide expressly for the laying of regulations before the Legislative Council, provisions relating to subsidiary legislation in the Interpretation and General Clauses Ordinance should require Legislative Council oversight.[762] Two regulations have been made. They are: the Environmental Impact Assessment (Appeal Board) Regulation (Cap 499 sub leg A); and the Environmental Impact Assessment (Fees) Regulation (Cap 499 sub leg B).

II. Technical Memorandum

606. The Secretary for the Environment may issue Technical Memoranda and so far only one Technical Memorandum has been issued, namely the Technical Memorandum on EIA Process.[763] The Ordinance explicitly provides that Technical Memoranda are not subsidiary legislation.[764] The nature of subsidiary legislation is that they must be within the power conferred by the parent legislation (the idea of being *intra vires*) and are subject to legislative control either by way of affirmative resolution – meaning that a subsidiary legislation may come into effect only if it is approved by an affirmative resolution – or by way of negative resolution – meaning that a subsidiary legislation comes into being unless it is disapproved by a negative resolution within a prescribed time. While Technical Memoranda are not subsidiary legislation, the Ordinance provides for legislative oversight of the making of Technical Memoranda.

A. Legislative Scrutiny

607. The Ordinance stipulates that a Technical Memorandum must be published in the Gazette and laid on the table of the Legislative Council at the next sitting after its publication; that the Legislative Council may by resolution repeal the Technical Memorandum, provided that such resolution is passed at a meeting of the Legislative Council held before the expiration of a period of twenty-eight days of the laying of the Technical Memorandum on the table of the Legislative Council, although this period stands extended in certain stated circumstances; that a resolution repealing a Technical Memorandum must be published in the Gazette normally within

760. The Environmental Impact Assessment Ordinance, s. 32.
761. *Ibid.*
762. *See* the Interpretation and General Clauses Ordinance (Cap 1) Part V (ss 28–37A).
763. *See* https://www.epd.gov.hk/epd/english/envir_standards/statutory/esg_stat.html.
764. The Environmental Impact Assessment Ordinance, s. 16(12).

fourteen days of its passing; and that a Technical Memorandum comes into effect after the expiry of the period for debate of it in the Legislative Council.[765]

608. The Legislative Council has the implicit power to request the Secretary for the Environment to reconsider a Technical Memorandum. For instance, the Legislative Council may have some serious reservations about a Technical Memorandum and may advise the Secretary that unless those concerns are addressed, it will vote against it. Such a request will most certainly be complied with since the Legislative Council has the express power to repeal the proposed Technical Memorandum unless it is amended accordingly.

B. Binding Nature of Technical Memorandum

609. The binding legislative nature of Technical Memoranda is illustrated by the provision that on an appeal, the Appeal Board cannot call into question the contents of a Technical Memorandum.[766] The Court of Final Appeal in the case of *Shiu Wing Steel Ltd v Director of Environmental Protection & Airport Authority of Hong Kong No 2*[767] rightly pointed out that Technical Memoranda, although they are not legislative instruments, impose duties and prescribe procedures and therefore occupy an important place akin to subsidiary legislation. The Court of Final Appeal asserted the importance of Technical Memoranda and explained that they fall to be interpreted as if they were subsidiary legislation, although rules of statutory interpretation might not be appropriate:

> The Technical Memorandum and the study brief are both technical instruments, to be understood as an expert risk assessor, properly understanding the legal requirements they create, would understand them. The Technical Memorandum and the study brief define the scope of the [Director's power to issue an environmental permit] and condition the exercise of that power, even though the meaning of those documents may have to be ascertained without employing the rules of statutory interpretation.

C. Contents of a Technical Memorandum

610. A Technical Memorandum may set out principles, procedures, guidelines, requirements and criteria for: (1) the technical content of a project profile; (2) the technical content of an EIA study brief or EIA report; (3) deciding whether a designated project is environmentally acceptable; (4) deciding whether an EIA report meets the requirements of the EIA study brief; (5) deciding whether the Director of Environmental Protection will permit an applicant to apply directly for an environmental permit; (6) resolving conflicts on the content of the EIA study brief and the

765. *Ibid.*, s. 16 various subsections.
766. *Ibid.*, s. 19(6).
767. (2006) 9 HKCFAR 478 (CFA), [23].

EIA report; (7) taking advice from other authorities; (8) deciding what is a material change, addition or alteration to an environmental impact or to a designated project; (9) the issue of environmental permits; and (10) the imposition of environmental monitoring and audit requirements for designated projects as conditions in environmental permits.[768] A Technical Memorandum may require or authorize the Director to follow the advice of the Secretary.[769]

D. Technical Memorandum as a Guide

611. The Director must refer to and be guided by any relevant Technical Memorandum in deciding matters under certain sections of the Ordinance.[770] They are: (1) issuing an EIA study brief to proceed with an environmental impact study for a designated project or to permit a person to proceed directly to an application for an environmental permit; (2) determining whether an environmental impact study report meets the requirements of the EIA study brief and Technical Memorandum and thereby is ready to be released for public consultation; (3) approving an EIA report; (4) determining whether to approve an environmental permit; (5) determining whether to grant a further environmental report necessitated by a change in the person responsible for the designated project; (6) determining whether to vary an environmental permit at the request of the person responsible for a designated project; and (7) deciding to cancel or vary an environmental permit.

612. What does it mean to say that the Director must 'refer to and be guided' by a relevant Technical Memorandum? In *Shiu Wing Steel Ltd v Director of Environmental Protection &Airport Authority of Hong Kong (No 2)*,[771] it was argued that a guide is not the same as a direction and that the repository of a power might depart from a guide but not from a direction. The Court of Final Appeal said:

> That distinction was drawn by Woolf LJ (as he then was) in *R v Secretary of State for Social Services, ex parte Stitt* (Lexis copy 21 February 1990; on appeal 3 July 1990 CO/1026/89). There may be good reason for departing from a guide in particular circumstances but the repository of a power is not at liberty to ignore, depart from or qualify the content of the provisions without cogent reasons: *R (on the application of Munjaz) v Ashworth Hospital Authority* [2005] UKHL 58 at paras 5, 21, 68 and 69.[772]

768. The Environmental Impact Assessment Ordinance, s. 16(1).
769. *Ibid.*, s. 16(2).
770. *Ibid.*, s. 16(4).
771. (2006) 9 HKCFAR 478 (CFA).
772. *Ibid.*, [26].

E. The Relevance of a Technical Memorandum

613. Is the requirement that an EIA report must comply with the relevant Technical Memorandum crucial to a decision by the Director to authorize the release of the report (under section 5) only or is it also crucial to the Director's decision to approve the report (under section 8)? In *Shiu Wing Steel Ltd v Director of Environmental Protection & Airport Authority of Hong Kong No 2,*[773] it was argued unsuccessfully in the Court of Final Appeal as follows: the relevant Technical Memorandum and the study brief are used as yardsticks when the Director of Environmental Protection decides under section 6 whether or not to approve an EIA report for the purpose of releasing it for public consultation; if that decision went unchallenged in a judicial review application, it is too late for a person who contests the validity of the approval of an environmental assessment report by the Director after public consultation under section 8 to argue that the report does not comply with the requirements of the Technical Memorandum or the study brief.

614. The Court of Final Appeal rejected that argument saying that the approval under section 6 is for a limited purpose – namely, public consultation – and that the determinative decision is taken under section 8 – namely whether to approve the environmental assessment report which will form the basis for the ultimate grant of an environmental permit. The Court of Final Appeal rightly decided that the Technical Memorandum and the study brief will continue to inform decisions taken by the Director under both section 6 and section 8. The Court of Final Appeal said:

> Approval of an Environmental Impact Assessment report, and the consequential placement by the Director of the Environmental Impact Assessment report on the register, fixes the entirety of the information which an applicant provides relating to the construction of a project, the applicant's assessment of the impact of the project on the environment and the measures which the applicant proposes to take for the protection of the environment. These issues are the issues prescribed by the Technical Memorandum and the study brief and they are the issues which the Director is bound to regard in determining whether to grant an environmental permit for the project.[774]

This view of the Court of Final Appeal is entirely consistent with section 16(4) – requiring the Director to be guided by the relevant Technical Memorandum in deciding certain matters, namely, issuing a study brief (section 5), approving an EIA report for public inspection (section 6), approving an EIA report (section 8), granting an environmental permit (section 10), issuing a further environmental permit (section 12), varying an environmental permit on the application of the permit-holder (section 13) and cancelling or varying an environmental permit by the Director of his own motion (section 14).

773. *Ibid.*
774. *Ibid.*, [19].

F. Interpreting a Technical Memorandum

615. Where the Director is required to determine whether an environmental assessment report 'meets the requirements of the environmental impact assessment study brief and Technical Memorandum',[775] what is the standard that must be applied to the Director's decision? Is it a subjective decision, namely that in the opinion of the Director the EIA report meets the requirements of the EIA study brief and Technical Memorandum? Or is it an objective decision, namely whether when objectively assessed – which is left to judicial determination – the impact assessment report meets the requirements of the EIA study brief and Technical Memorandum?

616. In Shiu Wing Steel Ltd v Director of Environmental Protection &Airport Authority of Hong Kong (No 2),[776] the Court of Final Appeal asserting that an objective test has to be applied said:

> If the Director, in approving an environmental impact assessment report, is found to have misunderstood the requirements of the study brief and the Technical Memorandum, his misunderstanding may suggest error in his decision that the requirements have been met (cf. *Henderson Real Estate Agency Ltd v Lo Chai Wan* (PC) [1997] HKLRD 258 at 267 although in that case and in *South Somerset District Council and Secretary of State for the Environment* [1993] 1 PLR 80 the misunderstanding of the governing guidelines was itself the ground of invalidity). But the question of the environmental impact assessment report's meeting the requirements of the study brief and the Technical Memorandum is for the Court to determine. It is a question of construction, albeit the Technical Memorandum and the study brief are to be construed not as legislative instruments but as they would be understood by an expert risk assessor. In other words, the court determines what the Technical Memorandum and the study brief require but technical evidence may be needed to show that an environmental impact assessment report meets or does not meet the requirements so determined. It is one thing to acknowledge that satisfaction of the requirements or proof of satisfaction calls for expertise; it is another to allow the Director or an expert risk assessor to define for himself or herself the requirements to be satisfied. The definition of the legal effect of the Technical Memorandum and the study brief is necessarily a matter of law but it is necessary to appreciate any special or technical meaning which experts may attribute to particular terms.[777]

775. Under s. 6(3) of the Environmental Impact Assessment Ordinance.
776. (2006) 9 HKCFAR 478 (CFA).
777. *Ibid.*, [30].

§3. Application of the Environmental Impact Assessment Ordinance

I. The Impact of the Ordinance on the Government

617. The Environmental Impact Assessment Ordinance is intended to apply to designated projects undertaken by any public or private body. Thus, just as the government would need to apply for planning permission before it can undertake any development for which planning permission is required, it must comply with the provisions of the Environmental Impact Assessment Ordinance before it undertakes any designated project falling within the scope of the Ordinance. In *Leung Hon Wai v Director of Environmental Protection*, the Court of Final Appeal held that an application for a designated project may be made by the Director of Environmental Protection.[778] The Court of Final Appeal observed that the Ordinance applied to the government and that a government department or agency which embarks on a designated project would be bound by the requirements of the Environmental Impact Assessment Ordinance, which provides that a person planning a designated project must go through the statutory procedure. A government agency would fall within the meaning of 'a person'. The argument before the Court of Final Appeal was whether the rules of natural justice would be breached if an application was made in the name of the Director of Environmental Protection and determined by the Director. The court observed that there was a separation of functions in the department. The application for the designated project, namely a project to construct and operate a municipal waste incinerator, was made by one division of the department, namely the Infrastructure and Planning Division, while the application was processed by the EIA Division exercising powers delegated to it by the Director. The application, if it is acceptable to that division, would eventually be approved by the Director. The Court observed that it is only where there is a potential conflict of interest that such a procedure would be invalid. It was held that under the Waste Disposal Ordinance the Director was the waste disposal authority and an EIA application had to be made in his name. Ribeiro PJ observed at paragraph 12: 'The evidence establishes that the present environmental impact assessment process was implemented by two functionally segregated sections of the EPD, scrutinised by the public and in judicial review proceedings. It is clear that the Director did not herself play any role in it. The fact that the complaints as to conflict of interest and apparent bias made by the appellant below are not pursued in this Court represents an implicit acceptance that the statutory process involving the Director as project proponent can occur, and did in this case occur, without giving rise to such objections.'

618. The Ordinance t binds the government.[779] However, section 3(2) provides that sections 26 and 27 do not have effect to permit proceedings to be taken against, or to impose criminal liability on, the government or on a person doing anything in the course of carrying out his duties as a public officer. It is difficult to envisage in

778. [2014] 5 HKLRD 194, [2014] HKEC 1459.
779. The Environmental Impact Assessment Ordinance, s. 3(1).

what circumstances a public officer can commit an offence under section 26 (constructing or decommissioning a designated project without or contrary to an environmental permit) or section 27 (resisting or obstructing a public officer or failure to provide information a public officer requires). A public officer is not personally liable for anything done or omitted to be done in the honest belief that such act or omission was required or authorized to discharge his functions under the Ordinance. While public officers are exempted from personal liability, the Ordinance does not exclude the possibility of government liability in tort for such act or omission of the public officer.[780]

619. Provision has been made, as in other environmental statutes, for administrative measures to be taken to prevent any environmental damage caused by government action and to take remedial measures. Where the Director of Environmental Protection considers that a public officer, in carrying out his duties in the service of the government, has contravened the Ordinance, the Director must report the matter to the Chief Secretary for Administration, unless the contravention has been immediately terminated to his satisfaction. On receiving the report, if the Chief Secretary for Administration's enquiry shows that the contravention is still continuing or likely to continue, he must ensure that best practicable steps are taken to stop the contravention or avoid the recurrence and to remedy any environmental damage that may have occurred.[781]

II. Key Personnel

A. The Chief Executive

620. In comparison to the other environmental statutes, the Environmental Impact Assessment Ordinance gives only a limited role to the Chief Executive. His only powers are: (1) the power to exempt a project from the provisions of the Ordinance, in the public interest;[782] (2) the power to suspend vary or cancel an environmental permit;[783] and (3) the power to appoint a panel of persons suitable for appointment as members of an Appeal Board.[784]

B. Chief Secretary for the Administration

621. The Chief Secretary has a role to play, where a public official has contravened the Ordinance and there is a need to prevent environmental damage. This has been discussed in paragraph 618 above. He has no other part to play under the Ordinance.

780. *Ibid.*, s. 31(1) and (2).
781. *Ibid.*, s. 3(3) and (4).
782. The Environmental Impact Assessment Ordinance, s. 30(1).
783. *Ibid.*, s. 14(1).
784. *Ibid.*, s. 18.

C. The Secretary for the Environment

622. The Secretary for the Environment has the power of a legislative nature to make regulations, to issue Technical Memoranda and to amend Schedules 2 and 3 which describe designated projects.[785] He may determine that contiguous projects which individually do not qualify as designated projects must be taken together as amounting to a designated project.[786] The Secretary may act in an advisory capacity, where any Technical Memorandum gives him such advisory power.[787] In giving such advice, the Secretary must ensure that the effect of his advice is to protect the environment. The Secretary has the power to authorize certain acts by the Director of Environmental Protection, such as the issuing by the Director of a cessation order.[788]

D. The Director of Environmental Protection

623. As in relation to other environmental legislation, the Director of Environmental Protection plays the central administrative role in implementing the Environmental Impact Assessment Ordinance. He has the power to set the form of any document required under the Ordinance,[789] such as the application for EIA study brief.[790] The Director is required to be guided by any Technical Memoranda issued by the Secretary when deciding selected matters under the Ordinance. Where the Ordinance so provides, he is required to act on the advice given by the Secretary[791] or other relevant authority.[792]

624. The Technical Memorandum on the EIA provides that Director may seek the advice of the Secretary: (a) where there is likely to be unresolved conflicts on the content of the EIA study brief or the EIA report: (b) where there is disagreement regarding the EIA findings and conclusions of the report between the Director and other relevant authorities (such as the Director of Planning) that he has consulted;[793] and (c) where the mitigation measures described in the EIA report lead to conflicts.[794]

785. *Ibid.*, ss 32, 16 and 4(2).
786. *Ibid.*, s. 4(4).
787. *Ibid.*, s. 16(2) and (3).
788. *Ibid.*, s. 24.
789. *Ibid.*, s. 33(1).
790. *Ibid.*, s. 5(1)(a).
791. *Ibid.*, s. 16(3).
792. Some of the relevant authorities are Director of Agriculture and Fisheries (on nature conservation, ecological assessment, agriculture, animal and plant health fisheries), the Director of Planning (on visual and landscaping aspects), the Commissioner of Transport (on traffic and transport matters) and the Director of Health (on human health matters). *See* 'Taking Advice from Other Authorities', Technical Memorandum on Environmental Impact Assessment Process, s. 9.
793. *See* 'Taking Advice from other Relevant Authorities', Technical Memorandum on Environmental Impact Assessment Process, s. 9.
794. Technical Memorandum on Environmental Impact Assessment Process, s. 10.

E. The Advisory Council on the Environment

625. The Advisory Council on the Environment performs an important advisory role in the EIA process. The Advisory Council's advice in relation to an application for an EIA permit, side by side with public comments, plays an important part in providing critical advice to the Director in arriving at his decisions, especially by commenting on project profiles and EIA reports

F. The EIA Appeal Board

626. Just as other environmental statutes, the Environmental Impact Assessment Ordinance provides for an administrative appeal against certain decisions made under the Ordinance. The Appeal Board is known as the Environmental Impact Assessment Appeal Board. The Chief Executive appoints a Chairman, a Deputy Chairman and members of the appeal panel for a renewable term of three years. The Chairman and the Deputy Chairman must be persons who are qualified to be appointed as a District Judge and members of the panel are such persons as the Chief Executive considers suitable for such appointment.[795] The Chairman has the power to appoint an Appeal Board consisting of such number of panel members, not less than three, as he considers appropriate to hear an appeal. An Appeal Board is chaired by the Chairman or Deputy Chairman. Public officers are disqualified from serving as members of an Appeal Board.[796]

§4. ENVIRONMENTAL IMPACT ASSESSMENT

627. United Nations Environment Programme defines EIA as a tool used to identify the environmental, social and economic impacts of a project prior to decision-making. It aims to predict environmental impacts at an early stage in project planning and design, find ways and means to reduce adverse impacts, shape projects to suit the local environment and present the predictions and options to decision-makers. By using EIA both environmental and economic benefits can be achieved, such as reduced cost and time of project implementation and design, avoided treatment/clean-up costs and impacts of laws and regulations.[797]

I. Identifying Projects That Are Subject to an EIA

628. An EIA is required for any designated project. The Ordinance defines environmental impact of a designated project as follows:

(1) an on-site or off-site change that the project may cause in the environment;

795. The Environmental Impact Assessment Ordinance, s. 18.
796. *Ibid.*, s. 19(5).
797. At http://www.unep.org/regionalseas/publications/reports/RSRS/pdfs/rsrs122.pdf.

(2) an effect of the change on: (a) the well-being of people, flora, fauna and eco-systems; (b) physical and cultural heritage; (c) a structure, site or other thing that is of historical or archaeological significance;
(3) an on-site or off-site effect on any of the things referred to in point (2) from activities carried on for the project;
(4) a change to the project that the environment may cause, whether the change or effect occurs within or outside the site of the project.[798]

629. Designated projects are listed in Schedules 2 (designated projects that require an environmental permit) and 3 (major designated projects that require an EIA report but not an environmental permit). The Secretary for the Environment may by order published in the Gazette amend the lists of designated projects by adding to or removing projects from the lists.

630. Designated projects are only those listed in schedules 2 and 3. There is no discretionary power given to an administrative agency to determine whether a particular project is likely to have such significant environmental impacts as to require thorough examination through the EIA process.

631. However, the Secretary for the Environment has discretionary power to order that a particular activity must be regarded as a designated project in a very limited context. The Secretary may direct that a project which, if individually taken, does not amount to a designated project, must be treated as a designated project taken together with other contiguous projects, which are proposed by the same person or associated persons. The Secretary may, after consultation with the Director of Environmental Protection, designate such contiguous projects as a designated project if he is satisfied that the purpose behind the separation of the projects is to avoid the purposes of the Ordinance.[799]

II. Designated Projects

632. Schedules 2 and 3 of the Environmental Impact Assessment Ordinance list designated projects. Schedule 2 lists designated projects which require an environmental permit. Designated projects listed in Schedule 2 are of two types: (i) projects to construct or operate a designated project; and (ii) projects to decommission a designated project. Schedule 3 lists engineering feasibility studies which require an environmental report but not an environmental permit.

798. Environmental Impact Assessment Ordinance, Sch. 1 'Interpretation'.
799. *Ibid.*, s. 4.

A. *Designated Projects That Require an Environmental Permit to Construct and Operate*

633. They are listed in Part I of Schedule 2 under the following heads: roads, railways and depots; airports and port facilities; reclamation, hydraulic and marine facilities, dredging and dumping; energy supply; water extraction and water supply; sewage collection, treatment, disposal and reuse; waste storage, transfer and disposal facilities; utility pipelines, transmission pipelines and substations; waterways and drainage works; mineral extraction; industrial activities; storage, transfer and trans-shipment of fuels; agriculture and fisheries activities; community facilities; tourist and recreational developments; residential and other developments; and miscellaneous.

B. *Designated Projects That Require an Environmental Permit for Decommissioning*

634. They are listed in Part II of Schedule 2. Decommissioning is defined in Schedule 1 (which defines words and phrases used in the Environmental Impact Assessment Ordinance) as 'ceasing production and demolishing an existing plant for the development or redevelopment of the site'. The listed decommissioning works include decommissioning of airports, oil refineries, electricity or gas generation plants, petrochemical works, explosives depots and waste incinerators.

C. *Designated Projects That Require an EIA Report but Not an Environmental Permit*

635. Schedule 3 of the Environmental Impact Assessment Ordinance lists two types of engineering feasibility studies of large-scale developments that must follow the environmental impact assessment process and obtain an EIA report. They are: (a) engineering feasibility study of urban development projects with a study area covering more than 20 ha or involving a total population of more than 100,000; and (b) engineering feasibility study of redevelopment projects with a study area covering more than 100,000 existing or new population. These call for the approval of an EIA report. Where a designated project is proposed in an area within such a feasibility study area, the approved EIA report will provide useful guidance and, if appropriate, the designated project may be submitted for an environmental permit on the basis of that EIA report.

III. Exemption of Designated Projects from the Environmental Impact Assessment Ordinance

A. Existing Projects

636. A designated project listed in Part I of Schedule 2 of the Environmental Impact Assessment Ordinance (such as a project to construct an airport or a railway) is exempt from the requirements of the Ordinance if it has been authorized, approved or permitted before the Ordinance came into effect. This provision has been made to safeguard any existing development rights. It is important to keep in mind that major projects of the type that the Ordinance is directed at might have been subjected to an EIA under the administrative arrangement that was in place before the enactment of the Ordinance.

637. A designated project is considered to have an existing authorization, approval or permit if it has had planning permission granted by the Town Planning Board; had consent for commencement of building works granted by the Building Authority under the Building Ordinance; had reclamation authorized under the Foreshore and Seabed (Reclamations) Ordinance; had road works authorized under the Roads (Works, Use and Compensation) Ordinance; been approved as a new development under the Country Parks Ordinance or the Marine Parks Ordinance; authorized under the Water Pollution Control (Sewerage) Regulation.

638. The Ordinance exempts designated projects which had commenced construction or been in operation before the Ordinance came into effect. Such projects do not need to have an environmental permit. Likewise, a project listed in Part II of Schedule 2 is exempt from the Ordinance so far as the decommissioning of a project is concerned if the demolition plan for it had been approved by the Building Authority before the Ordinance came into effect.

639. We saw in paragraph 622 above that the Secretary for the Environment has the power to amend Schedule 2 and Schedule 3 by adding to the list of designated projects. If a project which has already been approved, permitted or authorized by the relevant authority is added to one of the Schedules, then it would be regarded as an existing project and is exempt from the Ordinance. Similarly, the Ordinance exempts any existing project whose construction commences within six months of the addition of the project to a Schedule.[800]

B. Material Changes to Existing Projects Are Not Exempt

640. While existing projects are exempted, any changes in the project which is likely to have significant impacts which were not envisaged at the time the project was carried into effect need to be examined. The Ordinance provides therefore that

800. *Ibid.*, s. 4(3).

a material change[801] to an exempted project is subject to the Ordinance and requires an environmental permit. Section 9(4) provides that a material change to an exempted project is subject to the requirements of the Ordinance and requires an EIA to be carried out leading to an environmental permit. However, section 5(10) of the Ordinance provides:

> The Director may permit an applicant to apply directly for an environmental permit for a material change to an exempted project by notice in writing if the applicant satisfies the Director, having regard to the project profile, that the impact of the material change to the project and the mitigation measures described in the project profile meet the requirements of the Technical Memorandum.

C. *Exemption of Projects in the Public Interest*

641. The Chief Executive in Council may, by an order published in the Gazette, exempt a project from the provisions of the Ordinance if it is in the public interest to do so.[802] It is not clear what kinds of circumstances may give rise to such public interest in the absence of any guidelines or criteria in the Ordinance, Technical Memoranda or other administrative guidelines. Any exemption granted by the Chief Executive in Council may be subject to conditions and limitations;[803] may have effect for a period of time;[804] and may be partial in operation with respect to the project or to specified provisions of the Ordinance.[805] A person who breaches a condition or requirement imposed under an exemption order made by the Chief Executive in Council is deemed to have breached an environmental permit and triggers provisions of the Ordinance that apply to the breach of an environmental permit.

801. *Ibid.,* Sch. 1 'Interpretation': 'Material change means a physical addition or alteration to a designated project which results in an adverse environmental impact as defined in the technical memorandum.' Section 6 of the Technical Memorandum provides that a change is considered material only if it is significant. Section 6.1 provides that as a general rule, changes under the following circumstances are regarded as material changes to a designated project: a. a change to physical alignment, layout or design of the project causing an environmental impact likely to affect existing or planned community, ecologically important areas or sites of cultural heritage; b. a physical change resulting in an increase in the extent of reclamation or dredging affecting water flow or quality likely to affect ecologically important areas, or disrupting sites of cultural heritage; c. an increase in pollution emissions or discharges or waste generation likely to violate guidelines or criteria in this Technical Memorandum without mitigation measures in place; d. an increase in throughput or scale of the project leading to physical additions or alterations that are likely to violate the guidelines or criteria in this Technical Memorandum without mitigation measures in place; or e. a change resulting in physical works that are likely to affect a rare, endangered or protected species, or an important ecological habitat, or a site of cultural heritage.
802. *Ibid.*, s. 30(1).
803. *Ibid.*, s. 30(2)(a).
804. *Ibid.*, s. 30(2)(b).
805. *Ibid.*, s. 30(2)(c).

§5. THE EIA PROCESS

642. As shown above, a project proponent may directly apply for an environmental permit or apply for the approval of an EIA report leading to an environmental permit.

I. Application to Proceed Directly to Apply for an Environmental Permit

643. A person who is planning a designated project may, instead of applying for an EIA study brief to proceed with an EIA report, apply directly for an environmental permit in the following situations:

(1) where the Director of Environmental Protection is satisfied, having regard to the project profile, that the environmental impact of the project is adequately assessed in an assessment report in the register and that the information and findings of such report in the register are still relevant;[806]
(2) where Director is satisfied, having regard to the project profile, that the environmental impact of the project is unlikely to be adverse and that the mitigation measures proposed in the project profile meet the requirements of the Technical Memorandum;[807] or
(3) where the application is in respect to a material change to an exempted project, the Director is satisfied, having regard to the project profile, that the impact of such material change to the project and the mitigation measures proposed in the project profile meet the requirements of the Technical Memorandum.[808]

644. The Director must permit or refuse to permit the applicant to apply directly for an environmental permit, with or without conditions, within forty-five days of receiving the application or further information.[809] If the Director does not give written notice rejecting the application within such period, the Director is deemed to have given his consent.[810] The Director may impose conditions on a permission to apply directly for an environmental permit, and in imposing such conditions, the Director is guided by the relevant Technical Memorandum.[811]

II. Project Profile

645. The EIA process begins with the submission of a project profile. The purpose of a project profile is to enable the Director of Environmental Protection to determine the scope of the environmental issues associated with a designated

806. *Ibid.*, s. 5(9).
807. *Ibid.*, s. 5(11). The Director may so allow only with the consent of the Secretary for the Environment.
808. *Ibid.*, s. 5(10).
809. *Ibid.*, s. 5(7).
810. *Ibid.*, s. 5(8).
811. *Ibid.*, s.s. 5(12).

project which must be addressed in the EIA study, together with the technical and procedural requirements that the EIA study must meet.[812] If the application is directly for an environmental permit, the project profile will help the Director to decide whether the application should be granted. The project proponent must submit a project profile, whether he intends to apply for an EIA study brief as a prelude to the submission of an EIA report or to make a direct application for an environmental permit.[813] A project must comply with the Technical Memorandum on Environmental Impact Assessment Process. Guidance on preparing a project profile is given in Annex 1 of the Technical Memorandum, which sets out the information that must be included in a project profile: (a) basic information, such as the purpose and nature of the project, location and scale of the project, number and types of designated projects to be covered by the project profile; (b) an outline of planning and implementation programme, including the project timetable; possible impacts on the environment during the construction, operation or decommissioning of the project, including noisy operations, manufacture, storage, use handling, transport, or disposal of dangerous goods, hazardous materials or wastes, ecological impacts; (c) major elements of the surrounding environment, including existing and planned sensitive receivers and sensitive parts of the natural environment which might be affected by the proposed project, such as residential developments, health care facilities, places of religious worship, ground water resources, water catchment areas and gathering grounds, industries which are sensitive to pollution, and sites of cultural heritage; (d) environmental protection measures to be incorporated in the design and any further environmental implications, including pollution control technology, waste management systems and practices, acoustic barriers and insulation, buffer zones and landscaping, site layout and building design, and retention of natural environmental features.[814] Annex II contains guidance on preparing a project proposal for material change to a designated project.[815] The information that the applicant must submit are: and (a) basic information, including the nature of the project and the proposed addition, modification or alteration to the project; (b) possible impact on the environment including how the environment and the community might be affected by the proposed change and how the proposed modification addition or alteration deviates from or invalidates the assumptions in the previous EIA reports. Any additional or alternative types of information that the applicant considers useful in the evaluation of the proposed material change must also be provided in the profile. The information should include all existing and planned pollution sources and sensitive receivers to the best knowledge of the applicant at the time of the submission.

812. *Ibid.*, s. 2.1.1(a).
813. *Ibid.*, s. 5(2).
814. *See* the Technical Memorandum on Environmental Impact Assessment Process.
815. Section 6.2 of the Technical Memorandum on EIA provides as follows: 'The environmental impact of a designated project, for which an environmental permit has been issued, is considered to be materially changed if the environmental performance requirements set out in the EIA report for this project may be exceeded or violated, even with the mitigation measures in place.'

III. EIA Study Brief

646. Where the project proponent plans to go through the full EIA process (i.e., not applying directly for an environmental permit), he must apply to the Director of Environmental Protection for an EIA study brief. The Director must determine the application within forty-five days and issue to the applicant an EIA study brief and notify the Advisory Council on the Environment of his decision.[816] The project proponent must give notice of the availability of the project profile for public inspection.[817] A copy of the project profile must also be made available to the Advisory Council on the Environment.[818] Within fourteen days of the project profile being advertised, the Advisory Council on the Environment and any member of the public may comment on the project profile.[819] The Director must consider any comments received in drawing up the study brief.[820]

647. The preparation of the study brief by the Director of Environmental Protection Department is what is generally referred to as the 'scoping stage' of the EIA process. Scoping is the process of determining the content and extent of the matters which must be covered in the environmental information to be submitted by the applicant. The study brief sets out the purposes and objectives of the EIA study, the scope of environmental issues which must be addressed, the requirements that EIA study must fulfil, and the necessary procedural and reporting requirements.[821] The study brief may, where appropriate, prescribe the methodologies or approaches that the EIA study must follow, or the matters the EIA study must take into account.[822] Where necessary, the Director may prescribe in the study brief the assessment methodologies which are necessary for sound assessment of certain issues listed in the brief.[823]

648. In setting out the scope of the issues to be addressed, the Director must have due regard to the factors listed in the Technical Memorandum on EIA Process and other guidelines and criteria laid down in the Technical Memorandum. He must also have due regard to the following criteria:

(a) the scope of issues must be relevant to the project by virtue of its type, scale and location, or the likely emissions, discharges, waste generation, destruction, alteration or environmental changes that may result from the project;
(b) previous relevant EIA and environmental studies have identified such issues as being of relevance to the project and of having the potential for causing adverse environmental impacts;

816. The Environmental Impact Assessment Ordinance, s. 5.
817. *Ibid.*, s. 5(2).
818. *Ibid.*, s. 5(3).
819. *Ibid.*, s. 5(6).
820. *Ibid.*, s. 5(6).
821. Technical Memorandum on Environmental Impact Assessment Process, s. 3.1.
822. *Ibid.*, s. 3.1.
823. *Ibid.*, s. 3.6.

(c) the issues under consideration have been causes of environmental complaints in the past;
(d) experiences on actual implementation of similar projects, scientific researches or overseas experiences show that a particular aspect of the project has potential to cause serious environmental effects.[824]

649. A study brief must define the purposes, objectives and detailed requirements of the study and indicate the scope of issues, the timeframe of environmental issues if appropriate, and the framework in which the applicant shall carry out an EIA study to meet the requirements laid down in this Technical Memorandum. The study brief may stipulate the geographic and temporal boundaries of the assessment.[825]

650. A study brief may set out issues relating to the combined impacts of the entire project or the cumulative impacts of the existing, committed and planned developments in the vicinity of the project, but such issues must be limited to those that may have a bearing on the environmental acceptability of the project. Such assessment must be based on the best available information at the time of the assessment. Such information must be that which the applicant has access to or is as provided or referred to by the Director in the EIA.[826] A study brief must be limited to those issues for which compliance with the guidelines or criteria in the Technical Memorandum has not been demonstrated or where there are doubts about their compliance with the guidelines or criteria in the Technical Memorandum.[827] Where necessary, the Director may prescribe in the EIA study brief the assessment methodologies which are necessary for sound assessment of certain issues listed in the brief.[828] The EIA study brief may cover more than one designated project. The applicant shall state in the project profile the number and types of designated projects that shall be covered by the same EIA study.[829]

651. The importance of the study brief in the EIA process and how the relevant technical memorandum and the study brief are to be construed was explained in *Shiu Wing Steel Ltd v Director of Environmental Protection & Airport Authority (No 2)* as follows: 'Although the TM and the SB are not legislative instruments, they are expressed to impose duties and to prescribe procedures. To ascertain whether an EIA report meets their requirements, their provisions must be properly understood. The TM and the SB are both technical instruments, to be understood as an expert risk assessor, properly understanding the legal requirements they create, would understand them. The TM and the SB define the scope of the power under s.8(3)

824. *Ibid.*, s. 3.2.
825. *Ibid.*, s. 3.3.
826. *Ibid.*, s. 3.4.
827. *Ibid.*, s. 3.5.
828. *Ibid.*, s. 3.6.
829. *Ibid.*, s. 3.7.

and condition the exercise of that power, even though the meaning of those documents may have to be ascertained without employing the rules of statutory interpretation. The Director's opinion as to what the TM and SB require is not sufficient to establish a lawful exercise of the power of approval under s.8(3); s.6(1) makes what the TM and SB in fact require and the EIA report's meeting of those requirements the relevant criterion. As the scope of the s.8(3) power depends on, inter alia, a correct definition of what the TM and SB require, it is a question of law for the court if the Director's decision is being judicially reviewed.'[830] The Court of Final Appeal held that 'it is not a question whether the Director acted reasonably in attributing a given meaning to the TM and SB. The question the Director had to answer under s.6(3) had to be answered objectively'.[831] The need for objectively ascertaining the requirements of the Technical Memorandum and the study brief is of crucial importance because at the stage of approving an EIA report, the Director must be satisfied that the report meets those requirements: ' ... the question of the EIA report's meeting the requirements of the SB and TM is for the Court to determine. It is a question of construction, albeit the TM and the SB are to be construed not as legislative instruments but as they would be understood by an expert risk assessor. In other words, the court determines what the TM and the SB require but technical evidence may be needed to show that an EIA report meets or does not meet the requirements so determined. It is one thing to acknowledge that satisfaction of the requirements or proof of satisfaction calls for expertise; it is another to allow the Director or an expert risk assessor to define for himself or herself the requirements to be satisfied. The definition of the legal effect of the TM and the SB is necessarily a matter of law but it is necessary to appreciate any special or technical meaning which experts may attribute to particular terms'.[832]

IV. EIA Report

652. The major submission that the project proponent is required to make is the EIA report. Having received the EIA study brief from the Director of Environmental Protection, the project proponent must prepare an EIA report in accordance with the requirements of the EIA study brief and the relevant Technical Memorandum, namely the Technical Memorandum on EIA Process.[833] An EIA report refers to a document or a series of documents that provides a detailed assessment of the likely environmental impacts and environmental benefits of the project. Such assessment must be in quantitative terms, wherever possible, and in qualitative terms.[834]

---

830. *Shiu Wing Steel Ltd v Director of Environmental Protection & Airport Authority (No 2)* (2006) 9 HKCFAR 478 (CFA), [23].
831. *Ibid.*, [29].
832. *Ibid.*, [30].
833. The Environmental Impact Assessment Ordinance, s. 6(1).
834. Technical Memorandum on Environmental Impact Assessment Process, s. 4.1.

A. *Contents of an EIA Report*

653. The study brief sets out the project-specific study objectives and the detailed scope of any required EIA study. Issues that an EIA report is required to address include: (a) the proposed project and associated works together with the requirements and environmental benefits for carrying out the proposed project; (b) the elements of the community and the environment likely to be affected by the proposed project; (c) the likely adverse impacts of the project; (d) proposals for mitigation measures to minimize pollution, environmental disturbance and nuisance during construction, operation and, if applicable, decommissioning of the project; (e) environmental monitoring and audit requirements; and (f) the need for additional studies to implement mitigation measures.[835]

654. The report must describe the characteristics of the environment in a way sufficient for identification and prediction of environmental impacts. Where necessary, baseline environmental surveys must be carried out to determine the existing environmental conditions on the site and in all environs likely to be affected by the proposed project. The issues described in the EIA study brief must be investigated and would typically include existing water and sediment quality, air quality, the existing noise environment, ecology, the cultural heritage and the man-made environment. These surveys must normally include the site of the project, its access, and any other areas likely to be impacted during construction and operation (or decommissioning). The type and duration of baseline surveys must be such that there will be adequate information taking account of natural variation to define the existing conditions. This information forms the basis for predicting and evaluating the impacts from the project so that the study objectives can be met. Where appropriate, results from past studies can be used.[836] The report also must contain:

(1) an impact prediction;
(2) an impact evaluation; and
(3) an impact mitigation.

1. Impact Prediction Study

655. The impact prediction study must be capable of: (i) identifying potential impacts which may be harmful or beneficial to the environment; (ii) identifying receivers, habitats or resources which are vulnerable to change; (iii) defining the project/environment interactions; (iv) examining the chain of events or 'pathways' linking cause with effect; (v) describing and predicting the reasonable case scenario and/or the worst-case scenario, or such scenarios as required in the EIA study brief; and (vi) predicting the likely nature, extent and magnitude of the anticipated

835. Technical Memorandum on Environmental Impact Assessment Process, s. 4.2.
836. *Ibid.*, s. 4.3.1(a).

changes and effects such that an evaluation, in quantitative terms as far as possible, can be made with respect to the criteria described in Annexes 4–10 inclusive.[837]

2. Impact Evaluation Study

656. The impact evaluation study must be capable of addressing: (i) the existing or projected environmental conditions without the project in place; (ii) the projected environmental conditions with the project in place and the sum total of the environmental impacts taking into account all relevant existing, committed and planned projects; (iii) a differentiation between the environmental impact caused by the project and that caused by other projects, and to what extent the project aggravates or improves the existing or projected environmental conditions; (iv) the environmental impact during different phases of construction and development of the project; and (v) the evaluation of the seriousness of the residual environmental impacts.[838]

3. Impact Mitigation Study

657. The impact mitigation study must be capable of: (i) identifying and evaluating mitigation measures in order to avoid, reduce or remedy the impacts; (ii) assessing the effectiveness of mitigation measures; and (iii) defining the residual environmental impacts, which are the net impacts remaining with the mitigation measures in place.[839]

B. Model Contents of an Assessment Report

658. Annex 11 of the Technical Memorandum sets out the model contents of an EIA report as follows:

- Introduction: The background of the project, purpose of the EIA study and the approach.
- Description of the project: Key project requirements, Site location and site history, nature, scope and benefits of the project, size or scale, shape and design of the project, project timetable and phasing of the project, means by which the project will be implemented, any related projects, type, scope, scale, frequency and duration of the construction, operational or decommissioning (if relevant) activities, background and history of the project, including considerations given to different options, and the project's different sitting or alignment, description of scenarios with or without the project.

837. *Ibid.*, s. 4.3.1.(b).
838. *Ibid.*, s. 4.3.1.(c).
839. *Ibid.*, s. 4.3.1.(d).

- Environmental legislation: Policies, plans, standards and criteria (applicable environmental ordinances and regulations, applicable government environmental policies and plans, applicable environmental standards and criteria, other references).
- Description of the environment: Baseline environmental conditions, environmental trends.
- Description of assessment methodologies: Assessment methodologies, assumptions and criteria, including sample calculations and input and output files of a typical model run for all mathematical modelling.
- Identification of environmental impacts: Potential environmental impacts including the types, characteristics and estimated quantities of emissions, discharges, wastes, potential risks, disturbances or displacement associated with the activities relating to the project during construction, operation and decommissioning phases, description of resources or receivers which are vulnerable to change or environmental impacts.
- Prediction and evaluation of environmental impacts: Prediction of environmental impacts (including beneficial or adverse; direct or indirect; short term or long term; reversible or irreversible; transboundary; cumulative) evaluation of predicted environmental impacts against applicable environmental legislation, policies, plans, standards and criteria.
- Mitigation of adverse environmental impacts: Measures to eliminate, reduce or remedy adverse environmental impacts; Definition and evaluation of residual environmental impacts definition and evaluation of net environmental impacts with mitigation measures in place.
- Environmental monitoring and audit: Need for and scope of monitoring and audit, environmental monitoring and audit requirements, if found to be necessary, and the related environmental monitoring and audit programme.
- Conclusions and recommendations.
- A schedule of all mitigation measures recommended in the EIA report, listing out what the mitigation measures are, by whom, when, where and to what requirements, and including the key environmental monitoring and audit requirements.
- Response to comments must be appended to the report.

C. Consideration of the Report

659. The project proponent must pay the prescribed application fee and submit the EIA report to the Director of Environmental Protection for consideration. The Director may require the applicant to supply sufficient copies of the report so that the Director is able to circulate copies to relevant parties as defined in the Technical Memorandum.[840] The Director of Environmental Protection must decide whether or not the assessment meets the requirements of the study brief and the Technical

840. The Environmental Impact Assessment Ordinance, s. 6(2).

Memorandum on EIA Process.[841] In reviewing the quality of the EIA report, the Director must have regard to the guideline of the Technical Memorandum. It must be noted that what is required is substantial compliance with the study brief and the Technical Memorandum. Minor non-compliance would not invalidate the Director's decision. Any non-compliance must be serious enough to affect the validity of the approval.[842] As Chow J observed in *Ho Loy v Director of Environmental Protection*: 'if the Director approves a report which does not, in fact, fully meet the requirements of the Technical Memorandum and Study Brief, it is, I consider, strongly arguable that whether the Director's decision should thereby be treated as being a decision made without jurisdiction, or unlawful, should depend on the circumstances of the case, including the nature and seriousness of the non-compliance. In any event, whether to grant relief in any judicial review, even if a ground of review is made out, is discretionary. If the court comes to the view, for example, that the non-compliance (or breach) is purely technical and has no material impact on the decision or on the environment, the court is entitled not to grant any relief in the exercise of its discretion'.[843]

660. The report will be considered as adequate if there are no omissions or deficiencies identified which may affect the results and conclusions of the assessment. The Director must in particular consider the following:[844]

(a) whether the scope and extent of the project as presented in the EIA report covers all the phases and key sequences of the project which the application under consideration is intended to cover;
(b) whether the information and descriptions in the EIA report are factually correct;
(c) whether the assessment methodologies adopted in the EIA report are consistent with the methodologies set out in Annexes 12–19 inclusive and with the general principles laid down in section 4.3, and whether the evaluation of the predicted impacts is consistent with the criteria listed in Annexes 4–10 inclusive. Where specific methodologies are not listed in the annexes or where the methodologies for certain issues can only be established on a case-by-case basis, the Director will assess whether the proposed methodologies are consistent with the methodologies adopted for Hong Kong projects having similar issues or with methodologies accepted by recognized national and international organizations;
(d) whether the identification and descriptions of the potential environmental impacts in the EIA report are complete and whether all applicable criteria in Annexes 4–10 inclusive have been considered;
(e) whether the assumptions and methodologies used are sound and adequate;

841. 'The coverage and approaches adopted in the environmental Impact Assessment Report shall be reviewed against the Environmental Impact Assessment Study Brief and the guidelines in this technical memorandum': Technical Memorandum on Environmental Impact Assessment Process, s. 4.4.
842. *See Ho Loy v Director of Environmental Protection* [2016] HKEC 2751.
843. *Ibid.*, [57].
844. Technical Memorandum on Environmental Impact Assessment Process, s. 4.2.

(f) whether adverse environmental effects are avoided to the maximum practicable extent;
(g) whether the assessment has considered and compared the environmental benefits and disbenefits of various scenarios with or without the project;
(h) whether lessons learned from other similar projects are incorporated into the project;
(i) whether the report has sufficiently defined all environmental protection requirements and measures necessary to avoid or reduce the adverse environmental impacts to within the applicable standards or criteria;
(j) for impacts where there are no applicable quantitative standards or criteria, whether the report has defined the best practicable mitigation measures that shall be adopted for the project;
(k) whether the report has assessed and determined the feasibility, practicability, programming and effectiveness of the recommended mitigation measures;
(l) whether the report has adequately addressed the need for environmental monitoring and audit, and if it is considered to be necessary, whether it has sufficiently defined the required environmental monitoring and audit programme; and
(m) whether the report has listed out in a schedule the environmental protection requirements and mitigation measures that the applicant is prepared to implement.

D. Approval of the Report for Public Consultation

661. The Director of Environmental Protection must within sixty days of receiving the EIA report decide whether or not the report meets the requirements of the EIA study brief and the Technical Memorandum. The Director is deemed to have decided that the report meets the requirements of the EIA study and the Technical Memorandum if within sixty days of receiving the report the Director has not given notice in writing that the support does not meet such requirements.[845] If the Director decides that the EIA report does not meet the requirements of the study brief and the Technical Memorandum, he must advise the applicant of the reasons why the report is unacceptable.[846] The applicant has a right of appeal to the Appeal Board against such decision.[847]

E. Submission of the EIA Report for Public Inspection and to the Advisory Council on the Environment

662. If the Director of Environmental Protection determines that an EIA report meets the statutory requirements, he must advise the applicant when the report must be exhibited for public inspection and whether the advertisement must contain any

845. The Environmental Impact Assessment Ordinance, s. 6(5).
846. *Ibid.*, s. 6(6).
847. *Ibid.*, s. 17(1).

specific material. He must also advise whether a submission to the Advisory Council on the Environment or its Environmental Impact Assessment Sub-committee is required.[848] The applicant must, as soon as practicable after he has been notified that the EIA report is acceptable to the Director, make the report available at such locations as approved by the Director for public inspection free of charge for a period of thirty days; advertise in newspapers, as the Director requires, the availability of the report for public inspection; and provide free of charge sufficient quantities, as the Director may require, of the report for public inspection. The advertisement must set out the nature of the designated project and the location of the project site, the period for which and the places at which the report is available for inspection, that members of the public may give the Director written comments on the report before the expiry of the public inspection period and the address to which comments are to be sent and any other information that the Director may reasonably require relating to the project.[849]

F. Approval of the EIA Report

663. The Director of Environmental Protection may, within fourteen days of the expiry of the public inspection period, or the receipt of comments from the Advisory Council on the Environment, whichever is later, ask an applicant to give him any further information he requires to decide whether to approve an EIA report. The Director must supply the applicant with one set of written comments received from the members of the public and the Advisory Council on the Environment free of charge where comments have been received.[850]

664. The Director of Environmental Protection may approve, approve with conditions or reject the environment impact assessment report for the designated project, within the specified period.[851] He may approve the EIA report if: (1) the requirements in the study brief have been met; (2) the quality of the report meets the requirements as set out in the Technical Memorandum and the results and conclusions are technically sound and reliable;[852] (3) it addresses relevant environmental issues raised by the public and the Advisory Council on the Environment during

848. *Ibid.*, s. 6(4).
849. *Ibid.*, s. 7.
850. *Ibid.*, s. 8(1).
851. *Ibid.*, s. 8(3).
852. As the Court of Final Appeal explained in *Shiu Wing Steel Ltd v Director of Environmental Protection v Airport Authority (No 2)* (2006) 9 HKCFAR 478 (CFA) [29]: 'The lawfulness of the approval was not dependent on the Director's opinion if that opinion was objectively in error. If the EIA report in fact met the requirements of the SB and the TM, the Director's decision to approve the report is valid; if the EIA report did not in fact meet those requirements, the Director had no power to approve the report. It is immaterial whether the Director thought that the requirements were met. And, as the limits of the Director's power are a matter of law, it is for the Court to determine the meaning and scope of those requirements.' *See also* the discussion of this case above under 'III. EIA Study Brief'.

the public inspection period; and (4) all relevant environmental principles and criteria laid down in the Technical Memorandum can be met and the residual environmental impacts[853] are within the relevant criteria, with sound environmental justifications and without long-term serious environmental implications.[854] In case the report requires certain amendments but such amendments will not affect the validity of the assessment and the overall results and conclusions of the report, the Director may approve the report with conditions.[855]

665. If the Director is not satisfied that the report complies with the above-stated requirements, he may reject the report, giving reasons for the rejection.[856] The applicant may appeal to the Appeal Board against such rejection.[857]

666. The Director must make his decision of approval or rejection of the EIA report within thirty days of: (a) the expiry of the public inspection period; (b) the receipt of comments from the Advisory Council on the Environment, or (c) the receipt of further information from the applicant in response to comments from members of the public or the Advisory Council on Environment.[858] If the Director does not give notice of rejecting the report or approving it with conditions within the statutory period of thirty days, he is deemed to have approved the report without conditions.[859]

G. Placing Approved Report on a Register

667. The Director must place an approved EIA report on the register.[860] The placing of approved EIA reports on the register will be relevant for decisions that the Director may make. For instance, the Director may permit an applicant to apply directly for an environmental permit if he satisfies the Director, having regard to the project profile, that: (a) the environmental impact of the project is adequately assessed in an EIA report in the register; and (b) the information and findings of the EIA report in the register are still relevant.[861] A person who wishes to have constructed, construct or operate a designated project listed in Part I of Schedule 2 or to decommission a designated project listed in Part II of Schedule 2 must, when applying for an environmental permit, prepare and obtain approval for an EIA report or instead refer to an EIA report on the register.[862]

853. Residual environmental impacts refer to the net environmental impacts after mitigation, taking into account the background environmental conditions and the impacts from existing, committed and planned projects: Technical Memorandum on Environmental Impact Assessment Process, s. 4.4.3.
854. Technical Memorandum in Environmental Impact Assessment Process, s. 4.5.1.
855. *Ibid.,* s. 4.5.2.
856. The Environmental Impact Assessment Ordinance, s. 8(6).
857. *Ibid.*, s. 17(1).
858. *Ibid.*, s. 8(3).
859. *Ibid.*, s. 8(4).
860. *Ibid.*, s. 8(5).
861. *Ibid.*, s. 5(9).
862. *Ibid.*, s. 10(1)(b).

V. Environmental Permit

668. A person must not construct or operate a listed designated project or decommission a listed designated project without an environmental permit for the project; or contrary to conditions, if any, set out in the permit.[863] A person who wishes to have constructed, construct or operate a designated project or to decommission a designated project must apply to the Director of Environmental Protection for an environmental permit. In the application, he must: (a) refer to an EIA report on the register; (b) submit an EIA report approved by the Director for the project; or (c) refer to the permission he has received from the Director to apply directly for an environmental permit.[864]

A. Determination of an Application for Environmental Permit

669. In granting or refusing an environmental permit, the Director of Environmental Protection must have regard to the following:

(1) the approved EIA report;
(2) the attainment and maintenance of an acceptable environmental quality;
(3) whether the environmental impacts caused or experienced by the project might be prejudicial to the health or well-being of people, flora, fauna or ecosystems;
(4) any relevant Technical Memorandum;
(5) any EIA report approved under the Environmental Impact Assessment Ordinance or any conditions in an approval; and
(6) any comments submitted to him by members of the public or the Advisory Council on the Environment.[865]

670. The Technical Memorandum on the EIA Process states that the Director will grant an environmental permit to the applicant if an EIA report covering the project has been approved with or without conditions under the Ordinance. It also provides that any refusal of environmental permit shall only be on environmental grounds in accordance with the Ordinance and this Technical Memorandum, not on land-use grounds.[866] When considering whether or not to grant an environmental permit, the duty of the Director is not to appraise the wisdom of the proposal, but to consider the assessment and acceptability of the environmental impacts which may be caused by the project.[867] What matters the Director must take into account are clearly set out in the Ordinance, the Technical Memorandum and the study brief. Therefore, 'generally speaking, compliance with the express obligations imposed by the Ordinance (including the Technical Memorandum and the Study Brief created

863. *Ibid.*, s. 9(1).
864. *Ibid.*, s. 10.
865. *Ibid.*, s. 10(2).
866. Technical Memorandum on Environmental Impact Assessment Process, s. 7.1 and 7.6.
867. *Ho Loy v Director of Environmental Protection* [2016] HKEC 2751, [127].

under it) should be regarded as a sufficient discharge of the Director's duties in relation to the environmental impact assessment process, and the court should not readily impose additional obligations on the Director over and above what is expressly required by the Ordinance'.[868] There might however be circumstances where more is required from the Director such as that the Director, in the exercise of his statutory power, must ask himself the right question and take reasonable steps to acquaint himself with the relevant information to enable him to answer it correctly: This is commonly referred to as the '*Tameside* duty'.[869]

B. Imposition of Conditions

671. The Director may grant an environmental permit subject to conditions which he thinks fit and, without limiting the general nature of conditions which the Director may include in an environmental permit, he may include conditions relating to matters set out in Ordinance, but must be guided by the relevant Technical Memorandum. A condition specified in an environmental permit may be subject to a qualification, restriction or requirement concerning the location, time or period of the condition's application.[870]

672. The Director must not normally specify in an environmental permit a condition that might be imposed on an approval of any nature under another pollution control Ordinance.[871] He may, however, impose such a condition on an environmental permit if the condition is necessary to meet the requirements of the Technical Memorandum or the study brief or the EIA report of the project or the permission to directly apply for an environmental permit specifies expressly that the environmental permit may include such a condition.[872]

673. In determining the conditions to be imposed on a permit, the Director will use the following criteria: (a) the mitigation measures set out in the project profile or the findings or conclusions in the approved EIA report; (b) the conditions of

868. *Ibid.*, [45].

869. Taking its name from *Secretary of State for Education and Science v Tameside Metropolitan Borough Council* [1977] AC 1014.

870. The Environmental Impact Assessment Ordinance, s. 10(5), (6) and (7). An example of conditions imposed on an environmental permit may be taken from the environmental permit granted for the construction of the Third Runway of the Hong Kong International Airport. The conditions included the following: The applicant shall (1) in consultation with the Agriculture, Fisheries and Conservation Department, submit a marine park proposal including the proposed size and management plan of the marine park as recommended in the EIA report; (2) formulate a detailed Marine Ecology Conservation Plan for the conservation of marine life particularly Chinese White Dolphins and submit the plan to the Director for approval; devise a Marine Traffic Routes and Management Plan for high speed ferries of the SkyPier and submit the plan to the Director for approval; and submit a detailed Fisheries Management Plan in collaboration with fishermen for supporting the fishing industry and enhancing fisheries resources in the western Hong Kong waters especially the Lantau waters to the Director for approval.

871. *Ibid.*, s. 10(8).

872. *Ibid.*

approval of the assessment report; (c) the conditions of approval for directly proceeding to an application for an environmental permit; (d) the advice given to him by other relevant authorities; or (e) the measures that are necessary to meet the guidelines, standards or criteria laid down in the Technical Memorandum on the EIA Process.[873]

C. Informing the Applicant of the Outcome

674. The Director must advise the applicant and the Advisory Council on the Environment, where it has been consulted on the EIA report, of the grant or refusal of the environmental permit within thirty days of the later of: (a) the receipt of the application; (b) the expiry of the public inspection period of the EIA report; (c) the receipt of comments from the Advisory Council on the Environment on the EIA report; or (d) the receipt of further information from the applicant in response to comments made by the public or the Advisory Committee on the Environment on the assessment report.[874]

675. The Director is deemed to have granted an environmental permit if he has not within such thirty-day period rejected the application or approved it with conditions.[875] A refusal of an environmental permit must be accompanied by reasons why the permit is refused.[876] The applicant may appeal against such refusal to the Appeal Board.[877]

VI. Further Environmental Permit

676. There may be situations where the holder of an environmental permit may cease to be responsible for implementing the project, in which event he should surrender the permit he holds.[878] The person who assumes responsibility of the outgoing permit-holder can only continue the designated project if he has a valid environmental permit.[879] The application must be made in the form prescribed by the Director, and accompanied by the prescribed fee.[880] Such an application is referred to as an application for a further environmental permit.

873. Technical Memorandum on the Environmental Impact Assessment Process 7.2.
874. Environmental Impact Assessment Ordinance, s. 10(3).
875. *Ibid.*, s. 10(4).
876. *Ibid.*, s. 10(9).
877. *Ibid.*, s. 17(1).
878. *Ibid.*, s. 11 provides that a person who is issued with an environmental permit may surrender the whole or a part of the permit after ceasing to be responsible for implementing the whole or a part of the project.
879. *Ibid.*, s. 12(1).
880. *Ibid.*, s. 12(5).

A. Application for a Further Environmental Permit

677. A person applying for a further environmental permit is not required to submit an EIA report where he satisfies the Director that there has been no material change to the designated project since the previous environmental permit was issued.[881] The Director must issue a further environmental permit to the applicant within thirty days of receipt of the application if he is satisfied that: (a) there has been no material change to the designated project since the previous environmental permit was issued; and (b) the information and findings of the EIA report, if any, are still relevant and adequate.[882] The Director is taken to have issued a further environmental permit on the same conditions as the previous environmental permit if the Director has not given notice in writing rejecting the application or approving it with conditions within thirty days of the receipt of the application.[883]

B. Exemption from a Further Environmental Permit

678. The Director may exempt a designated project from the requirement to be further subject to an environmental permit if: (a) an environmental permit has been issued for the designated project and the terms of the environmental permit have been complied with; and (b) the designated project is not subject to any conditions under the environmental permit that are of an ongoing nature and require monitoring or other compliance.[884]

VII. Variation of an Environmental Permit at the Request of the Permit-Holder

679. The person holding an environmental permit may apply for a variation of the conditions of the environmental permit.[885] He must apply in the form approved by the Director and pay the prescribed application fee.[886] If the Director considers that it is necessary for the applicant to submit an EIA report for the variation, the applicant must be so advised within thirty days of the receipt of the application.[887] The Director is taken not to require an EIA report for the variations sought if the

881. *Ibid.*, s. 12(2).
882. *Ibid.*, s. 12(3).
883. *Ibid.*, s. 12(4).
884. *Ibid.*, s. 12(6).
885. *Ibid.*, s. 13(1).
886. *Ibid.*, s. 13(6).
887. *Ibid.*, s. 13(2).

Director does not notify the applicant within thirty days of the receipt of the application.[888] If the Director requires an applicant to submit an EIA report, the applicant may request that he be permitted to apply directly for an environmental permit, and if the applicant opts to submit for an EIA report, he must comply with provisions that apply to EIA.[889]

680. The Director may decide to amend the environmental permit without calling for an EIA report if the applicant satisfies him that: (a) there is no material change to the environmental impact of the project with the mitigation measures in place; and (b) the project complies with the requirements described in the Technical Memorandum.[890]

VIII. Cancellation or Variation of an Environmental Permit by the Director or the Chief Executive

681. The Director may, with the consent of the Secretary, suspend, vary[891] or cancel an environmental permit if he is satisfied that: (a) on the application for the environmental permit the applicant gave: (i) misleading information; (ii) wrong information; (iii) incomplete information; or (iv) false information; or (b) the applicant is no longer able to comply with the conditions of the environmental permit.[892] The Director must give written notice of his decision to suspend, vary or cancel an environmental permit under this section together with the reasons for the suspension, variation or cancellation and the conditions on which the permit can be reinstated.[893] *See Ho Loy v Director of Environmental Protection and the Chief Executive in Council*, [2014] HKEC 1358 for an unsuccessful judicial review application against the decision of the Director and the Chief Executive not to cancel or vary an environmental permit that the Director had granted. This case will be reviewed at the end of this chapter as the fifth case study.

682. The Chief Executive in Council may suspend, vary or cancel an environmental permit if he is satisfied that the continuation of the designated project is, or is likely to be more prejudicial to the health and well-being of people, flora, fauna or ecosystems than expected at the time of issuing the environmental permit.[894] The Chief Executive in Council must give the reasons for the suspension, variation or cancellation and the conditions on which the permit can be reinstated.[895]

---

888. *Ibid.*, s. 13(3).
889. *Ibid.*
890. *Ibid.*, s. 13(5).
891. *Ibid.*, s. 14(5) provides that 'vary' in s. 14 includes to delete, modify or add to the conditions of an environmental permit.
892. *Ibid.*, s. 14(1).
893. *Ibid.*, s. 14(2).
894. *Ibid.*, s. 14(3).
895. *Ibid.*, s. 14(4).

683. There is an appeal against a decision of the Director to suspend, vary or cancel an environmental decision.[896] Where the decision is taken by the Chief Executive in Council, there is no appeal. The only way that such a decision may be contested is by way of judicial review.

§6. MONITORING AND ENFORCEMENT

I. Environmental Monitoring and Audit

684. The environmental permit may impose requirements for monitoring the environmental impacts of the project for verification of predictions or the effectiveness of measures to mitigate its environmental impacts, whether such impacts occur within or outside the physical boundary of the project. The environmental permit may also impose requirements for the formulation of environmental audit requirements, including any necessary compliance and post-project audit programme, in order to review the environmental monitoring data, assess compliance with regulatory requirements, policies and standards, and identify any remedial works required to redress unacceptable or unanticipated environmental impacts. In determining the need for and the scope of the environmental monitoring and audit programme, the Director must have regard to the findings and recommendations in an approved EIA report.[897]

685. Generally implementation of a full environmental monitoring and auditing programme is required in the following circumstances: (a) the project has the potential of causing environmental impacts which are or are likely to be prejudicial to the health or well-being of people, the flora, fauna or ecosystem if the recommended mitigation measures are not properly implemented; (b) the project is situated in any area of high conservation value; (c) the project involves mitigation measures of which the effectiveness may require a long period to establish, e.g., compensatory planting of trees or mangroves; (d) the project involves an unproven technology; (e) the project involves unproven mitigation measures; (f) an otherwise familiar or routine mitigation measure is proposed for a new or unfamiliar environmental setting; (g) the analysis is based on a new technique or model, or there is other uncertainty about design assumptions and/or the conclusions; or (h) project scheduling is subject to change such that significant environmental impacts could result.[898]

896. *Ibid.*, s. 17(1).
897. Technical Memorandum on Environmental Impact Assessment Process, s. 8.1.
898. *Ibid.*, s. 8.3.

II. Offences

686. The Environmental Impact Assessment Ordinance creates a number of offences. Section 9 provides that it is an offence punishable by fine and imprisonment for anyone to construct or operate a designated project listed in Part I Schedule 1 or decommission a designated project listed in Part II of Schedule 2 in contravention of the Ordinance. Prosecution for a violation of section 9 is provided by section 26. In proceedings for an offence under section 26, the prosecution does not have to prove that the acts or omissions in question were accompanied by any intention, knowledge or negligence on the part of the defendant as any element of the offence.[899] A person does not commit an offence under section 26(1) if he carries out an action in response to an emergency and in the interests of public safety or public health.[900] A person does not commit an offence under section 26(1) arising out of a breach of conditions of an environmental permit if he proves that the offence was committed without his consent or connivance and that he exercised all such diligence to prevent the commission of the offence as he ought to have exercised having regard to the nature of his functions in that capacity.[901]

687. A person for whom a project is constructed, operated or decommissioned and who permits the carrying out of the project contrary to section 9 commits an offence.[902] A person does not commit such an offence if he proves that the offence was committed without his consent or connivance and that he exercised all such diligence to prevent the commission of the offence as he ought to have exercised having regard to the nature of his functions in that capacity.[903] A person who, alone or with associated persons, separates contiguous projects, which, if taken individually, do not qualify as designated projects but which collectively qualify as a designated project, to avoid the project being considered a designated project (and thus bypassing the requirement of securing an environmental permit), commits an offence if he permits the carrying out of any part of any of the contiguous projects without first applying to the Director under section 4(5) for a ruling that the proposed contiguous projects are not to be treated collectively as a designated project.[904]

688. Where a person convicted of an offence under the Ordinance is a body corporate and it is proved that the offence was committed with the consent or connivance of, or was attributable to any neglect or omission on the part of, a director,

899. Environmental Impact Assessment Ordinance, s. 26(7).
900. *Ibid.*, s. 26(2).
901. *Ibid.*, s. 26(3).
902. *Ibid.*, s. 26(4).
903. *Ibid.*, s. 26(5).
904. *Ibid.*, s. 26(6). Section 9 prohibits the carrying out of a designated project unless an environmental permit has been granted. Section 4(4) empowers the Secretary to specify that a collection of contiguous projects proposed by a person or associated persons must be treated collectively as one designated project, if he is satisfied that the purpose behind the separation of the projects is to avoid the purposes of this Ordinance.

manager, secretary or other person concerned in the management of the body corporate, the director, manager, secretary or other person also commits the offence.[905] Where a person convicted of an offence under the Ordinance is a partner in a partnership and it is proved that the offence was committed with the consent or connivance of, or was attributable to any neglect or omission on the part of, any other partner or any person concerned in the management of the partnership, the partner or the person concerned in the management also commits the offence.[906]

III. Enforcement Powers of Public Officers

689. The Director may in writing authorize a public officer to exercise the powers conferred on an authorized officer under Part VII 'Enforcement' as the Director may specify in the authorization.[907] A public officer exercising a power under this Part: (a) may obtain the assistance of persons he reasonably requires for the purposes of the discharge of his functions; (b) shall, if required, produce his identity card, together with his written authorization under this section.[908]

690. It is an offence for a person: (1) to wilfully resist, obstruct or delay any public officer or to fail without reasonable excuse to comply with a requirement duly made by a public officer, in the exercise of a power of entry and inspection which he is authorized to exercise; (2) in compliance or purported compliance with a requirement of a public officer under Part VII of the Ordinance to produce a drawing, record or document which he knows to be incorrect or inaccurate in a material respect or does not believe to be correct or accurate; or (3) to wilfully or recklessly give information which is incorrect in a material respect or withhold information as to any of the matters for which information is required to be given under Part VII of the Ordinance.[909]

A. *Power to Enter and Search*

691. An authorized officer may, without warrant and on production of his written authorization, enter and search a place where he reasonably believes an offence against the Environmental Impact Assessment Ordinance has been or is being committed, or there is some evidence of an offence against the Ordinance.[910] He may also enter a place to serve a notice under the Ordinance or to measure, inspect, take samples and test as he reasonably believes is necessary to determine if an offence against this Ordinance has been or is being committed.[911]

---

905. *Ibid.*, s. 29(1).
906. *Ibid.*, s. 29(2).
907. *Ibid.*, s. 22(1).
908. *Ibid.*, s. 22(2).
909. *Ibid.*, s. 27.
910. *Ibid.*, s. 23(1)(a).
911. *Ibid.*, s. 23(1)(b) and (c).

692. An authorized officer shall not, except with the consent of the occupier or person in charge of the premises, enter domestic premises without a warrant issued by a magistrate.[912] A magistrate will issue a warrant if he is satisfied that there is reason to believe that: (a) an offence against the Ordinance has been or is being committed on domestic premises; or (b) there is on domestic premises anything that is or is likely to constitute evidence that an offence against the Ordinance has been or is being committed.[913] He may also issue a warrant if he is satisfied that there is reason to believe that it is necessary for an authorized officer to enter domestic premises to serve a notice or to measure, inspect, take samples or test as the authorized officer reasonably believes is necessary to determine if an offence against the Ordinance has been or is being committed.[914]

693. An authorized officer who enters a place may require any person present at that place: (a) to give details of his identity, name and address and produce his identity card for inspection by the authorized officer; or (b) who appears at the time to be responsible for or in charge of that place, to give such information or render such assistance as may be necessary to enable the authorized officer to carry out his functions under Part VII of the Ordinance.[915]

B. Power to Order Cessation of Work

694. The Director of Environmental Protection may, with the consent of the Secretary for the Environment, issue an order requiring persons working on a designated project to cease working on the project until the order is withdrawn if: (1) an environmental permit has not been issued for the project; or (2) an environmental permit has been withdrawn from the project; or (3) there has been a breach of the conditions of an environmental permit for the project resulting in environmental damage.[916]

C. Power to Order Remedial Work

695. The Director may, with the consent of the Secretary, issue an order requiring persons working on a designated project to carry out work on the project to remedy environmental damage identified by the Director.[917]

912. *Ibid.*, s. 23(2).
913. *Ibid.*, s. 23(3).
914. *Ibid.*, s. 23(4).
915. *Ibid.*, s. 23(5).
916. *Ibid.*, s. 24(1).
917. *Ibid.*, s. 24(2).

D. Power to Take Remedial Action

696. Where an order for remedial work has not been properly complied with, the Director of Environmental Protection may order remedial work. He may, with the consent of the Secretary for the Environment, take direct action to remedy any environmental damage and may recover the costs of the remedial work from the owner of, or the operator or the contractor on, the site of the designated project. Costs certified by the Director are recoverable as a civil debt due to the government.[918]

§7. APPEALS

697. The Environmental Impact Assessment Ordinance has established an Appeal Board to hear appeals against certain decisions made by the Director of Environmental Protection.

I. Appealable Decisions

698. As provided in section 17, an appeal lies to the Appeal Board in the following circumstances:

(1) Where an applicant for an EIA study brief is aggrieved by the decision of the Director of Environmental Protection as to the content of the EIA study brief.
(2) Where an applicant for an environmental permit is aggrieved by the decision of the Director of Environmental Protection not to issue a permit.
(3) Where an applicant for permission to apply directly for an environmental permit is aggrieved by the decision of the Director of Environmental Protection not to grant such permission.
(4) Where an applicant for permission to apply directly for an environmental permit is aggrieved by the decision of the Director of Environmental Protection as to conditions imposed on the permission.
(5) Where an applicant for an EIA report is aggrieved by the decision of the Director of Environmental Protection not to approve the report.
(6) Where an applicant for an environmental permit is aggrieved by the decision of the Director of Environmental Protection to impose conditions on the permit.
(7) Where an environmental permit-holder is aggrieved by the decision of the Director of Environmental Protection to vary or cancel the environmental permit.
(8) Where an environmental permit-holder is aggrieved by the decision of the Director of Environmental Protection to claim costs incidental to remedying environmental damage.

918. *Ibid.*, s. 24(3).

II. Commencement of Proceedings

699. The notice of appeal must be lodged with the Chairman of the Appeal Board within thirty days of the receipt of the notice of the decision appealed against.[919] The Environmental Impact Assessment Ordinance makes provision to ensure that both parties to the appeal are given sufficient access, in a timely manner, to information, evidence and documents relating to the appeal. The appellant must, at the same time, serve a copy of the notice of appeal on the respondent,[920] and the Appeal Board may dismiss the appeal for failure to comply with this requirement.[921] The appellant must, together with the notice of appeal, submit a statement of particulars of appeal such as the details of the decision appealed against, the grounds of appeal and particulars of evidence and documents he relies on to support his case.[922] If the appellant fails to submit such a statement of particulars, the Appeal Board may dismiss the appeal.[923]

700. It is the responsibility of the respondent, within sixty days of receiving the notice of appeal, to inform the Appeal Board and the appellant of particulars of witnesses, documents and other things he proposes to introduce in support of his case.[924] The Appeal Board may allow the appeal if the respondent fails to furnish such particulars to the appellant.[925] Any party to the appeal may require further particulars from the other party, within twenty-one days after the service of notice of appeal on the respondent, and failure of the appellant to comply with such request made by the respondent may lead to the dismissal of the appeal.[926] Similarly, the failure of the respondent to comply with a request for further particulars made by the appellant may result in the Board allowing the appeal.[927]

701. Any party to the appeal has a right to inspect documents relating to the appeal, in the possession of the other party.[928] If any party fails to comply with the request of the other party to render a document for inspection, he will not be permitted to put that document in evidence unless he satisfies the Appeal Board that he had a reason for his failure to comply which the Appeal Board deems sufficient.[929]

702. Once there has been sufficient exchange of information between the parties, the Appeal Board is required to arrange an appeal hearing without delay. Following the expiration of sixty days from the service of notice of appeal on the respondent, or the supply of requisite particulars by the respondent, whichever is the

919. Section 17(3).
920. Section 14(1).
921. Section 14(1)(a).
922. The Environmental Impact Assessment (Appeal Board) Regulation (Cap 499 sub leg A) s. 4.
923. Environmental Impact Assessment Ordinance, s. 14(1)(b).
924. The Environmental Impact Assessment (Appeal Board) Regulation (Cap 499 sub leg A), s. 4(2).
925. The Environmental Impact Assessment Ordinance, s. 19(13).
926. The Environmental Impact Assessment (Appeal Board) Regulation (Cap 499 sub leg A), s. 5 and s. 14(1).
927. *Ibid.*, s. 14.
928. *Ibid.*, s. 6(1).
929. *Ibid.*, s. 6(2).

earlier, the Chairman must fix a date, time and place for the hearing of the appeal as soon as reasonably practicable and give at least twenty-eight days' notice of the hearing to the parties.[930] Not less than seven days before the date fixed for the appeal hearing, the appellant and the respondent must lodge with the Chairman a copy of witness statements, documents and other things to be produced in evidence.[931] At the same time, each party must copy such information to the other party.[932] Upon the application of any party to the appeal, the Chairman may issue witness summonses.[933]

III. Appeal Hearing

703. The Environmental Impact Assessment (Appeal Board) Regulation makes supplementary provision regarding the conduct of an appeal hearing.[934] Where a form or matter of practice or procedure of the Appeal Board is not provided for by the Ordinance or the Regulation, the Chairman may determine how the matter should be handled.[935] The parties may be legally represented[936] and the appeal hearing is required to be held in public unless the Chairman, of his own motion or upon the application of one of the parties, orders that all or any persons should be excluded from the whole or any part of the hearing.[937]

704. The Appeal Board has been given extensive powers to ensure that a full investigation may be carried out. It may: administer an oath and receive evidence on oath; admit or take into account a statement, document, information or matter whether or not it would be admissible in a court of law; and by notice in writing summon a person to appear before it to produce a document or to give evidence. A witness before the Appeal Board has the same immunities and privileges as if he were a witness in civil proceedings before the Court of First Instance.[938]

705. The Chairman has the power to certify in writing the contempt of a person to the Court of First Instance if such a person on being summoned as a witness before the Appeal Board fails to attend; or being in attendance as a witness refuses to take an oath required by the Appeal Board to be taken, or to produce a document under his power or control required by the Appeal Board to be produced by him, or to answer a question to which the Appeal Board may require an answer; or does any other thing which would, if the Appeal Board had been a court of law having power to commit for contempt, have been contempt of that court.[939] The Court of First

930. *Ibid.*, s. 7.
931. *Ibid.*, s. 9(a).
932. *Ibid.*, s. 9(b).
933. *Ibid.*, s. 8.
934. The Environmental Impact Assessment (Appeal Board) Regulation (Cap 499 sub leg A).
935. The Environmental Impact Assessment Ordinance, s. 19(3).
936. The Environmental Impact Assessment (Appeal Board) Regulation, s. 11.
937. *Ibid.*, s. 10.
938. The Environmental Impact Assessment Ordinance, s. 19(11).
939. *Ibid.*, s. 19(9).

Instance may enquire into the alleged contempt and after hearing: (i) the witnesses who may be produced against or for the person charged with the contempt; and (ii) any statement that may be offered in defence, punish or take steps for the punishment of that person in the same way if he had been guilty of contempt of court.[940]

706. The appellant may abandon the whole or any part of an appeal by notice in writing lodged with the Chairman.[941] If on the date and time fixed for the hearing of an appeal any party to the appeal fails to attend the hearing either in person or by legal representative, the Appeal Board may, if satisfied that the party's failure to attend was due to sickness or other reasonable cause, postpone or adjourn the hearing for such period as it thinks fit.[942] If there is no such valid reason for absence, the Appeal Board may proceed to hear the appeal and in the case of a failure by the appellant to so attend other than by reason of sickness or other reasonable cause, dismiss the appeal.[943] An appellant whose appeal has been so dismissed may apply to the Appeal Board, within thirty days after the making of the order for dismissal, to review its decision and the Appeal Board may set aside its decision if the appellant satisfies it that there is a reasonable excuse for his failure to attend the hearing.[944]

707. The Chairman has the authority to determine any question of law that arises in an appeal, and the Appeal Board may refer any such question of law to the Court of Appeal for its determination by way of case stated.[945]

IV. The Decision of the Appeal Board

708. The Appeal Board may confirm, reverse or vary the decision or requirement appealed against.[946] The Appeal Board may give directions to the Director of Environmental Protection as to the exercise of his functions relevant to the appeal, which the Director must comply with.[947] It may award costs of the appeal as is just and equitable in all the circumstances of the case.[948] The Chairman must take in writing a full minute of matters relevant to the appeal, including the grounds of appeal, the evidence, the decision of the Board and costs awarded.[949] It is the usual

940. *Ibid.*, s. 19(10).
941. The Environmental Impact Assessment (Appeal Board) Regulation, s. 11.
942. *Ibid.*, s. 13(1)(a).
943. *Ibid.*, s. 13(1)(b) and (c).
944. *Ibid.*, s. 13(2).
945. The Environmental Impact Assessment Ordinance, s. 21.
946. *Ibid.*, s. 19(7)(d).
947. *Ibid.*, s. 19(2).
948. *Ibid.*, s. 19(e).
949. The Environmental Impact Assessment (Appeal Board) Regulation, s. 15.

practice of the Environmental Appeal Board to award costs, based on the civil litigation principle that the costs follow the event, meaning that the unsuccessful party must pay the costs of the successful party.[950]

§8. PUBLIC ACCESS TO INFORMATION

I. The Register of Information

709. The Director of Environmental Protection must keep a register which is open for inspection by the public free of charge during normal office hours at such places as the Director may determine. The register must contain details of the following:

(1) project profiles he receives;
(2) EIA study briefs he issues;
(3) his decisions on the applications for permission to apply directly for an environmental permit;
(4) EIA reports he receives;
(5) his decisions on the EIA reports;
(6) EIA reports he held prior to the commencement of the Environmental Impact Assessment Ordinance;
(7) applications for environmental permits;
(8) his decisions on the applications for environmental permits; and
(9) matters required by regulations.[951]

II. Disclosure of Secret Information

710. Full disclosure of information and unqualified public participation being its objects, the Environmental Impact Assessment Ordinance does not authorize any person to withhold information from being placed on the register. However, an exception exists to protect secret information that has been collected by public officers from unauthorized disclosure. It is a punishable offence for any person to disclose to another person any information that concerns a trade, business or profession, that has come to his knowledge in the course of the discharge of his functions under the Environmental Impact Assessment Ordinance. Disclosure of such information is excused if the disclosure was made by a person in the discharge of his functions under the Ordinance or in connected proceedings; under a court

950. *See*, for instance, Appeal No. 2 of 2000, *Kowloon-Canton Railway Corporation v Director of Environmental Protection* where the Director was awarded costs. There, the Appeal Board upheld his decision to reject the environmental impact assessment report submitted by the railway corporation to construct a railway line. Subsequently the Railway Corporation submitted a new assessment report which was approved. Construction of the railway line was completed in 2007.
951. The Environmental Impact Assessment Ordinance, s. 15.

order to disclose such information, to serve justice of the case; or with the consent of all persons who appear to be interested in the confidentiality of the information.[952]

§9. Case Studies

711. An Appeal Board decision and five judicial decisions illustrate the operation of the Environmental Impact Assessment Ordinance in relation to the powers of the Director of Environmental Protection to approve EIA reports and to grant, suspend or cancel an environmental permit. Of these six case studies, the Appeal Board Decision resulted in the upholding of the decision of Director to reject an environmental assessment report. In one of the judicial decisions – arising out of a judicial review application brought by a directly affected neighbour – the Court of Final Appeal quashed the approval by the Director of an environmental assessment report. In three of the remaining reported cases – which arose from what can be properly described as judicial review applications brought in the public interest – the court upheld the validity of the approval of environmental reports. The last case concerned refusal by the Director of Environmental Protection and the Chief Executive to cancel or suspend an environmental permit that the Director had issued. We will briefly review these six cases in their chronological order which also shows how judicial views on EIA developed over time.

I. Kowloon-Canton Railway Extension Through an Area of High Ecological Value: Decision of the Appeal Board (2001)

712. In *Kowloon-Canton Railway Corporation v the Director of Environmental Protection* (Appeal No. 2 of 2000), the Appeal Board upheld the decision of the Director of Environmental Protection to reject an EIA report. The Director had refused to approve the impact assessment report submitted by the Kowloon-Canton Railway Corporation for a railway line extension linking the existing East Rail System from Sheung Shui station to a new border crossing into the Mainland of China at Lok Ma Chau, referred to as the Spur Line. The main ground of rejection was that the construction of a 700-metre-long section of the proposed 7.3 km long Spur Line passing through an area of high ecological value was unacceptable. The Director had determined that the construction of a viaduct through the area of high ecological value was unacceptable because: (a) the corporation had failed to prove that the proposed mitigation measures were sufficient to prevent serious damage to the area of high ecological value; and (b) the corporation had not proved the absence of practicable or reasonable alternatives the submitted proposal. Having refused to approve the EIA report, the Director also refused to grant an environmental permit. As we have seen above, an environmental permit is granted authorizing a proposed designated project, on the basis of an approved EIA report.

952. *Ibid.*, s. 28(1) and (2).

713. On appeal, the Railway Corporation presented submissions on a large amount of mitigation measures that it would propose to address the concerns of the Director and requested the Appeal Board to carefully consider the information made available to it and grant approval of the assessment report and the environmental permit subject to appropriate conditions which would ensure that the proposed mitigation measures are in fact implemented. The Appeal Board was not prepared to revisit the merits of the EIA report because the amendments to the report that the railway corporation placed before the Appeal Board were significant and in effect would turn the appeal into the making of a fresh application for an EIA report. It was of the view that the detailed amended EIA report had to be tested through the approval process, including public participation, as envisaged in the Ordinance.

714. We will focus on two issues in this case study. First, the nature of an appeal and what an Appeal Board may legitimately do in considering an appeal. Second, the views of the Appeal Board on the EIA process and related issues such as the precautionary principle.

715. The determination of the Appeal Board on its jurisdictional limits arose this way. At the commencement of the appeal, the Director of Environmental Protection sought a ruling from the Chairman of the Appeal Board on its jurisdictional remit.[953] Having heard submissions from both the parties, the Chairman ruled as follows: The Appeal Board may hear and receive evidence relevant to its determination whether to confirm, reverse or vary a decision appealed against but has no authority to entertain and decide on a new application. The Appeal Board may exercise such powers as the Director may exercise under the Ordinance, particularly it may receive information from the applicant (section 8(3)(c)), it may place an environmental assessment report on the register if it approves it on appeal (section 10(5)), and it shall give reasons if it rejects an EIA report (section 10(6)). Following upon this ruling, the Appeal Board concluded that the submissions made by the railway corporation and the supporting proposals it made went far beyond clarifying or explaining its failed EIA report application and that the corporation's appeal submission was virtually a new application. As the Appeal Board observed: 'The appeals are against the two decisions of the Director to reject the [EIA] report and not to grant [an environment] permit. Not against the general issue whether the whole project is environmentally acceptable as now proposed. We sit as an appellate tribunal not a tribunal of enquiry. The basic principle is that major proposals which are not assessed in the report must at least be the subject of a further assessment and an amended report. Normally, this will require further exhibiting of the amended report for public consultation and resubmission to [the Advisory Council on the Environment].'

953. Any question of law that arises before the Appeal Board has to be determined by the Chairman. Section 19(3) of the Environmental Impact Assessment Ordinance provides as follows: 'The opinion of the majority of the members hearing the appeal determines a question before the Appeal Board except a question of law which the Chairman determines.'

716. What the railway corporation asked the Appeal Board to do was to grant an environmental permit on the basis of the failed EIA report, which the Appeal Board was asked to approve on the basis of a large number of newly proposed conditions which the corporation proposed for the Appeal Board's consideration, running into at least fifty pages. This the Appeal Board found not possible to do because what the appellant-applicant was proposing to do was to amend the EIA report on the basis of some entirely new proposals and a long list of conditions, none of which had been duly considered by the Director in the first instance. To approve such a significantly different report would not be within its jurisdiction of confirming, reversing or varying the report which had been considered and rejected by the Director. The Appeal Board reasoned that: (1) the EIA report can be approved only if it amended to include new and far-reaching proposals; (2) accepting new proposals would affect the validity of the report that had been prepared and submitted for the Director's approval, which was not granted. The proposals are 'radical alterations and should be confirmed and assessed as part of the [EIA] study and report'; and (3) To accept the proposed new conditions on the basis of which to grant approval would be to 'circumvent the assessment process laid down in the Ordinance and the Technical Memorandum, [in particular, to circumvent] proper public participation and the participation of the Advisory Council on the Environment'.

717. In concluding that the Director's decision was the correct one to arrive at, the Appeal Board made important observations on the EIA process and the relevant principles. As mentioned above, the EIA report related to the proposed extension of the East Rail from Sheung Shui station to Lok Ma Chau Station, the border crossing point to Mainland China. This 7.3 km long extension, known as the Spur Line partly, would run through Long Valley, an area of high ecological value. The proposal was to build the railway over a 700-metre-long elevated viaduct when it passes through Long Valley. It is the passing of the railway through Long Valley that became the focus of objection to the project. The argument was that the construction of the railway through Long Valley would cause irreversible damage to the environment. The corporation had proposed both temporary and more permanent mitigation measures in recognition of the environmental impacts that would occur during the construction phase. Refusing to approve the environmental report, the Director had noted that the mitigation measures were not effective or practicable and that the corporation had not proved that there were no practicable or reasonable alternatives to a viaduct. The Appeal Board was not prepared to reverse the decision of the Director for the principal reason that to accept the appeal would be to grant approval on a wide range of untested proposals which needed to be tested through the EIA process, through the preparation of the study brief and environmental report with crucially important public participation.

718. As regards the EIA process, the Appeal Board made some significant observations. As the Appeal Board observed, the underlying aim of the impact assessment process is to ensure that no designated project is undertaken unless it is shown to be environmentally acceptable. The EIA process is set out in the Ordinance. The EIA Technical Memorandum sets out detailed criteria to be applied at each stage of EIA. Section 4.5.1 of the Technical Memorandum provides that an environmental report may be approved if: (a) the requirements in the study brief are met; (b) the quality of the report meets the requirements set out in section 4.4 (such as that assumptions and methodologies used are sound and adequate, adverse environmental impacts are avoided to the maximum practicable extent, feasibility, practicability, programming and effectiveness of recommended mitigation measures have been assessed and determined) and the results and conclusions are technically sound and reliable; (c) the report addresses relevant environmental issues raised by the public and the Advisory Council on the Environment during the public inspection period; and (d) all relevant environmental principles and criteria laid down in the Technical Memorandum can be met and the residual environmental impacts are within the relevant criteria, unless with sound environmental justifications and without long-term serious environmental implications.

719. Section 4.5.2 of the EIA Technical Memorandum provides that where the Director is satisfied that the above requirements are met but the report needs certain amendments, he may approve the report subject to conditions, provided that such amendments will not affect the validity of the assessment and the overall results and conclusions. The aim of section 4.5.2 is to remedy any minor oversights and omissions or to accommodate changed circumstances, where a rerun of the EIA process would not be necessary.

720. The Appeal Board examined the guiding principles set out in Annex 26 of the Technical Memorandum, which set out the general approach and methodology for assessment of ecological impact arising from a project or proposal. The general principles for ecological assessment are set out in section 3. They are: (i) areas of ecological importance must be conserved as far as possible; (ii) a project which is likely to have adverse ecological impacts in areas of ecological importance will not normally be permitted unless the project is necessary; (iii) it must be proved that there are no practical or reasonable alternatives to such a project; and (iv) where such a project is approved there are adequate off-site and on-site mitigation measures. Applying these general principles to the appeal before it, the Appeal Board agreed that there was an urgent public need to relieve congestion at the existing crossing point Lo Wu and therefore the construction of the Spur Line is necessary.

721. On the question whether the corporation had adequately considered viable alternatives to the proposed Spur Line, the Board concluded that the proposed railway extension was a matter of public policy and the corporation would not be at liberty to propose a solution which would be outside the approved government policy. Proceeding to the question whether there were alternatives to the construction of a viaduct through Long Valley, the Appeal Board found two alternatives: (1) a bored tunnel on the same alignment; and (2) using the proposed extension of the MTR railway line, the Northern Link. A bored tunnel was not a viable option because of the unacceptable high cost of implementation. The second alternative was not viable because it was the settled government policy to construct both the Spur Line and the Northern Link.

722. Having accepted that the elevated viaduct was the only viable alternative acceptable in principle, the Appeal Board considered that by adopting adequate mitigation measures likely adverse impacts during the construction stage could be prevented or greatly lessened. The Appeal Board observed: 'Our view is that with the expertise and long-term financial support available the mitigation is likely to succeed. But the [corporation] have fallen short of demonstrating on the evidence put forward on appeal that the mitigation proposed is feasible and effective and therefore likely to be successful.' Had the corporation succeeded in convincing the Appeal Board that the project could be implemented without causing undesirable adverse impacts of serious concern, on the basis of readily acceptable evidence, the Appeal Board would have been prepared to approve the project subject to some additional conditions. However, since the evidence was not entirely convincing, the Appeal Board decided that the submissions that the corporation made had to be thoroughly assessed through the EIA process with the expertise of the Environmental Protection Department and public involvement throughout the process as envisaged legislation and the Technical Memorandum. More importantly, the Appeal Board was concerned that it was not the appropriate body to consider the suitability and effectiveness of a large number of significant amendments that the applicant corporation proposed: The Ordinance envisaged a detailed process with adequate opportunity for public participation in the assessment of any amendments of the rejected environmental report.

723. The Appeal Board took the opportunity to make some important observations on the public policy considerations that guided the EIA process and some suggestions on better implementation of the assessment process.

On the public policy considerations, the Appeal Board said: 'There are two main matters of public interest involved. Both are important. The first is the public interest in the protection of the environment upon which the quality of like in Hong Kong will increasingly depend. The second is the public interest in ensuring that major designated projects are brought to fruition in a timely and efficient manner. The time constraints put upon the Director for steps in the process and for his decisions show that the [Environmental Impact Assessment] Ordinance aims to satisfy both interests. It is necessary in the implementation of the process that both should be kept in mind. This is so especially when major infrastructural projects (roads, railways, tunnels, reclamation works and the like) which may cause a variety of adverse environmental impacts are proposed.'[954]

---

954. This was quoted with approval by Tang VP in *Chu Yee Wah v Director of Environmental Protection* [2011] 5 HKLRD 469, [31] (CA). Chow J said in *Ho Loy v Director of Environmental Protection* [2016] HKEC 2751, [38]: 'It is apparent from the long title to the Ordinance that its main object is the protection of the environment. The Court of Final Appeal in *Shiu Wing Steel Ltd case* has expressed the view that such purpose should "inform", and even "govern", the interpretation of the Ordinance, which would include the instruments created under it (ie, the Technical Memorandum and the Study Brief). On the other hand, the aspect of the public interest … namely, that major designated projects should be brought to fruition in a timely and efficient manner is already inbuilt in the timetable laid down in the legislative scheme for the environmental impact assessment process. It is not, in my view, a separate or independent purpose of the Ordinance.'

On making the EIA process more productive, the Appeal Board emphasized the importance of 'open, ready and frank communication between the Director and the proponent' in order to ensure that the Director may not have any serious concerns about the EIA report when it is submitted to the Director for approval. We have seen in our discussion of the EIA process that the Director is required to decide within 60 days of receiving the report whether or not the report meets the requirements of the Technical Memorandum and the more project-specific study brief that the Director had given the project proponent. The Director would approve the report only if there are no omissions or deficiencies which may affect the results and conclusions in the report. The Appeal Board observed that it would immensely help the smooth working of the EIA process if the project proponent actively coordinates with the Director in preparing the EIA report. The Appeal Board made the following useful suggestions:

(1) At all stages of the process, there must be open, ready and frank communication between the project proponent and the Director.
(2) The more important three stages of the process are: drafting of the study brief; reaching a decision that the EIA report meets the requirements of the study brief and the Technical Memorandum; and seeking of more information by the Director after having conducted public consultation and sought the advice of the Advisory Committee on the Environment.
(3) The study brief is prepared by the Director after receiving comments from the public and the Advisory Committee on the Environment on the project proponent's project profile. It should reflect the public concerns as well as any further matters that the Director requires to be addressed. These concerns and matters should be specifically set out in the Director's communication. When the project proponent seeks any clarification, such requests should be readily and helpfully addressed.
(4) If the Director considers that the EIA report does not meet the requirements of the Ordinance and the Technical Memorandum, he should communicate with the project proponent to see if his concerns can be met. It is only when that matters cannot be resolved that the Director should refuse to accept it for public exhibition, leading to formal amendment of the report by the project proponent, if the project proposal is to proceed any further. If the Director fails to refuse to proceed to public consultation within the prescribed period of sixty days, by default the report must proceed to public consultation. If, however, the report does not meet the requirements of legislation and Technical Memorandum, public consultation will be a waste of time and resources because the Director has no authority to approve a report which does not satisfy the requirements of the Ordinance and the Technical Memorandum. Similarly, if the Director inadvertently decides to refer a report which does not satisfy those requirements and proceeds to public consultation, he would have no authority to approve it thereafter because he may approve only a report which is statute and Technical Memorandum compliant.[955]

955. In *Shiu Wing Steel Ltd v Director of Environmental Protection & Airport Authority(No 2)*, (2006) 9 HKCFAR 478, [19], the Court of Final Appeal succinctly explained the close connection between

(5) Once consultation with the public and the Advisory Committee on the Environment has been completed, the Director may seek further information from the project proponent. It is advisable for the Director to specify any information or clarification that he requires, and simply not refer to the project proponent comments made by members of the public or the Advisory Committee on the Environment and ask for any further information in response to those comments. The Director may seek further information on matters not directly arising from the public consultation if that would assist the approval process.

724. The Appeal Board saw the merits of the project in general but was not prepared to approve the report and grant an environmental permit because it was essential for the extensive material that the project proponent submitted to the Appeal Board be thoroughly assessed by the Director with necessary consultative input. The Appeal Board said: 'Our belief is that provided the concerns about the feasibility of the migration and the construction methods are overcome the project may be shown to be environmentally be acceptable.'

725. As shown above, the Appeal Board dismissed the appeal on the ground of the need for consideration by Director, in the first instance. Thereafter, the railway corporation submitted a new assessment report which was approved leading to the grant of an environmental permit in 2002. Interestingly, the corporation adopted a combined tunnel and viaduct scheme for the Spur Line. From Sheung Shui to Chau Tau, the railway runs through tunnels and thereafter runs on viaducts until it reaches Lok Ma Chau Station.[956]

---

the Director's decisions under ss 6 and 8: 'Approval is a pivotal point in the process. Approval of an Environmental Impact Assessment report and the consequential placement by the Director of the report on the register, fixes the entirety of the information which an applicant provides relating to the construction of a project, the applicant's assessment of the impact of the project on the environment and the measures which the applicant proposes to take for the protection of the environment. These issues are the issues prescribed by a technical memorandum and a study brief and they are the issues which the Director is bound to regard in determining whether to grant an environmental permit for the project. The critical step which brings information and proposals on these issues into the section 10 process is the decision to approve the environmental impact assessment report under s. 8(3). As s. 6(3) makes clear the legislative intention that an environmental impact assessment report must meet the requirements of a study brief and technical memorandum, it would be contrary to the Director's duty to approve a report that did not meet the requirements of the applicable study brief and technical memorandum. The power to approve an environmental impact assessment report can be exercised only in respect of a report that meets those requirements. Section 4.5.1(a) and (d) of the technical memorandum make approval of an environmental impact assessment report conditional on its meeting the requirements of the study brief and the environmental principles and criteria in the technical memorandum. As the decision under s. 8(3) can be made only after the period of public exhibition of the report and only after consideration of any comments submitted by the public or by the Advisory committee on the Environment, a decision to approve an environmental impact assessment report must be the final decision that the report meets the requirements of the applicable study brief and technical memorandum. A final decision under s. 8(3) that an environmental impact assessment report be approved subsumes the earlier decision under s. 6(3) that the report meets the requirements of the study brief and technical memorandum.'

956. For documentation relating to this case *see* http://www.epd.gov.hk/eia/english/alpha/aspd_226.html.

II. EIA of an Aviation Fuel Storage Facility: Decision of the Court of Final Appeal (2006)

726. Shiu Wing Steel Ltd v Director of Environmental Protection & Airport Authority of Hong Kong (No 2)[957] concerned an environmental assessment exercise in relation to the proposed construction by the Hong Kong Airport Authority of a permanent aviation fuel storage facility, a designated project. The applicant company which operated a steel mill on an adjacent site and used extremely hot processes was concerned about the risk of fuel spillage from the aviation fuel storage facility into the mill where a conflagration would pose danger to life and property. It considered that the EIA had not thoroughly assessed the possible risk of having a fuel storage facility right next to a steel works site, and therefore the EIA report was defective and should not have been approved by the Director of Environmental Protection. The application for judicial review challenging the legality of the Director's decision to approve the EIA report and to grant an environmental permit was unsuccessful in the Court of First Instance and in the Court of Appeal. However, this view was overturned by the Court of Final Appeal.

727. As we shall see, the Court of Final Appeal laid down some important ground rules for the conduct of an EIA. Appreciating the need for a thorough assessment of all environmental risks as guided by the relevant Technical Memoranda and the project-specific study brief, as well as the critical importance of public participation in the assessment process, it stressed how important it is for the impact assessment to be conducted in strict compliance with the Technical Memorandum and the study brief. In relation to these procedural matters, the Court of Appeal set out the following principles:

(1) Technical Memoranda are not, strictly speaking, legislative in nature (as we have seen above, the Ordinance expressly states that a Technical Memorandum is not subsidiary legislation, but a Technical Memorandum has to be placed before the Legislative Council which has the power to repeal it).
(2) Not being subsidiary legislation, Technical Memoranda are not to be interpreted in strict compliance with rules of statutory interpretation.
(3) Technical Memoranda lay down important technical rules and requirements which must be strictly complied with if an EIA is to be genuine and meaningful.
(4) A Technical Memorandum can be strictly followed only if the requirements it lays down are properly understood. Because of the importance of Technical Memoranda, it is crucial that there is a single meaning to each of the requirements of a Technical Memorandum.
(5) The interpretation of the Technical Memorandum is a matter of law, and if there is a doubt about any provision in a Technical Memorandum, such doubts have to be cleared by a court of law.
(6) The Director of Environmental Protection is not the proper authority to decide such a question of law, and if the Director misunderstood the requirements of

957. (2006) 9 HKCFAR 478 (CFA).

a Technical Memorandum, his decision based on such a misunderstanding may invalidate his decision, if it is affected by such mistake in a material way.

(7) Since the Technical Memorandum is a technical document meant to guide administrators of the EIA, the court must view the Technical Memorandum in the way professionals would.

728. In the light of these principles, the Court of Final Appeal reviewed the decision of the Director to approve the impact assessment report and the consequent decision to grant an environmental permit. The Court concluded that the Director had acted on a grave misunderstanding of the Technical Memorandum and quashed his decisions. The error that the Director had fallen into was his belief that the Technical Memorandum and the study brief required the project proponent to conduct a project-specific risk assessment only, whereas on a true construction the Technical Memorandum required a generic risk assessment too.

729. The study brief had directed the Airport Authority to make an assessment of hazard to life in order especially to identify all hazardous scenarios associated with the operation of the storage facility, which might cause fatalities and to carry out a quantitative risk assessment. The applicant argued that the EIA report did not contain a quantitative risk assessment in respect of all hazard to life risk scenarios because the quantitative risk assessment only addressed risks which were project specific. The assessment report had identified a 100% loss scenario but did not go only to assess that risk because the Director had indicated to the project proponent that it was not a credible one in relation to the designated project in question.

730. The Court of Final Appeal held that on a proper interpretation the Technical Memorandum required not only a project-specific risk assessment but also a generic risk assessment. The quantitative risk assessment was 'generic', taking into account scenarios from the history of other projects of the same genus, and project specific. As a generic quantitative risk assessment, the scenarios to be identified included those in the history of projects of the same genus which seemed incredible in relation to the specific project. So identification was not limited to scenarios that were 'predicted', 'expected or anticipated', and so judged to be 'credible', in a specific project. Otherwise, the risk of a scenario, which had occurred earlier in another fuel storage facility, occurring at the proposed designated project caused by an unknown, unforeseen or unexpected cause, would not be quantified. Having noted that there were actually records of incidents of catastrophic releases from storage vessels, but a quantitative risk assessment was not undertaken, the Court of Final Appeal had no hesitation in deciding that the assessment report failed to satisfy the requirements of the Technical Memorandum.

731. While recognizing that the Technical Memorandum – a technical document which applied to all designated projects – and a study brief – which is directed at a specific designated project – were not legislative instruments, the Court of Final Appeal emphasized that the adequacy and legality of an EIA depended on a correct understanding of their meaning. There could be only one meaning of what is required by them, and it was for the court to determine this meaning. On this question of construction, the Technical Memorandum and study brief were technical instruments to be construed as they would be understood by an expert risk assessor. Since the Director had misunderstood the requirement in relation to quantitative risk assessment, his approval of the report and the consequent grant of the environmental permit were of no legal effect.

732. The Court of Final Appeal pointed out that the invalidation of the project approval because of the quantitative risk assessment would not cause any serious delay to the implementation of the project because all that was required was the conduct of a proper quantitative risk assessment. And if, when the required quantitative risk assessment was made, it appeared that there was no unacceptable risk to human life, a new approval and permit could follow within a reasonable time. But if it appeared that further mitigation measures ought to be taken to eliminate an unacceptable risk to human life, delay to achieve that end must be accepted.

733. In 2007 the Airport Authority submitted a new EIA report which was approved after public consultation. The aviation fuel storage facility was completed and commenced operations in 2010.[958]

III. An Alleged Failure to Comply with the Technical Memorandum: Decision of the Court of Appeal (2011)

734. Chu Yee Wah v Director of Environmental Protection[959] is a case where the adequacy of an EIA was questioned by way of judicial review for alleged failure to comply with the relevant Technical Memorandum, Technical Memorandum on Environmental Impact Assessment. The Court of Appeal willingly followed the views expressed by the Court of Final Appeal in *Shiu Wing Steel* case, but found on facts of the case that there was sufficient compliance with the Technical Memorandum. The applicants' arguments centred on the alleged requirements of the Technical Memorandum for the proposed designated project to be subjected to a 'stand alone' assessment.

735. The major concern the applicant expressed in this case was that the implementation of the designated project would have serious adverse impacts on Hong Kong's already poor air quality. The applicant argued that the current air quality objectives that the assessment used as a reference point were not fit for the purpose. On this point, both the Court of First Instance which decided in favour of the applicants and the Court of Appeal which overturned that decision agreed that the court was not in a position to decide the suitability of air quality objectives, that being a matter within the policymaking sphere that belonged to the legislature.

958. *See* http://www.hongkongairport.com/eng/business/about-the-airport/aviation/fuel-service-system.html.
959. [2011] 5 HKLRD 469, [2011] HKEC 1275 (CA); [2011] HKEC 555 (CFI).

736. The designated project in question was the construction of the Hong Kong section of the proposed Hong Kong-Zhuhai-Macau Bridge project, which was completed in 2018. The bridge, which connects Hong Kong, Zhuhai City in China and Macau Special Administrative Region, is part of the construction project known as the 'National High Speed Road Network Planning'. The Hong Kong section of the Bridge project consists of three main parts, namely: (a) the Hong Kong Boundary Crossing Facilities; (b) the link road in Hong Kong which will connect the Bridge and North Lantau Highway; and (c) the Tuen Mun – Chek Lap Kok Link Road in Hong Kong. Each of these sections is a designated project.

737. The project proponent was the Highways Department which submitted the project profile for the Link Road in October 2003, the project profile for the TM-CLK Link in November 2007 and the project profile for the Boundary Crossing Facilities in March 2008. The Director of Environmental Protection issued three study briefs, which were quite similar in content. The three EIA reports were submitted to the Director in June and August of 2009, who advised the project proponent on 13 August 2009 that the reports were suitable for public inspection. During the public consultation over 2,700 public comments were received. Having requested and considered further information on air quality assessment, the Advisory Council on the Environment, in October 2009, endorsed the project subject to conditions. The Highways Department then provided further clarifications principally to address the concerns raised by the Advisory Council, and in November 2009 the Director granted an environmental permit.

738. The applicant challenged the Director's decision to approve the EIA reports for the Boundary Crossing Facilities and the Link Road, and his subsequent decision to issue environmental permits. The Court of First Instance granted the judicial review application, accepting the applicant's argument that the Technical Memorandum required a stand-alone assessment, meaning that the project proponent was required to compare the environmental impact that the construction of the project would cause with the air quality situation if the project was not carried out at all (the baseline situation).

739. At the first instance as well as on appeal, the Director submitted that the Environment Impact Assessment Ordinance was not concerned with the minimization of pollutants from a designated project; it was sufficient that the increases in a particular air pollutant did not exceed the limits specified in applicable guidelines. The judge was of the view that the fact that the increases in a particular air pollutant did not exceed the limits specified in the applicable guidelines could not be the sole determining factor in deciding whether to grant an environmental permit. The judge quashed the decisions, adopting a purposive approach and finding that it was only by knowing the starting point, i.e., the stand-alone position, that a project's environmental footprint could be measured and the Director could decide what mitigating measures should be adopted.

740. The Court of Appeal rejected the submission made by the Director that the Environmental Impact Assessment Ordinance was not concerned with the minimization of pollution. The Ordinance, through the Technical Memorandum and study briefs, required the minimization of pollutants and also imposed limits on the quantities of polluting emissions. However, the Court of Appeal rejected the applicant's argument that a stand-alone assessment was required. Both the Technical Memorandum and the study briefs required a project proponent to minimize pollution. This duty did not depend on the extent of the footprint of a designated project: whatever the footprint, pollution has to be kept to a minimum. Accordingly, it was not necessary to construe the Technical Memorandum and the study briefs as requiring a stand-alone assessment in order that the Director could decide what mitigating measures should be adopted. The Court of Appeal concluded that, on a true interpretation, the Technical Memorandum and the study briefs did not make it mandatory for the project proponent to carry out a stand-alone assessment.

741. The important new principle that the Court of Appeal set out in this case was that, although it was a matter of construction for the court to decide what was required by the Technical Memorandum and the study brief, it was often a question of professional judgment what information was required to be contained in an impact assessment report to enable the Director to perform his duties. Where the Director cannot be faulted for his understanding of the requirements of the Technical Memorandum or study brief, the court would not second-guess the Director's decision. The court would intervene only if his decision was *Wednesbury* unreasonable.

742. While the judicial review application failed, it has had an important impact on the environmental standards that have been adopted in Hong Kong. As we saw above, in *Chu Yee Wah* case severe criticisms were levelled against the prevailing air quality objectives, which led Fok J to say that 'no one can seriously question that air quality in Hong Kong is a matter of concern'.[960]

743. The government responded and amended the Air Pollution Control Ordinance in 2013 to come into effect on 1 January 2014. The Ordinance was amended by adding a new section 7A which requires the Environmental Protection Department to review air quality objectives every five years, with 2014–2019 earmarked as the first period. In addition, the Department published a new set of air quality objectives to be effective from 1 January 2014.[961]

960. *Chu Yee Wah v Director of Environmental Protection* [2011] HKEC 555, [31].

961. *See* http://www.epd.gov.hk/epd/english/environmentinhk/air/air_quality_objectives/air_quality_objectives.html.

See also the Legislative Council Brief on Air Pollution Control (Amendment) Bill 2013: https://www.legco.gov.hk/yr12-13/english/bills/brief/b06_brf.pdf.

IV. An Alleged Failure to Comply with the Technical Memorandum and the Study Brief: Unsuccessful Judicial Review Application in Court of First Instance, Affirmed by the Court of Appeal and the Court of Final Appeal

744. Leung Hon Wai v Director of Environmental Protection[962] is a judicial review application which was unsuccessful both in the Court of First Instance and on appeal in the Court of Appeal. The applicant unsuccessfully challenged three decisions relating to the proposed project for the construction and operation of Phase 1 of the Integrated Waste Management Facilities, namely a municipal wastes incinerator. The three impugned decisions were: (1) The decision of the Director of Environmental Protection (the Director) to approve the Environmental Impact Assessment Report (2) the Director's decision to grant an environmental permit; and (3) the Town Planning Board's decision not to uphold the objections to the draft outline zoning plan relating to the proposed project and to submit it to the Chief Executive in Council for approval. The Court of First Instance upheld the first two decisions and found as a result that the third question did not need to be examined, for the reason that the third decision would be invalid only if the first two decisions on which it relied were invalid. The Court of Appeal agreed with the decision of the Court of First Instance and dismissed the appeal.[963] The principal arguments against the validity of the approval of the EIA report and the grant of an environmental permit for the designated project were that: (a) the assessment report was not made in compliance with various provisions or requirements set out in the Technical Memorandum and the relevant study brief; and (b) the Director's decision was *Wednesbury* unreasonable. The relevance of these two grounds of challenge has already been considered and decisively clarified in *Shiu Wing Steel* case and the *Chu Yee Wah* case. Therefore, the *Leung Hon Wai's* case did not raise any new legal arguments.

745. The applicant argued in the Court of First Instance that the project proponents had not complied with the requirement for an ecological assessment set out in the Technical Memorandum. It was argued that the project did not satisfy the requirements set out in paragraph 3.1 of Annex 16 of the Technical Memorandum which provides that any project that is likely to result in adverse ecological importance shall not normally be permitted unless:

(1) the project is necessary, in that it has been proven that no other practical and reasonable alternatives are available; and
(2) adequate on-site and/or off-site mitigation measures are to be employed; and

---

962. [2013] HKEC 1166 (CFI) affirmed by the Court of Appeal [2014] 5 HKLRD 194, [2014] HKEC 1459 (CA). The other important case decided in 2014 is *Ho Loy v Director of Environmental Protection* [2014] HKEC 1398, which is examined in the fifth case study.

963. The Integrated Waste Management Facilities project is currently underway. *See* the reply to a Legislative Council Member's question in the following press release: 'LCQ: Integrated Waste Management Facilities Phase 1', dated 20 January 2021. https://www.info.gov.hk/gia/general/202101/20/P2021012000273.htm

(3) any off-site measures shall be determined during the EIA study in accordance with the guidelines laid down in the Technical Memorandum, in particular Annexes 8 and 16.

It was argued that as the project would adversely affect finless porpoises the EIA report ought to have provided adequate off-site mitigation measures as required by Annex 16 of the Technical Memorandum. Paragraph 5.4.2 of the Technical Memorandum provided that 'all mitigation measures recommended shall be feasible to implement within the context of Hong Kong. The effectiveness of the proposed mitigation measures shall be carefully evaluated and the significance of any residual impacts after implementing them shall be clearly stated'. Paragraph 5.4.5 set out the guidelines for determining the need for and the type and scope of off-site mitigation measures to be adopted for a particular project.

746. Rejecting the argument that the EIA report failed to comply with the requirements in the Technical Memorandum regarding off-site mitigation measures, Thomas Au J said:

> What the Technical Memorandum requires ... is that all mitigation measures recommended shall be 'feasible' to implement. Given that the nature of an environmental impact assessment report is to assess the impact of a designated project on the environment, and the requirement of compensatory measures is to minimise any such impact, properly construed in that context, I am of the view that the meaning of the word 'feasible' means that the proposed measures are reasonably possible to be practically implemented. This construction is consistent with the nature of the scope and type stipulated to be required of these measures ... , which focuses on practicability and feasibility.[964]

The judge had no hesitation in accepting that the proposed off-site mitigation measures by way of a commitment to designate a 700 ha marine park, subject to the completion of the statutory process of the Marine Parks Ordinance, was one that was reasonably possible to implement. The judge also rejected the argument that the assessment report failed to conduct an adequate health risk assessment.

747. In view of his finding that the EIA had carried out a thorough and satisfactory assessment exercise, the judge summarily dismissed the allegation that the Director had unreasonably approved the EIA report.

748. The applicant also raised an objection to the propriety of the Director's decision-making, on the ground of breach of the second rule of natural justice, namely that the Director was judge of her own cause when she acted as both the project proponent and the decision-maker. This objection was rejected on the grounds that: (a) the Director had to be the project proponent because the project in question was proposed by a government agency which was under her direction; (b) the Director's duties in relation to functions under the Ordinance especially those

---

964. *Leung Hon Wai v Director of Environmental Protection* [2013] HKEC 1166, [53].

relating to approval of EIA reports and the grant of environmental permits had been delegated to officers of the Environmental Protection Department; (c) there was in place a statutory process with the legislation and Technical Memorandum prescribing both substantive requirements and various procedural requirements that had to be complied with, including active public participation and; (d) the availability of an appeal on merits to the Appeal Board.

749. The applicant appealed unsuccessfully against the decision of the Court of First Instance. The Court of Appeal held, affirming the view expressed by the Court of First Instance, that whether an EIA report met the requirements of the Technical Memorandum and the study brief was to be determined objectively. The Technical Memorandum and the study brief were to be construed not as legislative instruments but as they would be understood by an expert risk assessor and should be read in a 'down-to-earth way'. The Technical Memorandum applied generally to all designated projects, while the study brief was project-specific and set out the agenda for the rest of the process. The study brief should follow the general requirements set out in the Technical Memorandum and guide the project proponent on specific issues that the Director is required to address. It was often a question of professional judgment what information the project proponent must provide in the EIA report sufficient for the Director to determine whether the report meets the requirements of the study brief and the Technical Memorandum.

750. The Court of Appeal agreed that Thomas Au J in the Court of First Instance was correct to construe the words 'all mitigation matters recommended shall be feasible to implement' occurring in the Technical Memorandum as meaning that proposed off-site mitigation measures had to be 'reasonably possible to be practically implemented'. Those words did not suggest that a project proponent was required to establish with absolute certainty, at the stage when the report was submitted for approval, that such mitigation measures could be implemented.

751. The Court of Appeal affirmed the findings of the Court of First Instance that the proposed off-site mitigation measure by way of a commitment to designate a marine park, subject to the statutory process of the Marine Parks Ordinance (Cap 476) was 'reasonably possible to be practically implemented'. The Director had consulted with and secured the support of the Director of Agriculture, Fisheries and Conservation, who was responsible for making recommendations to the Chief Executive in Council on designating marine parks. Further, possible objections under the Marine Parks Ordinance would not render the designation infeasible because the interests of aggrieved stakeholders could be provided for by the Director of Agriculture, Fisheries and Conservation by imposing appropriate conditions when granting the necessary permits and licences.

752. As regards the determination of the Director of Environmental Protection, the Court of Appeal agreed with the Court of First Instance that unless the determination was *Wednesbury* unreasonable, the Court would not interfere. For this proposition the Court found support in *Belize Alliance of Conservation Non-Government Organisations v Department of the Environment* [2004] Env LR 38,

PC; *Shiu Wing Steel Ltd v Director of Environmental Protection & Airport Authority (No. 2)* (2006) 9 HKCFAR 478, CFA; and *Chu Yee Wah v Director of Environmental Protection* [2011] 3 HKC 227 (CA).

753. The Court of Appeal held, with McWalters JA dissenting, that the Ordinance applies to the government and there was nothing in the Ordinance to prevent the Director of Environmental Protection from making an application for a government project which is within his managerial responsibility, just as any private project proponent. The fact that the Director was responsible for implementing the provisions relating to EIA did not necessarily mean that he could not be a project proponent. The Court of Appeal reasoned that though the Director plays the role of the decision-maker in terms of the approval of the EIA report and the issue of an environmental permit (note these powers are delegated to officers in his department), it is also a process in which other stakeholders participate actively and the Director's power is circumscribed. The process is highly transparent with full opportunity for interested parties (including members of the public concerned about environmental issues) to put forward their comments. The decisions of the Director can be challenged on their merits by an independent appeal procedure and also on their legality by court proceedings. It could be said that in the view of the Court of Appeal there is no threat of 'systemic bias' in the Director determining an application made by the Director as project proponent, and it is only when there is a suspicion of a breach of the rules of natural justice in a particular case, that he would be found disqualified as having acted in these two capacities. Neither in the Court of First Instance nor in the Court of Appeal was the concept of 'systemic bias' referred to but it appears that this case is a good illustration of absence of systemic bias just as *Kwan Kong Company Ltd v Town Planning Board* [1996] 2 HKLR 363 (CA). There it was held that the membership and participation of government officials such as the Director of Planning, the Secretary for Transport and the Director of Environmental Protection did not by that fact alone mean that the Town Planning Board was biased towards the government.

The applicant appealed to the Court of Final Appeal from the decision of the Court of Appeal only in respect of its determination that it was proper for the Director to have been the project proponent. Rejecting the appeal, the Court of Final Appeal held that there was nothing in the Environmental Impact Assessment Ordinance to exclude the Director from being 'a person' who proposes a designated project for approval by the Director, the approving authority. The Director thus acts in two different capacities with a number of built in safeguards to prevent a breach of the rules of natural justice. Tang PJ observed that there was an actual separation of functions in the EPD, and that there was no breach of natural justice and agreed with the majority's description in the Court of Appeal of the complaint as being 'more or less of a formalistic nature'. Tang PJ observed that in fact the applications were made by a deputy director to another deputy director under authority duly delegated by the Director. Tang PJ reasoned as follows:

> 24. McWalters JA [the dissenting judge in the Court of Appeal] was right to be concerned about the Director's duties under the Waste Disposal Ordinance. Both before and after the enactment of Environmental Impact Assessment

Ordinance, the Director was the waste disposal authority under the Waste Disposal Ordinance. The facilities which are waste disposal facilities were the responsibilities of the Director under Waste Disposal Ordinance.

25. However, McWalters JA concluded that because the legislative purpose of the Environmental Impact Assessment Ordinance was that particular projects should go through an environmental impact assessment process which is presided over and enforced by the Director and that in a real sense the Director is the guardian of the environment:

> [138] It is my view that standing back and looking at the Environmental Impact Assessment Ordinance as a whole and having regard to the Ordinance's legislative purpose, the important public interest that purpose is designed to protect and the importance of the Director performing his regulatory and enforcement duties in an independent way as a means of achieving that purpose, it would be contradictory and illogical for the Director to himself be a project proponent.

26. With respect, I cannot agree. As Lam V-P and Kwan JA pointed out in their joint judgment [in the Court of Appeal], the approval process is highly transparent and during the approval process other stakeholders (including members of the public concerned about environmental issues) have full opportunity to comment and state their views. As these and other proceedings have shown there is also the possibility of recourse to the courts by way of judicial review. Moreover, as the organisational chart shows so clearly, the functions of Environmental Assessment Division and the Infrastructure Planning Group divisions are clearly separated. Indeed, they are housed in separate premises.

27. With respect, McWalters JA failed to have sufficient regard to the fact that Au J had found that having regard to the actual and effective separation of function in the Environmental Protection Department there was no real or apparent bias in the application and decision process. The majority in the Court of Appeal was of the same view. Indeed, McWalters JA said that the legislature could have expressly enacted 'a scheme of which the Director was regulator and enforcer and also a participant as a project proponent'. No doubt the legislature could have done so. No doubt, any such scheme would have provided for actual separation of function. If one compares what was actually done in the separation of function with what the legislature might have chosen to do, it is clear the actual separation is not deficient in any way. Were it otherwise, relief might have been obtained by judicial review. With respect, it begs the question to say that the legislature had implicitly rendered illegitimate a scheme which had actually provided for functional separation.

28. McWalters JA said:

> [140] There is nothing within the Environmental Impact Assessment Ordinance that would suggest that it was ever contemplated by the legislature that the Director would participate as a project proponent in a scheme designed to protect a particular public interest over which he presides as regulator and enforcer.

29. Waste removal facilities were mentioned expressly in Schedule 2 and made designated projects such that applications would have to be made in respect of such facilities under Environmental Impact Assessment Ordinance. The legislature must have been aware of the Director's duties under the Waste Disposal Ordinance. Moreover, as the organizational chart clearly shows, the Environmental Protection Department included a division dealing specifically with waste management which was involved with waste management policy, infrastructure, facilities and reductions, for which the legislature had voted the necessary funds. They provide the context in which the Environmental Impact Assessment Ordinance should be construed. They inform the clear separation of function in the Environmental Protection Department. I have no doubt it was clearly envisaged by the legislature that the Director, as waste disposal authority under the Waste Disposal Ordinance and proponent of waste disposal facilities, might apply for an environmental permit under the Environmental Impact Assessment Ordinance.

V. An Unsuccessful Attempt to Have an Environmental Permit Cancelled: Decision of the Court of First Instance (2014) and Court of Appeal (2016)

754. Ho Loy v Director of Environmental Protection [2014] HKEC 1358, concerned the power of the Director of Environmental Protection and the Chief Executive in Council to suspend, cancel or vary an environmental permit that she has granted. Both the Director and the Chief Executive in Council had rejected requests by the applicants to suspend or cancel an environmental permit that the Director had granted. The applicants made this judicial review application to challenge those decisions. This case concerned the grant of an environmental permit for the Civil Engineering and Development Department to construct a bathing beach at Lung Mei, Tai Po.

755. The applicants had requested the Director to suspend or cancel the environmental permit for the reason that the project proponent had submitted misleading or wrong information in their application for an environmental permit, to the effect that 'Lung Mei did not appear to serve as critical/unique habitats for species of conservation importance, or support significant populations of species.' The applicants argued that the study area was an important habitat for spotted seahorses and the construction of a bathing beach would endanger this species. Thomas Au J, in rejecting the application, observed that the Director had received sufficient information and had reviewed them with the assistance of expert or professional advice, and it was not irrational for her to have concluded that the study area did not constitute a habitat that supported a significant population of spotted seahorses, and that as a result, it was not mandatory for the project proponent to have carried out a specific ecological impact assessment of spotted seahorses. Therefore, the lack of such a study did not render the statement misleading or wrong. Nor did the judge think that the statement gave the misleading impression that the findings in the project proponent's EIA report were based on an ecological impact assessment specifically of spotted seahorses. All that the statement was saying was that *Lung Mei itself:* (a) did not serve as a critical habitat for any species of conservation importance or (b) support significant populations of such species.

756. The court rejected the argument that the Chief Executive in Council had acted unlawfully or irrationally when he refused the request to cancel or suspend the environmental permit. As provided in section 14(3) of the EIA, 'The Chief Executive in Council may suspend, vary or cancel an environmental permit if he is satisfied that the continuation of the designated project is, or is *likely to be more prejudicial* to the health and wellbeing of people, flora, fauna or ecosystems than expected at the time of issuing the environmental permit.' Thomas Au J, adopting a purposive interpretation, held that what was required was not merely being more likely but *seriously or significantly* more likely. For the same reasons that the Director's decision was justifiable in relation to the alleged impact on sea horses, it was held that it could not be said that there was any evidence for the Chief Executive to conclude that refusal to suspend or cancel the environmental permit would prove *seriously or significantly* more likely to be prejudicial to the environment. Nor could it be said that the Chief Executive had acted irrationally when he refused to uphold the applicants' objection to the continuation of the environmental permit.

757. The appeal to the Court of Appeal was unsuccessful,[965] where Kwan J observed as follows at [39]: 'Whether an ecological impact assessment specifically of spotted seahorses is required and whether sufficient information is available to enable a determination to be made are matters for the public authority, subject to review by the court on Wednesbury principles […]. The Director's Decision was based on the professional judgment that was made after taking advice from Agriculture, Fisheries and Conservation Department, and where the existence or non-existence of a fact is left to the judgment and discretion of a public body, it is the duty of the court to leave that fact to the public body entrusted with the decision-making power, save where it is obvious that the public body, consciously or unconsciously, is acting perversely […].11 As the Director has taken expert advice from Agriculture, Fisheries and Conservation Department sensibly and rationally at every stage, there is no room for any doctrine of vicarious unreasonableness in these circumstances.' Regarding the decision of the Chief Executive in Council, Kwan J said at [54]: 'The powers are engaged when the Chief Executive in Council is satisfied that the continuation of the project is or is likely to result in any serious or significant increase in the adverse effect on the fauna or ecosystem. The Chief Executive in Council had considered the effect of the continuation of the project on the well-being of the spotted seahorses, cowfish and dragonet subsequently found at Lung Mei, as rightly found by the Judge. Taking into account all the matters […] the Chief Executive in Council concluded that the answer is in the negative and exercised his discretion accordingly. There is no basis in the contention that the Chief Executive in Council's Decision was not made in accordance with the law. There is no merit in [the] contention that the Chief Executive in Council's assessment of the ecological value of Lung Mei, relying on the professional view of the Agriculture,

965. *Ho Loy v Director of Environmental Protection* [2016] 2 HKLRD 417.

Fisheries and Conservation Department, is not a consideration of any prejudice to the ecosystem or fauna that may result from the continuation of the project.'

VI. Unsuccessful Attempt to Challenge the Approval of an EIA Report and the Grant of an Environmental Permit to Construct a Third Runway at the Hong Kong International Airport: Court of First Instance (2016)

758. Ho Loy v Director of Environmental Protection[966] concerned the legality of the approval of an EIA report and the consequent grant of an environmental permit for the construction of a third runway.[967] To put the matter in context, the Hong Kong International Airport was originally planned with two runways. The airport commenced operations in 1998 with one runway and the second runway came into operation in 1999. In 2011 the Hong Kong Airport Authority consulted the public extensively on possible alternatives for airport extension: (i) maintain and develop the existing two runways or (ii) construct a third runway. Later that year, the Airport Authority submitted for the government's consideration the two development options with its recommendation for a new third runway. In 2012 the Chief Executive gave in principle approval for the third runway. In the same year, the Airport Authority submitted a project profile and the Director of Environmental Protection issued a study brief. In April 2014, an EIA report was submitted which the Director approved in November that year. At the same time, the Director granted an environmental permit.

The judicial review application, which was rejected by the Court of First Instance, challenged the approval of the EIA report and the grant of an environmental permit on a number of grounds. They may be summarized as follows:

(1) The EIA report failed to comply with the Technical Memorandum and the study brief for the reason that the following assumptions that the report made were untested: (a) the airspace in the Pearl River Delta area would be available for air traffic into and out of Hong Kong; (b) airport operational data used for noise impact assessment (NIA) were not confirmed by the Civil Aviation

966. [2016] HKEC 2751.

967. The third runway system is said to be almost equal to building a new airport next to the existing one. It involves seven core projects: (1) reclaiming approximately 650 hectares of land using non-dredge methods; (2) building the third runway passenger building and an associated apron; (3) building a new, 3,800-metre-long runway and its supporting taxiway, necessitating the reconfiguration of the existing second runway; (4) expanding Terminal 2 to provide full-fledged passenger services including arrival and departure facilities; (5) Building a new, 2 600-metre-long Automated People Mover (APM) system that will connect Terminal 2 with the new passenger building. The new APM system will operate at a top speed of 80km/h and transport up to 10 800 passengers per hour; (6) Building a new Baggage Handling System (BHS) linking Terminal 2 with the new passenger building. The new BHS will be capable of handling 9 600 bags per hour; and (7) Building other associated airport support infrastructure, road network and transportation facilities. The project is expected to see completion in 2024 with the commissioning of the three-runway system. *See* https://www.threerunwaysystem.com/en/three-runway-system/project-timeline/.

Department. The applicant also argued that the grant of an environmental permit was flawed because the Director had failed to sufficiently enquire whether Pearl River Delta area might be available for use by air flights to and from Hong Kong.

(2) The report did not adequately compare the two alternatives for airport extension.

(3) The ecological impact assessment was flawed in that it failed to provide compensatory measures for the progressive destruction of habitat during the construction of the runway and to consider the cumulative impact on the Chinese White Dolphins by the project taken together with other exiting, committed or proposed developments, namely the Hong Kong-Zhuhai-Macau Bridge project and the Lung Kwu Tan reclamation project. The applicant also argued that the failure to conduct a fair public consultation on those matters constituted procedural irregularity.

(4) The Director failed to disclose the 'Marine Ecology and Fisheries Enhancement Plan', which was prepared by the project proponent, for public consultation.

The Court of First Instance had no hesitation in rejecting all the submissions made in support of the judicial review challenge. We could helpfully summarize the judge's views on the EIA process and the judicial review process, leading to the rejection of the arguments against the validity of the approval of the EIA report and the environmental permit.

(1) While the governing objective of the Environmental Impact Assessment Ordinance is the protection of the environment, the well-structured and defined EIA process is meant to ensure that designated projects could be brought to fruition in a timely and efficient manner.[968]

(2) The Ordinance sets out a detailed procedure for public consultation. There is therefore ordinarily no need to require more to be done. There might be instances where the common law may require more measures to be taken to satisfy the requirement of public consultation. This was not a case where anything more than compliance with statutory process was required. In the instant case, there was adequate adherence to the statutory process.

(3) The EIA report must be prepared in accordance with the requirements of the study brief and the Technical Memorandum. This did not mean that there must be strict compliance with those documents in the sense any technical and insignificant non-compliance will invalidate the report. The judge did not find support for the argument that there has been any significant non-compliance in respect of the making of assumptions that the report had allegedly made to support its conclusions.

968. On this point *see* the relevant discussion in the first case study above: *Kowloon-Canton Railway Corporation v Director of Environmental Protection*, Appeal Board.

(4) The requirements of the Technical Memorandum must be understood not in such a way as to impose an unreasonably high degree of responsibility to provide information, justifications and solutions to potential problems. So understood, the project proponent had provided adequate information on potential impacts on the environment and preventive, minimizing or compensating measures it proposes.

(5) Similarly, consideration of cumulative impacts of a proposed project must be done in a sensible way. In the instance case, the court was satisfied that in relation to likely impacts of the proposed project on Chinese White Dolphins, it was unnecessary to consider impacts on the environment caused by the section of the Hong Kong-Zhuhai-Macau Bridge located outside Hong Kong.

(6) Once a public consultation has been concluded and the Director requires further information to be submitted by the project proponent, there is no strict requirement that such submissions must be put before the public for consultation. Where the effect of the information is to clarify or substantiate what was already stated in the report, or to propose additional measures not strictly required for the project to be approved, there is no need for public input on them.

(7) The requirement in the study brief that the project proponent must consider alternative development options meant that the project proponent must consider alternative ways of implementing the third run way. It did not mean that the project proponent must engage in a comparison of airport expansion with or without a third runway. The development of the airport by constructing a third runway had been decided upon as a matter of government policy. The EIA is not concerned with the wisdom of government policy: it is concerned with how best to implement a designated project with minimal adverse impacts on the environment.

§10. Judicial Attitude Towards EIA

759. The six case studies we have set out above reflect the judicial attitude to the process and outcome of EIA. At the outset, it is important to bear in mind that the first case study is an appeal against the decision of the Director to the Appeal Board, where the appeal process is statutory spelt out. The other five case studies concerned judicial review applications challenging the decisions of the Director, and in one case of the Chief Executive, in relation to the approval of an EIA report, grant of an environmental permit, or refusal to revoke or suspend an environmental permit. Unlike a statutory appeal under the Environmental Impact Assessment Ordinance where the Appeal Board has the jurisdiction to look into merits of the decision appealed from with a view to affirming, reversing or varying the decision appealed from, a court of law in determining a judicial review application exercises a supervisory jurisdiction to ensure that a public body stays within its power. Judicial review concerns legality and not merits of a decision. A review of the above case studies shows that courts have asserted the need to protect our environment but have at the same time fully appreciated the need for the implementation of major infrastructural projects effectively and in a timely fashion. The following observations may be made:

(1) Judicial review is not a proper forum to question merits of government policy. In the first case study *Kowloon-Canton Railway Corporation v Director of Environmental Protection*, the Appeal Board took into consideration the fact that the government policy was to implement two different railway schemes. In that light, the Appeal Board considered it unwise to consider the option of combining both schemes into one because the government policy would not be in favour of such option. In *Chu Yee Wah v Director of Environmental Protection*[969] where the applicants were questioning the serious adverse impacts the designed project would cause to the environment, Fok JA observed thus in the Court of First Instance. 'Nor is this case a debate about the adequacy of the air quality objectives currently in force in Hong Kong under the Air Pollution Control Ordinance (Cap 311). That is a matter of policy and, so long as lawfully determined and executed, policy is not a matter for the courts. No one can seriously question that air quality in Hong Kong is a matter of concern. But, as Reyes J said in *Ng Ngau Chai v Town Planning Board* ([2007] HKEC 1207), para. 28: I fully sympathise with [the applicant's] concerns about the deteriorating quality of the environment … where he lives. But the Court can only apply law. The Judiciary cannot manage the environment. That is the role of the Executive.' In *Reid, Peter Anthony v Environmental Bureau* where the applicants unsuccessfully challenged how waste management is handled in Hong Kong, Zervos J emphasized that while waste management is an important matter of public interest judicial intervention is justified only if there are clear legal issues to be considered. The present application was ill-prepared, did not articulate what 'public law wrongs' had been committed, and was time-barred.

(2) The function of the judiciary in the exercise of its supervisory jurisdiction is to consider whether a public authority has transgressed the boundaries of its legal powers. In determining whether a public authority, in our cases the Director of Environmental Protection, has acted within his statutory power, the courts would enquire into the legislative intention as appearing from the legislative language. While the courts can have reference to the object or the purposes of a statute they can only assist in implementing such object or purpose so long as the substantive provisions of the statute support it. Chow J made the following helpful observations in *Ho Loy v Director of Environmental Protection*:[970]

> 39. 'This having been said, there is a clear limit on the use that may be derived from the legislative purpose when one is engaged in the interpretation of a statute. It must be borne in mind that ultimately, when interpreting a statute, "the

969. [2011] HKEC 555, [31], affirmed by the Court of Appeal [2011] 5 HKLRD 469, [30].
970. [2016] HKEC 2751, [39–40]

court's task is to ascertain the intention of the legislature as expressed in the language of the statute" (per Li CJ in *HKSAR v Cheung Kwun Yin* (2009) 12 HKCFAR 568, [11])'.

40. As observed by Lord Millet in *China Field Ltd v Appeal Tribunal (Buildings) (No 2)* (2009) 12 HKCFAR 342, [36]: 'There can be no quarrel with the principle that statutory provisions should be given a purposive interpretation, but there has been a distressing development by the courts which allows them to distort or even ignore the plain meaning of the text and construe the statute in whatever manner achieves a result which they consider desirable. It cannot be said too often that this is not permissible. Purposive construction means only that statutory provisions are to be interpreted to give effect to the intention of the legislature, and that intention must be ascertained by a proper application of the interpretative process. This does not permit the Court to attribute to a statutory provision a meaning which the language of the statute, understood in the light of its context and the statutory purpose, is incapable of bearing.'

(3) Courts are mindful of the importance of protecting the environment but are also acutely aware of the pressing need for development. Their task is to balance these competing public interests and determining whether the public authority has acted lawfully and rationally and not in a way unauthorized by law, arbitrarily or unreasonably. For instance, while the Director must not approve an EIA report that does not comply with the requirements of the Technical Memorandum or the study brief, a mere technical or insignificant non-compliance does not amount to a legal defect.[971]

(4) Public participation is a crucial feature of the EIA process and the Ordinance provides sufficient provision for effective public participation. In light of that courts are reluctant to add any further requirements of public consultation into the process. For instance, in *Ho Loy v Director of Environmental Protection*,[972] Chow J held that there was no need in the instant case to engraft onto the statutory process any common law duty to consult, if such existed. He also doubted whether ordinarily there would be room for what is popularly known as the Tameside duty, which meant that 'a decision-maker exercising a statutory power must ask himself the right question and take reasonable steps to acquaint himself with the relevant information to enable him to answer it correctly'.[973] The manner in which he acquaints himself with the necessary information is a matter for him, on which he could be called to account only where he had acted irrationally, or he had acted as no reasonable person would have acted.[974]

971. Chow J said in *Ho Loy v Director of Environmental Protection* [2016] HKEC 2751, [55]: 'It is, of course, well established that the Director's power to approve an environmental impact assessment report can be exercised only in respect of a report that meets the requirements imposed by the Technical Memorandum and Study Brief (*see Shiu Wing Steel Ltd v Director of Environmental Protection & Airport Authority (No 2)* (2006) 9 HKCFAR 478, (CFA), [19]). It does not necessarily

(5) A decision made by a public authority may be questioned not only where there has been non-compliance with the legislative and other requirements, such as when the Director has approved an EIA report which does not meet the requirements of the Technical Memorandum or the study brief, but also where there has been a procedural unfairness. As Chow J observed in *Ho Loy v Director of Environmental Protection*: 'if the decision-maker decides to embark upon a public inquiry or consultation, such exercise can, depending on the facts, be challenged on the ground of procedural unfairness (*PCCW-HKT Telephone Ltd v Telecommunications Authority* [2008] 2 HKLRD 282)'.[975]

(6) While questions of fact, for instance, determining whether an EIA report complies with the requirements of the Technical Memorandum is for the Director, determining the meaning of such a requirement is a matter of law for the courts. As the Court of Final Appeal held in *Shiu Wing Steel Ltd v Director of Environmental Protection and Airport Authority (No 2)*: 'It is not a question whether the Director acted reasonably in attributing a given meaning to the Technical Memorandum or the study brief. The question the Director had to answer under section 6(3) had to be answered objectively. Equally, the condition on which the environmental impact assessment report could have been lawfully approved had to be objectively determined. The lawfulness of the approval was not dependent on the Director's opinion if that opinion was objectively in error. If the EIA report in fact met the requirements of the study brief and the Technical Memorandum, the Director's decision to approve the report is valid; if the EIA report did not in fact meet those requirements, the Director had no power to approve the report. It is immaterial whether the Director thought that the requirements were met. And, as the limits of the Director's power are a matter of law, it is for the Court to determine the meaning and scope of those requirements.'[976]

(7) It is not an inaccurate assessment of the judicial role in the area of EIA that courts have been sympathetic to the public interests in the protection of the environment but at the same time has been benevolent in considering the environmental soundness of major designated projects such as airport construction and expansion, waste management, and provision of strategically important

---

follow, however, that any deviation or non-compliance from or with the Technical Memorandum and Study Brief, however minor, insignificant or inconsequential, would result in the invalidation of the Director's approval of the report.'

972. [2016] HKEC 2751.

973. *Ibid.*, [51]. '*Tame side* duty' is the principle derived from *The Secretary for Education and Science v Tameside Metropolitan Borough Council* [1977] AC 1014 (HL). The court will exercise its unusual power to imply a duty to consult only if it is clear that the statutory procedure is insufficient to achieve justice and that to require additional steps of consultation would not frustrate the apparent purpose of the legislation: *Tomorrow Finances Ltd v Director of Fire Services* [2019] HKEC 4134, an unsuccessful application for judicial review of the validity of a fire hazards abatement notice.

974. *Ibid.*, [53]. As Laws LJ explained in *R (Khatun) v Newham London Borough Council* [2005] QB 37, [35], it is for the decision-maker and not the courts, subject to *Wednesbury* review, to decide upon the manner and intensity of enquiry to be undertaken into any relevant factor accepted or demonstrated as such.

975. [2016] HKEC 2751, [54].

976. (2006) 9 HKCFAR 478, [29].

railway links. Courts have however not given a complete free hand to the administration which is evident from the thorough review of the EIA process in each of the cases.

Chapter 6. The Conservation of Nature

§1. INTRODUCTION

760. Being an affluent, modern and densely populated city state, Hong Kong has to find ways to meet its increasing need for infrastructural developments in such a way as to minimize environmental degradation and the inevitable threat to nature conservation. Although generally perceived as a densely built area, only 25% of Hong Kong's land has been developed. Most of the undeveloped areas are country parks or under other statutory protection. Hong Kong has a landscape rising from sandy beaches and rocky foreshores to a height of almost 1,000 metres and is rich in woodlands. Its topography and subtropical climate provide a wide range of habitats supporting a rich variety of flora and fauna. The Agriculture Fisheries and Conservation Department is the most directly involved government agency in nature conservation. A quick view of its achievements provides a valuable background to the legislative framework.

761. The Agriculture Fisheries and Conservation Department adopted a new nature conservation policy in 2013, with a view to regulating, protecting and managing natural resources that are important for the conservation of biological diversity of Hong Kong in a sustainable manner, taking into account social and economic considerations.[977] The policy has the following objectives: to identify and monitor the important components of biological diversity; to identify, designate and manage a representative system of protected areas for the conservation of biological diversity; to promote the protection of ecosystems and important habitats, and the maintenance of viable populations of species in natural surroundings; to identify, monitor and assess activities that may have adverse impacts on biological diversity and to mitigate such impacts; to rehabilitate degraded ecosystems and promote the recovery of threatened species where practicable; to promote the protection and sustainable use of natural resources that are important for the conservation of biological diversity; to provide opportunities for people to appreciate the natural environment; to promote public awareness of nature conservation; to collaborate with, the private sector, including the business community, non-governmental organizations and the academia, to promote nature conservation, and to conduct research and surveys as well as to manage ecologically important sites for such purpose; and to cooperate with and participate in regional and international efforts in nature conservation.

762. In order to implement its nature conservation policy, the Department has introduced two important initiatives: Management Agreement Scheme and Public-Private Partnership scheme. The management agreement scheme encourages non-governmental organizations to enter into management agreements with landowners to preserve and enhance the ecological value of areas of special conservation interest. For instance, Mai Po Inner Deep Bay area, which is a Wetland of International Importance under the Ramsar Convention, is managed by the World Wide Fund for

977. The following information is taken from the Department's website. http://www.afcd.gov.hk/eindex.html.

Nature Hong Kong under the management agreement scheme. The objective of the Public-Private Partnership initiative is to encourage landowners of sites of conservation interest to restrict developments to an ecologically less sensitive portion of a site while preserving and managing the ecologically more sensitive area. In assessing proposals, due consideration is given to the net benefit of the proposal in terms of conservation and possible adverse environmental impacts arising from the proposed development.

763. The Agriculture Fisheries and Conservation Department has adopted conservation plans to protect important habitats and species. For example, a conservation management plan was adopted in 1988 under which Mai Po Inner Deep Bay Ramsar Site has been managed to promote conservation and wise use of its wetlands and to raise public awareness about their importance.

764. An important policy that the Department has adopted is the 'habitat approach', namely protecting important habitats through various conservation designations, including country parks, special areas and conservation zonings. It has designated thirteen areas as country parks and fifteen areas as designated special areas (eleven of which are in country parks) extending to a total area of about 41,600 hectares. They cover over 60% of the forests, 55% of the shrub land, 40% of the grassland, all the freshwater reservoirs and most of the stream origins in the territory, and the fauna and flora associated with these habitats. The Department has 6,600 hectares of land as sites of special scientific interest, conservation areas and coastal protection areas.

765. There are four broad categories of protected land in Hong Kong. They are:[978]

(1) Country parks and special areas. These will be discussed below under country parks.
(2) Water gathering grounds, which are protected under the Waterworks Ordinance, Cap 102. A gathering ground means any surface of land in or by which rain or other water is collected and from which water is, or is intended to be, drawn for the purposes of a supply and which is mapped as a gathering ground under the Ordinance. When demarcating any area as a gathering ground, the Water Authority must give careful consideration to the preservation of traditional rights of any person to take water for agricultural or domestic purposes. We may provide a brief account of the Ordinance which is important in relation to conservation and regulated use of water and the protection of the gathering grounds. Section 2 of the Waterworks Ordinance, Cap 102, the interpretation section, states that the Water Authority has the custody and control of waterworks and all water therein; and that waterworks means any property occupied, used or maintained by the Water Authority for the purposes of

978. *See* publication ISE06/16-17 of the Hong Kong Legislative Council 'Country Parks and Protected Areas in Hong Kong'. http://www.legco.gov.hk/research-publications/english/essentials-1617ise06-country-parks-and-protected-areas-in-hong-kong.htm.

this Ordinance and any gathering ground. Section 3 provides that the Water Authority is responsible for supplying water from waterworks in accordance with the Ordinance, acquire and conserve water, supervise and regulate consumption and ensure proper administration and management of the waterworks. Section 28 provides that a person who wastes or misuses a water supply is guilty of an offence. Section 30 makes it an offence to pollute water forming part of the waterworks. Gathering ground means any surface of land in or by which rain or other water is collected and from which water is, or is intended to be, drawn for the purposes of a supply; and is mapped as a gathering ground. Part V of the Ordinance deals with gathering grounds. Section 24 provides that the Chief Executive may require a lessee of land within a gathering ground to drain, treat, or develop his leased land, in such manner as the Chief Executive may specify, for any purpose connected with the waterworks, including the prevention, control or rectification of contamination or damage to the waterworks. Section 25 provides that where the lessee carries out necessary work to comply with such a requirement, the Water Authority must pay him the reasonable cost of such work. If the lessee fails to carry out such work, the Water Authority may carry out such work at its own expense. Section 26 provides that where the lessee suffers any damage or loss because of the work so carried out by him or the Water Authority, he is entitled to receive compensation.

(3) Conservation-related zonings. They include sites of specific scientific interest, conservation area and green belt (GB) areas. These are created by land-use plans in accordance with the principles stipulated in the Hong Kong Planning Standards and Guidelines.[979] The notes of a zone in a land-use plan (typically an outline zoning plan) contains notes which set out the planning intention for the zone and set out uses that are always permitted in the land covered by the zone and uses which may be permitted in that zone with planning permission. GBs are the most extensive in area which prevent urban sprawl. We may briefly explain these zonings:

   (a) *Cites of special scientific interest* are areas where, for instance, rare plants or animals or fossils are found. Mai Po marshes are the most well-known site of special scientific interest (SSSI). The Town Planning Board may designate sites of special scientific interest as zones in a land-use plan. Such a zone typically sets out the zone's planning intention to be 'to conserve and protect the features of special scientific interest such as rare or particular species of fauna and flora and their habitats, corals, woodlands, marshes or areas of geological, ecological or botanical/biological interest which are designated as Site of Special Scientific Interest (SSSI). Its intention is to deter human activities or developments within the SSSI. There is a general presumption against development in this zone. No developments are permitted unless they are needed to support the conservation of the features of special scientific interest in the SSSI, to maintain and protect the existing character of the SSSI, or for educational and research purposes'.

979. *See also* below '§3. The Role Planning Law in Nature Conservation'.

(b) *Conservation areas* are too designated and regulated by land-use plans made under the Town Planning Ordinance. Chapter 10 'Conservation' of the Hong Kong Planning Guidelines and Standards states that Hong Kong's nature conservation policy is to regulate, protect and manage natural resources that are important for the conservation of biological diversity of Hong Kong in a sustainable manner, taking into account social and economic considerations, for the benefit and enjoyment of the present and future generations of the community. It sets out the principles of conservation in land-use planning as follows: (i) retain significant landscapes, ecological and geological attributes and heritage features as conservation zones; (ii) restrict uses within conservation zones to those which sustain particular landscapes, ecological and geological attributes and heritage features; (iii) control adjoining uses to minimize adverse impacts on conservation zones and optimize their conservation value; and (iv) create, where possible, new conservation zones in compensation for areas of conservation value, which are lost to development. A conservation zone of a land-use plan typically explains its planning intention to be 'to protect and retain the existing natural landscape, ecological or topographical features of the area for conservation, educational and research purposes and to separate sensitive natural environment such as Site of Special Scientific Interest or Country Park from the adverse effects of development. There is a general presumption against development in this zone. In general, only developments that are needed to support the conservation of the existing natural landscape or scenic quality of the area or are essential infrastructure projects with overriding public interest may be permitted'.

(c) *GB Zones* in a land-use plan typically explain that their planning intention in urban areas is 'primarily for the conservation of the existing natural environment amid the built-up areas/at the urban fringe, to safeguard it from encroachment by urban type development, and to provide additional outlets for passive recreational activities. There is a general presumption against development within this zone'. In relation to rural areas and New Town, the notes of the zone typically state that 'the planning intention of this zone is primarily for defining the limits of urban and sub-urban development areas by natural features and to contain urban sprawl as well as to provide passive recreational outlets. There is a general presumption against development within this zone'.

(4) *Wild animal protection areas.* The Wild Animals Protection Ordinance, Cap 170 makes provision in this regard. Section 4 of the Ordinance provides that no person shall, except in accordance with a special permit, hunt or wilfully disturb any protected wild animal. Similarly, no person shall, except in accordance with a special permit, take, remove, injure, destroy or wilfully disturb a nest or egg of any protected wild animal (section 5). Section 13 prohibits the entry of any person other than in accordance with a permit granted by the Director of Agriculture, Fisheries and Conservation. The Ordinance provides

for the appointment of wardens, creates offences intended to protect wild animals and restricted areas and provides for effective enforcement. There are three such restrictive areas.

The following discussion of relevant legislation will throw further light on the above broad categories and provide further supplementary information.

§2. LEGISLATIVE FRAMEWORK

766. The principal statutes which relate to nature conservation are the following: Country Parks Ordinance (Cap 208), Forests and Countryside Ordinance (Cap 96), Plant (Importation and Pest Control) Ordinance (Cap 207), Protection of Endangered Species of Animals and Plants Ordinance (Cap 586), Wild Animals Protection Ordinance (Cap 170), Public Health (Animals and Birds) Ordinance (Cap 139), Marine Parks Ordinance (Cap 476), Fisheries Protection Ordinance (Cap 171), Marine Fish Culture Ordinance (Cap 353), Whaling Industry (Regulation) Ordinance (Cap 496), Waterworks Ordinance (Cap 102) and the Protection of the Harbour Ordinance (Cap 531).

I. Country Parks

767. Out of Hong Kong's 1,108 km of land about three-quarters is countryside. The Country Parks Ordinance provides for the designation, control and management of country parks and special areas to preserve countryside and enable the community to enjoy the amenities of countryside. Country parks have been designated for the purposes of nature conservation, countryside recreation and outdoor education, while special areas are created mainly for the purpose of nature conservation. Designation of area as country parks and designated areas began in the 1970s, with the enactment of the Country Parks Ordinance in 1976, and they now cover an area of 443 square metres. Within country parks are scenic hills, woodlands, reservoirs and coastline. Currently, there are twenty-four country parks and twenty-two special areas. Country parks are managed by the Agriculture, Fisheries and Conservation Department, which is responsible for tree planting, litter collection, firefighting, development control and provision of recreational and educational facilities. Country parks are very popular. There are several hiking trails are situate within country parks, most popular among them being the MacLehose trail (100 km) and the Lantau trail (70 km).[980]

768. Designation of country parks: The Country Parks and Marine Parks Authority (Authority) may designate areas as country parks. The procedure begins when

980. Hong Kong: The Facts–Country Parks and Conservation on the Agriculture, Fisheries and Conservation Department. http://www.afcd.gov.hk/english/country/cou_lea/the_facts.html.

the Authority recommends to the Chief Executive that a certain area may be designated as a country park or a special area. When directed so by the Chief Executive, the Authority may make and publish for public consultation a draft map together with explanatory or descriptive material showing or making provision for such facilities and services it considers appropriate for the country park. The draft country park map must be published for consultation, and the effect of gazetting a draft map is that no new development[981] may be carried out within the proposed country park area without the prior approval of the Authority. During the public inspection period of sixty days, any person who is aggrieved by the making of the draft map may object to the draft map and the Board must conduct an objection hearing. The Board may reject the objection amend the map. The next step is for the Authority to submit the draft map to the Chief Executive in Council, who may approve or refuse to approve the draft map or refer it to the Authority for further consideration and amendment. Where the Chief Executive in Council approves a draft country park map, he must designate the area shown in the map as a country park.[982,983] The creation of country parks serves an important public interest and therefore loss of any private interest is justified by that public purpose. Section 18 of the Country Parks Ordinance thus provides that no compensation is payable to any owner of or any person interested in any land because it is situated within or is affected by a country park. However, where the Authority refuses approval to carry out a new development or requires a person to discontinue or modify a use, inconsistently with the landowner's property rights under the lease or other agreement (such as a licence), he is entitled to compensation for any resultant loss or damage or costs.[984]

769. Designation of special areas. The Chief Executive may by order in the Gazette designate any area of government land outside a country park as a special area for the purposes of the Country Parks Ordinance; and the Authority may designate an area of government land within a country park as a special area.[985] While a country park may include government land and private land, a special area may only consist of government land. Ma Shi Chau special area may be taken as an example of a special area. The Ma Shi Chau (Special Area) Order of 1999 designated four islands in Tolo Harbour as Ma Shi Chau special area, an area well known for its rich geological features, fossils and nesting site for egrets. Two of these islands had previously been registered as sites of special scientific interest. Once an area is designated as a special area, it comes under the control and management of

---

981. New development means any development other than development in respect of which all the necessary approvals and permissions had been obtained prior to the date of publication in the Gazette of a notice under s. 9(1). Country Parks Ordinance, Cap 208, s. 10(3). 'Development means the carrying out of building, engineering, mining or other similar operations in, on, over or under land, or the making of any material change in the use of any buildings or other land.' Section 10(3).
982. *See* Part III 'Designation of Country Parks', Country Parks Ordinance, Cap 208.
983. *See* Country Park Ordinance, Cap 208, Part II 'Duties of Country and Marine Parks Authority and Establishment of Country and Marine Parks Board'.
984. *See* Country Parks Ordinance, Cap 208, Part V 'Compensation'.
985. Country Parks Ordinance, Cap 208, s. 24.

the Authority. The Board must consider and advise the Authority on policy and programmes for the area in order to prevent incompatible development in or near it.[986]

770. Exclusion from country parks and special areas. The Chief Executive may by order published in the Gazette exclude any of the following areas or places from a country park or a special area: village areas, traditional burial grounds, temples and other religious buildings; any area in respect of which a lease is issued or to be issued by the Director of Lands, after consultation with the Authority, for the purposes of recreation or tourism; and any place, building, site or structure that has been declared a monument under section 3 of the Antiquities and Monuments Ordinance (Cap 53).[987] As we shall see below, village areas when so excluded from a country park are known as country park enclaves, meaning private land protected from control and management of country parks. The extent of the power of the Chief Executive to exclude an area from a country park through his power to amend an approved country park map was reviewed in *Lai Pun Sung v The Director of Agriculture, Fisheries and Conservation* [2009] HKEC 1425. This was an unsuccessful application for leave to proceed with a judicial review application concerning the amendment of an approved country park map designating a part of the country park as a landfill. The applicant argued that the power of amendment whereby a part of an existing country park is excluded may be exercised only where the excluded area is no longer suitable for country park use. Lam J in the Court of First Instance held that section 15 of the Ordinance imposes no such restriction and expressed the view that exclusion of an area from a country park is lawful so long as the reason for such exclusion is proportionate to a problem of waste management that is sought to be addressed. In the instance case, the power has been properly exercised since there was an overriding need for the use of the land as a landfill. Lam J emphasized the importance of taking a balanced view when exercising the powers under the Ordinance: 'I wish to add that country parks are valuable natural heritage to be preserved for those living in Hong Kong. … [T]there is a legitimate expectation that they would not be excised unless it can be demonstrated that there is a need to do so. That may involve showing that the excise of the country park is a proportionate response to the problem at hand' (*Lai Pun Sung v The Director of Agriculture, Fisheries and Conservation* [2009] HKEC 1425, [13]).

771. Country parks and special areas are managed and controlled by the Country and Marine Parks Authority. The Ordinance has set up a Country and Marine Parks Board to advise the Authority, whose functions are to (a) act as a consultative body to advise the Authority upon any matter referred to it by the Authority; (b) consider and to advise the Authority on, the policy and programmes prepared by the Authority in respect of country parks and special areas, including proposed country parks and special areas; and (c) consider any objections that may be lodged under section 11 (objections to a draft country park map) or section 17 (objections to an

986. *See* Legislative Council Brief on the Order, http://www.legco.gov.hk/yr98-99/english/subleg/brief/93_brf.pdf.

987. Country Parks Ordinance, Cap 208, s. 25.

order requiring an occupier to discontinue or modify a land use which would substantially reduce the enjoyment and amenities of a country park).

772. The Authority acts in accordance with established principles and criteria in deciding whether to designate an area as a country part. Such criteria include among other things, landscape quality, recreational potential, conservation value, size, land status, and management effectiveness of the site. The Country and Marine Parks Board may from time to time elaborate on the applicable criteria. In 1989 the Board prepared a policy paper describing the applicable principles and criteria. This paper noted that generally it is government land, and not private land, that was recommended for designation as country parks. The reason being that including private land in a country park would involve conflicts with indigenous landowners who would assert their rights to the land. When large areas of land are designated as country parks, it is the general practice to carve out of the country park any private land situate within the country park limits. Such excluded private lands are known as 'country park enclaves'. Currently, there are seventy-seven country park enclaves with a total area of 2,076 hectares. There are about 460 hectares of private land which have been incorporated into country parks in the absence of objections from the landowners.

773. The detection of unauthorized excavation work in the country park enclave of Sai Wan in 2010 gave rise to much public concern about undesirable land developments in enclaves. At that time fifty-four of the seventy-seven enclaves had not been covered by outline zoning plans made under the Town Planning Ordinance and thus were not subject to planning controls. As many of the relevant land leases contained little prohibition against undesirable land uses, the exclusion of these enclaves from country parks control gave them a fairly free hand to embark on development. Sai Wan was soon brought under planning control by making a draft Development Permission Area plan.

774. Responding to public concern fanned by the Sai Wan incident, the Chief Executive in his 2010 Annual Policy Address promised to either include enclaves into country parks or determine their proper use through statutory land-use planning. The Authority's response was to conduct a comprehensive review of existing principles and criteria for designating new country parks or for extending the area of country parks. The Authority submitted a working paper on these issues 'Review of the Criteria for Designating Country Parks and Proposed Measures for Protecting Country Park Enclaves' to the Board for its advice, which was duly endorsed. Thereafter the Authority embarked on assessing fifty-four enclaves. Some of which were considered suitable for inclusion into the surrounding country park. As regards six enclaves, the Authority decision being that they were not suitable for incorporation into the surrounding country park, it decided not to recommend them to the Chief Executive in Council for incorporation, on the ground that they had come under planning control of outline zoning plans.

775. In *Chan Ka Lam v Country and Marine Parks Authority*,[988] Chan Ka Lam, a founding member of 'Save Our Country Parks', questioned the legality of the Authority's decision not to include those six enclaves into the surrounding country parks. The principal question was whether the Authority was required to seek the advice of the Board whenever it took a decision regarding the incorporation or non-incorporation of an enclave. Answering the question in the negative, the Court of First Instance distinguished between the referral of 'policy and programmes prepared by the Authority in respect of country parks and special areas, including proposed country parks and special areas' and making a decision in respect of a particular country park or special area. The provisions relevant to determining the question were subsections (a) and (b) of section 5 of the Country Parks Ordinance, which provides that the Country and Marine Parks Board shall: (a) act as a consultative body to advise the Authority upon any matter referred to it by the Authority; and (b) consider and advise the Authority on, the policy and programmes prepared by the Authority in respect of country parks and special areas, including proposed country parks and special areas. It was held that reading these two subsections together, the Authority has a duty to consult the Board in relation to matters referred to in subsection (b), and observed that the Authority had in fact referred its policy paper to the Board.[989] The applicant's complaint that the Authority ought to have consulted the Board before it came to a decision not to include the six enclaves into the surrounding country park was rejected by the Court of First Instance for the following two reasons: (i) the decisions did not fall within the meaning of 'policy and programmes' and therefore fell outside the scope of section 5(b); and (ii) the Decisions were not made in respect of any country park or proposed country park as the enclaves were situated outside any country park or proposed country park. As regards whether the decisions of the Authority were caught by the words 'policy and programmes prepared by the Authority' Au J said that 'policy' means 'a course or set of general principles to guide the conduct' and a programme means a 'plan or scheme that is of general and broad nature'. Au J observed that 'the Authority did refer those proposed revised principles and criteria to the Board for advice, and the Board has endorsed them'. By contrast, a specific assessment the Authority makes in order to decide whether an enclave must be brought under the control of a country park could not be regarded as part of 'policy or programme'.

776. The applicant's argument founded on section 5 failed, but his argument succeeded on the ground that the Authority had not taken all relevant considerations into account when deciding not to recommend the enclaves into the surrounding country parks. Au J in *Chan Kam* case usefully set out the relevant legal principles drawn from previous Hong Kong and English judicial decisions and held that the consultation undertaken by the Authority fell short of what is expected. Au J emphasized that the Authority was under legal obligation (a) to consider the legislative purpose of the Country Parks Ordinance and the Authority's statutory obligations; (b) to ensure that its decisions properly give effect to relevant policy considerations;

988. [2017] HKEC 841.
989. *Ibid.*, [34]–[36].

(c) act in a manner so as not to frustrate any legitimate expectations; (d) and to take all relevant consideration and not be prompted by irrelevant considerations.

777. The applicant appealed against the decision of the Court of First Instance that section 5 did not require the Authority to have consulted the Board in deciding not to incorporate the six enclaves into the neighbouring country parks. The Court of Appeal dismissed the appeal and upheld the decision of the Court of First Instance on the first reason given by the judge, namely that, having regard to the clear difference between the formulation of policy and programmes, on the one hand, and their execution and implementation, on the other, the decisions on whether or not to incorporate the six enclaves did not fall within the ambit of section 5(1)(b): 'There is a clear distinction between the formulation of policy and programme on the one hand and their actual execution and implementation on the other. Whilst s.5(1)(b) provides that the Board should consider and give advice on the former, it could not be the legislative intent that the Board, playing an advisory role, should be involved in the execution or implementation of policy or programme.'[990] The Court of Appeal observed that the Authority is required to consult the Board at the stage of formulating policy and programmes which will guide the Authority in determining how the question of enclaves be decided and that once a decision has been taken to bring an enclave within a country park area, the Authority must, as provided by section 8(4), consult the Board in preparing a draft map for that purpose. The Court of Appeal thought the legislative intention could not have been that in the intermediate step of making a decision in respect of each enclave too the Board must be consulted.[991] The Court of Appeal did not consider it necessary to consider the second reason given by the judge, that is a decision not to incorporate an enclave in a country park was not a matter in respect of any country park or proposed country park.[992]

On further appeal, the Court of Final Appeal disagreeing with the Court of First Instance and the Court of Appeal held that the decision in question fell within the ambit of section 5(a) and (b). It also considered the second ground and disagreeing with the Court of First Instance held that the words 'in respect of country parks and special areas' were wide in scope to cover the question whether an enclave should be incorporated into a surrounding country park: 'the assessment programme was clearly in respect of the neighbouring country parks in that the purpose of the assessments was to decide whether the enclaves should be absorbed into these country parks. Looked at from another angle, the assessments were also in respect of proposed country parks in the sense that the enclaves were to be assessed for designation as country parks'.[993]

In determining that the word 'programmes' was wide enough to include within it an assessment of circumstances in deciding whether or not to incorporate an enclave into the neighbouring country park, the Court of Final Appeal reasoned as follows: 'The word "programme" is less general or broad in nature [than policy], being more

990. *Chan Ka Lam v Country and Marine Parks Authority* [2009] 2 HKLRD 1198 (CA), [57].
991. *Ibid.*, [61].
992. *Ibid.*, [68].
993. *Chan Ka Lam v Country and Marine Parks Authority* [2020] HKEC 3188 (CFA).

specific in terms of what is sought to be achieved. It connotes a plan of action, a project or scheme or … a series of planned activities, events or future actions. A programme is a suitable term to employ if it seeks to implement the effect of a policy by a series of intended activities, events or actions. There is no justification artificially to cut down the scope of what a programme can contain and exclude "executive acts" from a programme. For the same reason, it is unhelpful to say categorically that an act to carry out or implement a programme does not form part of the programme, for it begs the question as to what the programme comprises in the first place. … It makes no sense to confine the Board's consideration and advice only to a plan or outline and not to the substance of the activities, events or actions thereunder.'[994]

778. In 2009, the Agriculture, Fisheries and Conservation Department launched a 'Country Parks Plantation Enrichment Programme', with the following main objectives: to increase biodiversity and ecological value of exotic plantations in country parks; to enhance the sustainability of the plantations; and to improve the health of trees within and reduce the chance of pest outbreaks.[995] It is also engaged in afforestation work.

779. The Country Parks and Special Areas Regulations[996] contain a number of regulatory measures to protect the tranquil nature of country parks. It is an offence for any person to bring into a country park any vehicles, animals, and hunting or trapping appliances, without a permit. The Department has adopted strict policies in relation to the grant of permits. For instance, a permit to bring vehicles into a country park will be issued only to residents of the country park, persons carrying out official duties or works and other activities approved by the Department. Applications for recreational purposes will not be considered.

780. The Regulations also creates offences to prevent cutting trees, cultivating or disturbing the soil, causing fires or polluting any area within a country park or a special area. The Authority may, in the interests of good management, close any part of a country park or a special area.

II. The Forests and Countryside Ordinance

781. This Ordinance consolidates the law relating to forests and plants, and provides for the protection of the countryside. It is an offence for anyone, without lawful excuse, to cut grass, remove turf or earth; pluck or damage any bud, blossom or leaf; trespass or pasture cattle or goats; or destroy trees or fell, cut, burn or otherwise destroy any trees or growing plants in any forest or plantation. It is also an

994. *Ibid.*, [35], [39].
995. *See* https://www.afcd.gov.hk/english/country/cou_how/whats_new_pep.html/plantation_PEP.html.
996. Cap 208 sub leg A.

offence for anyone to light a fire in or near a forest, plantation or open countryside, unless it is reasonable to do so and he takes reasonable precautions to prevent damage by fire to the surrounding area.[997]

III. The Plant (Importation and Pest Control) Ordinance

782. This Ordinance provides for the control of the importation of plants, plant pests and soil, and for the prevention of the spread of plant pests. The importation of certain specified plants is prohibited except under licence to ensure that plants are imported only if they are free from plant pests. Similarly, no soil, plant pests or any plant infected by or infested with a plant pest may be imported save in accordance with the terms of an authorization. These offences are strict liability offences. Accordingly, the prosecution is not required to prove that the accused knew of the existence of the offending goods, but the accused could rely on the common law defence on a balance of probabilities that he did not know the offending goods existed, and he honestly and reasonably believed that the offending goods did not exist. The statutory defence to the offence importing pest infected plants is 'reasonable excuse' and the accused who relies on it bears an evidential burden of proof.[998] The Ordinance provides for the control of plant pests particularly through seize and destroy powers. It also provides for the creation and maintenance of quarantines.[999]

IV. The Protection of Endangered Species of Animals and Plants Ordinance

783. In 2006, this Ordinance (Cap 586) repealed and replaced the Animals and Plants (Protection of Endangered Species) Ordinance (Cap 187). The repealed Ordinance was enacted to give effect to the 'Convention on International Trade in Endangered Species of Wild Fauna and Flora' (CITES), which was signed in 1973. It was ratified by the UK in August 1976 both for itself and for Hong Kong. The English Endangered Species (Import and Export) Act came into force in November 1976 and the Hong Kong Ordinance was passed on 6th August 1976. The repealed ordinance did not expressly declare that its aim was to incorporate the CITES in Hong Kong, unlike the UK Act of 1976. Certain defects in the provisions of this Ordinance were highlighted in the 1988 case of *Attorney-General v Yau Kwok-Lam, Johnny*[1000] where the Department of Agriculture and Fisheries, in order to follow a resolution passed at the 1987 conference of the contracting parties to the CITES that party states should adopt more stringent measures to control ivory trade, issued a circular making it more difficult to export ivory that had been worked in Hong Kong. In *Yau Kwok-Lam* case, the Court of Appeal held that worked ivory meant ivory that had been skilfully prepared, so that exporting partially prepared ivory pieces was not prohibited. Hunter JA gave a strong dissenting opinion emphasizing

997. The Forests and Countryside Ordinance (Cap 96), s. 16.
998. *HKSAR v Diao Rui* [2015] 4 HKLRD 187.
999. The Plant (Importation and Pest Control) Ordinance (Cap 207).
1000. [1998] 2 HKLR 394 (CA).

the need to give a purposive interpretation to the provisions of the Ordinance to make meaningful implementation of the Convention, observing that the roughly worked pieces of ivory would be finished into ornaments by skilled craftsmen in Africa to which they are re-exported (re-export was not covered by the Ordinance). The 2006 Ordinance was enacted to address difficulties in the 1976 Ordinance such as this and to bring it up-to-date in compliance with later developments in relation to the implementation of the Convention. The 2006 Ordinance which is now in force regulates the import, export, re-export, and possession or control of certain endangered species of animals and plants and parts and derivatives of those species. Contraventions of provisions regulation the import, export and re-export of (a) live or dead animals and any derivatives and (b) plants or parts of plants and any derivatives, are offences punishable by fine and imprisonment. The 2006 amendment has substantially increased the penalties for these offences and 'this remarkable increase in maximum sentence shows the government's commitment to convey a clear message to the society that there is a strong determination to combat illegal trafficking of endangered species'.[1001] *HKSAR v Goron Jomar Osal*[1002] illustrates the strict view of any breach of these regulatory provisions, where the judge said at [34]: 'As a party in the international convention for protection of endangered species, Hong Kong must take effective measures to ensure its compliance. A sentence of sufficient deterrence has to be imposed.' A similarly hard-line approach to sentencing was taken in the case of *HKSAR v Fung Tak Cheung*,[1003] where the judge observed that the substantial increase in the level of punishment in 2006 shows the government's strong commitment to protect the endangered species and to stop illegal trading and that in order to reflect the legislative intent, it would be appropriate to recognize the importance of a deterrent sentence. Courts have observed that it is important to set a fine that would be sufficient to reflect the value of the imported animal or plant specimens and the deterrent objective of the statute.[1004]

784. The Ordinance sets out, as did its predecessor, but in much greater detail, a licensing system to regulate the import, export, re-export or introduction from the sea of such plants and animals. No licence will be approved if such approval would contravene any Convention requirement, and in granting a licence, the Director of Agriculture, Fisheries and Conservation may impose conditions, including conditions that are more stringent than any requirement under the Convention.[1005] The Director may cancel a licence if any condition of the licence is contravened or the Director is satisfied that the licence was issued, extended, renewed or varied as a result of a false representation of fact made by the applicant or an unlawful act of

1001. *HKSAR v Hiraguchi Naoki* [2019] HKEC 1810 (DC).
1002. [2021] HKEC 90 (DC).
1003. [2020] HKEC 3264 (DC). *See also HKSAR v Muller Canlyn Yolande* [2020] HKEC 2520 (DC), *HKSAR v Rasolonirina Marie Yvon Aljymiand* [2020] HKEC 483 (DC), *HKSAR v Tshirobo Confidence* [2020] HKEC 782 (DC), *HKSAR v Schlögl Leopold* [2019] HKEC 2358, *HKSAR v Zhao Zhengxin* [2019] HKDC 223 (DC).
1004. *HKSAR v Schwendinger Glenn Harry Patrick* [2020] HKEC 1095 (DC).
1005. The ability to impose restrictions more stringent than requirements under the Convention upholds the dissenting view of Hunter JA in *Attorney-General v Yau Kwok-Lam* which we discussed immediately above.

the applicant. An applicant whose application for a licence has been rejected or whose licence has been cancelled may appeal against such decision to the Administrative Appeals Board, established in 1994 by the Administrative Appeals Board Ordinance (Cap 442).[1006]

785. Part VI of the Ordinance deals with enforcement powers. Authorized officers have power to require production of documents or other evidence to show compliance with the Ordinance, to require production of things for inspection, to inspect and enter place or premises, to search, detain and seize anything which is liable to seizure, and to detain a person suspected of an offence for a reasonable period of time while the officer enquires about the suspected commission of the crime. Part 7 of the Ordinance provides circumstances in which things seized in the exercise of enforcement powers may be returned or forfeited and the manner in which forfeited things will be disposed of.

V. The Wild Animals Protection Ordinance

786. The object of this Ordinance is the conservation of wild animals. The Ordinance prohibits the hunting or disturbing of any protected wild animal or disturbing, removing or destroying any nest or egg of any protected animal without a special permit. Possession, sale or export of dead or live protected wild animals is an offence unless a special licence has been issued for that purpose. The Ordinance prohibits the entry into a restricted area, such as the Mai Po Reserve, without a special permit. It provides for the appointment of nature wardens and gives authorized officers powers of entry, search and detention, and associated powers for purpose of enforcement.[1007]

VI. Prevention of Disease among Birds and Animals

787. Public Health (Animals and Birds) Ordinance (Cap 139) consolidates the law relating to quarantine and the prevention of disease among animals and birds, makes provision relating to the regulation of livestock keeping and provides for the protection and safety of the public at places where wild animals and birds are exhibited. The Ordinance prohibits the importation into Hong Kong of any animal or bird suffering from disease and authorizes the Chief Executive to regulate the movement of animals or birds within or from an infected area. It makes provision for the safety of the public at places where wild animals and wild birds are exhibited. Section 8 of Public Health (Animals and Birds) Ordinance (Cap 139) provides that: 'The senior veterinary officer, or any person acting under his direction, may seize any animal, bird or thing dealt with in contravention of this Ordinance or of any regulation

1006. That is the Protection of Endangered Species of Animals and Plants Ordinance No. 3 of 2006 (Cap 58) *see* Legislative Council Brief, 'Protection of Endangered Species of Animals and Plants Bill', File Ref: EP 55/25/01 Pt 14 https://www.legco.gov.hk/yr04-05/english/bills/brief/b17_brf.pdf.
1007. Wild Animals Protection Ordinance (Cap 170).

thereunder, and may order the forfeiture of such animal, bird or thing, and the same shall thereupon be destroyed, sold or otherwise disposed of as the senior veterinary officer may direct.' Such forfeiture is not a contravention of Article 105 of the Basic Law which provides that 'The Hong Kong Special Administrative Region shall, in accordance with law, protect the right of individuals and legal persons to the acquisition, use, disposal and inheritance of property and their right to compensation for lawful deprivation of their property. Such compensation shall correspond to the real value of the property concerned at the time and shall be freely convertible and paid without undue delay.'[1008] The Public Health (Animals and Birds) Regulations provide detailed provisions to give effect to the Ordinance.[1009] *Kowloon Poultry Laan Merchants Association v Department of Justice*[1010] is a case where the Court of First Instance upheld the decision of the Director, under the Regulations, to declare a poultry market an infected place during the Avian Influenza outbreak in 2000.

VII. Marine Parks Ordinance

788. This Ordinance provides for the designation, control and management of marine parks and marine reserves. These parks and reserves are a means of conserving marine life, protecting breeding grounds for fish stocks and providing opportunities for scientific research. A marine park is an area of the sea set aside for conservation and recreation purposes, whereas a marine reserve is an area of high conservation value set aside for scientific and educational study. The Country and Marine Parks Authority controls and manages marine parks and marine reserves. The Authority may take measures for the protection and management of marine parks and marine reserves.

789. The following activities are prohibited in both marine parks and marine reserves: fishing, hunting, removing or taking away any animal or plant except in accordance with a permit or in a special zone; conducting any fish culture operations; water skiing, jet skiing or water scootering except in a special zone; speeding power-driven vessels; obstructing waterways or causing water pollution; unauthorized commercial activities. Swimming, diving and boating are prohibited in marine reserves.[1011]

VIII. The Fisheries Protection Ordinance (Cap 171)

790. This Ordinance promotes the conservation of fish and other forms of aquatic life within the waters of Hong Kong and regulates fishing practices. The Ordinance imposes a number of general controls on fishing: (i) No person may be

1008. *Mo Chun Hon v Agriculture, Fisheries and Conservation Department* [2008] 1 HKCLRT 386 (CA).
1009. Public Health (Animals and Birds) Ordinance (Cap 139).
1010. [2001] HKEC 702.
1011. Marine Parks Ordinance (Cap 476).

engaged in fishing with the use or aid of a vessel in any area of the waters of Hong Kong, other than in a fish pond or reservoir, unless (a) the person holds a valid research fishing permit,[1012] or (b) the vessel has a valid operating licence and is not designed or equipped to be used primarily for fishing or (c) the vessel is a registered fishing vessel and is not engaged in fishing in breach of section 15.[1013] A person aggrieved by a decision of the Director, such as to refuse an application for registration of a fishing vessel (under section 14), or imposing conditions on a registration (under section 16 or section 25(3)), or cancellation of a registration (under section 24) or refusal to grant a research fishing permit (under section 29), may appeal to the Administrative Appeals Board.[1014] It provides for the appointment of fisheries inspectors and authorized officers for the purpose of carrying into effect the provisions of the Ordinance, for example, by exercising powers of search and seizure.[1015] The Fisheries Protection Regulations prohibit the use for fishing of any explosives or toxic substances, and such fishing apparatus as may be prescribed by the Director of Agriculture, Fisheries and Conservation. The Director may grant exemptions from any or all of these prohibitions where he is satisfied that such exemption is reasonably necessary for the purpose of carrying out any scientific research or any bona fide business of fish culture in fish ponds or artificially enclosed waters.[1016]

IX. The Marine Fish Culture Ordinance

791. This Ordinance was enacted to regulate and protect marine fish culture (meaning any operation involving the maintenance, propagation or promotion of growth of fish in captivity within the waters of Hong Kong). The Director of Agriculture, Fisheries and Conservation has the authority to designate any area of waters of Hong Kong to be a fish culture zone. It is unlawful for any person to engage in fish culture within the waters of Hong Kong outside a fish culture zone except for the purposes of scientific research and for the maintenance of fish in captivity for purposes other than the propagation or promotion of growth of such fish. A person may engage in fish culture within a fish culture zone only with a licence. The Director has the power to instruct licensees on any matter concerning fish culture.

792. Several offences have been created to protect fish culture zones. For instance, it is an offence for any person to deposit any chemical or any other matter likely to injure fish or pollute waters in any fish culture zone. It is also an offence to interfere with any raft or impoundment within a site or any fish within such raft or impoundment. It is an offence for any person to cause or permit any vessel to

1012. On research fishing permits *see* Part 6 of the Fisheries Protection Ordinance (Cap 171).

1013. Fisheries Protection Ordinance (Cap 171), s. 11.

1014. *See Wan v Director of Agriculture, Fisheries and Conservation* [2017] 5 HKLRD 141 (CA) regarding the correctness of an interpretation of the Ordinance by the Administrative Appeals Board.

1015. *Ibid.*, Part 2 'Appointment and Powers of Officers and Making Subsidiary Legislation' and Part 3 'Search, Seizure, Arrest and Evidence'.

1016. Cap 171 sub leg A.

enter or remain in a fish culture zone except for the purposes of or in connection with fish culture operations; when authorized in writing by the Director; or in a case of emergency or stress of weather to save life or property or for the safety of the vessel concerned.[1017]

X. The Whaling Industry (Regulation) Ordinance

793. This Ordinance implements the International Convention for the Regulation of Whaling of 1946. Its objects are to prohibit the taking, towing or treating of whales within the waters of Hong Kong; to prohibit the taking, towing or treating of whales by any Hong Kong ship or Hong Kong aircraft outside the waters of Hong Kong without a licence or permit; to provide measures for the conservation and utilization of whales elsewhere; and for purposes connected with such matters.[1018]

794. The master of a ship which is used within the waters of Hong Kong for taking, towing or treating whales commits an offence. If any person on board or belonging to a Hong Kong ship or aircraft while outside the waters of Hong Kong to kill or take a right whale or grey whale, an immature whale or a female whale accompanied by a calf, that person, the master of the ship or the commander of the ship or aircraft each commit an offence. Treating whales in a factory situated in Hong Kong, or using any Hong Kong ship or aircraft for taking, towing or treating whales outside the waters of Hong Kong is an offence unless such activity is authorized by a licence. There is special provision for a permit to take and treat whales for scientific purposes. The relevant authority in the Central People's Government may grant to any person a permit authorizing that person to kill, take and treat whales for the purposes of scientific research or for other exceptional purposes, subject to such restrictions as to the number, and subject to such other conditions, as it thinks fit. Whale fishery inspectors have been given wide powers of inspection for the purpose of enforcing the Ordinance.

XI. Protection of the Harbour Ordinance

795. Protection of the Harbour Ordinance (Cap 531) was passed at a time when there was widespread community concern about extensive and uncontrolled reclamation of the harbour.[1019] The aim of the Ordinance is to protect and preserve the harbour by establishing a presumption against reclamation in the harbour.

1017. Marine Fish Culture Ordinance (Cap 353). *See also* Marine Fish Culture Regulations, Cap 353 sub leg A. *See HKSAR v Special View Ltd* (2018) 21 HKCFAR 562 (CFA) where the Court of Final Appeal upheld that validity of the decision of the Agriculture, Fisheries and Conservation Department not to renew a licence to operate a raft upon its expiration. The conviction for operating a raft after the expiration of the licence was upheld.

1018. Whaling Industry (Regulation) Ordinance (Cap 496).

1019. Protection of the Harbour Ordinance (Cap 531).

796. Town Planning Board v Society for the Protection of the Harbour Ltd[1020] arose out of a decision of the Town Planning Board to submit an outline zoning plan to enable reclamation of 26 hectares from Victoria Harbour to the Chief Executive in Council for approval. The Society for the Protection of the Harbour Ltd successfully challenged the decision on the ground that the Town Planning Board had misinterpreted the Protection of the Harbour Ordinance, in particular section 3, which provides as follows:

(1) The harbour is to be protected and preserved as a special public asset and a natural heritage of Hong Kong people, and for that purpose there shall be a presumption against reclamation in the harbour.
(2) All public officers and public bodies shall have regard to the principle stated in subsection (1) for guidance in the exercise of any powers vested in them.

797. The Court of First Instance upheld the challenge and the Town Planning Board appealed directly to the Court of Final Appeal, without exhausting its appeal to the Court of Appeal, in view of the urgency and public importance of the matter. It argued that it had correctly interpreted that section to mean that the decision-maker must consider the presumption against reclamation as one of the material considerations and must weigh it against other material considerations to decide whether the public benefit of the proposed reclamation outweighed the need to preserve the harbour.

798. The Court of Final Appeal rejected the contention that the presumption against reclamation is only one of the many material considerations that the Board may take into account. The Court reasoned as follows: Section 3(1) established a statutory principle recognizing the harbour as a special public asset and a natural heritage of the Hong Kong people and prescribing that it was to be protected and preserved as such an asset and such a heritage. By representing the harbour in such special terms, the legislature was giving legal recognition to its unique character and the great public need to protect and preserve it having regard to such character. The legislative intent so expressed was to establish the principle of protection and preservation as a strong and vigorous one and that the presumption against reclamation may only be rebutted by establishing an overriding public need for reclamation.

799. The Court observed that a need – be it economic, environmental or social – is overriding only if it is a compelling and present need. Such need goes far beyond something which is desirable, preferable or beneficial, but it would be going too far to describe it as a last resort or something which the public would not do without. Where there is a reasonable alternative, an overriding need for reclamation would not be made out. In considering what is a reasonable alternative, all the circumstances must be considered, including the economic, environmental and social

1020. [2004] 1 HKLRD 396, CFA.

implications. The overriding public need being a demanding test, there must be cogent and convincing material before the decision-maker to satisfy that the test has been satisfied.

800. The nature of the presumption against reclamation, and especially whether it would apply to a temporary reclamation to support the carrying out of an infrastructure project, came up for decision before the Court of First Instance in *Society for the Protection of the Harbour v Secretary for Justice.*[1021] There, the government had proposed to build a trunk road along the foreshore. The road would include a tunnel running under the seabed and under a typhoon shelter for mooring small craft. Construction would involve extensive temporary reclamation works of the foreshore and seabed for tunnel construction over six years and require additional temporary reclamation to build temporary breakwaters farther out in the harbour for displaced vessels. The government took the view that the construction of the tunnel was not subject to the constraints of the Protection of the Harbour Ordinance because: (i) there was no reclamation within the meaning of the Ordinance as the purpose of the works was to form a 'working platform' and not 'land'; and (ii) the works were of a temporary nature and would be removed and the foreshore and seabed reinstated.

801. The Society for the Protection of the Harbour brought judicial review proceedings seeking a declaration that the government had erred in law. The Court of First Instance disagreed with the Board's argument and held that, even though the end result was constructing a tunnel, reclamation was part of that process. Since the applicant had only asked for a declaration that the presumption against reclamation applied not only to permanent reclamations but also to temporary reclamations, the court did not venture to consider whether there was a compelling and overriding public interest to justify the proposed reclamation work. Hartman J, however, observed that:

> as a common sense observation, and no more, it must surely be the case that the presumption against reclamation can much more easily be rebutted when it is shown, first, that the works are temporary in nature and, second, that the very purpose of the works is to avoid the need for permanent reclamation.

802. The Presumption against reclamation applies only to Vitoria harbour. Any reclamation of land in the sea surrounding Hong Kong elsewhere remains unaffected by this rebuttable but strong presumption. Aware of the public concerns, the government is unlikely to take reclamation lightly and would be well advised to take adequate measures to mitigate any ill effects of reclamation on the natural environment.

1021. [2008] 4 HKLRD 417.

§3. The Role Planning Law in Nature Conservation

803. Hong Kong's planning system revolves around land use zoning and planning permission. The Town Planning Board has power to make land-use plans for any areas of Hong Kong. Most areas of Hong Kong have been brought under land-use plans, which are commonly referred to as outline zoning plans. As the name suggests, what an outline zoning plan does is to designate a selected geographical area for specified purposes such as residential, commercial or agricultural use. Where the Board has not decided on an appropriate broad use for an area, but wishes to bring that area under planning control, it is possible to designate the zone as an undetermined zone. Once an area has been zoned for a specific purpose such as residential or commercial, no developments may be undertaken in any land situated in that area, unless: (i) the proposed land use or development is an always permitted use, for instance, a village house in a Village Zone, or (ii) the proposed use is specified in the plan as a use which may be permitted with planning permission, and such permission has been obtained.

804. In making land-use plans, the Town Planning Board gives effect to government's planning policies. The Planning Department which has responsibility of adopting planning policies and strategies prepares strategic development plans at territorial, regional and district levels. In accomplishing this task, the Planning Department is guided by the Hong Kong Planning Standards and Guidelines,[1022] Chapter 10 of which is titled 'Conservation'. That chapter sets out four principles that guide development plans for nature conservation: (i) retain significant landscape, ecological and geological attributes and heritage features as conservation zones; (ii) restrict uses with conservation zones to those which sustain particular landscapes, ecological and geological attributes and heritage features; (iii) control adjoining uses to minimize adverse impacts on conservation zones and optimize their conservation value; and (iv) create, where possible, new conservation zones in compensation for areas of conservation value which are lost to development.

805. The Hong Kong Planning Standards and Guidelines have specified several zonings which are relevant to nature conservation that the Town Planning Board may adopt. They are:

(a) *Coastal Protection Areas.* They are to conserve, protect and retain the natural coastlines and the sensitive coastal natural environment, including attractive geological features, physical landform or area of high landscape, scenic or ecological value, with a minimum of built development; and to cover areas which serve as natural protection areas sheltering nearby developments against the effects of coastal erosion, with a general presumption against development.

(b) *Sites of Special Scientific Interest.* They are intended to conserve and protect features of special scientific interest such as rare or particular species of fauna and flora and their habitats, corals, woodlands, marshes or areas of geological,

1022. *See* http://www.pland.gov.hk/pland_en/tech_doc/hkpsg/index.html.

ecological or botanical/biological interest and to deter human activities or developments within such sites, with a general presumption against development.

(c) *GB Zones*. They are intended primarily to conserve the existing natural environment amid the built-up areas/at the urban fringe, to safeguard it from encroachment by urban-type development, to define the limits of urban and suburban development areas by natural features, to contain urban sprawl as well as to provide passive recreational outlets, with a general presumption against development.

(d) *Conservation Areas*. They are intended to protect and retain the existing natural landscape, ecological or topographical features of the area for conservation, educational and research purposes and to separate sensitive natural environment such as SSSI or Country Park from the adverse effects of development. There is a general presumption against development in this zone.

(e) *Conservation Areas (Wet Land only)*. They are intended to discourage new development unless it is required to support the conservation of the ecological integrity of the wetland ecosystem or the development is an essential infrastructure project with overriding public interest.

(f) '*Other Specified Uses (Comprehensive Development and Wetland Enhancement Areas)*'. They are intended for conservation and enhancement of ecological value and functions of the existing fishponds or wetland through consideration of application for development or redevelopment under the 'private-public partnership approach' The 'no-net-loss in wetland' principle is adopted for any change of use in this zone.

(g) '*Other Specified Uses (Comprehensive Development to include Wetland Restoration Areas)*'. *They are intended* to provide incentives for the restoration of degraded wetlands adjoining existing fish ponds through comprehensive residential and/or recreational development to include wetland restoration area, and to phase out existing sporadic open storage and port backup uses on degraded wetlands.

806. The Town Planning Board has adopted a master schedule of plans which it uses as a guide to preparing notes on outlines zoning plans. The notes of a zone contain a section on planning intention which is a guide to interpreting the notes. The Master Schedule of Plans follows Chapter 10 'Conservation' of the Hong Kong Planning Standards and Guidelines and elaborates on the planning intention for the above zones. For instance, the suggested wording for the planning intention of conservation area zone is as follows:

> This zoning is intended to protect and retain the existing natural landscape, ecological or topographical features of the area for conservation, educational and research purposes and to separate sensitive natural environment such as Sites of Special Scientific Interest or Country Parks from the adverse effects of development. There is a general presumption against development in this zone. In general, only developments that are needed to support the conservation of the existing natural landscape or scenic quality of the area or are essential infrastructure projects with an overriding public interest may be permitted.

807. The Town Planning Board makes use of guidelines that it publishes for the benefit of planning applicants to explain the importance of conservation in the above zones. There are two relevant guidelines: TPB PG-No. 10 Application for Development within GB Zone under section 16 of the Town Planning Ordinance, and TPB PG-No. 12C Application for Developments within Deep Bay Area under section 16 of the Town Planning Ordinance.

808. The Guidelines for GB zones provide as follows: The planning intention of the GB zone is primarily to promote the conservation of the natural environment and to safeguard it from encroachment by urban-type developments. The main purposes of the GB zone include the following: (a) to conserve existing landscape features, areas of scenic value and areas of recognized *fung shui* importance; (b) to define the outer limits of urbanized districts and to serve as a buffer between and within urban areas; and (c) to provide additional outlets for passive recreational uses. To preserve the character and nature of the GB zone, the only uses which will always be permitted by the Town Planning Board are compatible uses which are essential and for public purposes such as waterworks, water catchment areas, nature reserves, agriculture, forestry and certain passive recreational uses. Other uses, including government/institution/community, residential development and public utility installations, will require planning permission from the Board and each proposal will be assessed on its individual merits. Applications for development will be considered by the Board according to the criteria set out in the Guidelines. They include the following: (i) there is a general presumption against development (other than redevelopment) in a GB zone. In general, the Board will only be prepared to approve applications for development in the context of requests to rezone to an appropriate use; (ii) an application for new development in a GB zone will only be considered in exceptional circumstances and must be justified with very strong planning grounds. The scale and intensity of the proposed development including the plot ratio, site coverage and building height should be compatible with the character of surrounding areas. Any proposed development should not involve extensive clearance of existing natural vegetation, affect the existing natural landscape, or cause any adverse visual impact on the surrounding environment.

809. In order to protect the Mai Po Nature Reserve and the areas around the Deep Bay, the Guidelines for the Deep Bay Area have created two zones. Zone 1, which comprises existing and contiguous fish ponds, is designated a wetland conservation area. No developments, other than those required to support the conservation of the ecological value of the area and essential infrastructure projects, will be permitted. The other zone, Wetland Buffer Area Zone, runs along the Wetland Conservation Area. Some residential or recreational developments may be permitted in this area, as an incentive to remove the undesirable open storage uses and to restore fish ponds that have been filled. The Guidelines explain that in considering any application for planning permission, the Board applies the precautionary principle of preserving fish ponds. No development may be permitted unless it can guarantee that there will be no net loss of wetlands. Any proposed development must be supported by an ecological impact assessment, which must show in particular that it will not increase pollution of the Deep Bay.

§4. CULTURAL RESOURCES

I. Antiquities and Monuments

810. There is quite a variety of historic buildings in Hong Kong, ranging from traditional Chinese ancestral halls and Western residences to functional structures such as waterworks facilities. The architectural styles, selections of sites and building materials as well as types of buildings to be constructed are all governed by social beliefs, traditions, ideas and cultures.[1023]

811. The Antiquities and Monuments Ordinance (Cap 53) makes statutory provision for the preservation of objects of historical. archaeological and paleontological interest.[1024] The Ordinance vests power in the Secretary for Development, who is the Authority for the purposes of the Ordinance, to implement the Ordinance in consultation with the Antiquities Advisory Board, which represents different sections of the community but does not necessarily consist of persons with expertise in antiquities or heritage conservation.[1025] The Advisory Board is assisted by the Antiquities and Monuments Office, the executive arm of the Authority. The Antiquities and Monuments Office is headed by a Chief Curator as its Executive Secretary and it has thirty-six curator grade officers. They all have professional training and knowledge in heritage conservation.[1026] The Ordinance envisages that the Advisory Board advises the Secretary on the relative importance of historical buildings on a grading system. The Advisory Board is guided by advice given by the Antiquities and Monuments Office.[1027]

812. In 1996, the Antiquities and Monuments Office, which provides assistance to the Advisory Board, carried out a four-year territory-wide survey of historic buildings, recording some 8,800 buildings. About 1,000 buildings of higher heritage value were selected for more in-depth study. These buildings were graded as follows: Grade I: Buildings of outstanding merit (every possible effort should be made to preserve); Grade II: Buildings of special merit (efforts should be made to preserve them selectively); Grade III: Buildings of some merit (preservation in some form would be desirable and alternative means could be considered if preservation is not practicable). Buildings were graded using six criteria: historical interest, architectural merit, group value, social value and local interest, authenticity, and rarity. As recommended by Members of the Antiquities Advisory Board, an Expert Panel of historians and members of the Hong Kong Institute of Architects, Hong Kong Institute of Planners and Hong Kong Institution of Engineers was formed in 2005 to undertake an in-depth assessment of the heritage value of these buildings.

1023. *See* for an informative and critical account of heritage preservation in Hong Kong, http://www.heritage.gov.hk/en/index.htm.
1024. The Antiquities and Monuments Ordinance (Cap 53) Long Title.
1025. *Chu Hoi Dick & Another v Secretary of Home Affairs* [2007] HKEC 1471, [19].
1026. *Ibid.*
1027. *See* http://www.amo.gov.hk/en/index.php.

813. The more important buildings of historical value which deserve preservation, and placed in Grade I by the Advisory Board, may be declared as monuments. Section 3(1) provides that the Authority may, after consultation with the Board and with the approval of the Chief Executive, by notice in the Gazette, declare any place, building, site or structure, which the Authority considers to be of public interest by reason of its historical, archaeological or palaeontological significance, to be a monument historical building or archaeological or palaeontological site or structure. The Authority must give notice of its intention to declare any place or structure as a monument and, if it is within private land, the landowner may object to the proposed declaration (*see* sections 2A, 2B, 2C and 4). Compensation is payable to a landowner affected by such a declaration (section 8). Government may make financial grants for the preservation and maintenance of a monument (section 7).

814. In the case of *Chu Hoi Dick & Another v Secretary of Home Affairs*,[1028] the Court of First Instance had the opportunity to comment on the statutory provisions relating to declaration of monuments. The Court of First Instance observed that the Antiquities and Monuments Office carries out studies and advises the Advisory Board on the importance of buildings, structures and places for the purposes of preservation. The Board is thus in a position to advise the Authority on how the Authority should exercise his powers.

815. The Court pointed out that the Authority, while it respects the advice given by the Advisory Board, takes decisions in its own right:

> The function of the Board is to provide advice. It is not the function of the Board to make decisions. As to how its advice would be weighed in the light of other relevant matters, it is a matter for the decision maker. In the context of a declaration under Section 3, the primary decision-maker is the Authority although a declaration cannot be made without the approval of the Chief Executive. Whilst the Board may give advice even on its own volition, it would be acting ultra vires if it purports to dictate the Authority as regards whether a Section 3 declaration should be made. Likewise, the Board could not direct the Authority on how he should proceed with his assessment in considering whether to exercise his power under Section 3 in the light of a Grade I classification by the Board. Although the grading system stems from an administrative scheme instead of the Ordinance, the Board's role is still confined to an advisory one in the context of a Section 3 declaration (at [29]).

816. In *Chu Hoi Dick* case, it was argued that the Authority had acted ultra vires when it decided not to declare the Queen's pier as a monument, when the Advisory Board had a by a majority vote placed Queen's Pier in grade 1. The declaration of a monument has the serious consequence under section 6 in that the government would not have been able to demolish the pier and relocate it, without a permit from the Authority. Lam J explained:

1028. [2007] HKEC 1471.

> But it does not follow that the Authority has to make a declaration once he is satisfied a place, building, site or structure has some historical, archaeological or palaeontological significance. After all, the declaration of a building as a monument would entail consequences under Section 6 and that may in some cases result in serious interference with property rights (at [47]).

The court decided that the Authority had not applied a test stricter than required for determining whether a particular building should be declared a monument and had not acted unreasonably. After this litigation, the government dismantled the pier and plans are now underway to reassemble it close to the Star Ferry.[1029]

II. Historical and Cultural Sites

817. It is the duty of the Country and Marine Parks Authority to preserve and maintain buildings and sites of historic or cultural significance within country parks and special areas, but without prejudice to the Antiquities and Monuments Ordinance. Under the Mining Ordinance (Cap 285), there is a duty, while mining or prospecting, not to injure or destroy any tree or other thing which is an object of veneration.

1029. At http://www.construction-post.com/queens-pier-reassembly-slated-2016/.ss

Selected Bibliography

Cooray, Anton. 'Environmental Torts'. In *Tort Law and Practice in Hong Kong,* edited by Kemal Bokhary. 2nd edn. Sweet & Maxwell, Hong Kong, 2011, 625–652.

Cooray, Anton. 'Environmental Litigation in Hong Kong: The Role of the Judiciary and Statutory Tribunals'. In *Law and Development: Facing Complexity in the 21st Century,* edited by John Hatchard & Amanda Perry-Kessaris. Cavendish, London, UK, 2003, 226–245.

Cooray, Anton. 'Environmental Offences'. Chapter 40 of *Archbold Hong Kong: Criminal Law Pleading Evidence and Practice.* Sweet & Maxwell, Hong Kong, 2021.

Cooray, Anton. 'Environment'. In *Halsbury's Laws of Hong Kong.* LexisNexis, 2020,461-837.

Lin, Jolene. 'Creating a Market for Clean Air: The Air Pollution Control (Amendment) Ordinance 2008'. *Hong Kong Law Journal* 39, no. 2 (2009): 269–284.

Table of Cases

The numbers here refer to paragraph numbers.

Hong Kong Cases

UK Cases

Australian Cases

Table of Hong Kong Statutes

The numbers here refer to paragraph numbers.

Table of Hong Kong Statutes

Index

The numbers here refer to paragraph numbers.

www.ingramcontent.com/pod-product-compliance
Lightning Source LLC
LaVergne TN
LVHW011111300926
849160LV00008B/352